Susan M. Boyan, LMFT
Ann Marie Termini, LPC

The Psychotherapist As Parent Coordinator in High-Conflict Divorce
Strategies and Techniques

Pre-publication
REVIEWS,
COMMENTARIES,
EVALUATIONS . . .

"**A**lthough this book is designed for therapists who act as parent coordinators, it should be mandatory reading for all professionals involved in any level of divorce. A parent coordinator should be mandated in every high-conflict divorce where the children are suffering, and this book sells the model. I hope that the effort continues to grow and that this book launches a renewed interest by professionals in protecting children whose voices are too often not heard.

The book contains simple suggestions that any professional can share with high-conflict parents. Too many parents do not realize that they are taking a position rather than an interest and become entrenched in their distorted beliefs about the other parent. The book is all-encompassing in dealing with parents who suffer emotional problems and addiction and offers practical tips on how to deal with the most challenging situations. One of the most useful aspects of the book is that it does not take a one-size-fits-all approach, but recognizes that all families are different. Nonetheless, regardless of the family dynamics or level of dysfunction, this book offers hope for the children."

Melody Z. Richardson, JD, PC
Family Law Attorney
and Guardian Ad Litem,
Atlanta, Georgia

"**B**oyan and Termini have written a comprehensive and important book on parent coordination. This book will be very useful for beginners in the field who want to understand the value of parent coordination and who are looking for assistance in developing their career in this field. Most useful are the sections on working within the legal system and the techniques and strategies in the field."

Philip M. Stahl, PhD
Psychologist and Custody Evaluator,
Danville, California

More pre-publication
REVIEWS, COMMENTARIES, EVALUATIONS . . .

"**B**oth new and experienced therapists will find that this book provides a wealth of legal and psychological knowledge for establishing a practice as a parent coordinator within the context of the legal system. It is unprecedented in the extent to which it provides the necessary guidelines, practical strategies, and techniques for helping parents communicate and coordinate on behalf of their children in the most difficult and vulnerable families—those entrenched in high-conflict divorce. It is the product of the authors' extensive experience with these families, and it incorporates and advances the most recent developments in the field. Most important, it shows how to set up the necessary structure to help mental health professionals avoid the pitfalls and traverse the minefield of practice in this forensic context. The authors are to be congratulated for their substantial contribution!"

Janet R. Johnson, PhD
Professor, Department
of Justice Studies,
San Jose State University;
Co-author, *Impasses of Divorce:
The Dynamics and Resolution
of Family Conflict*

The Haworth Clinical Practice Press
An Imprint of The Haworth Press, Inc.
New York • London • Oxford

The Psychotherapist
As Parent Coordinator
in High-Conflict Divorce
Strategies and Techniques

HAWORTH *Practical Practice in Mental Health*
Lorna L. Hecker, PhD
Senior Editor

101 Interventions in Family Therapy edited by Thorana S. Nelson
and Terry S. Trepper

101 More Interventions in Family Therapy edited by Thorana S. Nelson
and Terry S. Trepper

*The Practical Practice of Marriage and Family Therapy:
Things My Training Supervisor Never Told Me* by Mark Odell
and Charles E. Campbell

*The Therapist's Notebook for Families: Solution-Oriented Exercises
for Working with Parents, Children, and Adolescents* by Bob Bertolino
and Gary Schultheis

*The Therapist's Notebook for Children and Adolescents: Homework,
Handouts, and Activities for Use in Psychotherapy* edited by
Catherine Ford Sori and Lorna L. Hecker

*The Therapist's Notebook for Lesbian, Gay, and Bisexual Clients:
Homework, Handouts, and Activities for Use in Psychotherapy*
edited by Joy S. Whitman and Cynthia J. Boyd

Collaborative Practice in Psychology and Therapy edited by David A. Paré
and Glenn Larner

A Guide to Self-Help Workbooks for Mental Health Clinicians and Researchers
by Luciano L'Abate

*Using Workbooks in Mental Health: Resources in Prevention, Psychotherapy,
and Rehabilitation for Clinicians and Researchers* edited by
Luciano L'Abate

*The Psychotherapist As Parent Coordinator in High-Conflict Divorce: Strategies
and Techniques* by Susan M. Boyan and Ann Marie Termini

The Psychotherapist
As Parent Coordinator
in High-Conflict Divorce
Strategies and Techniques

Susan M. Boyan, LMFT
Ann Marie Termini, LPC

The Haworth Clinical Practice Press
An Imprint of The Haworth Press, Inc.
New York • London • Oxford

Published by

The Haworth Clinical Practice Press, an imprint of The Haworth Press, Inc., 10 Alice Street, Binghamton, NY 13904-1580.

TR: 6.22.05

PUBLISHER'S NOTE
Identities and circumstances of individuals discussed in this book have been changed to protect confidentiality.

Cover design by Marylouise E. Doyle.

Library of Congress Cataloging-in-Publication Data

Boyan, Susan.
   The psychotherapist as parent coordinator in high-conflict divorce : strategies and techniques / Susan M. Boyan, Ann Marie Termini.
      p. cm.
   Includes bibliographical references and index.
   ISBN 0-7890-2214-1 (alk. paper)—ISBN 0-7890-2215-X (pbk. : alk. paper)
   1. Divorced parents. 2. Interpersonal conflict. 3. Parenting, Part-time. 4. Parenting. 5. Children of divorced parents. 6. Divorce—Psychological aspects. I. Termini, Ann Marie. II. Title.
HQ759.915.B69 2004
306.89—dc22
                                                                                          2004004259

CONTENTS

ABOUT THE AUTHORS

Susan M. Boyan, LMFT, and **Ann Marie Termini, LPC,** are co-founders of the Cooperative Parenting Institute and the National Parent Coordinator's Association (NPCA). Since 1996 they have been providing extensive parent coordination training and supervision throughout North America. They also co-authored *Cooperative Parenting & Divorce*—a video-based psychoeducational program for divorced parents, and they have self-published *Parents R Forever: Everything You Need to Know to Help Your Young Child Adjust to Divorce.* Widely known for their expertise in the area of divorce, parental alienation, parent coordination, and the family, the authors train and consult with family law and mental health professionals.

COOPERATIVE PARENTING INSTITUTE
RESOURCES FOR PARENT COORDINATORS

- Parent coordination training opportunities
- Parent coordination marketing materials
- Parent coordination assessment materials package

DIVORCE-RELATED RESOURCES

Cooperative Parenting & Divorce: A Parent's Guide to Effective Co-Parenting

A 199-page parent guide to effective coparenting, this book offers valuable information about the process of divorce and practical skills necessary to create a two-household family.

Cooperative Parenting & Divorce Group Kit

The group kit is designed for use by therapists, social workers, and parent educators. It includes a 200-page leader's guide, a thirty-six-minute companion video, and one copy of *Cooperative Parenting & Divorce: A Parent's Guide to Effective Co-Parenting*. In addition, the kit contains a disk with marketing and assessment materials. The group format incorporates skill development, large and small group discussion, role-plays, application, and homework assignments. The proven-effective activities can be implemented in eight two-hour sessions.

For more information or to purchase materials, contact the authors at

<www.cooperativeparenting.com>

or

The Cooperative Parenting Institute
2801 Buford Highway T-70
Atlanta, GA 30329
(404) 315-7474 ext. 1

Preface

Experienced therapists recognize all too well the negative impact of high-conflict divorce on their clients' welfare. It is especially frustrating to witness the countless children of divorce who are trapped in the throes of endless parental tension and warfare. As family therapists, we have encountered children receiving psychotherapy due to their parents' pending divorce. It is also common for parents to seek services for their children years postdivorce who are still exhibiting symptoms ranging from stomachaches, aggression, and anxiety disorders to failing grades and much more. However, it generally becomes apparent fairly quickly that the child's symptoms are related to the parents' inability to navigate the process of family separation in such a manner as to shield their child from parental conflict. Unfortunately, many parents are unwilling to address their own issues and would prefer to keep the focus of treatment on their child. After years of attempting to work within the parameters set by resistant parents, it became evident that neither education nor psychotherapy was enough to make a difference in the quality of life for high-conflict families. As we were coming to this painful realization, other frustrated professionals working with divorced families were coming to the same conclusion. Legal and mental health providers have recognized the necessity for a new and unique type of service provider. In response to this critical need, the role of parent coordinator was created.

In 1994, as an extension of this movement, we founded the Cooperative Parenting Institute (CPI) in Atlanta, Georgia. Since then we have dedicated our resources, time, and expertise to the development of programs for divorcing families. As an outgrowth of our work in Georgia, we provided coparent groups and coparent counseling. After experiencing the limitations of these services for high-conflict families, we developed parent coordination. The model that evolved is now referred to as the *cooperative parenting model*. Through the years we continued to refine our model based on our clinical experiences, the limited information available on the subject, collaboration with legal professionals, and consultation with prominent researchers in the area of high-conflict divorce. Initially, we fashioned our approach after the early work of Carla Garrity and Mitchell Baris (1994), *Caught in the Middle: Protecting the Children of High-Conflict Divorce.*

Over time, divorced parents experiencing moderate to severe levels of parental conflict have been ordered by juvenile court, family court, and superior court judges to participate in parent coordination. Recognizing the value of this approach, attorneys, mediators, guardians ad litem, custody evaluators, physicians, and psychotherapists have referred parents to the program. Some parents include the services of parent coordination in their settlement agreement.

As court jurisdictions throughout the country appointed parent coordinators, it became apparent that three areas critical to the ongoing development of parent coordination would need to be explored. Psychotherapists working as parent coordinators found the work challenging yet recognized the need for unique training and professional support in order to provide competent assistance to these challenging families. Consequently, professionals contacted us to request training based upon our unique approach. Therefore, in 1996, we began sharing our ideas by providing national training workshops several times per year. Ultimately, it is our hope that states will begin mandating more extensive training for coordinators as a way to ensure the growth and improvement of parent coordination.

Furthermore, the evolution of parent coordination as a viable service necessitates the development of uniform standards for the profession. As a starting point, we developed standards that guide the services we provide at the Cooperative Parenting Institute. These standards are outlined in the Appendix. One of our long-term goals has been to create an organization that can be a unifying force in the creation of national standards that define the field of parent coordination. In 1999, we cofounded the National Parent Coordinators Association (NPCA) by pulling together the professionals we previously trained. Still in its infancy, the overall goals of the association are to clarify the role and responsibilities of parent coordinators, provide professionals the needed support from other providers, and identify uniform standards for the profession.

Finally, the growth of parent coordination relies upon both public and legal awareness of the profession. Although some courts utilize parent coordinators, many jurisdictions are still becoming aware of this unique service and its benefits for both families and the court system. However, in order to adequately educate the court system and promote the field, interested professionals representing the various disciplines involved in the arena of divorce, including the parents we serve, must collaborate to further define and regulate this service. Consequently, the purposeful evolution of the field will demand that each of the essential elements be addressed and result in the establishment of protocols to ensure ethical services.

As a way to provide general and specific information, this book has been organized to benefit both the novice and the experienced psychotherapist.

The first section offers up-to-date research regarding the impact of divorce, particularly high-conflict divorce, on families and children. In addition, information on custody, time sharing, and the legal system is offered.

The second section provides the history, role, responsibilities, and protocols of parent coordination. Our unique CPI model is thoroughly discussed. Information regarding how to set up and market this type of practice is also provided. The CPI model offers a step-by-step approach to parent coordination along with suggestions on how to integrate other family members into the process. Unlike other resources to date, specific techniques and strategies for managing the angry and the impaired parent are addressed at length. Parental alienation is discussed, including suggestions for effective interventions. The last section on standards, located in the Appendix, is an invaluable resource for both legal professionals and parent coordinators.

We believe that you will benefit from our extensive experience, whether you set up a new professional service such as parent coordination or simply use the skills in your general psychotherapy practice. It is our hope that you will consider the importance of working in collaboration with the legal system as a way to truly advocate for children of divorce.

As you develop parent coordination in your community, we hope that you will gain a sense of personal satisfaction in reaching out to families in emotional distress. As a dedicated psychotherapist you play a vital role in the restructuring of the family unit. Your ongoing involvement with these parents and their children will not only assist troubled families but also educate the community regarding the needs of separating families. By pooling our expertise and experience, we can preserve and strengthen the family structure. These are troubled families in need of powerful solutions. It is up to all of us.

Chapter 1

The Impact of Divorce

Family relationships do not disappear when a marriage ends in separation or divorce. Divorce does not dissolve the family; it reorganizes it from a one-home structure to a two-home structure. Parental functioning and the ability of parents to interact with each other greatly influence a child's adjustment. It is how parents navigate the separation of the family that colors the impact of divorce on the children. Parental interaction characterized by hostility and conflict is the single most common cause of poor adjustment in children following a divorce (Garrity and Baris, 1994; Hess and Camara, 1979; Mnookin, 1992; Wallerstein, 1989). It places a greater strain on a child's development than any other single factor in divorce. Therefore, for the sake of their children, divorcing parents must continue to interact with their former spouses in matters of child rearing. Ultimately, divorcing parents need to learn to parent in a two-household structure that emphasizes collaboration and a focus on the children.

Currently the rate of divorce is fairly stable. It is estimated that 40 to 60 percent of the current marriages will end in divorce (Ahrons, 2004). More than 1 million children each year are affected by divorce (Hirczy de Mino, 1997). Half of these children will be raised in families where parents remain in conflict, while 60 percent of the children will feel rejected by at least one parent. Although only approximately 10 percent of custody cases (Ahrons, 2004) reach the courtroom, these cases tend to be highly litigious and damaging to the innocent children caught in the middle of their parents' intense hostility. Approximately 20 to 30 percent of divorcing couples have been identified as exhibiting high-conflict behaviors (Maccoby and Mnookin, 1992). Many of these same parents engage in ongoing litigation over their children for years. Although these parents represent a minority of the divorcing parents, the high conflict poses grave concerns for legal and mental health professionals. Consequently, many professionals have focused their attention on eliminating the adverse effects of high-conflict divorce on families.

PROFESSIONAL REACTIONS TO DIVORCING FAMILIES

Historically, professionals in the field of domestic relations have attempted to meet the needs of families experiencing the devastating effects of divorce. This proactive stance has led to the development and implementation of voluntary and mandated programs utilized by separating parents. Movement toward mandated parent programs that meet the specific needs of divorced parents have increased dramatically. Judges across the nation have signed orders mandating two- to four-hour educational seminars focusing on the effects of divorce on children. These time-limited seminars are helpful in reducing some of the adverse effects of divorce on the child's healthy adjustment, but they do not meet the unique needs of those children caught in the middle of their parents' intense hostility. These seminars are limited in their ability to address the crippling tension, implicit and explicit differences of opinions, and impaired communication and conflict-resolution skills characteristic of antagonistic parents in the throes of divorce. Under these circumstances, it is imperative that divorcing parents develop anger management techniques, effective communication and conflict-resolution skills, and empathetic understanding of their children's needs.

Most professionals agree that a call for policies, procedures, and resources that reduce adversarial approaches to custody and favor alternative methods of dispute resolution such as mediation, educational programs, parent coordination, and therapeutic services are warranted. Once it is recognized that divorcing parents are at high risk of remaining in conflict, parents should be encouraged and even mandated to become involved in programs designed to reduce the child's exposure to parental warfare. Regardless of whether parents have been given sole or joint custody, establishing a cooperative relationship between separating parents can decrease or even prevent the severity of emotional and behavioral problems in children. If parental conflict is not treated, serious psychological difficulties in children will probably continue into adulthood. Children who are raised in a cooperative atmosphere both during and after their parents' divorce are more likely to cope successfully and develop a healthy attitude toward relationships.

Although parental conflict is one aspect of the divorce process in which parents can exercise some control, they may not have the necessary skills or knowledge to reduce parental hostilities without professional assistance. Even in an atmosphere of unrelenting conflict, both parents are convinced that they are invested in their child's best interest. Neither parent recognizes that their child is being torn apart. To circumvent that potential conflict, services focusing on prevention and intervention can lead the binuclear family toward a healthy coparenting relationship. Extensive psychoeducational services, such as the Cooperative Parenting and Divorce group program and parent coordination, play a pivotal role in easing the child's transition from one to two homes.

Increased interest in programs focusing on the complex issues of divorce is supported by research and the authors' experience indicating that the majority of parents can learn to work with each other to some degree (Ahrons, 1990, 1994; Blau, 1993; Garrity and Baris, 1994; Marston, 1994; Ricci, 1980; Wallerstein, 1991; Williams, 1987). The Stanford Custody Project (Maccoby and Mnookin, 1992) revealed that a significant number of divorced parents were able to establish and maintain a cooperative parenting arrangement on behalf of their children.

THE ADULT PERSPECTIVE

Divorce is a painful experience for men and women regardless of the circumstance. Most experts agree that divorced individuals need about two years before they are back on their feet again. In fact, it has been suggested that an eighteen- to twenty-four-month period of postseparation adjustment occurs, involving personal and interpersonal turmoil for the divorcing couple (Hetherington, Cox, and Cox, 1982; Wallerstein and Kelly, 1980). Adjustment is complicated because the divorce sets off a chain of stressful events that endures over an extended period of time. Studies suggest that other than the death of a spouse, divorce requires more reorganization than any other transition in life (Clapp, 1992).

As the marriage ends, parents are faced with the enormous task of reorganizing their lives. Each spouse must accept the end of the marriage and emotionally disengage from the marital relationship. While breaking from the past, they must separate their parenting interaction from their feelings and interactions as former spouses. During the transition, they need to discover their identity and gain confidence in their ability to live alone. Despite the pain of making the transition, divorcing spouses must let go of the old marital relationship in order to thrive as separate individuals.

The pain and fear of letting go can be so great for some people that they put all their efforts into staying attached to the marital relationship. For instance, a parent may stay negatively attached to a former spouse through negative emotions such as anger and bitterness. A divorcing couple engaged in revenge takes action not because it is advantageous for the children but often to inflict emotional pain on the other parent. The children are placed between the adults and, unfortunately, often manipulated to create tension in the other parent.

Others may stay attached to the marital relationship by hoping for a reconciliation. In these situations, decisions are based not on the needs of the child but on the opportunity of staying attached to the former spouse. They refuse to give up their dreams. They wanted a perfect marriage and a perfect family. Letting go means having to accept the death of these dreams. Either situation prevents parents from establishing a new life for themselves and places the children in jeopardy of ongoing emotional stress. Clearly, remaining engaged causes significant problems for the parents as well as the children.

Separating parents must define the type of relationship they will maintain with their former spouse. Clear boundaries are essential. Part of that distinction requires them to determine how much personal information, if any, they will share with each other. Creating clear expectations and boundaries helps the parents distinguish between their life as an individual and their life as a partner in parenting. It is difficult to realign the parental relationship when one or both parents are still grieving the end of the marriage. The sooner parents can clarify boundaries and expectations, the smoother the relationship will become. This will facilitate the family's transition. For instance, parents may mutually decide that unannounced house visits will not take place and the sharing of parental social activities will not be part of their parenting discussions. Developing a parenting partnership framed within a business relationship limits the emotional involvement of the two parties. Although it is advantageous to create a business relationship, some parents will never achieve the comfort of coparenting in an unemotional manner.

During the transition from married to single, it is not uncommon for men and women to rush into a new romantic relationship during or soon after the divorce. Rather than face being alone, the individual enters a relationship to prevent loneliness, and this interrupts the grief process. After years of a long marriage, it is difficult for parents to think of themselves as single. Constance Ahrons (2004) reported that over 50 percent of men and 33 percent of women remarry within a year of their legal divorce. Within three years of the divorce, 75 percent of women and 83 percent of men remarry. Divorce rates jump to 75 percent among stepfamilies. Thus parents should be cautioned about entering an intimate relationship prematurely, if not for their own sake, then at least for the sake of the family's children.

Divorced parents must also restructure parent-child relationships. When the child's living arrangement is being considered, physical changes take place, and there are emotional and psychological effects on the parent. Just as children become distressed over the disappearance of a parent in their lives, parents become anxious over the impending removal of the child from their daily life. Furthermore, the circumstances and demands placed on divorcing parents interfere with their ability to support their children's physical and emotional needs as well as provide consistent discipline and structure. Additional hardships can be created for the family if guilt begins to erode consistent discipline. At the same time, parents must separate their own needs from those of their children. Parents may become dependent on their children for emotional support and develop an enmeshed relationship. As a result of meeting these numerous demands, many adults have a diminished capacity to parent.

The new family alignment will dictate the extent to which parent-child relationships are transformed. Women are faced with distinguishing their role as mother from their role as wife. Often this is a formidable task for women, since the two roles are typically intertwined with their core identity. Some women may need to return to work or increase their hours in order to provide financially for their children. Overwhelmed by their financial responsibilities, mothers may focus less on nurturing their children or providing adequate discipline. These factors can create an additional loss for both mother and child. Women appear to be at greater risk of feeling guilty over the quality of time spent with their children than men.

Similarly, the new family arrangement may alter the role a father plays in his child's life. Some men may need to adjust the parent-child relationship very little. If a father did not actively participate in his child's life during the marriage, his role when divorced may not change. He may continue to be the breadwinner and maintain a limited fathering role. On the other hand, the father may have to minimize his role as breadwinner and focus more on the nurturing and disciplinary tasks of being a single parent. The father who was not a primary parent during the marriage is suddenly faced with having to develop a new and unfamiliar relationship with his child. Regardless of the family circumstance, more and more men are attempting to be active figures in their children's lives. Similar to women, men may also feel the loss of daily contact with their child.

THE BINUCLEAR FAMILY PERSPECTIVE

Family separation ignites a chain of stressful events that endures over an extended time. It requires each family member to cope with numerous losses, conflicting emotions, and ongoing change. Divorce disrupts the old family structure and creates a new relationship among all family members. The family must leave behind familiar routines, rules, and structures and establish new patterns in a relatively short time. Former spouses must let go of their marital relationship while at the same time realign their parenting relationship. Children must recognize and accept the fact that their parents' marital relationship has ended but their relationship as parents continues. As the binuclear family (Ahrons, 1990) transitions from one to two homes, the roles and routines each family member assumes have the potential of offering the family the stability and predictability that will help them navigate the transition in a more secure manner.

In any family system, the members function according to a set of roles, routines, and rules. The parental roles established in an intact family will no longer apply to the binuclear family. In each household, the parents individually assume the role of the primary authority figure rather than sharing these responsibilities with the other parent. Each parent is now met with the sole responsibility of maintaining order and control. Depending on the nature of the parental role in the intact family, parents are likely to encounter a difference in the degree of authority that they will need to establish in order to provide the children with a stable environment. Mothers and fathers must shift their parenting style to accommodate this change in role. As a result, the relationship between the parent and the child will also shift and require a different way of interacting with each other.

Many rules originating in the intact family may or may not be duplicated in the two-household family. As the family adjusts to their new structure, children are likely to experience different rules in each household. The structure of the children's living arrangement may dictate the design of the rules in each household. For instance, as a function of the demands placed on children of school age, those who live primarily in one household during the week may experience more rigid rules and routines, while children living in the other household primarily on weekends may encounter more flexible rules and routines. Similarly, the responsibilities placed on the child in these different living environments are generally associated with the amount of time the child spends in each household. Once again, children who maintain a primary residence with one parent are usually expected to perform chores on a daily and weekly basis, whereas children living with a parent on alternating weekends may not be responsible for meeting such demands. Not only does the difference in lifestyle influence the parental role, but the difference in expectations also impacts the parents' relationship with each other. The children's relationship with each of their parents is obviously also affected.

Furthermore, the boundaries between households will need to be clarified. Highly conflicted divorces have benefited from clearly delineated guidelines and responsibilities. In the future, these high-conflict families may find that less formal agreements may be adequate. Defining the two-home structure in very specific and concrete terms helps diminish any misunderstandings that can lead to conflict. Ahrons (1994) warned that arbitrary boundaries lead to power struggles between parents. As a result, children walk on eggshells waiting for the next explosion to occur between their parents. They become confused and anxious. However, rigid boundaries that do not take into consideration the necessary interdependency of parenting and the unexpected events that are sure to arise can lead to the child living in a compartmentalized world. In this situation, the child is often forced to choose between his or her parents, creating devastating loyalty binds. During the transition, family members are likely to adjust more easily if some degree of predictability and continuity is established between households.

Realignment for parents following divorce implies forming a relationship that differs in structure from the former parenting relationship. The new relationship is built solely on the principle of addressing the needs of the children. A structure needs to be established that allows the two parties to communicate about their child's welfare, solve problems, negotiate solutions, and share valuable information in order for both parents to obtain their mutual goal of providing for the emotional and physical well-being of the child. This structure must clarify the boundaries in such a way that clearly delineates the responsibilities of each parent. Parents need to be clear about how much of the parenting they will share and what they will accomplish on their own when the children are living with them. Just as in a healthy marriage, the importance of verbalizing expectations and specifying parental responsibilities is vital for the two-household family to effectively function. Although this shift is difficult, it is essential that divorcing parents clarify the new parental structure.

In any family, some decisions about the welfare of the child are made independently while others are made between parents. Although the number of decisions made together and those made separately may differ from those prior to the divorce, the most important fact is that some decisions still need to be made together. Parents may no longer confer with each other about minor decisions that affect the child while the child is under one parent's direct supervision. But in a healthy binuclear family, some decisions are still made by both parents. More often than not, the judicial system awards joint legal custody to separated parents. Joint legal custody requires parents to consult with each other regarding major decisions impacting on their child's life.

THE EXTENDED FAMILY PERSPECTIVE

Extended family members may play an integral role in the realignment of the family structure. Depending on the involvement of the extended family member, a divorce or separation may directly impact the extended family member's relationship with parents as well as the children. A custody conflict often leads to division even when family members attempt to remain neutral. This may create further stress on the divorcing parent who demands total loyalty from his or her family of origin. On the other hand, extended family members may feel caught in a tug-of-war as they support their family member while, at the same time, maintain contact with their former in-laws.

Physical changes may take place that affect the two-generational family. For instance, a parent and children moving into the extended family member's home may create more intimate contact between the members of the family. Parents may look toward their extended family members to offer both physical and emotional support. New demands may be placed on family members in the form of providing child care, car pools, meals, and a sympathetic ear. Independent grandparents may now need to be more accessible to their child and grandchildren, resulting in a change of lifestyle. The roles, routines, and responsibilities in the household must shift in response to the physical changes.

On the other hand, the physical changes placed on the family may lead to erratic contact between the family and extended family members. For instance, grandparents may have more limited contact with their grandchildren if the parent's time with his or her children has dramatically decreased. In addition, the former in-laws may experience the loss of their own extended family. A mother-in-law may lose her son- or daughter-in-law. They become an "ex" while their long-term history and feelings may remain intact. These family relationships, in a high-conflict divorce, die along with the dream of an extended family. Furthermore, the loss of stepparents, stepchildren, stepsiblings, and steprelatives is often a common casualty of divorce, especially when working with conflicted divorced families. Everyone involved is likely to become distressed over the shift in physical contact.

The children's new living arrangement may greatly influence their ability to participate in special events celebrated by both sides of their extended family. Holiday traditions may need to be altered to accommodate the children's vacation and visitation schedule. Children may not be able to participate in all extended family activities as they once may have with each parent. Time with each parent has been regulated, interfering with their ability to sustain a close and satisfying relationship with both sides of their extended family. No matter how they spend their time, everyone is likely to feel a sense of loss.

Clear boundaries between the separated parents, the family, and the extended family must be re-created. Realignment for parents may mean forming a relationship with their own parents that greatly differs from their previous interaction. Moving back in with a parent may cause great strain on an otherwise healthy two-generational relationship. Boundaries may be blurred and lifestyles may be changed dramatically, not only for the divorced parent and child but for the grandparent as well. In these situations, creating clear boundaries and establishing parental responsibilities are vital for the family to recover from their numerous loses. Creating clear boundaries begins with the parents. Parents must distinguish and sometimes educate extended family members regarding the effects of divorce on children and how to best support both themselves and the children through the process of divorce. The importance of establishing appropriate boundaries between parents and other significant individuals should be addressed as soon as possible.

THE TRIBAL PERSPECTIVE

Tribal warfare is a term coined by Johnston and Campbell (1988, p. 47) to describe the interaction of the larger social system influenced by the divorce. The tribe involves the extended family members as well as neighbors, significant others, attorneys, various members of the legal and social arena, and societal norms and expectations.

Typically, extended family members either promote or sabotage the parents' efforts at collaboration. In some cases, the extended family members do not recognize how their negative behaviors impact the restructuring of the family. Others may or may not be fully aware of their influence. Because of their own inability to disengage from the situation, family members may sabotage the parental subsystem by (1) undermining the decision making of one or both parents, (2) engaging in inappropriate behavior in front of the children such as denigrating one or both parents, and (3) instigating conflict between the parents.

Professionals working with the family, such as attorneys, mental health workers, and social agencies, play a significant role in the restructuring of the family. Their influence can either invite or derail collaboration between the parents and extended family members. Courtroom antics may set the standard of behavior for parents and their extended family members. Well-meaning attorneys, advocating for their clients' rights, may inadvertently pit mother against father and vice versa. Custody evaluators, by the very nature of their role, often endorse one parent over the other. Likewise, mental health workers and social service agencies may align themselves with one parent while overlooking the interactional nature of relationship of the parents. Therefore, it is imperative that every member of the system, family members and professionals alike, recognize the interactional and reciprocal nature of the various components of the family and social system so as to not provide additional fuel for the conflict.

NEVER-MARRIED-PARENTS PERSPECTIVE

Each family redefines itself with its own unique circumstances. There may be differences in the type of relationship the couple has experienced. Sometimes the parents may have had very short-term relationships, perhaps even a one-night stand. Others may have lived together for an extended period but never married. Still others may have decided to maintain separate households from the beginning of the child's life. As a consequence of these many variables, never-married parents bring a different perspective to the realignment of the family.

Many factors may affect the never-married couple's ability to create and maintain a parenting partnership. The conception of the child may have been unexpected, unplanned, and never discussed. Depending on the length and circumstances of the relationship, parents may have limited, if any knowledge about each other's personal characteristics or ability to physically, emotionally, and financially provide for a child. Some men may be left totally in the dark about fathering a child until asked to provide child support. Others may learn they have a child only to be asked to relinquish parental rights so the mother's new spouse can adopt the child.

Never-married couples are often young and inexperienced. Due to their age, they may not have even established themselves; creating a secure environment for a child is foreign to them. They often blur their parenting relationship with the desire to establish an intimate relationship. Sometimes the child is used as a pawn in a game of love and hate. Their resources are often limited and, if available, they may enlist the aid of extended family members. Thus tribal warfare is a common phenomenon. The challenges for never-married parents mimic those of married couples while bringing additional obstacles to be overcome.

Ultimately, parental functioning, whether the parents were married or not, and the ability to interact with each other greatly influences their child's adjustment. Separation and divorce ignite a chain reaction which challenges each family member to reorganize his or her life. They must learn to cope with numerous losses, conflicting emotions, and continuous change. Professionals working with the family, such as attorneys, mental health workers, and social agencies, play a significant role in the restructuring of the family. Each of these individuals, along with extended family and friends, can either support or sabotage collaboration between the parents. A structure needs to be established that allows parents to communicate about their child's welfare, solve problems, and negotiate solutions. They must be willing to share parenting information to obtain their mutual goal of providing for the emotional and physical well-being of the child. Although children are always affected by their parents' divorce, the child caught in the middle of parental conflict suffers the greatest loss and most long-reaching consequences. Chapter 2 further explores the child's perspective on divorce and the devastating effect of parental warfare.

Chapter 2

Divorce and Parental Conflict: The Child's Perspective

Most couples experience some hostility in the first year or two following the breakup of their relationship. Although the conflict experienced by divorcing couples may be part of the process of uncoupling, children still need to be shielded from the cross fire. Often it is intense before resolving itself into a low level of tension. However, for some couples the conflict drags on and on and settles into a negative and destructive pattern. Years later, these parents still cannot be in the same room without problems erupting. Some couples experience an intensity of conflict that does not subside. Conflicted parents often struggle with issues of fairness, equality, retaliation, and betrayal. These behaviors and their destructive emotions can wreak havoc on the binuclear family. According to Maccoby and Mnookin (1992), most divorcing parents are engaged in fierce warfare during the first year of separation. They noted that for half of these couples, the battles will involve physical violence even when it was absent from the marriage. They observed that by the second year, most divorced parents become accustomed to a postdivorce arrangement. By the third year, couples who have realigned their relationship and started to heal emotionally minimize their conflict.

REACTIONS OF CHILDREN

Research shows that many factors determine a child's reactions to divorce. Some are inherent and cannot be altered, such as the child's age at the time of the divorce, the child's gender, and temperament. Other factors, however, can be controlled. Management of these factors is held in the hands of the child's parents. Parents are in a powerful position to influence their child's long-term recovery from the injury of divorce. For instance, Marston (1994), maintained that five requirements must be met to influence a child's healthy adjustment and development during and after the separation of the family:

1. Children must be shielded from their parents' conflict.
2. Children must be given permission to love both parents.
3. Children must be able to maintain relationships with both parents without being caught in the middle of parental warfare.
4. Parents must be able to realign their relationship from that of former spouses to coparents.
5. Parents must successfully cope with the effects of divorce and reconstruct their lives.

In a similar fashion, Wallerstein (1983) identified six psychological tasks a child of divorce must accomplish in order to accept the change in the family structure. The child must

1. acknowledge the end of his or her parents' marriage;
2. disengage from the parents' conflict and focus on his or her own needs;
3. resolve his or her personal loss;
4. overcome self-blame for the breakup of the marriage;
5. accept the permanence of the new family structure; and
6. acknowledge hope for the future.

Some children escape the trauma of divorce nearly unscathed, adjusting quickly to their new circumstances and going on to function well throughout adulthood. Others, however, are severely scarred by the experience and exhibit a multitude of problems years after the divorce.

FACTORS THAT INFLUENCE
CHILDREN'S ADJUSTMENT

Garrity and Baris (1994) identified seven major factors that influence a child's adjustment to divorce: age, gender, temperament, environmental stability, parental stability, parental access, and parental relationship.

Age of the Child

The age of the child at the time of the divorce often affects the child's reaction to it. In general, children under the age of five show their pain most keenly at the time of the divorce but ultimately tend to adjust best of all the age groups. They have fewer memories of their birth family and easily transition to membership in a stepfamily. Children between the ages of five and twelve generally react with hostility in the immediate aftermath of the divorce. Many symptoms indicate the degree of stress these children experience. The most telling, perhaps, is the frequency with which their academic grades plummet during the first year after the family breakup.

Although teenagers do not wear their feelings on their sleeve, they often harbor painful currents underneath. Adolescents navigate the treacherous waters of divorce with trepidation, already dealing with the normal insecurities of peer relationships, sexuality, obsession about their bodies, and normal separation from parents. The added stress of divorce at this time can precipitate serious consequences. Some act out, battling everyone and everything around them; others turn the battle inward and become acutely depressed.

So although age does not determine the long-term mental well-being of the child, it does profoundly influence the child's reaction. Wallerstein and Lewis (1998, p. 380) conclude that "at each developmental stage the impact (of divorce) is experienced anew and in different ways." The following age-group information is based on several sources, including Arbuthnot and Gordon (1993), Berger (1983), Clapp (1992), Kalter (1990), and Marston (1994).

Infants and Toddlers

Infants and toddlers depend upon their parents for their basic care as well as their emotional stability. Toddlers are likely to develop significant anxiety over being separated from a parent. Divorce interferes with an expected sense of predictability and stability in their lives. Three factors generally add to their state of confusion and anxiety: (1) dramatic changes in daily routines and schedules, (2) the emotional distress of one or both parents, and (3) conflict between parents. The young child's life feels unpredictable, confusing, and frightening. Very young children reflect the emotional state of their parents. Infants and toddlers may

- exhibit a loss of developmental accomplishments, such as returning to the bottle, waking in the night, crawling, and refusal of enjoyable food;
- demonstrate fear by becoming clingy and refusing to separate from the parent, by shying away from activity with familiar adults, and/or by not taking pleasure in exploring their environment;
- exhibit intense feelings of frustration and anger through yelling, biting, hitting, throwing toys, or banging their head;
- become extremely angry when their basic needs are overlooked or when caretaking schedules are unpredictable; and/or
- appear listless and withdrawn.

Preschoolers

Preschoolers begin developing some capacity for abstract thinking, yet they lack the cognitive skills to fully understand the concept of divorce. They also have difficulty distinguishing reality from fantasy. Consequently, preschoolers may believe that if Daddy left them, Mommy may also leave them. They may also come to the conclusion that the parent who left the home no longer loves them. It is common among preschoolers to believe that their misbehavior is responsible for the divorce. Frequently, they exhibit a sense of responsibility for the events surrounding the divorce. Therefore, the child may believe that the parents' distress, fighting, and separation are their fault. A common remark includes, "I'll be a good girl so Mommy and Daddy can live together again." Preschool children struggle for independence, but their emotional and social independence is still shaky. Preschoolers continue to rely on their parents' protective role to adequately consolidate their independence. In general, they become anxious over the separation from one or both parents, experience fears of abandonment, and may worry about the well-being of the absent parent. As a result, the parents' emotional turmoil and unpredictable behavior will threaten the preschooler's security. Under these circumstances, children often experience fear, confusion, and guilt. In addition, preschoolers may

- exhibit a loss of developmental accomplishments, such as returning to a bottle, soiling, refusing to play with peers, and regressing to baby talk;
- cry frequently;
- complain of stomachaches;
- display anger through aggression toward parents, siblings, and other children;
- exhibit more temper tantrums;
- have difficulty separating from parent;
- lose interest in pleasurable activities, food, or candy;
- eat less or eat more;
- worry about who will take care of them and where they will live; and/or
- appear subdued, joyless, listless, and withdrawn.

Early Elementary School Children (Ages Six to Eight)

Children between the ages of six and eight depend upon the security of their family structure. They develop love and trust in their family unit. Children this age depend on parents for safety, security, and self-esteem. When the security of a dependable home environment is disrupted by divorce, a child's emotional well-being is threatened. The primary desire is for parents to reunite. The child is likely to be aware of the conflict that occurred prior to the divorce as well as those battles that continue after the separation. At times children may find themselves caught in the middle of their parents' warfare. They are likely to experience an emotional tug-of-war.

The eight-year-old child may struggle to maintain allegiance to both parents. In the real world, this will play out by telling each parent what he or she wants to hear, which may exacerbate the conflict between the parents. In addition, children who try to please their parents generally do so at their own expense. In order to maintain their loyalty to each of their parents they adopt their parents' views and learn to deny their own thoughts and feelings. Gradually, they may lose a sense of who they are. They may continue to believe that they are responsible for the divorce. Children may assume the role of messenger, exchanging the complaints of angry parents. Likewise, children this age may be enlisted as spies, responding to frequent questions from one parent about the other parent. Six- to eight-year-olds may

- be preoccupied with feelings of guilt, loss, sadness, rejection, fear, and insecurity;
- deeply fear that they will be replaced by a new stepparent, stepsibling, or a significant other;
- cry easily, act cranky, and become anxious;
- become distractible and have difficulty concentrating;
- perform poorly academically;
- develop somatic complaints;
- attempt to reunite their parents (develop problems that require parents to work together); and/or
- assume the role of the absent parent in an attempt to support or comfort the residential parent.

Nine- to Twelve-Year-Olds

As children mature, they become acutely aware of what is going on around them. They are interested in the content of parental conflicts. Children this age actively seek information by asking adults questions and eavesdropping on adult conversations. They draw their own conclusions about who and what they believe. Nine- to twelve-year-olds are likely to side with one parent over the other. They have a strong sense of loyalty and may tend to rescue and side with the "wronged" parent. They may align themselves to this parent for a long time. Similarly, children at this age may be very critical of their parents. Believing that their parents are capable of working out their differences, they often accuse them of being selfish and inconsiderate of the needs of their children. Consequently, they experience immense anger directed at one or both parents. In addition, children this age struggle to define who they are and often feel threatened by the possibility of losing their friends or changing schools. Peer relationships become much more critical at this age. Preteens strive to fit in with a peer group. They fear that news of their family separating may alienate them from their peers. This age group tends to be easily embarrassed and may pretend to act "cool" in front of their parents and peers. The nine- to twelve-year-old may

- feel and express intense anger through verbal and at times physical acts;
- become rebellious by engaging in stealing, lying, or refusing to go to school;
- deny, displace, or intellectualize feelings;
- develop somatic complaints;
- perform poorly academically;
- begin dating early and become involved in sexual behavior; and/or
- assume an adult role.

Adolescents

Adolescence is a time of dramatic growth in each aspect of the child's life. Teenagers become aware of their physical growth, sexuality, the complexities of their environment, and their sense of independence. Because of the overwhelming changes, adolescents need love, emotional support, and consistent and firm guidance from their parents. Although teenagers strive for independence, they are still very aware of how much they need their parents for support. When parents divorce, adolescents face not only the changes that are associated with the separation of the family but also the changes that normally occur during this period of development. Adolescents are generally surprised when they discover that their parents are separating. On the one hand, they may be disappointed in their parents' inability to keep the family together. On the other hand, they may assume responsibility for the breakup of their family. In high-conflict situations, the teenagers may actually announce that they are happy about the separation. This does not mean that they are not hurt or frightened by the changes. Similar to other children, parental hostility can be extremely upsetting to teenagers. Most teenagers deeply wish for their parents to reunite. This age group is extremely susceptible to their parents' attempts to enlist them as spies and messengers. Adolescents may

- talk less and temporarily withdraw to cope with their feelings and emotions;
- exhibit angry and rebellious behaviors through physical fighting, verbal hostility, destruction of property, and self-injuring behavior;
- demonstrate chronic depression (feelings of worthlessness, sleep disturbance, eating disorders, constant fatigue);
- develop somatic complaints;
- use drugs and alcohol as a way to escape;
- become sexually active;
- perform poorly academically and skip school;
- become preoccupied with a sense of family and adopt a caretaking role; and
- run away from home.

Chapter 7 revisits the stages of child development and how each of the stages influences time-sharing arrangements.

Gender of the Child

The child's gender may indicate differences in responses to the divorce. Research shows that boys often have more difficulties in the first few years following the divorce in social and personal adjustment as well as in academic performance. However, long-term studies show that girls who appear at the time to adjust well to the divorce have more significant problems later in life.

Temperament of the Child

Some children have an easygoing personality or temperament from birth. These children have always adjusted easily to new or unfamiliar food, strange places, and each developmental stage. They usually adjust fairly well to the disruptions caused by the divorce as well. This resilient characteristic allows them to move between households with minimal difficulty. On the other end of the scale, "reactive children" (sensitive children) fare less well. These children navigated each developmental stage as though they were in stormy waters. They tend to be more inflexible when faced with the changes forced upon them by divorce. For these youngsters, divorce is a very arduous life experience (see Chapter 7).

Environmental Stability

Divorce involves a number of changes. The more changes in a child's life in a short period of time, the greater the risk of a negative influence on the child. Children fare better if changes are kept to a minimum, even when these changes are perceived as positive. Children benefit greatly from remaining in the same house, neighborhood, school, and religious institution. The continued support of a familiar network, including their extended family, helps ease their adjustment.

Parental Stability

Divorce directly affects parents' ability to provide continued structure, support, and nurturance to their children. The primary parent's psychological and economic stability is one of the most poignant influences on a child's adjustment. Parents having difficulty navigating the process of divorce may overlook the needs of their children. For instance, parents may seek emotional support, share adult information with their children, and ask their child's opinions on matters regarding dating and legal procedures. Children who assume an adult role become "parentified," which prolongs the grief process. It is crucial that children receive support as they cope with the separation of their family. Children make a better adjustment if at least one parent can provide the child extra support and guidance during this trying time. Parents need to provide continued discipline and routine in order to create a stable and predictable environment for their children.

Parental Access

The most fortunate children are those who are allowed to maintain close and satisfying relationships with each significant family member after the divorce. Not only is the relationship with each parent important, but relationships with the extended family members are important as well. Research suggests that a meaningful relationship with one or both parents appears to greatly decrease the negative effects of the divorce on a child's behavior. Experts unanimously agree that in all but a few extreme cases, children need both parents.

Parental Relationship

The ongoing postdivorce relationship between parents is one of the major influences on a child's adjustment following the separation of his or her family. Although this is difficult for many parents, shielding children from parental conflict is the most influential element on a child's adjustment. Parents who are able to set aside their personal differences and develop a co-operative parenting arrangement contribute greatly to their child's healthy development. Under these circumstances, children can receive the love and guidance from both parents, grow up in a stress-free environment, and be protected from the tension of the parents' differences.

COPING STYLES OF CHILDREN OF DIVORCE

Two major research teams concentrating on the impact of divorce on a child's adjustment, Johnston and Campbell (1988) and Hetherington, Hagan, and Anderson (1989), have identified a classification system to describe the personality styles of children of divorce. Johnston and Campbell characterized the behavior of children into four categories: maneuvering, equilibrating, merging, and diffusing.

> *Maneuvering* children were described as master manipulators. Typically, these children profit from their parents' conflict by using it for their own purposes and needs. Hence, they lack empathy, especially toward their parents, and are inclined to develop shallow attachments to others.
>
> *Equilibrating* children enroll themselves as referees or mediators. They are capable of withstanding a high degree of conflict. These children often appear to be functioning well on the surface but generally experience high anxiety.
>
> *Merging* children converge with the familial conflict and, therefore, lose their sense of self. They are unable to identify their own thoughts and opinions and, instead, imitate the emotions of people in their presence. These children are at risk for being recruited into their parents' battles. As a result, they will align themselves with one parent or the other or with both parents as they continually maneuver themselves across battle lines.
>
> *Diffusing* children are generally not strong enough to cope with the high-conflict characteristic of the family separation. They are unable to develop the coping mechanisms needed to protect themselves against parental conflict. These children often decompensate and are referred to psychological treatment. Johnston and Campbell identified these children as the most dysfunctional and disorganized.

In a similar fashion, Hetherington and colleagues classified three types of personality styles that emerge in children: aggressive/insecure, opportunistic/competent, and caring/competent. *Aggressive/insecure* children were described as demonstrating low self-esteem and poor academic performance. According to Garrity and Baris (2002) these children were characterized either as "bullies" or "victims." They exhibited aggressive and impulsive behavior in both their home and school environments. As a consequence, 70 percent of these children were unable to preserve close friendships. This group of children represented three times as many boys as girls.

The *opportunistic/competent* child resembles Johnston and Campbell's classification of an "equilibrating" personality. Children in this classification were perceived as being very influential and calming even when faced with a high degree of conflict manifested by those around them. Although these children are diplomatic and able to make friends easily, they have difficulty maintaining any depth of peer or adult relationships or attachments.

Hetherington identified the third style as *caring/competent.* She viewed these children as well adjusted, living in intact families exposed to limited familial conflict. Children manifesting this style are often required to take care of their younger siblings. They are able to establish and maintain healthy relationships with others characterized by affection and compassion. This group is represented mainly by girls raised by a single-parent mother.

Other clinicians and researchers have focused their attention on those children who cope successfully, build character from adversity in their lives, and possess optimism in spite of their difficult living situations (Katz, 1997; Rutter, 1987; Seligman, 1996). Four factors have been identified as providing children of divorce protection from the conflict associated with family separation:

1. *A supportive relationship with at least one parent* (Camara and Resnick, 1989; Gelman, 1991)—This factor provides children with a safe and predictable environment in which they can express their worries and concerns without the fear of rejection or retaliation. They are helped to make sense of a contradictory world by receiving accurate and objective answers to their questions. The unconditional positive regard demonstrated by the parent eases their sense of abandonment.
2. *The presence of siblings*—Siblings offer one another support and understanding as well as assist in navigating the changes associated with divorce. Moreover, they collectively absorb the consequences of their parents' warfare. Cowen, Pedro-Carroll, and Alpert-Gillis (1990) and Kempton and colleagues (1991) discovered that children with sib-

lings grasp a more realistic view of their parents' separation and a decreased sense of causing the divorce.

3. *Sensitive caregivers in the role of grandparents, teachers, friends, and day care providers*—Resources outside of the family that foster nurturing social support have a strong impact on a child's adjustment to divorce. Katz (1997) reported that both the quality and quantity of time spent with caregivers are important variables.

4. *Participation in group therapy*—This element benefits children when the focus of therapy includes providing information, sharing feelings, and developing coping skills.

PARENTAL CONFLICT

Children who experience their parents' frequent or ongoing conflict have a much longer road to recovery. Hostility breeds painful consequences for the children. The more intense the conflict, the greater the potential for damage, and the longer it lasts, the greater the chance of a child who is severely marred. When both of these factors are present, a lengthened period of hostility and high intensity of the conflict, children experience severe disruption, even into their adult lives. Such difficult divorces produce children at greater risk of long-term injury.

Definition of Parental Conflict

Parental conflict is any action, deed, or word that creates anxiety, places a child in the middle, or forces a child to choose. Conflict can be as subtle as tone of voice, hostile body language, eye rolls, ignoring, jokes, and sarcasm, to threats of violence, verbal attacks, and physical abuse. The fear of losing a parent is the most painful and agonizing alternative for children. Parental conflict is often heightened by value differences and issues of competition, power, and control (Ahrons, 2004).

Impact of High Conflict on the Child

Unfortunately, children are often put in the middle of their parents' negative interactions and frequently become messengers, scapegoats, manipulators, spies, and/or parentified children. Garrity and Baris (1994) estimated that one-third of all children of divorce are caught in the middle of their parents' animosity. Parental warfare forces children into a position for which there is no acceptable solution. In essence, a child caught in the middle assumes excessive responsibility for his or her parents by emotionally and/or physically caring for one or both parents. Children run the risk of betraying one parent while trying to please the other. The child may be crippled no matter how he or she responds.

Parental warfare is harmful to children because it interferes with responsible parenting necessary for healthy psychological development. It alters the nature of the parent-child relationship, threatens the parents' protective role, frightens children, leads to anxiety and distress, and influences the child's identity formation (Garrity and Baris, 1994). Moreover, parental hostility places a greater burden on a child's development than any other single factor in divorce. Ongoing parental conflict denies children permission to love both parents. In efforts to cope with parental hostility, children are forced to make many compromises in their own development. As a result, children live in an atmosphere of tension, fear, uneasy alliances, and feelings of abandonment. According to Johnston (1997) children caught in highly conflicted divorce are two to five times more likely to experience emotions and behaviors that are characteristic of clinical disturbances as compared to national norms.

Shear, Drapkin, and Curtis (2000) maintained that parental conflict does not necessarily cause maladjustment in children. They reviewed twenty-six research studies and concluded that 97 percent of this correlation was below .50, and 77 percent was below .30. Furthermore, they stated that exposure to parental conflict does not have uniform effects on children. They alleged that the correlation between parental conflict and a child's adjustment to separation is often misleading and does not always lead to negative outcomes for children. In support of this, they noted that children cope with stressors differently and are not as fragile as typically represented. Yet Shear and colleagues identified three factors that appear to contribute to the greatest perceived threat to children (fear of escalation or of being drawn into the conflict): (1) overt verbal or physical aggression (level of hostility), (2) incomplete conflict resolution, and (3) child-centered content.

Even if parents are not openly hostile, they can create internal conflict for the child by asking him or her to choose between Mom and Dad. Parents can carry this out either deliberately or unconsciously. For instance, the father may purposely say, "You do not really want to see your mother, do you?" Or he may say, "Your mother may not be able to spend a lot of time with you this weekend because her boyfriend is in town." Many children who are struggling with a loyalty bind walk the thin line of "fairness." It is extremely stressful to be vigilant enough to protect both parents at all times. These children maximize the positive qualities of each parent and rarely identify the weaknesses or inappropriate parental behaviors. Essentially, they deny their real experience in order to remain faithful to both parents.

On the other hand, some children caught in the middle of their parents' games will either play both parents against each other or align themselves with one parent while rejecting the other. All these options create an emotional dilemma for the child. Aggression, behavior problems, and depression are common early reactions to being caught in the middle of unrelenting animosity between parents (Blau, 1993; Johnston, Campbell, and Tall, 1985).

Long-Term Consequences for Children

Children who observe intense hostility between their parents are not only caught in loyalty binds; they are at high risk for future emotional and behavioral consequences (Allison and Furstenberg, 1989; Camara and Resnick, 1988; Garrity and Baris, 1994; Hetherington, Cox and Cox, 1985; Marston, 1994; Sandler, Wolchik, and Braver, 1988; Stolberg et al., 1987; Wallerstein and Blakeslee, 1989; Wallerstein and Kelly, 1980), particularly being vulnerable to future problems with adult relationships (Garrity and Baris, 1994). These children are frequently unable to maintain their own successful marriages because they grow up without appropriate role models for loving relationships. They do not learn the skills of communication, cooperation, and dispute resolution (Garrity and Baris, 1994). These children lack problem-solving strategies and tools for handling conflict in their own intimate relationships. Children of divorce are four times as likely to experience marital failure than children in intact families (Silvestri, 1991). Dr. Judith Wallerstein followed a group of children of divorce into adulthood to determine the long-term impact of divorce. Contrary to professional opinion, this twenty-five-year study indicated the children's emotinal scars were far reaching and negatively influenced their growth and development.

However, in a recent follow-up study by Ahrons (2004), she interviewed a group of 173 adult children of divorce and found that approximately 80 percent believed that their parents' divorce was a good decision for everyone involved. The remaining 20 percent did not fare well and reported that the divorce hurt their lives. Ahrons reported that this group had more parents with psychological problems, as well as a higher degree of alcoholism and violence in their families.

The more intense the conflict between parents, the greater the likelihood that one parent will walk out of the child's life (Garrity and Baris, 1994). Because the father is still frequently designated as the noncustodial parent, if one parent is absent from the child's life, it is generally the father. In studies associating postdecree financial issues and visitation access, parental involvement for noncustodial fathers often decreases over time. Past studies (Ahrons, 1979; Grief, 1979; Pasley and Ihinger-Tallman, 1987) indicated that as postdecree years increased, noncustodial father-child involvement decreased. Children whose fathers are absent experience greater stress and suffer more psychological and emotional distress than children whose fathers remain active in their lives (Hetherington and Arasteh, 1988; Hewlett, 1991; Lewin, 1990; Marston, 1994). Research pairs father absence with poor academic performance, higher incidence of drug abuse, teenage pregnancy, and suicide (Marston, 1994). A father's commitment to his children is instrumental in a child's healthy adjustment to the restructuring of the family. Although there is less documentation on the effects of mother absence, the emotional impact would no doubt be equally significant.

Garrity and Baris (1994) developed a conflict assessment scale to assist professionals working with separated families to evaluate the level of conflict demonstrated by the parental team. In addition, they used the conflict scale to design visitation plans for children based on both the child's age (infancy to eighteen years) and level of conflict manifested by the parents. The Conflict Assessment Scale is illustrated in Figure 2.1. Visitation plans are enumerated in Chapter 7.

THE ROLE OF PARENTS IN CHILDREN'S RECOVERY

Divorce poses significant consequences for all children. Depending upon the child's coping mechanisms and other factors, the reactions vary. However, when the normal adjustment to divorce is interrupted by high-conflict patterns, children pay the highest price: their childhood. When parental lines are drawn, the results are uneasy alliances, crippling tension, and painful loyalty binds. This type of divorce produces children at greatest risk.

Parents are in a powerful position to influence their child's long-term recovery. They have the power to minimize the damage of parental conflict. Unfortunately, some parents become so caught up in their own pain that they lose sight of the impact of their own behaviors. Some refuse to change because they enjoy the fight and/or the ability to inflict pain on their former partner. Thankfully, there are also parents who would shield their children if they knew how to alter their own behaviors. Ultimately, parents must learn to disengage, improve their communication, work toward a new coparenting relationship, and become proactive in reducing their child's stress.

For high-conflict families, the appointment of a parent coordinator may be the only viable solution. Parent coordination can offer parents the opportunity to learn new behaviors while being held accountable for any inappropriate ones. Through education, skill development, and new ways of interacting with each other, conflicted parents can make a choice to heal and release the past. As parents recover, so do most children.

Minimal	Mild	Moderate	Moderately Severe	Severe
Cooperative parenting Ability to separate children's needs from own needs Can validate importance of other parent Conflict is resolved between the adults using verbal exchange with only occasional expressions of anger Negative emotions quickly brought under control	Occasionally berates other parent in front of child Occasional verbal quarreling in front of child Questioning child about personal matters in life of other parent Occasional attempts to form a coalition with child against other parent	Verbal abuse with no threat or history of physical violence Loud quarreling Denigration of other parent Threatens to limit access of other parent Threats of litigation Ongoing attempts to form a coalition with child against other parent around isolated issues	Child is not directly endangered but parents are endangering to each other Threatening violence Slamming doors, throwing things Verbally threatening harm or kidnaping Continual litigation Attempts to form a permanent or standing coalition with child against other parent (alienation syndrome) Child is experiencing emotional endangerment	Endangerment by physical or social abuse Drug or alcohol abuse to point of impairment Severe psychological pathology

FIGURE 2.1. Conflict Assessment Scale (*Source:* Reprinted with permission from C. Garrity and M. Baris, *Caught in the Middle: Protecting the Children of High-Conflict Divorce*, p. 43, Table 4-1. Copyright © 1994, Jossey-Bass, a subsidiary of John Wiley & Sons, Inc.)

Chapter 3

The Role of Parent Coordinator

Parent coordination is a form of dispute resolution for high conflict that goes beyond mediation, psychotherapy, and a multitude of other family services. Parent coordination is a nonconfidential, child-centered process for parents "for whom mediation is inappropriate due to high levels of conflict or domestic abuse in the relationship" (Baris et al., 2001, p. 220). Parent coordinators (PC) are usually trained psychotherapists who are designated to work with select families.

Parent coordination is a response to the significant number of children caught in the middle of custody battles and postdivorce litigation. "Perhaps the most rapidly growing interventions for high-conflict cases are parental coordinators and special masters" (Neff and Cooper, 2004, p. 101). According to the Association of Family and Conciliation Courts Task Force on Parent Coordination (2002), "Parent coordination is an innovative approach which has been repeatedly recommended in the professional literature as a means to deal with high conflict and alienating families in domestic relations proceedings before the court." In the broadest sense, a parent coordinator can be viewed as a high-conflict manager for the family.

THE PROBLEM AND THE SOLUTION

The legal system has become overburdened with the needs of high-conflict families. Furthermore, the courts have begun to recognize the limitations of referring these families to standard psychotherapy. More often than not, traditional psychotherapeutic services do not significantly impact the behaviors of high-conflict divorcing parents. Many of the parents in this population return to the courtroom unchanged. Meanwhile, the children in these conflicted families are growing up without the necessary relief they so desperately need.

Peggie Ward discussed the limitations of traditional court referrals for high-conflict families at a 1997 conference sponsored by the Association of Family and Conciliation Courts in San Francisco. In an effort to heighten the awareness of these limitations, Ward (1997) considered three essential factors:

1. The power given to each professional as defined by the court system to authorize court orders
2. The professionals' accessibility to the family
3. The therapeutic skills and expertise of each professional to promote behavioral change

As illustrated in Table 3.1, Ward demonstrated the relationship between the three factors necessary to alter behaviors characteristic of high-conflict families with the professional's ability to function within each domain. Judges, attorneys, guardians ad litem, and psychotherapists are constrained by the standards of their profession and, accordingly, cannot successfully address the families' needs. It became apparent that a professional with both the ability and authority to work with the family was necessary to facilitate positive change within the system. Parent coordination is a service that offers the most promising solution to eliminate the adverse effects of parental warfare.

As noted, the only professional with the ability to practice within the three essential components needed to truly assist the high-conflict family is the parent coordinator. Even when parents are ordered into coparent counseling, they may or may not choose to adhere to the treatment plan. As soon as the parents hear something they do not like, they will terminate treatment. Psychotherapists without some form of authority will fail more often than they succeed (Boyan, 2000). In addition, since therapy is a confidential process, noncompliant behaviors cannot be reported to the court. Therefore, parent coordinators are in the best position to influence the family system when they are granted some basic authority as a means of reducing conflict and increasing cooperation.

TABLE 3.1. Methods to Assist High-Conflict Divorced Parents

Professional	Authority	Access	Clinical Skills
Judge	Yes	?	No
Attorney	No	No	No
Guardian ad Litem*	Some	Yes	No*
Psychotherapist	No	?	Yes
Parent Coordinator	Some	Yes	Yes

Source: Ward (1997, p. 24).
*Assuming the guardian is an attorney

HISTORY AND GROWTH OF PARENT COORDINATION

In the early 1990s, California designed the first model of parent coordination. This model borrowed from statutes previously developed for special masters and mediators. As an outgrowth of this movement, professionals in California were also the first to develop a detailed order outlining the appointment of a parent coordinator. In 1992, a group of ambitious Denver mental health professionals and family lawyers assembled in an effort to further clarify the role of a parent coordinator. Two of these professionals, Carla Garrity and Mitch Baris (1994), wrote the first book on parent coordination, titled *Caught in the Middle: Protecting the Children of High-Conflict Divorce.*

According to Garrity and Baris, a parenting coordinator is a professional with a varied background in both family law and psychotherapy. In their model, the parenting coordinator has multiple functions such as helping parents develop a parenting plan and/or monitoring the parents' compliance with the agreement; mediating disputes between the parents; teaching parents how to minimize conflict; and informing parents about children's issues in divorce and child development. In addition, Garrity and Baris believed it was necessary for the parenting coordinator to consult with other professionals working with the family.

Janet Johnston and Vivienne Roseby (1997) expanded upon Garrity and Baris's earlier work. They identified a similar role that they referred to as "coparenting arbitrator." Specifically, these authors suggested that the role of a coparenting arbitrator be utilized in the following circumstances:

- "Parents with severe personality disorders who are locked in enduring impasses and are chronically litigating
- Parents who have great difficulty making important mutual and timely decisions and require assistance coordinating their parenting efforts but possess minimal characterological disorders
- Potentially abusive situations where there are ongoing but unsubstantiated allegations of abuse
- Parents who have demonstrated intermittent mental illness." (Johnston and Roseby, 1997, p. 246)

In September 2000, the American Bar Association, Family Law Section, released a conference report and action plan that recommended "[p]arent monitors, coordinators, or masters who are professionals trained to manage chronic, recurring disputes, such as visitation conflicts, and to help parents adhere to court orders be provided as a fundamental service within the court system."

In 2001, Baris, Coates, Duvall, Garrity, Johnson, and LaCross collaborated on the book *Working with High-Conflict Families of Divorce*. This text outlines how to assess conflict and identify parental alienation, and it provides a comprehensive intervention model of parenting coordination. In addition, Boyan and Termini founded the National Parent Coordinators Association, a nonprofit organization to advance the profession of parent coordination. The NPCA is active in developing protocols and standards as well as providing support mechanisms, education, and supervision to parent coordinators throughout the country. The Association of Family and Conciliation Courts has also become very active in defining the role of parent coordinators. They created the first task force on parent coordination and wrote a document titled "Parenting Coordination: Implementation Issues" (May, 2002). This document was later published in the *Family Court Review* in October 2003.

Numerous states have instituted the practice of parent coordination to assist high-conflict families. Jurisdictions in the following states are currently using parent coordinators: Arizona, California, Colorado, Florida, Georgia, Idaho, Kentucky, Maryland, Massachusetts, Michigan, Minnesota, New Mexico, North Carolina, Oklahoma, Ohio, Oregon, Pennsylvania, Tennessee, Texas, and Vermont. Many states and parts of Canada have also begun exploring the use of parent coordinators.

To date, no uniform standard of practice exists for parent coordination. Some states outline the role of parent coordination based on local statutes and legislation. Others rely on mental health workers to define the role of the coordinator.

STATUTORY AUTHORIZATION

Although parent coordination is increasing in popularity, statutory authorization is limited. Currently, statutes defining the role and function of a parent coordinator exist in only Oklahoma, Oregon, and Idaho. Vermont has taken initial steps to develop an acceptable code of behavior that delineates the essential quality of parent coordination. Even though this state has not enacted legislation that authorizes the role of a PC, the state legislature has granted funds to the Vermont Court Administrator's Office for the development of a PC model and to partially finance participant fees for service (Coates et al., 2003).

Oklahoma's Parenting Coordinator Act was enacted in June 2001. This legislation specifies that a parent coordinator may be appointed when the court determines that a case involves high conflict. Oklahoma defines high conflict as

> any action for divorce, paternity, or guardianship where minor children are involved and the parties demonstrate a pattern of ongoing (a) litigation, (b) anger and distrust, (c) verbal abuse, (d) physical aggression or threats of physical aggression, (e) difficulty in communicating about and cooperating in the care of their children, and (f) conditions that in the discretion of the court warrant the appointment of a parenting coordinator. (Oklahoma Parenting Coordinator Act, May 2003; see Oklahoma Statutes, Title 43, Section 120.1, available at <http://www.oscn.net>)

In 2001, Oregon passed legislation that permits the appointment of a PC "to assist the court in creating parenting plans or resolving disputes regarding parenting time and to assist parents in creating and implementing parenting plans" (see Oregon Statutes, available online as "ORS Chapter 107" at <http://www.leg.state.or.us/ors/home.htm>). On July 1, 2002, House Bill 541 was signed into law by the Idaho legislature.

"Other states have borrowed the authority of a related statutory concept to authorize parent coordinators; e.g., using existing statutory authority for guardians ad litem, mediators, referees or special masters" (Coates et al., 2003, p. 536). For example, Arizona uses a new civil rule that requires the parties in every case to participate in arbitration or another form of alternative dispute resolution. Parents are required to utilize the services of a mediator or a family court advisor (FCA). The role of the FCA is very similar to the role of a PC.

In Arizona, the FCA has been given the authority to make binding recommendations on behalf of the family. In the event that the parents choose not to comply with a recommendation, the court conducts a hearing. The areas in which the FCA can make a recommendation include child-rearing matters such as transportation of the child. The FCA does not "order" compliance; he or she simply advises the court of any noncompliance.

APPOINTMENT OF THE PARENT COORDINATOR

More often than not, the appointment of a PC is either ordered by the court or as a stipulation of the parties. However, the AFCC task force (2003) reported that the court might not be authorized to demand parents to participation in parent coordination. Thus, parents are often asked by the judge or guardian to stipulate to the appointment. In most states, PCs must be appointed pursuant to the stipulation of the parties if the range of the PC's authority includes arbitration.

Professionals in one jurisdiction in Oregon maintain that the court does have limited authority to appoint a PC even over the party's objection when exceptional circumstances exist. They are that

- "one or both parents are unable to work cooperatively to engage in joint decision making for their child;
- that due to the existing level of parental conflict, the child's relationship with father/mother has been seriously disrupted; and
- that the only way the child will be able to develop a normal relationship with and spend time with both parents is through the use of a coordinator with the power to coordinate parenting time, parenting exchanges, communication, and exchange of information and records." (Marion County Family Law Advisory Committee, 2002)

Since parent coordination is a rapidly growing field, it is hoped that clearer standards and greater protection will arise out of this movement. According to the AFCC Task Force (2002):

> The parent coordinator is a hybrid role, functioning on the interface of the contrasting cultures of law and psychology. Working with highly conflicted, litigious cases in this adversarial-collaborative interface is one of the most difficult (and risky) emerging roles for professionals. (Coates et al., 2003, p. 558)

REFERRAL SOURCES

Self-Referral

Parents can enter the process of parent coordination through different referral avenues. Occasionally, parents may voluntarily agree to work with a parent coordinator. They may choose to locate a PC and sign a stipulation of the parties, or they may include it in their settlement agreement. However, unless they are strongly committed to the process, parents generally terminate their involvement in the program once they believe the coordinator to be biased against them. If parents volunteer, it is recommended that they sign the stipulation as well as notify their attorneys of their involvement in the program. The PC should send copies of stipulation to both attorneys as soon as the parents become involved in the process.

When parents agree to include parent coordination in their settlement agreement, it is imperative that the agreement include the parent coordination order. In the event that a settlement agreement lacks this information, the coordinator should contact the attorneys to request that the settlement agreement be modified to include the necessary language.

Attorney Recommendation

Once attorneys become familiar with parent coordination, they may suggest participation in the service to their clients. Under these circumstances, the attorneys generally discuss this option with the opposing attorney prior to their appearance in court. If both parties agree, the attorneys will notify the court of their clients' request; the court usually supports the decision of the parents and finalizes it in a court order. Again, it is imperative that the order include a comprehensive description of the responsibilities of both the coordinator and the parents, similar to the form in the Appendix.

Mediator Recommendation

During the process of mediation, a mediator may recommend parent coordination. Under these circumstances, the parents are not required by law to comply with this request. They may, however, include participation in parent coordination in their settlement agreement developed through the process of mediation. Once the settlement agreement is reduced to a court order, then the parents' participation becomes mandatory. However, the settlement agreement may not outline the process of parent coordination. Then it becomes necessary to execute a parent coordination stipulation prior to beginning the program. Likewise, if the parents agree to voluntarily participate in the program as part of a mediated agreement that does not become reduced to a court order, the stipulation should still be executed between the parents.

Guardian ad Litem Recommendation

Although most jurisdictions recognize the role of a guardian ad litem as an advocate for the children, their responsibilities and power may differ from jurisdiction to jurisdiction. Most guardians can request that a family member or family participate in ancillary services such as psychotherapy, substance abuse evaluation, and parent education. Some parents may abide by the guardian's recommendation without being ordered by the court. At times, parents may not be willing to accommodate the guardian's request. In these circumstances, the guardian generally makes a formal request to the court to compel the family to take part in a specific service. In either situation, the role of a parent coordinator may or may not be clarified for the parents in a written document. If the referral is not accompanied with an order delineating the parent coordinator's role, the coordinator should contact the guardian in order to determine the guardian's expectations for services prior to meeting with a parent. During this conversation, the coordinator can discuss the benefits of a comprehensive court order and make arrangements with the guardian to execute an order prior to the initiation of the service. Otherwise, the PC should request the parents sign a stipulation before offering PC services to them.

Judge's Order

Obviously, judges will not order parent coordination unless they are familiar with the process. However, even if they are familiar with the process, they may not completely understand the function of a parent coordinator. Thus their orders may be vague. If the order is vague, contact the attorneys through a memo to discuss the situation and request their support in enlisting their clients' cooperation in submitting the parent coordinator order to the court. The PC should not begin the program until the role is clearly defined.

Some judges may be uncomfortable mandating parents to work with a parent coordinator but recognize the need for such a service. Therefore, they may strongly recommend this option to the parents and their attorneys. In order to stay in the good graces of the judge, most attorneys will advise their clients to agree to participate in the service. Under these circumstances, the parent coordination process becomes a "stipulation of the parties" but may still be reduced to a court order.

AREAS OF DECISION-MAKING AUTHORITY

Typically, each jurisdiction defines the area and degree of decision-making authority granted to the PC. "A common limitation on PC authority is that s/he can not make changes to a custody determination, make relocation orders or substantially alter existing access schedules" (Coates et al., 2003, p. 534). In addition, in most but not all states, the PC does not have the authority to determine which religion the children will practice.

As noted, the authority given to the PC to make decisions on behalf of the children varies from state to state. In Vermont, the PC may make recommendations that relate to time-sharing schedules, transportation arrangements, and other parenting matters. In some states, the PC may make recommendations regarding supervised visitation.

The parent coordinator's authority to draft binding orders varies significantly from state to state and from judge to judge. California utilizes standard orders that delineate the areas of authority that may be granted to the PC. This checklist allows the parent coordination process to be tailored to meet the unique needs of each family. However, in Arizona, Georgia, and Pennsylvania, parent coordinators are prohibited from creating binding orders.

Orders and stipulations can vary in the degree of authority granted a parent coordinator. This authority falls along a continuum from no authority to arbitration. Some orders may grant the PC the authority to make temporary decisions while others may grant the authority to make binding decisions on specific parenting matters. Regardless of the degree of authority granted to the PC, each coordinator, including the professional with no authority, can still facilitate change by the very nature of their ability to make recommendations, monitor parental behaviors, and provide status reports to attorneys and the court.

Although the degree of authority granted to the PC may vary from case to case, it is imperative that this professional remain neutral and impartial when evaluating the family's needs as well as when offering recommendations. In order to offer additional objectivity and clarification, the order appointing a PC should distinguish between the professional's authority to make a decision versus a recommendation.

Since a document authored by a PC can influence the outcome of the court's decision, procedural guidelines outlining the nature and process of written documentation should be outlined in the court order or stipulation. Jurisdictions across the nation have identified different procedures for the PC to follow when submitting reports, recommendations, and objections. Most require the PC to put any decision into writing unless the issue is of such a small matter as not to need immediate attention. Oregon recognized that generating and filing documents with the courts after each parenting matter was resolved would impose excessive work for the PC. As a result, the PC does not have to file a report with the court unless a decision would change the parenting plan. In most states in which the PC is granted some authority to intervene, the PC decision remains in effect pending a hearing unless otherwise stipulated in the order.

COMMON PRACTICES

Because parent coordination is a relatively new profession, this role has been referred to by different names across the country. A study conducted by the AFCC Task Force (2003) revealed that a variety of terms have been used to identify the profession. In California a parent coordinator is referred to as a *special master,* while Colorado uses the term *med-arbiter.* In New Mexico the PC is called a *wiseperson,* while in Hawaii they are called *custody commissioners.* Arizona calls their PC a *family court advisor,* and Oklahoma a *resolution coordinator.* Oregon used to call their PC a *parenting referee.* Other jurisdictions use the term *coparenting arbitrator.* Most states refer to either *parenting coordinator* or *parent coordinator.* Consistently, however, parent coordinators are strongly discouraged from having multiple relationships. Custody evaluators or psychotherapists involved with a family should not shift their role to a PC even if they meet all the qualifications.

Parent coordination may be initiated at any stage of the divorce process. In some jurisdictions, the parent coordination model is utilized only after a parenting plan has been written and agreed upon by all parties. In other states, the PC may be appointed at the onset of the process in order to assist with the development of the parenting plan. Under these circumstances, the PC may also be responsible for monitoring and enforcing the parenting plan once it has been entered as an order of the court.

In most circumstances, the process yields the most optimal results once the parents have participated in mediation, been involved in the court process, and finalized a parenting plan or a settlement agreement. At this juncture, the PC is appointed to assist the family in complying with the agreements. A judge may also appoint a parent coordinator during the divorce process while additional data are collected about the family's dynamics. In high-conflict cases this is generally addressed through some form of custody evaluation or guardian investigation. Since custody evaluations tend to take several months to complete and the custody evaluator does not function as a helper for the family, a parent coordinator may be appointed to assist the family with day-to-day living while providing valuable feedback to the evaluator. In a similar fashion, those guardians working for the court may not have adequate time or the necessary skills (attorney as guardians) to identify and interrupt the dysfunctional behavior patterns of the family. However, the guardian can compel the family to follow the recommendations made by the PC. In the most acrimonious family situations, the collaborative efforts of the two professionals may be the most effective means of managing the family.

Training requirements necessary to function as a parent coordinator differ from jurisdiction to jurisdiction. At a minimum, most, if not all, jurisdictions require training and expertise in the following domains: child developmental theory, child and adult adjustment issues to divorce, adult psychopathology, family systems theory, communication and conflict resolution, time sharing, parenting plans, domestic violence, family mediation training, and legal aspects of divorce.

In Santa Clara County, California, the local rules designate that special masters are required to meet the same qualifications as supervising or associate counselors of family court services. In addition, they are required to demonstrate training in family code, domestic violence, and local court protocols. Three full days of training is strongly recommended for professionals who have the desire to work in this county (AFCC Task Force, 2000).

In metropolitan Atlanta, and Scranton, Pennsylvania, parent coordinators are presently mental health professionals with family mediation training and extensive training and supervision in the model developed by the Cooperative Parenting Institute. In Ohio, both attorneys and mental health providers function as PCs. In an attempt to teach attorneys more about family dynamics and therapists more about the legal process, they developed a team training approach. Attorneys and mental health providers are paired together until they are qualified to operate on their own.

Oklahoma requires the PC to have a master's degree in mental health, a license in their field, and additional training plus five years of experience. They created a quality assurance panel in order to monitor the integrity and quality of the PC program as well as review complaints. Although Vermont offers only eight parent coordination sessions, the state requires parent coordinators to have 160 hours of training. Arizona requires yearly training for FCAs.

Ordinarily, a parent coordinator is appointed for a two-year term unless the court extends the appointment. Even so, after the expiration of the professional's term, a PC may be reappointed. In Georgia, the parents participate in parent coordination indefinitely and utilize the services as new problems arise. However, in Georgia, the parents may jointly terminate the services at any point or request to receive services on an "as-needed basis." Most jurisdictions outline procedures for the resignation, removal, or substitution of a PC.

According to the AFCC task force (2003) most states grant their coordinators quasi-judicial immunity. However, alleged improprieties or unethical conduct of the parent coordinator may be brought to the attention of the court in a written document. Furthermore, immunity does not preclude a parent from filing a licensing board complaint against the PC. Most licensing boards are unfamiliar with the role of a parent coordinator. Unless the professional educates the licensing board regarding the role and responsibilities of a PC, the professional may be judged according to the ethical standards of practice in which he or she maintains licensure.

More often than not, parent coordination is not a confidential process. Most PC models provide that the parents and their attorneys may communicate with the PC ex parte. In Arizona, communication between the PC and the attorneys is limited to discussions addressing simple scheduling matters. Most states do allow the PC to communicate with the two attorneys via telephone conference and/or memo regarding any pertinent information. Most states do not allow the PC to communicate ex parte with the court. In a child-focused emergency, a parent coordinator may be permitted to have direct access to the judge in some jurisdictions. However, some areas adamantly oppose any ex parte communication with the judge.

PARENT COORDINATORS VERSUS OTHER HELPING PROFESSIONALS

Therapist versus Parent Coordinator

Although most parent coordinators are therapists by training, it is important to recognize that parent coordination is not psychotherapy. Parent coordinators do not have the luxury to take all the time necessary to ensure change. The PC must push parents to make as much progress as possible, often at a time when parents are highly resistant. Parent coordinators must be direct and authoritative at times. Therapists are not required to hold parents accountable for their behaviors, nor are they granted authority to require clients to seek additional services or to make temporary modifications. Refer to Box 3.1 for a more specific comparison of these two positions.

Coparent Counselor versus Parent Coordinator

In most areas, psychotherapists who work with divorced parents are calling themselves coparent counselors or custody counselors. Most coparent counselors prefer not to testify in court. Under these circumstances they may require parents to sign contracts stipulating that they will never subpoena the professional's testimony. Even when a client does hold privilege, these contracts may not be legally binding and may be disregarded by attorneys. Unlike parent coordinators, coparent counselors do not typically notify the court or attorneys of their clients' noncompliance with treatment recommendations or develop a detailed parenting plan or settlement agreement.

Similar to parent coordinators, coparent counselors are committed to improving the coparent relationship and minimizing stress on the child. In addition, both professionals discuss behavior-management techniques, developmental issues, and age-appropriate behaviors with parents. Since co-

BOX 3.1. Therapy versus Parent Coordination

Therapy*	Parent Coordination
Confidential	Nonconfidential
Voluntary	Voluntary, mandated, or stipulated
No client accountability	Client accountability
No monitoring	Required monitoring
Based on client's needs	Based on child's needs
Based on past and present	Based on present and future
Client in charge of treatment	PC in charge of session
Empathic	Directive and confrontational at times
Unlimited number of sessions	Limited number of sessions
Unstructured	Highly structured
Minimal expectations	Maximum expectations
"Change" optional	"Change" required
May use third-party reimbursement	No third-party reimbursement
No reporting to attorneys	Reports progress to attorneys
No authority	Limited authority
No mediation component	Utilizes mediation skills
No parenting plan created	Parenting plan created/submitted

*Therapy styles vary based upon training, education, and setting.
Source: Boyan, 2002.

parent counseling is considered psychotherapy, the parents may use third-party reimbursement.

When working with high-conflict families, a coparent counselor may be at a serious disadvantage. First, either parent may terminate the coparent counselor as soon as he or she does not like or agree with the counselor's recommendation. This means that the coparent counselor will have to be exceptionally cautious to keep the parents committed to treatment, which increases the number of sessions (and overall cost) it will take to complete the process. Second, when the process is unsuccessful, it is imperative that the courts understand the reason for the lack of success. The intervention can be discontinued without anyone knowing what has happened until the case returns to court. Some divorced parents may successfully work with a coparent counselor; however, high-conflict cases must have a parent coordinator appointed or the case will end in a stalemate.

Special Master versus Parent Coordinator

A special master may be a therapist or a family-law attorney. He or she may work in a fashion similar to a parent coordinator but almost always has the authority to arbitrate a binding decision. Special masters are generally appointed for a one- or two-year term and are utilized by parents only as issues arise.

Mediator versus Parent Coordinator

Obviously, parent coordination is much more than basic conflict resolution. However, since the professional employs mediation, it is important to distinguish between traditional forms of divorce or custody mediation and parent coordination. Divorce mediation is typically a short-term and problem-focused resource designed to facilitate disputes. It may or may not be limited to custody issues. Mediation may focus on financial issues such as alimony, child support, and the division of property. The overall emphasis of mediation is to promote a fair, acceptable resolution between the parties. In most cases, issues such as custody, child support, and alimony have already been determined before parents begin the parent coordination process. Thus similar to traditional forms of mediation, parent coordination uses the techniques of mediation to facilitate disputes but directs attention strictly to child-focused matters.

The degree to which emotional issues are addressed varies with the model of mediation practiced by the professional. Some time-limited models intentionally avoid the exploration of emotional issues (Saposnek, 1983) while others recognize the need to address emotional factors (Gold, 1992) in the context of mediation. The Cooperative Parenting Institute's model of parent coordination addresses emotional factors to the degree that they create an impasse blocking effective communication and constructive negotiation. As already mentioned, each parent's unresolved negative beliefs about the other will often interfere with mediation.

The role of mediator and parent coordinator varies considerably. Typically, a mediator facilitates the process of communication in a manner that promotes parental resolution of disputes rather than making decisions for parents. A mediator encourages the parents' authority and decision-making power. A PC also promotes parental authority but assumes responsibility for the decision-making process. This is especially true when the PC is also appointed to arbitrate a divorce impasse. In these situations, the PC actively intervenes as the expert.

The concept of self-determination is used in mediation to refer to the facilitating process in which both parents are encouraged to make their own decisions for their family rather than give the power to someone outside the family. Although parent coordination is far more directive and confrontational, the CPI model does encourage parents to solve their own problems. The major difference is that if the parents are making poor decisions or are off track, the parent coordinator is in the position to advise them.

In contrast with the CPI model of parent coordination, the aim of mediation is not to educate, monitor, or assist the parents to renegotiate their relationship, although proponents of mediation hope to positively enhance the parental relationship as a consequence of the mediation process. Last, and most important, mediation is generally a confidential process, whereas parent coordination is generally not confidential. In most cases parent coordination is a service utilized by the courts and the court may request information regarding any case. The CPI model stresses the mediation component of parent coordination particularly in predivorce cases. It is important to make a distinction between *mediator* as a noun, and *mediate* as a verb. Parent coordinators are not mediators, but they do practice a form of high-conflict mediation. Some PCs do not use the term *mediation* at all and instead make reference to dispute resolution.

Guardian ad Litem versus Parent Coordinator

A guardian ad litem is appointed as a child advocate and/or as the child's attorney. Some states select attorneys as guardians, while others designate mental health professionals. When the guardian is a therapist with similar background and training to a PC, then the differences between the two professions may not be as significant. Parent coordinators generally conduct joint sessions to assist parents to develop effective communication and conflict-resolution skills. However, in situations in which abusive behavior is demonstrated by one or both parents that interferes with the coordinator's ability to provide a safe environment, individual sessions or shuttle mediation may be utilized. Guardians, on the other hand, generally do not engage in joint sessions. Usually, a guardian is not responsible for teaching parents the skills of communication and conflict resolution. Therefore, meeting with parents in joint sessions in order to observe and enhance the parents' style of communication is not a routine practice since the guardian's goal is not to improve the communication process.

Numerous distinctions can be made between an attorney versus a mental health professional in the role of guardian. Attorneys appointed as guardians collect information through interviews, collateral reports, and court documents. This information is usually compiled into a report submitted to the court which includes recommendations for auxiliary services and, at times, a recommendation for custody. Although parent coordinators may make recommendations for outside services, they do not make custody recommendations. Attorney guardians, rarely, if ever, educate parents regarding parenting matters or communication skills or mediate child-friendly agreements. Most monitor parental compliance with court orders and ensure that the parents are acting in the best interest of their child. Guardians who are also attorneys may be allowed to cross-examine witnesses, including the parent coordinator. The parent coordinator does not function in this capacity. Nevertheless, both professionals are considered an advocate for the child.

No matter what their professional background, guardians are often overworked, understaffed, or working pro bono. Therefore, some may have only limited contact with the family over a short time, while others may complete an extensive investigation including a home study. More jurisdictions across the country are developing guidelines and standards of practice for guardians in their areas, yet most jurisdictions do not have comprehensive training for guardians.

Custody Evaluator versus Parent Coordinator

The custody evaluator's role to make a recommendation regarding custody is the most obvious difference between an evaluator and a coordinator. In addition, custody evaluators administer tests to parents to assist them with the determination of custody. Although some models of parent coordination also support the coordinator implementing testing, the CPI model does not. The CPI model advises the parent coordinator to refer the parent(s) and children for testing by a qualified professional even if the PC is qualified to administer the tests. Ultimately, the evaluator and the PC should share observations and concerns prior to a final report being submitted to the court by the custody evaluator.

The PC should never assume the role of custody evaluator. However, if the program is initiated prior to a final custody decision, it is likely that the parent coordinator will be asked to make a recommendation regarding custody. It is essential that the coordinator not fall into this trap. A parent coordinator who makes a custody recommendation is overstepping the limits of his or her role.

THE COOPERATIVE PARENTING INSTITUTE MODEL

Qualifications

A therapist working as a parent coordinator within the model of the Cooperative Parenting Institute is an experienced licensed clinician with at least a master's degree. If master's-level therapists are not recognized for licensure in their state, they generally have extensive experience and supervision comparable to licensure in other states or have obtained a clinical membership in a professional organization such as in the American Association of Marriage and Family Therapy. Although the CPI model for parent coordination is rooted in systems theory, the skills associated with family therapy are not enough while working with conflicted postdivorce families. Additional techniques and knowledge are also essential. Parent coordinators should have training and experience in the following disciplines:

1. Family systems theory
2. Adult psychotherapy
3. Developmental psychology
4. Child and adult divorce recovery
5. Parental alienation
6. Mediation and conflict resolution
7. Communications theory
8. Basic legal aspects of divorce
9. Parenting plans and time-sharing options
10. Domestic violence and substance abuse
11. Psychotherapeutic interventions designed for high-conflict parent coordination, such as the Cooperative Parenting Institute model

As different states provide parent coordination it is important to learn what requirements apply in that jurisdiction and if any statutes are used to appoint parent coordinators. For example, some states allow all therapists to call themselves parent coordinators. In other areas, the PC must be trained in family mediation. In some communities specific parent coordination training is expected but not required.

Role and Responsibilities

Occasionally the PC will step out of the traditional "therapeutic" role and assume a more authoritative role, thus the term *parent coordinator,* rather than *therapist,* more accurately defines the role and responsibilities of the professional. The parent coordinator must be able to actively intervene in the system. At times, this means that the PC is forceful in order to evoke the necessary change in the system. Not all parents will respond to logic, reality, or appeals to reason. Consequently, the PC must have thick skin and be able to structure situations in very concrete behavioral terms. The PC must remain focused on the present interactions demonstrated by the parents and avoid exploring issues related to the past, family of origin, or symptomology, particularly in joint sessions.

A parent coordinator working in the CPI model must maintain his or her maneuverability at all times and during all phases of the process. According to Fisch, Weakland, and Segal (1982, p. 22) "maneuverability implies the ability to take purposeful action despite fluctuating obstacles or restriction." Given the multilevel system with varying levels of hierarchy, the parent coordinator must work to ensure that his or her options are always open, shifting within the ecosystem as the situation demands.

A parent coordinator who is unaware of the characteristics of high-conflict divorce and the impact of parental alienation can unintentionally maintain or escalate the conflict between parents. Parents may engage in very subtle forms of alienation that can go unnoticed by naive and uneducated professionals. Many parents are quite convincing and adept at forming coalitions with the parent coordinator. The unsuspecting coordinator is also an easy target for children. The children's stories can be quite convincing, leading the parent coordinator to support the alienation of the parent. The parent coordinator must look at the behaviors in the context of the family and larger system as well as how the PC's own behavior may be helping or hurting the progress of the family.

The role of the PC working in the CPI model is to assist the parents as well as other significant individuals in resolving conflict in a manner that is beneficial to the children. Essentially, parent coordinators function as an impartial party safeguarding the child's best interest rather than advocating for either parent.

The Cooperative Parenting Institute has been providing parent coordination services since 1993 which has evolved into a specific training program known as the CPI model. The techniques and strategies contained in this text have been derived from the experiences of the authors.

Responsibilities for Parent Coordinators

The following list describes the responsibilities of the parent coordinator as outlined in the CPI model. However, depending upon the authorization granted through the court order, the parent coordinator may or may not be able to practice all of the following responsibilities:

1. To educate
   - Educate parents regarding the impact of parental conflict on their child's development
   - Teach parents anger management, communication, and negotiation skills and explain children's issues in divorce
   - Cover the concepts highlighted in *Cooperative Parenting and Divorce: A Parent Guide to Effective Co-Parenting*
2. To assess
   - Assess the family's overall functioning
   - Evaluate the child's emotional functioning and the emotional impact of parental behaviors on the child
   - Evaluate each parent's overall personal functioning (intrapsyche)
   - Appraise the coparent relationship and degree of cooperation (intrapersonal)
   - Appraise the degree of outside influence, especially from grandparents and stepparents (tribal warfare)
   - Determine impasse patterns
   - Assess the need for outside referrals
3. To intervene as case manager
   - Assist parents in shifting their role from former spouse to coparent
   - Reduce emotional attachment to the marital relationship
   - Help parents identify their contribution to conflict while increasing impulse control
   - Identify the impasses to effective communication and each parent's negative belief system
   - Record and monitor family progress and compliance
   - Consult with all professionals involved with the family
   - Identify the therapeutic needs of family members and makes recommendations for additional educational or therapeutic resources and evaluations such as parenting classes, filial therapy, supervised visitation, individual and play therapy, sexual deviance assessment, drug and alcohol assessment, random drug and alcohol screening, Alcoholics Anonymous (AA), as well as domestic violence groups.
4. To monitor
   - Ensure parental compliance with the settlement or court order
   - Assess and maintain the children's emotional and physical safety

- Monitor time-sharing arrangements and, when necessary, modify the plan as a means of reducing parental conflict
- Ensure parental access to the children
- Maintain appropriate parental behaviors

5. To mediate
   - Mediate parenting concerns in order to reach a consensus
   - Work with parents in developing a detailed plan for issues such as time sharing, discipline, decision-making procedures, communication, etc.

6. To arbitrate (only if clearly outlined)
   - If authority is granted by the parents, the parent coordinator may arbitrate any issue in which parents reach an impasse by following the guidelines described here and those outlined in the court order or stipulation of the parties.
   - If authority is granted by the judge then the parent coordinator may *temporarily* arbitrate an impasse. However, each jurisdiction varies. A judge may not be in a position to dictate arbitration. In some cases, it may be entered into only if the parties stipulate to arbitration. Otherwise, it may be considered a violation of the parents' due process rights.

Arbitration differs from mediation and negotiation. In arbitration, an impartial third party renders a binding or nonbinding decision that cannot usually be appealed. The parent coordinator must protect a child from physical, emotional, and sexual harm. Physical harm is considered to be any action or lack of action that may jeopardize a child's physical safety. For instance, lack of parental supervision may result in underage drinking or burns resulting from inappropriate use of the stove. Excessive corporal punishment may result in bruising and scarring. Physical harm may also be caused by a parent's lack of adherence to safety measures such as using a car seat and placing young children in the backseat of the car. Emotional harm includes any action that continually places a child in a loyalty bind, results in the alienation of one parent, or is of such degree and duration that the child manifests symptoms of acute distress. Finally, sexual harm is any behavior that results in a child being exposed to inappropriate sexual content or touch. Examples include inappropriate nudity within the family, inappropriate touch, observation of adult sex, and pornography. Second, the parent coordinator should arbitrate only when parents have agreed to it or the court has granted the coordinator permission to determine a temporary outcome to resolve disputes.

In the CPI model, whenever a parent coordinator functions as an arbitrator, the arbitrated decision must be carefully recorded as a temporary change, stating the reasons for acting on the child's behalf. A copy of the arbitrated decision should be sent immediately to both attorneys. The judge should also receive a copy if this provision is specifically stated in the court order. This information must be faxed the same day. If a guardian is involved, it is politically wise to consult with him or her prior to making a recommendation. Most attorneys are resistant to the parent coordinator functioning as an arbitrator and may block this function until they become more comfortable with the process.

With or without arbitration, the order or settlement agreement should stipulate that the parent coordinator has full discretion regarding program implementation including, but not limited to, recommendations of additional educational or therapeutic resources for parents and children; evaluations; and therapeutic or supervised visitation. It is understood that the parent coordinator cannot alter the legal custody status of the children. As a means of reducing parental conflict, temporary changes may be required. However, any temporary change to the schedule cannot increase or decrease either parent's time. The CPI model was designed to provide protection for the parent coordinator, clarify expectations, and encourage parents to commit to the process in good faith. The goals of parent coordination include the following:

- Assess the emotional impact of parental conflict on the child
- Safeguard the emotional and physical needs of the child
- Monitor and modify time-sharing arrangements as a means of reducing conflict and loyalty binds for the child
- Observe family progress and compliance with court orders
- Mediate parenting concerns in order to reach a consensus
- Assist parents to create a detailed Cooperative Parenting Plan
- Balance the needs of the family with the requirements of the court

Clarifying the Coordinator's Role in the Legal Document

Before initiating contact, the parent coordinator must have a clear idea of his or her role and responsibilities. This may be stipulated in a court order or settlement agreement. If a court order neglects to clarify the role of the parent coordinator, it is imperative to specifically address the court's expectations in written form. Otherwise, it will jeopardize the relationship with the family or one's own credibility. When a court order or settlement agreement is unclear, consider one of the following options:

- Contact both attorneys by fax or phone encouraging them to revise the court order or settlement agreement and replace it with the sample stipulation appointing a parent coordinator.
- If the judge recommends parent coordination, contact the law clerk and explain the situation. It is never a good idea to contact the judge directly about any case. This is considered ex parte communication.
- Encourage the parents to contact their attorneys requesting that their agreement or the order be changed to reflect the elements of an order or stipulation appointing a parent coordinator.

The court order is generally written by one of the attorneys and approved by the other attorney before it proceeds to the judge for final authorization. However, the judge may request certain stipulations in the order. Usually the attorney who is more invested in the contents of the order will assume the responsibility for its execution. The content of the court order will reflect the stipulations ordered by the judge and/or agreed upon by the parents and their attorneys. To avoid ambiguous orders regarding parent coordination, provide the legal professionals with a sample order designed for the appointment of a parent coordinator. When marketing the program, it is essential to gain the professional's understanding of the necessity for a clear and detailed order outlining the elements in the sample order so it will not conflict with the services provided by the parent coordinator.

Likewise, it is equally important to get a clear understanding of the court's support. The parent coordinator must know exactly how much leverage he or she has to request specific behaviors from the parents. Over time, the parent coordinator will learn how certain judges will view their recommendations.

In situations of parental alienation, it benefits the parent coordinator to know what sanctions will be executed by the court under conditions of noncompliance on the part of one or both parents. Sanctions may include fines, community service, attorney's fees, modification of time sharing, and jail time. Without the judge's support, a parent coordinator may have limited influence over the family system and the attorneys. When sanctions are not in place or enforced by the court, the compliant parent initiates contempt proceedings against the noncompliant parent. Other than a report noting the noncompliance of one or both parents, the parent coordinator should not contact the judge. The only exception is in the case of an emergency. The parent coordinator can send a memo to both parents' attorneys to request an emergency hearing to address the situation. Legal proceedings adversely affect the process of parent coordination, so parents are discouraged from initiating any legal proceedings when they are involved in the program.

A comprehensive order or stipulation of the parties that clearly defines the role of the parent coordinator offers several advantages. First, it requires that all parties adhere to the guidelines set forth in the document. Second, requiring the participation of both parents and any significant individuals in the life of the family increases cooperation among family members and lessens the likelihood of coalitions between parent, parent coordinator, or between generations. Third, the document can protect the PC and minimize confusion for the attorneys. Finally, a detailed order may reduce the chance of litigation and future time spent in court. Once the parent coordinator has received a signed copy of a detailed order or stipulation of the parties the process can proceed.

Parent Coordinator: Central and Essential to the Team

Families in crisis often work with multiple professionals. The parent coordinator plays a crucial role in the integration of services. The PC works as a case manager in order to reduce parental confusion, encourage professional consensus, prevent the duplication of services, and avoid any unnecessary costs. The parent coordinator should always advise the parents of his or her attempts to consult with professionals. When gathering the information, the coordinator should consider that generally no "real truth" exists, just several different perspectives generated by each member of the system.

Figure 3.1 depicts the CPI coordinator as a communication link between the multiple professionals involved with the family. As noted by the double arrow, the PC may collect information from collateral sources such as professionals working with the family as well as share details with others as necessary (two-way communication). The single arrow indicates those contacts in which the PC may only receive information (one-way communication). Until stepparents or other family members become directly involved in joint sessions, information may only be gathered.

Confidentiality

The nature of confidentiality as it pertains to parent coordination is substantially and qualitatively different from confidentiality as it pertains to therapist-client privilege in situations of psychotherapy. However, a parent coordinator is still required by law to reveal information to other persons or agencies without permission from the participant:

If a person threatens grave bodily harm or death to self or another person

If any reasonable suspicion exists that a minor is being neglected or abused

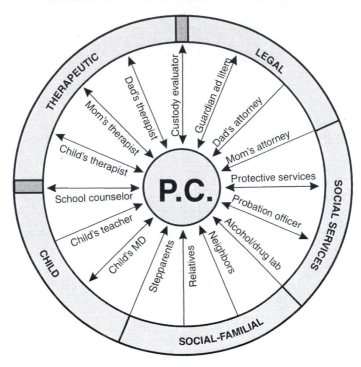

FIGURE 3.1. The Coordinator As Communication Link

The PC must clarify confidentiality and other limitations through the legal document, office policies, and the program material. Since the parent coordinator functions as a case manager, it is necessary for the PC to have access to all professionals and possibly the extended family members in the life of the family. Therefore, by executing a release form, all therapists, attorneys, guardians ad litem, visitation supervisors, physicians, child care providers, significant others, educators involved, and previous or current evaluators should be authorized to release information directly to the PC. Although issues discussed during sessions might be discussed with other professionals, the principle of confidentiality as it relates to parent coordination implies that all consultations are intended for the direct benefit of the children. This arrangement should never be exploited or abused. An authorization for release of information specifies the name of the individual as well as the content of the information to be shared. A release from one parent does not cover his or her former partner. When sessions are video- or audiotaped, every participant in the room must sign taping release forms.

The CPI model discourages parents from requesting that the parent coordinator produce notes or appear in court for the purposes of litigation unless a subpoena orders the PC to do so. It is not the intention of parent coordination to gather information that can be used in the attempt of one parent to discredit the other. The parent coordinator is not employed for the benefit of either parent. The CPI model for parent coordination provides services designed to promote a cooperative relationship between parents on behalf of the children. Therefore, the PC who is called by the judge to testify in either a court of law or by deposition must do so only on the children's behalf and pursuant to their best interests. All testimony requested from the parent coordinator should be focused solely on the interactions observed between coparents or between parents and children. However, when the parent coordinator is called to court, the testimony may indeed impact one parent or the judge's ultimate decision regarding custody.

The parent coordinator reserves the right to share information that has been provided by one parent about the other parent when conflicting information is received from the coparenting team. Verbal reports given by parents to others may not accurately reflect exactly what happened in any given situation. The parent coordinator must rely on interviewing skills, information from others, and direct observations in attempting to uncover the truth or something that resembles the truth. For these reasons, the PC should avoid frequent individual sessions or private conversations with either parent. Nonetheless, individual sessions may be warranted for the purposes of caucusing or coaching a parent. Chapter 11 contains information on coaching and caucus.

Personal Characteristics of a Parent Coordinator

The personality and abilities of the parent coordinator significantly impact the family's progress. The professionals at CPI have identified characteristics that may offer some indication as to the type of professional best suited to work as a PC.

Child focused	Empathic
Committed	Establishes appropriate distance
Competent	Ethical
Confrontational	Highly structured
Creative	Knowledgeable of the legal arena
Decisive	Patient
Determined	Proactive
Diplomatic	Problem solver
Directive	Realistic
Effective case manager	Vigilant

Professional Response

The PC functions as a neutral party appointed to safeguard the child's best interest rather than advocate for either parent. The Cooperative Parenting Institute has been instrumental in developing the first comprehensive parent coordination model including standards of practice. Chapter 4 highlights additional components of the CPI model of parent coordination.

Chapter 4

Implementing
a Parent Coordination Program

The first portion of this chapter provides an overview of the Cooperative Parenting Institute model of parent coordination. Implementing a program based upon this model is addressed in the second half of the chapter.

CPI PARENT COORDINATION MODEL OVERVIEW

The orientation adopted by the Cooperative Parenting Institute focuses on the interdependence of such environmental elements as the child, the family, the legal system, various social agencies, the culture, and the family and extended family in the life of the child. For instance, the interaction between father and child affects the interaction between mother and child at times of transition. The CPI advocates that the problems as well as the solutions appear to be in the interactional social context in which divorce is embedded. Such an approach is essential to planning and implementing therapeutic programs for two-home families.

In order to address the relationship between separate family households, the CPI program focuses on the communication process taking place between parents as they interact with each other. Discussions may focus on

1. parental behavioral expectations,
2. mutual respect,
3. the changing family structure and roles,
4. children's issues in divorce,
5. living arrangements and time-sharing plans,
6. effective communication skills,
7. problem solving and conflict resolution,
8. loopholes and corrections of the previous agreement/order, and
9. the development of a parenting plan.

The overall emphasis is to provide the children of divorce an environment free from the parents' intense hostility.

The CPI model, as outlined in this text, cannot adequately account for all situations, particularly the variety of abuse claims frequently made in high-conflict divorce. Since research indicates that approximately 25 to 50 percent of abuse allegations are substantiated in high-conflict cases, it is imperative that the professional seeking appointment has sufficient knowledge and training in multiple areas such as domestic violence, substance abuse, sexual abuse, and prevention techniques. Relying on the basic domestic violence information provided in most family mediation training will not adequately prepare the parent coordinator for working effectively with this population.

Due to the limitations inherent in any single text, continued postgraduate study is strongly recommended, including advanced parent coordination training, supervision, and further research beyond the scope of this text. Nonetheless, the CPI model has been successfully adapted to address the specific needs of families in which allegations of abuse have been claimed or documented. Additional information and specific CPI protocols are provided through advanced CPI training. The training topics include domestic violence, child abuse, Munchausen's by proxy, safety issues, and the impact of cultural influences on the process of parent coordination.

GENERAL SYSTEMS PERSPECTIVE

The CPI model endorses a systemic perspective. This perspective focuses on the interpersonal quality of families. It addresses the interfaces and communication processes taking place within the family. General systems theory emphasizes the reciprocal and interactive nature of each individual in the family. The focus is on understanding a position of shared responsibility and mutual cause. Since families do not end with the separation of a marriage, it is imperative that professionals working with binuclear families adopt a systems orientation in order to assist parents realign the family structure. Divorcing parents have a common bond between them. Therefore, for the sake of their children, divorcing couples need to continue to be involved with their former spouses in matters of child rearing. Parents must continue to parent together in spite of their unresolved grief and the fact that they no longer live together.

Ecological Considerations

An ecological perspective suggests a broader view of the family system. This perspective focuses on the significant environmental elements, the relationships among these elements, and the family's interaction with them

(Termini, 1991). In keeping with an ecosystemic view, the CPI model acknowledges that divorce involves the larger social network that is brought together in an attempt to alleviate the problematic situation in mutual, simultaneous interaction. Accordingly, an ecological orientation considers the interdependence of the family, legal and mental health systems, various social service agencies, neighborhoods, and the cultural orientation of the family.

Built within the ecological perceptive is an awareness that system components constrain and are constrained by other systems in which the family participates and in which the family and other systems are embedded (Termini, 1991). Although each of the systems in which the divorcing family participates has its own internal organization, it operates within, and/or in conjunction with, the other systems. Since family difficulties impact the legal system, and difficulties in the courtroom affect the family's ability to restructure, the two systems are interrelated and recursively influential. To understand the effect of divorce on the family requires a focus on all persons and relationships that come together. The ecological approach is an overall framework for understanding and treating the psychological and social problems of binuclear families.

PROGRAM COMPONENTS

The CPI model of parent coordination consists of three overlapping phases. These phases are not mutually exclusive and generally occur simultaneously: assessment, education, and conflict resolution. The assessment phase is a continual process and helps guide the course of the program. The model is circular in nature and is easily adapted to the individual needs of the family.

In addition, the CPI model stresses both process and outcome. The parent coordinator is not only interested in the outcome of the parents' decisions but is always watchful of the overall communication pattern taking place between parents. Parents tend to overfocus on the details of their issues and lose sight of the communication process. Thus the PC must balance outcome with process while interrupting ineffective communication patterns.

Ideally, the CPI model works best when the legal process of divorce has been concluded. In this situation, it is less likely for parents to use parent coordination as a process to gather information to use against each other in court proceedings, and the attorneys are less likely to interfere. In predivorce situations, the parent coordinator may not witness "reality" but rather a manipulation by the parents to look good in the eyes of the PC.

On the other hand, it appears that parents who enlist the services of a parent coordinator early in the divorce process seem to have less opportunity to become polarized in fixed positions. Otherwise, prior to any intervention, divorcing parents become locked into both their positions as they relate to each other and in their style of communication. The literature appears to support the notion that early intervention is central to a positive outcome (Amato and Keith, 1991; Camara and Resnick, 1988; Kelly, 1988; Maccoby, Depner, and Mnookin, 1991). Early intervention may maximize parental cooperation while decreasing the likelihood that children will be caught in the middle of their parents' negative interactions.

FINANCIAL CONCERNS AND TIME COMMITMENT

In the context of parent coordination, financial issues such as alimony, child support, and the division of property are not addressed. Financial matters in most cases have already been determined by a court of law or through another form of alternative dispute resolution. Because financial matters are routinely determined by state law, it is assumed that the legal arena is the best suited for financial disputes. However, it is not unusual for both parents to want to discuss a financial issue in hopes of resolving the matter within a joint session. Attempting to resolve financial issues may negatively affect the coparent relationship and break down communication. On the other hand, not addressing a financial impasse may actually aggravate the situation. The scope of the issue, the length of time to commit to the resolution of the problem, and clinical judgment will determine whether the issue should be addressed. If the financial concern can be addressed in fewer than two sessions, then it may be worthwhile to mediate that specific issue.

We do not recommend addressing any financial matter if the case is predivorce, since other financial arrangements may need to be considered first. However, if it is a postdivorce case and the parents choose to clarify a financial question, then the PC may choose to proceed. For instance, simple financial matters such as registration fees for an extracurricular activity may be resolved through the process of parent coordination.

The CPI model of parent coordination consists of an average of ten to sixteen eighty-minute sessions. The sessions are held over a period of approximately six to twelve months. Sessions are scheduled in this manner to better ensure a positive transition over an extended time. The PC generally reserves the right to adjust the schedule based on the unique needs of the family. In addition, the parent coordinator may deem it necessary to request that the family members attend additional sessions. However, some parents complete the program in a timely fashion and are then seen on an as-needed basis. Other important individuals (grandparents, aunts, significant others) in the life of the child may be asked by the parent coordinator to attend the sessions. See Chapter 8 for detailed information regarding the inclusion of other individuals in the sessions. After the completion of the initial sessions, the program also includes follow-up sessions scheduled at one, three, six, and twelve months as necessary. In addition, parents, as part of their final parenting plan, agree to return in the future as new issues arise. Both parents agree not to litigate until they have scheduled a minimum of two joint sessions focused on problem resolution.

THEORETICAL PRINCIPLES

The goal of parent coordination is to foster a constructive postdivorce parental alliance. The aim is to simultaneously assist parents to

1. disengage from the physical and emotional relationship of the marriage,
2. clarify new boundaries for relating to each other,
3. effectively manage conflict,
4. make effective mutual decisions,
5. increase positive collaborative behaviors, and
6. understand the impact of divorce and parental conflict on their children.

The overall emphasis of the program is to offer children of divorce the opportunity to grow in a home environment free from being caught in the middle of parental hostility. The objective is to initiate a change in the system by giving parents the tools they need to gain control of themselves and their families. The program strives to put children first while creating promising solutions that focus on education, intervention, mediation, and the prevention of parental conflict.

The CPI model of parent coordination focuses on the following:

- Safeguarding the child's emotional and physical needs
- Resolving the presenting problems and conflict between parents rather than developing client insight
- Emphasizing a position of shared responsibility and mutual cause rather than focusing on individual pathology
- Addressing the impact of the larger social network on the family and realigning the whole system in a manner that supports collaboration between coparents

Although pathology is not a primary focus, parents exhibiting personality disorders and/or addictions are often part of the high-conflict population. Personality disorders and addictions take a serious toll on the ability of coparents to effectively communicate and negotiate child-friendly agreements. In situations of psychopathology, the authors recommend that the PC adjusts the approach to accommodate the specific needs of that family. Extensive information on this subject can be found in Chapter 12.

Principles that guide the basis of the CPI model include the following:

- Child's functioning and needs as the primary focus of intervention
- Focus on present child-rearing matters rather than past marital issues
- Recognition that parental interaction may cause great distress for the child or promote a positive adjustment to the divorce
- Recognition and appreciation of the power of each parent's negative and positive assumptions about each other and their influence on a constructive postdivorce parental alliance
- Awareness that barriers at three levels (individual, interactional, ecosystemic) adversely affect the parents' ability to build a cooperative relationship
- Position that parents may not effectively use communication skills until they have grieved, reached some acceptance of the end of the marital relationship, realigned their relationship to focus on the child, and dealt with their emotional impasses
- Acknowledgment that secondary gain from symptoms and interpersonal advantage gained from a conflictual relationship serve to exacerbate postdivorce problems
- Appreciation of parental strengths in order to build on parental cooperation and healthy parent-child relationships
- Belief that parents should retain the power and the responsibility to make decisions about their child's well-being themselves; self-determination encouraged and expected
- Recognition that parents' active participation in the decision-making process is likely to yield more satisfaction with parenting agreements and compliance
- Belief that parents may get caught in an adversarial role because it is promoted and expected by society; divorcing parents pursue avenues derived from societal norms and sanctions of the legal system
- Acknowledgment of the power of the larger system and its tendency to shape and maintain the problematic behavior through social interaction as well as its potential to contribute to powerful solutions (recognizing that the practitioner is part of the system)

The primary goal is to improve the relationship between parents in order to minimize stress for the child. The unit of direct intervention is the parental team, while children are the beneficiaries of the parent coordination service. The predominant feature of the model is to focus on the needs of the children. Contrary to a healthy marital relationship, the purpose of the parents' relationship in a divorce is only to benefit the child. In this situation, the child is what brings the parents together. By keeping the focus on the child, the professional can acknowledge the parents' mutual concern and interest for their child. This sets the stage for positively aligning the parents in meeting the mutual goal of promoting the welfare of their child.

METHODOLOGY

Although the program adopts a systemic orientation, several treatment approaches have been integrated into the model. The CPI format is more than a random borrowing of techniques from various methodologies. The strong conceptual framework enables the parent coordinator to borrow ideas, methods, and techniques systematically from different theories and integrate them into the principles and framework of the program.

As an active agent of change, the parent coordinator considers what is in the best interests of the child and takes the necessary steps to motivate the parents to make changes on their child's behalf. Unlike traditional psychotherapy, parent coordination is a highly structured and often intrusive process. The parent coordinator actively and purposefully orchestrates each session while maintaining firm rules of communication and conflict resolution. Therefore, the process is not client driven, as in psychotherapy, but instead guided by the parent coordinator in the quest of decreasing conflict while increasing cooperation. To this end, the CPI model incorporates various methodologies:

> *Psychoeducational:* Parent training in communication, anger management, negotiation skills, and conflict resolution; the use of homework assignments, video instruction, and bibliotherapy to expand the parents' knowledge and skills
>
> *Interpersonal:* Communication and decision analysis, clarification of role expectations, experimentation with communication skills and direct confrontation
>
> *Cognitive-behavioral:* Cognitive restructuring, identification of automatic thoughts, self-monitoring, role reversal, and problem solving
>
> *Behavioral:* Role-play, behavioral contracting and rehearsal, contingency contracting, and self-monitoring and homework

Experiential: Gestalt techniques such as "empty chair" and exaggeration of behavioral problems and guided imagery

Strategic family therapy: Reframing, strategic questioning, and the use of paradox

Structural family therapy: Pattern interruption, solution focus, family sculpture, definition and respect of boundaries, coalitions, and alliances

Other: Case management, crisis intervention when the situation or event adversely affects the children emotionally or physically, use of video and/or written feedback, referrals to programs designed to address issues such as addiction and violence

For specific techniques and strategies in each category see Chapters 9, 10, and 11.

EDUCATIONAL FOUNDATION

Cooperative Parenting and Divorce: A Parent Guide to Effective Coparenting, by Boyan and Termini (1999), was originally created as a component of the Cooperative Parenting and Divorce group program. This guide has also been used effectively by coparent counselors and parent coordinators as a tool to introduce parents to the complex issues of family separation. The educational material is processed over time using as many weeks as necessary to address the concepts and skills highlighted in each chapter. The PC balances the educational material with the current and unique needs of the parents. The educational material focuses on the following broad concepts:

In Chapter 1, parents learn to recognize parental hostility and discover how conflict impacts their child's development. Factors that influence a child's adjustment to divorce are presented. The notion of "child focused" versus "self-focused" is proposed and stressed throughout the program. The divorce rules are covered along with a "commitment to caring" agreement and the steps to coparenting.

In Chapter 2, parents learn that when they attempt to put down the coparent they are hurting their child's developing self-esteem. For the sake of their child, parents learn to view their former spouse from their child's perspective. Although it is very difficult for some parents, they are expected to identify the positive and valuable qualities of the child's other parent. They learn to create two homes, minimize stress at transitions, and make visitation a less stressful time for their child. Parents determine the obvious and not so obvious ways they inadvertently put their child in the middle of their conflict. Parents discover the importance of loyalty and the ways children struggle to avoid a loyalty bind. The importance of allowing children access to their extended families is also addressed.

In Chapter 3, parents examine their attachment to their former spouse. They discover that their anger and bitterness keep them emotionally attached to each other in much the same way their love once did. They identify their level of attachment and learn ways to disengage or let go physically and emotionally from the marital relationship. The grief process, forgiveness, and the value of rituals are discussed.

In Chapter 4, parents clarify their personal choices and identify a personal path. The term *realignment* is introduced to assist parents to create a new role as coparents. Obstacles to realignment are examined and the notion of secondary gains and the noninterference principle are presented. Characteristics of a business relationship are taught as they apply to a coparenting relationship. The STP-A (stop, think, pause-act) technique is demonstrated. Parents realize that they are separate but equal partners in their role as coparents.

In Chapter 5, parents explore the emotion of anger. They determine what anger is, the internal and external signals of anger, constructive versus destructive anger, anger triggers, and the consequences of harboring anger. Parents recognize their distorted beliefs and how their negative assumptions create negative outcomes with the coparent. The anger connection (cognitive restructuring) is presented to teach parents how their thoughts create their feelings. These skills empower parents to make personal change rather than wait for their coparent to change. Parents are exposed to a variety of strategies to manage their own anger as well as their child's anger.

In Chapter 6, parents examine the cycle of conflict using the concepts of fire prevention. Barriers to effective conflict resolution are highlighted and techniques to overcome these barriers are practiced. Parents identify ways to defuse conflict for themselves and their child. They learn effective communication and listening skills. Parents identify their contribution to the communication pattern and identify obstacles to successful parental interaction. Tips for dealing with unreasonable expectations and limit-setting techniques are taught and practiced.

In Chapter 7, problem-solving techniques and business relationship skills are examined from the divorced parent position. Parents learn that negotiating on behalf of their child does not necessary mean that one parent wins. They learn that if their child "wins" then everyone is a "winner." A seven-step method for negotiating agreements is demonstrated. Parents learn how to prepare for and organize business meetings with their coparent. As they negotiate agreements, parents learn techniques to help them focus on their child's best interest rather than their own interests.

In Chapter 8, parents are introduced to techniques to determine the validity and seriousness of their concerns. Parents use the negotiation skills in the joint sessions until they are able to successfully address an issue without the parent coordinator's assistance. At this point, coparents are given assignments to negotiate specific issues with the coparent by phone and in person. Their ability to meet this requirement determines their overall success and length of the program.

GETTING STARTED

Before setting up a parent coordination practice the professional should be adequately prepared to work within the CPI model by

- meeting the qualifications of a parent coordinator,
- thoroughly reading this text,
- having prior experience with separating families,
- understanding the concepts of alienation and its various forms, and
- participating in a training program with a minimum of thirteen continuing education credits such as the training offered by the Cooperative Parenting Institute.

The second step is to develop a business plan to cover all the following points:

- Create a reasonable fee structure
- Develop or purchase parent coordination assessment and marketing forms
- Establish a supervisory relationship with an experienced parent coordinator
- Create relationships and consult with professionals in the areas of family law, guardian ad litem, and custody evaluators
- Prepare attractive referral and parenting packets

When determining the fee schedule, the limited financial resources of single parents should be considered. More often than not, parent coordinators also charge parents for professional consultations with attorneys and mental health professionals as well as extended telephone calls and after-hour emergencies. However, keeping fees reasonable is very important.

MARKETING YOUR PROGRAM

After the professional has met all the criteria listed, he or she is ready to market the new service as a parent coordinator.

Step 1. Network—Know Your Community: Parent coordinators should become familiar with the agencies and services already being offered in the area. The PC plays a pivotal role in educating the community regarding the needs of separating families and the programs available designed to meet their unique needs. Also, the PC should concentrate efforts on establishing a collaborative relationship with the following professionals who will be primary sources of referrals: juvenile, family, and superior court judges, family-law attorneys, guardians ad litem, custody evaluators, and parent educators.

Step 2. Professional Referral Packets: Provide each referral source with an attractive and neatly organized referral packet. Consider including the following information: a parent coordination brochure, parent coordination Q&A, standards of care, sample order or stipulation, a professional article on parent coordination, and your vita.

Step 3. Mail Parenting Packets: After receiving a referral, the coordinator should send a packet to each parent. Consider including the following information in the parent packet: dear parent letter, parent checklist of intake requirements, directions to office, program description, intake application, and assessment forms.

Step 4. Review Parent Paperwork: Parents should complete and return paperwork prior to the intake sessions and within the designated time frame stipulated in the court order. Once the paperwork has been returned, it should be reviewed carefully. Whenever possible, have a parent or an attorney mail or fax a copy of the divorce or settlement agreement along with the document appointing the parent coordinator to determine the degree of authority granted to the parent coordinator.

Step 5. Schedule Intake Appointment: After the paperwork has been returned by both parents, contact each parent and schedule their separate intake sessions as soon as possible. Do not include any significant others in the initial interview. Additional information regarding intake appointments can be found in Chapter 8.

Although it would be inappropriate for a therapist to pursue a client, it is the responsibility of a parent coordinator to contact parents to schedule intake and joint sessions. If a parent is resistant to scheduling a session, the PC can contact the client's attorney, explain the situation, and attempt to enlist the attorney's support in scheduling a session with the reluctant client. If this technique is not successful, the PC can write a short memo to the parent notifying him or her to contact the PC by a certain date or the appropriate contacts would be notified of the parent's noncompliance. This memo should be copied to both attorneys as well as the compliant parent.

Set the Stage to Begin

Professionals can purchase CPI assessment and marketing materials directly from the institute's Web site <www.cooperativeparenting.com>. Otherwise, the parent coordinator can create his or her own forms. We recommend having the following items.

Intake Form

The intake form elicits factual information about the family and the divorce. The data include information about the parental relationship and the extent of conflict that may have been experienced by the family prior to or during the divorce. Important information such as drug and alcohol use, prior treatment, and history of violence are also included. For instance, it requests the parents to report any altercations with the law or family protective agencies. Important legal information is also included.

CPI Parent Coordination Assessment(s)

In order to assess the level of parental conflict, the child's adjustment to the divorce, the nature of the parent-child relationship, and the parents' ability to use communication and conflict-resolution skills, an informal assessment tool has been designed by the Cooperative Parenting Institute. It is used as a preassessment instrument. Ideally parents should complete the assessments prior to their initial interview. The CPI assessments are divided into the following sections:

1. *Self-assessment*—The parents individually assess their emotions, attitudes, beliefs, behaviors, and communication patterns.
2. *Coparent assessment*—The parents identify the behaviors they believe the coparent is demonstrating that contribute to the conflict. This section also addresses parental alienation and the extent to which children are placed in loyalty binds.
3. *Conflict assessment*—The parents provide information regarding the types and frequency of conflict. The subcategories include content, behaviors, and outcome. This assessment highlights the parents' ability to take responsibility for their personal contribution to the conflict.

4. *Relationship assessment*—This section is used to determine the parents' ability to effectively work together on behalf of their child. The assessment evaluates six elements of a coparent relationship: communication, trust, respect, cooperation, child rearing, and parent-child relationships. Parents rate their behaviors on a continuum of 1 to 10. Lower scores reflect weaknesses while the higher scores reflect strengths. Quickly glancing at the form provides a preview of the relationship dynamics. Generally the results revealed through the CPI assessment have corresponded to the behaviors observed through the program.

5. *Child assessment*—The child assessment provides the parent coordinator information regarding the child's functioning through each parent's perspective. Information such as the number of additional losses/changes experienced by the child, the child's reaction to the separation, transitional behaviors, and parenting style are assessed.

6. *Child behavioral checklist*—The second portion of the child assessment focuses on the child's functioning and adjustment to the binuclear family. Each parent identifies the behaviors that have started or increased since the family separation or the initiation of litigation. It also offers some indication of the parents' ability to separate themselves from the child and to perceive the needs of their child. Some parents will minimize their child's behaviors in an attempt to imply that the child is making a healthy adjustment to the divorce. Often these parents will also imply that the child does not exhibit any behavioral difficulties in "their" presence, therefore proving they must be the better parent. Parents involved in custody litigation or threatening to return to court may underrate or overrate their child's behaviors depending on their motive. The behavioral checklist is used to identify any problem behaviors that the child may be experiencing. Many of the behaviors are developmentally normal and some are more problematic. The information is useful in determining the child's response to the parental conflict. Similar to other aspects of the CPI assessment forms, parents may perceive the child's functioning and adjustment very differently. In addition, several researchers (Campbell and Johnston, 1986; Saposnek et al., 1984; Steinman, 1984) discovered that during the first year or two after the family's separation, parents seriously distort their views of their children's adjustment to the divorce process. Saposnek (1991) maintained that at least one parent, usually the parent most satisfied with the custody arrangements, reported that their children were coping well with the divorce. On the other hand, the parent who is most distressed about the divorce tends to indicate more behavioral problems for the children.

7. *Stepparent assessment (optional).*
8. *Domestic violence and abuse checklist (optional)*—This form is not
   completed by every parent. It is used only as a screening tool after one
   or both have indicated on their assessment forms or during their intake
   appointment that domestic violence has been documented. Also,
   based on the information gathered, the PC may request one or both
   parents complete the checklist in order to gain a clearer understanding
   of the situation. The checklist focuses on physical, emotional, and financial abuse. It also reveals the last occurrence of any of the behaviors. The appendix at the end of this chapter provides a bibliography
   of sources regarding the specific problem of domestic violence.

The CPI assessment forms have provided more information than originally expected. The perceptions of parents are not always the same. At
times, individual parent scores do not reflect the same levels or the same areas of conflict. Often, one parent has accurately reflected the circumstances
while the other has not. Or, one or both parents may have minimized or distorted the dynamics occurring in the relationship. Parents may underesti-
mate the level of conflict between them to present a situation that is better
than it is or to imply they are model coparents. More often than not, the parent that minimizes the child's distress is the parent that initiated the divorce.
In addition, when scores are polarized it is a strong indication that parents
will demonstrate this behavior during sessions. This preliminary information is useful to help generate hypothesis and direct inquiry.

Professional Liability

A parent coordinator should carry additional liability insurance that is
designed specifically for the profession. Currently at least two agencies offer insurance to parent coordinators. Contact mediation insurance providers
for additional information.

In response to a licensing compliant, PCs should make sure that their records are legible and organized for the investigator. Audiotapes of hostile
voice messages, parent-to-parent conversations, or other audio- and videotapes should be reviewed by the PC prior to any investigation. The PC may
select a vignette for the investigator's review that accurately reflects the
general behavior of the complaining parent. This tape may expedite the investigation. It is also helpful to prepare a time line enumerating the services
received by the family as well as the agreements made during the process of
parent coordination. If the licensing board has not previously responded to

a complaint regarding PC, it is judicious to copy a brochure and other literature for the investigator to educate the board on the process of parent coordination. Signed documents associated with the services of parent coordination should be provided to the investigator. Copies of the complaining
parent's invoice will also be helpful, particularly if the parent is angry due to
a fee dispute.

Record Keeping

The field of parent coordination is relatively new and is therefore often
misunderstood by professionals, licensing boards, and even parents. Thus,
the PC must determine the type and quality of records to keep on each case.
At a minimum, the parent coordinator should document (1) the date and
time of each telephone contact as well as the details of the message, (2) the
date and details of each session including parental behaviors, (3) the date
and detailed description of the agreements reached during mediation,
(4) parental compliance of agreements and modifications to agreements,
and (5) recommendations for referrals.

In the most severe cases, the PC may also decide to record (6) the parents' exact words and the coordinator's response to these statements, (7) messages from parents and others left on voice mail, and (8) feedback given to
parents during the session. Agreements and modifications to the parenting
plan must be documented in written form and provided to both parents,
their attorneys, the guardian ad litem, and, if applicable, the court.

At times the parent coordinator may be instructed to or may wish to write
memos highlighting the parents' behaviors and interaction, observations of
the children, extent of compliance, and referral recommendations. When
memos are written, they should reflect concrete observations that support
the parent coordinator's impressions of the family. However, once a memo
is written and distributed, it may be used as a weapon by one parent and his
or her attorney against the other parent. In addition, parents may use this information to interrogate their children. Any information included about the
children needs to be carefully considered. A memo should not place a child
in a compromising position. Consequently, the parent coordinator must
weigh the advantages and disadvantages of any memo before writing one.

It is useful to prepare a multiclip folder for each parent coordination
case. The separate sections reduce confusion and help to organize the extensive paperwork. We recommend sorting paperwork into the following
categories:

Legal Section

This section contains all the legal documents, such as the court order or stipulation of the parties, original order/settlement agreement, custody evaluations, and other legal documents.

Correspondence

This section contains copies of all legal correspondence and letters and e-mail from parents.

Child Section

This section includes all relevant child material such as teacher reports, consultations with other professionals, and the child's intake session notes.

Parent Section

This section of the file would include assessment forms, releases, intake notes, and feedback sheets.

Joint Session Notes

This section would include the agreement/expectation form, mutual goals, joint session case notes, and dated agreement sheet (a different color for this form makes it easily accessible).

File Cover Sheet

For convenience and as a quick reference, use a summary sheet stapled to the outside of the folder. This one-page form should highlight significant information such as the parents' names, billing address and telephone number, attorneys' names and phone numbers, as well as the names and ages of the children.

Phone Log

Documentation enumerating phone contact between the PC and parents as well as other professionals working with the family is contained in this section.

Child's Photograph

Keep the child's photograph loose so it can be removed from the folder during each session. Purchase clear plastic sleeves to store the photographs. Also, use 8 x 10 clear plastic sign holders that stand upright to display the child's photo during joint sessions.

Final Preparation

The CPI model of parent coordination was built upon a conceptual framework that includes sound theoretical principles and familiar methods used in psychotherapy. An educational component serves as a resource for both the parent and the parent coordinator. To successfully implement a program, several prerequisites are necessary. Once the parent coordinator has a sound understanding of the service, he or she will need to consider potential referral sources. Another prerequisite that adds cohesiveness is the development of a method of record keeping that ensures that the PC has gathered the necessary data to prepare for the beginning phase of the service. As part of the process, parents are requested to complete assessment forms designed by the CPI that evaluate different aspects of the family's functioning. The assessment forms furnish the PC with vital information necessary to implement the beginning phase of the program.

Furthermore, the PC must also have a comfortable understanding of domestic law prior to beginning work with high-conflict families. To successfully interface with the legal profession, parent coordinators must expand their knowledge base beyond the field of mental health. For example, a thorough understanding of legal terminology, court and divorce procedures, and limits of confidentiality are essential to program success. It is also advantageous to identify the potential pitfalls commonly encountered by parent coordinators. Chapter 5 offers a brief yet critical overview of the legal system.

APPENDIX: RESOURCES FOR UNDERSTANDING
FAMILY VIOLENCE

The bibliography provided here lists several sources regarding family violence. For more information about different forms of child abuse and their symptoms, contact U.S. Department of Health and Human Services, Administration for Children and Families, National Clearinghouse on Child Abuse and Neglect Information.

Austin, W. (2000). Assessing credibility in allegations of marital violence in high conflict child custody cases. *Family and Conciliation Courts Review* 38(4): 462.

Briere, J. and Elliot, D. (1997). Psychological assessment of interpersonal victimization effects in adults and children. *Psychotherapy* 34(4): 353-364.

Depner, C., Leino, E., and Chun, A. (1992). Interparental conflict and child adjustment. *Family and Conciliation Courts Review* 30(3): 323-341.

Faller, K. (1999). Focused questions for interviewing children suspected of maltreatment and other traumatic experiences. *The APSAC Advisor* 12(1): 14-18.

Gelles, R. and Strauss, M. (1988). *Intimate Violence*. New York: Simon and Schuster.

Graham-Bermann, S.A. (2000). Evaluating interventions for children exposed to family violence. *Journal of Aggression, Maltreatment, and Trauma* 4: 191-216.

Hilton, N. (1992). Battered women's concerns about their child witnessing wife assault. *Journal of Interpersonal Violence* 7(1): 77-86.

Holden, G., Geffner, R., and Jouriles, E. (Eds.) (1998). *Children Exposed to Marital Violence*. Washington, DC: American Psychological Association.

Johnston, J. (1993). High conflict and violent divorcing families: Findings on children's adjustment and proposed guidelines for the resolution of disputed custody and visitation. San Francisco: Judicial Council of the State of California.

Johnston, J. and Campbell, L. (1993a). A clinical typology of interpersonal violence in disputed custody divorces. *American Journal of Orthopsychiatry* 63: 190-199.

Johnston, J. and Campbell, L. (1993b). Parent-child relationships in domestic violence families disputing custody. *Family and Conciliation Courts Review* 31(3): 282-298.

Mandal, D. (2002). Working with batterers as parents: What would a curriculum look like? *Issues in Family Violence* 4(3). Available at <www.endingviolence. com/>.

McGill, J., Deutsch, R., and Zibbell, R. (1999). Visitation and domestic violence: A clinical mode of family assessment and access planning. *Family and Conciliation Courts Review* 37(3): 315.

Pearson, J. (1997). Mediating when domestic violence is a factor: Policies and practices in court based divorce mediation programs. *Meditation Quarterly* 14(4): 319-335.

Van Horn, P. and Lieberman, A. (2002). *Domestic Violence and Parenting: A Review of the Literature*. San Francisco: Judicial Court of California, Administrative Office of the Courts, Center for Families, Children and the Courts.

Chapter 5

The Legal System

Divorcing parents pursue avenues derived from societal norms and sanctions of the legal system. Because divorce is a legal process, many individuals make the assumption that the divorce itself has to be adversarial. When parents abdicate their power to the judge to determine the structure of their family, the courtroom becomes fertile ground for battle. Under these circumstances, the judge and attorneys expect to see conflict between divorcing parents and sometimes even encourage it though courtroom dramatics. However, even if the attorneys are not adding fuel to the fire, sometimes parental anger does. Pressure from angry family members who are offering to pay for the legal expenses can also fuel litigation. Anger often encourages ongoing litigation. Nonetheless, extended and heated battles adversely affect the child's adjustment. Consequently, the child's needs are sacrificed in the cross fire.

Within the legal profession a systems perspective is often missing. More often than not, legal professionals view the plight of the divorcing family in a linear cause-and-effect chain of events. Although most attorneys are undoubtedly conscientious and concerned about children, they are obligated by the standards of their profession to vigorously represent their client's interests. They do not represent the coparent, and unfortunately they do not directly represent the children. Mother is pitted against father and vice versa in order to determine who is best suited to care for the children. Consequently, this stance encourages an all-or-nothing attitude and a "good parent" versus "bad parent" mind-set. Sande (1997, p. 22) stated, "Your attorney is expected to make you look faultless and to paint your opponent as the one that is entirely responsible for the problem—which is seldom the case." In most cases it is difficult to declare a winner without causing considerable harm to the family. A systems perspective calls upon those in the court to give up the notion of finding individual deficits in one or both parents and replace this focus with an understanding of the interactional nature of the family system. Several legal trends have contributed to this movement: the unified family court, therapeutic jurisprudence, and the collaborative law movement.

EMPLOYING A SYSTEMS PERSPECTIVE

Unified Family Court

Although the movement toward a unified family court began in the 1920s (Page, 1993), the ideology has recently reemerged throughout the United States, Australia, and Canada. The fundamental premise of the unified family court is that a single, highly trained judge presides over family-related matters with the help of a network of social service, mental health, and dispute-resolution professionals. The unified family court operates on the principle that it functions as both a resource for legal services and a gateway to obtain support such as various therapeutic services, parent education, mediation, psychological and custody evaluations, and alternative dispute resolution. In keeping with an ecosystemic view, this perspective focuses on the significant environmental elements, the relationships among these elements, and the family's interaction with them. Accordingly, the unified family court considers the interdependence of the family, legal and mental health systems, various social service agencies, neighborhoods, and the cultural orientation of the family. The court's intention is to simultaneously resolve the family's legal matters while alleviating the problematic situation that led to the family's involvement with the legal system.

The unified family court operates according to a set of criteria for judicial administration which is executed differently in different judicial arenas. According to Burhans and colleagues (1998), however, the central, recurring themes of the unified family court are an emphasis on centralized planning, increased funding, and specialized family law training for the judiciary. They maintained that these three components must be adequately addressed in order to meet the criteria for a productive unified family court. Although in general the family courts are more family friendly, they are often no less adversarial.

Therapeutic Jurisprudence: The Law's Healing Potential

Professors Bruce Winick and David Wexler are cofounders of the school of social enquiry known as "therapeutic jurisprudence." In the late 1980s, the professors defined therapeutic jurisprudence as the study of law's healing potential. Therapeutic jurisprudence strives to evaluate the therapeutic and antitherapeutic consequences of law and legal proceedings and promote legal change designed to increase therapeutic consequences while decreasing countertherapeutic outcomes. It is a point of view that considers the law a social force that produces behaviors and consequences:

It is a mental health approach to law that uses the tools of the behavioral sciences to assess law's therapeutic impact, and when consistent with other important legal values, to reshape law and legal processes in ways that can improve the psychological functioning and emotional well-being of those affected. (Winick, n.d.)

Although therapeutic jurisprudence advocates that the legal system's role as a potential therapeutic agent should be recognized and studied, it does not imply that therapeutic concerns are more important than other elements of the system. A comprehensive bibliography of therapeutic jurisprudence books and articles is enumerated on the Web site of the International Network on Therapeutic Jurisprudence <www.therapeuticjurisprudence.org>.

Therapeutic jurisprudence studies the therapeutic and anti-therapeutic nature of the law in action. Wexler (n.d.) identified three categories: "(1) legal rules, (2) legal proceedings, such as hearings and trials, and (3) the roles of the legal actors and the behavior of judges, lawyers, and of therapists performing in a legal context." Child custody disputes are an example of a legal procedure that can be easily analyzed through the lens of therapeutic jurisprudence. The traditional adversarial process embedded in the legal system's approach to child custody illustrates how legal procedures can be countertherapeutic to the family system. Consequently, these actions sabotage a working relationship between the parents, who need to develop and maintain some type of alliance for the well-being of their children. Not only is the parental relationship damaged, but the results are often traumatic to the children. Conversely, therapeutic jurisprudence focuses on resolving child custody issues through alternative dispute resolution practices such as mediation, parent coordination, and collaborative law.

Therapeutic jurisprudence seeks to uncover innovative and promising resources and to incorporate them into the legal arena. In essence, therapeutic jurisprudence attempts to accomplish therapeutic goals through the structure of the legal system.

The Collaborative Law Movement

Collaborative law grew out of the recognition that the adversarial process is often a destructive approach to conflict resolution. The Collaborative Law Institute (Webb, 1998) defines collaborative law as "a way of practicing law whereby the attorneys for both of the parties to a dispute agree to assist in resolving conflict using cooperative strategies rather than adversarial techniques and litigation." In this way, the conflict resolution process does not rely on court-imposed interventions. Instead, all parties agree to work collaboratively and in good faith to determine creative solutions that meet the fundamental needs of the family and, if necessary, to compromise and reach a resolution of all matters outside the court system. The clients are actively involved in the decision-making process that directly affects their lives. The result is not only greater compliance with the terms of the collaboratively reached agreement but also an increased investment in the coparenting relationship.

Collaborative law attorneys work cooperatively with one another and their clients during informal meetings focused on reaching satisfactory settlements in an efficient, cost-effective manner. Each party makes a formal commitment not to litigate while agreeing to participate in good faith, disclose all pertinent information, and reach a negotiated agreement that addresses each party's interests. In the event that one party terminates involvement in the process and initiates litigation, all parties withdraw and the clients must seek new counsel. Although this approach may have a positive effect on the family, it is often difficult to encourage parents to adopt an alternative to litigation.

Because the process of collaborative divorce is nonadversarial, the attorneys most likely to work in this manner tend to be those who take the child's needs into consideration. These attorneys also tend to see the value in referring their clients to parent coordination. Unlike the collaborative attorney, adversarial attorneys tend to be focused on winning and posturing for their clients.

WORKING WITH THE LEGAL SYSTEM

Since parent coordinators establish a collaborative relationship with the legal system, it is necessary to become familiar with legal terms commonly used during the divorce process. Some divorcing parents may be very familiar with these terms. Gaining an understanding of them will help the parent coordinator communicate more effectively with both legal professionals and parents.

Selected Legal Terms

affidavit: A written declaration or statement of facts given under oath and made before an authorized official.

alternative dispute resolution (ADR): A form of resolving disputes without the assistance of legal intervention. It has many forms, including arbitration, mediation, parent coordination, and the use of a special master.

arbitration: A form of dispute resolution in which an impartial third party (arbitrator) executes a decision after a hearing. During this hearing both parties have the opportunity to be heard. In situations of voluntary arbitration, the parties generally select the arbitrator, who has the authority to execute a binding decision.

deposition: A statement under oath, taken down in writing by a court reporter. The deposition is conducted outside the courtroom. This statement is used in a court of law in place of the spoken testimony of the witness. It may also be used by an attorney as part of the discovery process. Both attorneys are present and question the witness. The parents may also be present, but they are usually prohibited from speaking or giving testimony.

ex parte: A judicial proceeding, court order, stipulation, and/or communication is referred to as ex parte when it is taken or granted for the benefit of one party only and without notice to the opposing party. An appointed coordinator attempting to communicate with the judge without involving the attorneys would be considered an inappropriate ex parte communication.

expert witness: A professional who has been determined by each individual judge presiding over the case to be an expert in his or her field by reason of education or specialized experience.

guardian ad litem (GAL): A person entrusted by law to protect the child(ren)'s best interests. A guardian is usually appointed by the judge and may be an attorney or mental health professional. Different states outline different criteria. Guardians may be requested to write reports and make custody recommendations. Some individuals appointed as guardians may have limited knowledge of child development.

quasi-judicial immunity: "Quasi-judicial" is a term applied to the action of public administrative officers who have been appointed to investigate the facts, consider evidence, and reach conclusions. In situations of divorce, guardians ad litem are often appointed in this capacity. In most jurisdictions, individuals functioning under quasi-judicial immunity are protected from civil liability.

settlement agreement: A legal document noting the agreements made between the parents outlining their rights and responsibilities that is written by both parents or by the parents' attorneys, or is agreed upon through mediation. These agreements may reflect parental decisions regarding child support, alimony, distribution of property, and custody. Once the agreements are reached, the document is submitted to the court for approval and the parents are required to comply with the agreement.

special master: A professional role characterized by a neutral, third-party decision maker. This professional generally has the authority to make decisions regarding the best interest of the child. However, he or she does not have the authority to make changes to physical or legal custody. A special master can function as a fact finder, case manager, investigator, or med-arbiter. Some may take on the same responsibilities of a parent coordinator and maintain an ongoing relationship with a family. However, their role generally goes beyond the role of a parent coordinator. A special master may function as a private judge.

subpoena: A summons to court or a deposition. When an individual is subpoenaed, he or she must respond to the request or be present during the legal procedure. A subpoena generally outlines the requirement for professionals to provide their records. If specified, the professional must follow the stipulation of the subpoena and bring the records to the court or deposition. However, if this request is not made, the professional does not have to provide written documentation.

temporary order: An order of the court that outlines temporary stipulations. The parents are obligated to comply with this order until further court proceedings result in a permanent order or settlement agreement.

visitation: The amount of time the children are required to visit with the noncustodial parent. The visitation schedule is stipulated in the divorce decree or settlement agreement or in a separate court order. Visitation differs from custody because the noncustodial parent and child do not live together in a legal sense. Many states have a stipulation that designates an age at which the child may decide to change primary residence or alter the visitation schedule.

CONFIDENTIALITY VERSUS PRIVILEGE

Confidentiality is held by therapists as part of their licensing and professional guidelines. It refers to an expectation that a client's information is to remain private. This information is not intended to be shared without specific permission from the identified client. Other professionals with a duty to maintain a confidential relationship with their clients may include CPAs, psychotherapists, attorneys, and clergy. Also, medical, bank, and employment records are considered confidential documents. Since the practice of parent coordination is not a confidential process, parents must be reminded of this important distinction. However, parents should know that the professional will not share information with anyone outside the family's involvement or the process of parent coordination.

Records and Parent Coordination

A therapist working with a minor child must ensure confidentiality via the child's parent or guardian. Parents are entitled to their child's records. However, in situations of divorce only those parents who hold legal custody may request their child's therapy records. If the parent making the request has legal custody but is in the process of litigation, then a judge or guardian may determine if the requesting parent has a "self-interest" which may not be consistent with the child's interest. Some parents obtain therapeutic services for their children prior to going to court in order to gain access to their child's records. Also, their agenda may be to subpoena the therapist to provide an avenue in which the child's private notes can be shared with the court. This is sometimes known as securing a hired gun. It is not uncommon for parents to behave in this manner during the divorce or postdivorce litigation process.

As part of the parent coordination process, the PC may meet with the children. It is not unusual for highly litigious parents to demand copies of the notes from their child's meeting. To determine whether the child's records should be released to the parents, the guardian ad litem can be consulted if one has been assigned to the case. However, since the primary role of the PC is to shield the child from unnecessary stress, sharing the child's notes is generally discouraged. To do so would likely place the child in a compromising position within the family. The parent coordinator may request a court order to refuse to release the child's records or simply wait until the case goes back before the judge to rule on the matter.

Privilege

Privilege is a legal term granted by the Supreme Court and applies only to court proceedings. Privilege is a legal right of the person who generated the information. It is his or her privilege to determine if the information should go beyond the original professional. Since the client holds the privilege he or she can choose to waive privilege or not. If privilege is waived then the therapist may testify. If the client does not waive privilege, the therapist is barred from testifying. Therefore, privilege does not even become a factor until the case goes to court.

Because parent coordination is usually a nonconfidential process, privilege is automatically waived by the parents. Thus the language of the order appointing the parent coordinator must be clear on this point. This allows the parent coordinator to send memos to the attorneys and to testify in court if supoenaed to do so.

Privilege and Minor Children

The client, as the holder of the privilege, must be competent to assert privilege or waive it. Privilege does not automatically apply with a minor child. The natural guardian is the holder of the child's privilege. The guardian can waive privilege unless it is determined that he or she cannot be neutral because his or her own issues diverge from the child's best interest. When this is not clear, it is recommended that the court appoint a special guardian simply to determine if the parents can waive their child's right to privilege as a third party.

The terms of confidentiality and privilege can vary from state to state. For example, some states have what is referred to as a "mature minor" (i.e., sixteen years old and older). However, most states have one exception that may be determined by the answer to the following question: Is this a custody question and is the question at hand more important than confidentiality?

Although parent coordination is not a confidential process, parent coordinators working in the CPI model do not share any information received from the children with their parents unless the child grants the PC permission to release this information. However, the professional is mandated to report abuse. Also, at times the PC may be required by the judge to release the children's notes. However, more often than not, judges maintain the children's confidentiality.

HANDLING A SUBPOENA

As defined earlier in this chapter, a subpoena is a summons to court or a deposition. Not all subpoenas are signed by the judge. Some are drafted by the attorneys and indicate the court date and time. A parent coordinator must respond to this request or be available during the legal procedure.

In situations in which an attorney has requested the PC to testify in court, the PC should send a contract to the attorney designating fees and the requirement for a retainer from the attorney's client one week prior to the court date. If the PC is not available for the court date due to an unavoidable situation, such as another court hearing on that date, he or she should alert all parties, including the judge, through written documentation that includes the reason for the inability to attend the proceeding. No other information should be included in this memo. More often than not, the attorney who issued the subpoena will request a change in the court date. If the attorney who has subpoenaed the PC is not willing to reschedule the hearing, the coordinator must hire an attorney to file a motion to quash. Subpoenas must always be taken seriously.

Generally, a subpoena also includes a demand for the PC's records. Records usually include session notes, phone notes, and tapes, if they exist. When this is part of the subpoena, it is important to bring a very organized file to court. Each section of the PC file should be clearly delineated so that the PC can get to any necessary paperwork while testifying to avoid rummaging through the file. If the records are requested, it is prudent to have any notes or drawings from the children in a separate file. If asked to release or reveal any information from the child's material, the PC should ask the judge if the information must be released.

WORKING WITH ATTORNEYS

During the divorce process, parents tend to relinquish their power and control to their respective attorneys and ultimately the judge. They allow individuals outside their family to make decisions that will greatly impact the lives of each family member. The adversarial system employed in most courtrooms today easily sets the parents up for abdication of their parental responsibilities. Parent coordination attempts to move the parents away from the courtroom to an atmosphere where mutual decision making is based on the best interest of the child. Ultimately, it is the parents who must come to some agreement on the general care of their children. Through parent coordination, the professional attempts to place the power back in the hands of the parents. Parents should assume parental authority for their children rather than giving this precious job to those who are the least familiar with their family needs and unique circumstances. The parent coordinator must encourage the parents to take responsibility for their own decisions and restore their executive and protective functioning.

The parent coordinator should always be aware of the relative influence the attorney has over his or her client. After all, parents seek legal advice during a time when they are especially vulnerable and in need of legal guidance. Parents often rely on their attorneys to guide them in the right direction. The attorney's point of view and purpose will have a profound impact on the parent's perception of reality and decision making. Attorneys may discourage their clients from participating in parent coordination out of fear of losing control over their client's actions and due process rights. Some attorneys may also be concerned about the potential for a reduction of fees for their services. When first working with any family-law attorney, it is advantageous to contact the attorney directly to ask for input regarding the specific case. This will be viewed as respectful and diplomatic. This conversation may indicate how supportive the attorney will be of the process and how the attorney may view his or her own client. If the attorney shares information only about the other parent, this may be an indication of the attorney believing everything the client says. Attorneys who share slightly negative information about clients may be able to view the case in a neutral fashion.

Although parent coordinators are advised to become familiar with the laws and terms associated with divorce, the parent coordinator should never provide legal advice to parents. The parent coordinator must not lose sight of the role of the attorney in the process. Some parents will not act unless they have the opportunity to consult with their attorney. This will, however, slow down the process. Other parents may prefer to leave their attorneys out of the process. In either case, the PC must always make it clear to the parents that they have the option of consulting with their attorneys prior to finalizing any agreements.

It is often difficult for some attorneys to let go of the power and influence over their clients and they will adamantly object to the client making any decisions without their input. Under these circumstances, the parent coordinator may be able to move the agreement along by taking the time to explain the process to the attorney. Furthermore, the coordinator can routinely advise the attorney about the progress being made by his or her client. However, unless the parent coordinator is authorized to speak to the attorney about the client's partner, information about the coparent should not be shared with the attorney.

Furthermore, some attorneys may advise clients not to resolve or mediate any child-rearing matters in joint sessions. In this situation the PC might encourage both parents, especially the resistant client, to consider the following factors:

1. The attorney is working for the parent and therefore the parent should be in charge of the process, not the other way around.
2. The order or settlement agreement requires parents to participate in the PC mediation and mutual problem solving.
3. Lack of compliance with the court order and an uncooperative stance may not be viewed favorably by the judge in the event that the case goes before the court.

As attorneys become familiar with the process of parent coordination and learn to trust the practices of the coordinator, they generally become a tremendous asset to the process. Attorneys can encourage resistant and noncompliant clients to cooperate with the process. The attorney can empathize with the client while at the same time highlighting the benefits of parent coordination. Yet it will become very clear which attorneys will support parent coordination and which will not. Just as the mediation movement was initially met with resistance and fear, parent coordination is sometimes met with attorney resistance and interference. To establish credibility and develop a working relationship with attorneys, the following techniques might be useful:

- Establish and maintain an impartial stance with the attorneys who represent the parents. Do not align yourself with either attorney. Remain objective, avoid all alliances, always employ professional courtesy, and refrain from inappropriate, spontaneous remarks.
- Call each attorney before meeting with the parents. Ask the attorney to highlight his or her client's position and concerns regarding the case. Consulting with the attorneys in this manner communicates your respect for their role and involvement in the case.
- Share the parent coordination stipulation/order with the attorney. Clarify any points which may be ambiguous.
- Send a copy of the parent coordinator standards and a signed expectation form to the attorneys. The expectation form highlights the importance of refraining from litigious action. Explain the reason for this guideline to the attorneys and request that they contact you in the event that they are considering legal intervention.
- Provide the attorneys with written notification of their clients' initial compliance with the process after the first joint session by noting the dates of service. This memo could include the mutual goals and be sent to both attorneys.
- Under certain circumstances the PC may contact the attorney to discuss concerns regarding his or her client and the impact of the client's behavior on the process. Engage the attorney as an adviser and convey empathy for the client's situation.
- When it is necessary to communicate with an attorney, the PC should discuss only that attorney's client or the general process. Information about both parents should be conveyed by scheduling three-way conference calls or through written communication. Communication between the guardian and parent coordinator can be kept confidential. It may not be necessary to share this information with each parent's attorney. However, each attorney will have different expectations. Try to accommodate their preferences as much as possible, but minimize the amount of contact with legal counsel.

- Notify the attorneys through a memo prior to making a referral for additional services. Discuss the reason and purpose for the referral.
- Arrange a lunch date to discuss the attorney's concerns regarding parent coordination.
- Utilize the assistance of the guardian assigned to the case. The guardian may have established a relationship with the attorney and be able to facilitate communication between the attorney and parent coordinator.

WORKING WITH A GUARDIAN AD LITEM

In high-conflict situations the judge may appoint a guardian to represent the child's best interest. This appointment may be made prior to the appointment of a parent coordinator, or both professionals may be appointed simultaneously. In the first situation a guardian rarely "recommends" parent coordination in a written document. Thus it is important for the parents to sign a stipulation of the parties. Otherwise, request the GAL to clarify the expectations of the parents and the authority of the parent coordinator prior to proceeding with the service. Under these circumstances, the parent coordinator can clarify his or her role in the form of a letter to the guardian or can request that the guardian submit the parent coordination order to the court.

When a guardian and coordinator are appointed at the same time, the guardian may not be familiar with the process of parent coordination. Under these circumstances, it is imperative that the coordinator contact the guardian as soon as possible to establish a collaborative relationship and clarify each person's role. The responsibilities of both professionals may overlap. Therefore, it is necessary to define the role each will play in the life of the family as well as how the two professionals will work together to assist the family. Generally, when both a guardian and coordinator are working together, the guardian may have more power and influence over the family. Furthermore, the guardian's recommendations may have more impact on the attorneys and the judge. The guardian may demand all authority over recommendations and the decision-making process and consider the coordinator to be working for the guardian. As a result, parent coordinators may have to tread lightly when working with guardians unknown to them.

By working together, the guardian and parent coordinator can have a significant impact on the family and the legal system. However, since a guardian's role has been established in the legal system, the coordinator may have to initiate contact with the guardian. A guardian can be helpful to the parent coordinator in several ways. First, the guardian can assist the parent coordinator by requiring the parents to authorize the release of legal, educational, medical, and psychological documents. Second, the guardian can clarify for resistant or hesitant parents the consequences of their noncompliance with program requirements. Third, the guardian can support the coordinator's recommendations and thereby add credibility to the coordinator's role. Fourth, the guardian is in a unique position to interface directly with the judge by enlisting his or her support in insisting that the parents follow through with agreements. Fifth, the guardian can function as a liaison between the parent coordinator and the judge since direct communication between the two is not possible. Finally, the guardian can facilitate communication and cooperation among all the professionals working with the family. Usually, the guardian is perceived as an extension of the court by other professionals. Accordingly, the guardian has a direct impact on promoting cooperation among the professional team. For instance, when the parent coordinator is meeting with resistance from one of the other professionals, the coordinator can enlist the support of the guardian by requesting that the guardian arrange an interdisciplinary meeting with the professionals working with the family in an attempt to ensure the coordination of services.

In addition, a parent coordinator can be a helpful resource to the guardian. Since many guardians are legal professionals with limited knowledge of family dynamics and the psychological consequences of divorce on the family, a psychotherapist performing the role of a parent coordinator can share his or her knowledge and expertise with the guardian. This results in a better understanding of the family system, leading to more appropriate recommendations for ancillary services. As a result, the coordinator can assist the guardian in the determination of additional services for the family as well as be a resource for competent referral options. Also, the coordinator can gain essential information for the guardian by exploring his or her concerns during joint or family sessions. Under circumstances in which the guardian is meeting parental resistance, the parent coordinator may facilitate a solution with the parents and enhance their relationship with the guardian. Together, the guardian and parent coordinator can significantly assist the family to experience positive change.

THE LEGAL PERSPECTIVE

Traditionally, the legal arena has focused on the individual deficits in one or both parents in order to determine a custody arrangement that is in the child's best interest. Recognizing that the adversarial process promotes parental conflict, the legal system has developed alternative methods of conflict resolution. As an extension of these trends, parent coordinators have also established collaborative relationships with various professionals working in the legal system.

It is beneficial for the inexperienced professional to become familiar with the legal terms commonly used during the divorce process. Chapter 6 addresses custody options, the essential elements of successful custody and time-sharing arrangements, and potential barriers to parental cooperation. A thorough understanding of custody, court orders, and settlement agreements is essential to the professional seeking to be appointed in this capacity.

Chapter 6

Custody and Cooperation

Over the years, the United States has moved away from the trend of the "tender-years" doctrine or parental preference to the "best-interests-of-the-child" presumption. The tender-years doctrine focused on the parents' rights, while the current focus is upon the child's individual needs. Political/social trends and research on child development have provoked much debate with regard to the best interests of the child. The modern view of best interests refers to an individualized plan that best suits a particular child, rather than favoring a one-size-fits-all approach. This movement was predicated on the ideology that custody determination should consider many factors, such as the child's current developmental needs, the parents' ability to provide for these needs, and the current life circumstances of the family.

There has also been a major shift from granting one parent sole custody to a preference for joint custody. In the early 1980s California added the term *joint legal custody* as an option to involve both parents in raising the child. The overall emphasis at this time was twofold: to create a social and legal norm of shared parenting, and to encourage parents to refrain from manufacturing conflicts as the basis for sole custody. More often than not, litigation during this period resulted from the sociolegal paradigm shift as mothers perceived sole legal and physical custody as their right (Shear, Drapkin, and Curtis, 2000). Mothers were not motivated to share their authority with fathers since they were accustomed to the court awarding them sole custody.

CUSTODY OPTIONS

Although several common terms are used to designate a type of custody arrangement, no standard definition has been adopted. State statutes and case law define custody differently. Yet in an attempt to provide a common language, the legal system has adopted a set of terms to define the various custody options available to separating families. However, in reality, custody arrangements can and have been structured in many creative ways despite the legal system's attempt to pigeonhole the family structure into distinct categories. The custody terms that follow may vary from state to state.

custodial parent: The parent designated as the person primarily responsible for the children. The children reside with this parent. The noncustodial parent is awarded "visitation." School attendance is usually determined by the address of the custodial parent. The term custodial parent may also refer to the parent who is responsible for the care of the child at any given moment.

sole custody: One parent is recognized as the custodial parent. The children reside with this parent on a full-time basis. The noncustodial parent is awarded "visitation."

split custody: The custody is split between the two households. In other words, one or more children may live with one parent while the other children live with the other parent. Many courts refuse to grant split custody unless compelling reasons suggest that the children would benefit from such an arrangement. When split custody is granted, the children usually spend the weekends together. This allows for maximum sibling contact.

joint legal custody: Both parents are required to make mutual decisions on the child(ren)'s behalf. However, one parent may be appointed as the custodial parent and one appointed as the noncustodial parent, or they may share joint physical custody of the child(ren). In most states joint legal custody has become a fairly standard practice. Some states have designated this type of legal custody as "shared parental responsibility." Joint legal custody generally refers to access to the child's records (school, medical, etc.) and both parents are required to discuss mutual parenting decisions on the child(ren)'s behalf. In some states the parents must agree. In other states, if the parents disagree, decision-making power may be designated such as divided power assigned according to parenting issue; equal power using mediation when necessary to overcome an impasse; or equal power with one parent assigned final decision-making power to overcome an impasse

tiebreaker with joint legal custody: In some states one parent may be known as the "tiebreaker." This indicates that one parent has the authority to make the final decision in any nonemergency parenting impasse. Even when one parent has 51 percent of the power to make decisions, he or she is still required to discuss parenting issues with the other parent prior to making the final decision. In states that use tiebreakers, if neither parent is designated in the legal document it automatically falls with the primary custodial parent. However, when a tiebreaker is designated it may be defined as one of the following methods:

1. *Primary custodial parent:* The parent with physical custody is the tie-breaker based on default.
2. *Time period:* The mother is the tiebreaker in even years and the father in odd years.
3. *Specific child:* Father shall be tiebreaker on disputes regarding their daughter and mother shall be tiebreaker on disputes regarding their son.
4. *Category:* Divided authority is assigned according to impasse category (i.e., education, medical, psychological, extracurricular activities, and religion).

Today joint legal custody is considered an entitlement of both parents. As a result, shared custody and postdivorce coparenting has become acknowledged as a universally accepted alternative. Still, some families are poor candidates for a joint legal arrangement. Under the following circumstances, joint legal custody should be seriously questioned: (1) when families make poor decisions, (2) when decisions are not made for the children because both parents must agree, (3) in cases of high conflict, and (4) when domestic violence has occurred (Shear, Drapkin, and Curtis, 2000). Shear, Drapkin, and Curtis (2000, p. 37) advocated, "Joint legal custody may work best when both parents have the capacity to make non-coerced, timely, and cooperative decisions for their child." They concluded that parental decision-making power that maintains and exacerbates parental tension is contrary to the intent of a joint legal custody arrangement. Under these circumstances, it negatively impacts the parents' ability to make reasonable decisions for their children in a timely fashion. Many states are amending their custody statutes to insert presumptions against the granting of joint or sole custody to parents who have abused their partners (Shear, Drapkin, and Curtis, 2000). Presumption for joint legal custody requires careful examination of whether joint legal custody is in the child's best interest in situations of alleged domestic violence.

Parent coordinators cannot always rely on custody evaluators to query about domestic violence. Even if evaluators do routinely assess this area, parent coordinators should still make provisions in their intake and assessment questionnaires as well as during individual interviews to explore the issue of domestic violence. The type, severity, and frequency of the alleged abusive acts should be determined. A supplemental domestic violence questionnaire has been developed by the CPI. This information is used by the PC to assist parents in developing agreements that minimize potential violence.

joint physical custody: The residential care of the children is shared by both parents. In essence, the child resides with both parents. However, the time spent with each parent may vary. For instance, a child may live with his or her mother during school months and father during the summer months, or the child may alternate between homes every other week. Other time-sharing arrangements may include a 70/30 split or a 60/40 split. The term *joint custody* has also been referred to as *shared parenting, joint parenting, co-custody, shared custody, concurrent custody,* and *joint managing conservators* (Folberg, 1991). Joint physical custody generally includes joint legal custody.

When parents have a joint physical custody arrangement they must designate a primary home for the purposes of public school zoning. Therefore, one parent must be designated as the primary parent even when both are granted joint physical custody and share the children's time equally. More often than not, attorneys and mediators have avoided the use of the term *primary parent* for joint 50/50 arrangements in favor of designating which home will be considered the primary one rather than appointing a parent as primary. This is an attempt to keep the parents on an equal playing field.

THE LABEL OF CUSTODY

The custody debate usually centers on the amount of time and the degree of authority granted to each parent to make decisions regarding the children's welfare. Most parents initially fight over custody for financial or emotional reasons. Rather than using the term *custody* some professionals will use the following terms: *the child's living arrangements, the child's schedule, parental responsibilities,* and *parental roles.* Some jurisdictions are also attempting to avoid using the term *custody.* In Florida, for example, they refer to *shared parental responsibility* rather than joint legal custody. In the same way, some parents will find the use of the word *visitation* offensive and replace it with phrases such as "Mom's time" and "Dad's time."

For the purposes of this text, the term *joint custody* shall refer to joint physical custody. The terms *shared* and *coparenting* are used to represent a type of parenting relationship used by divorcing parents regardless of the form of custody arrangement assigned to define the family. When using these two terms, it will not refer to any specific type of custody arrangement.

LIVING ARRANGEMENTS

The period in which divorcing parents negotiate custody and living arrangements is usually one of severe emotional stress. Parents are involved in the immediate turmoil of the separation and often are unable to anticipate the evolution of their own postdivorce lives let alone what their children may need. They possess a very limited ability to anticipate and prepare for the continuous changes brought on by divorce when the issue of custody is first raised. Most parents believe that they can assume all the child-rearing responsibilities even if they have never taken part in child care during the marriage.

Even the best researchers exploring the impact of custody arrangements on children of different ages cannot say with certainty what is in the best interest of the child. Each family must consider not only the age of the child but other factors including the child's temperament, ability to adjust to change, gender, relationship with each parent prior to family separation, the primary bond, and the amount of cooperation between the parents. Taking a child to and from a home in a limited amount of time may cause unnecessary stress and confusion. Among other issues, frequent contact between a parent and a child should be weighed against the number of transitions. Some children are unable to cope with frequent exchanges, particularly when their parents are in conflict. With the guidance of a trained professional, parents are encouraged to come to terms with what they can realistically accomplish in a two-household family and determine what arrangement meets the needs of their children. For additional information see Chapter 7 on time-sharing options.

JOINT CUSTODY: WHAT WORKS AND WHAT DOESN'T

Joint custody arrangements have become very popular in recent years. Statutes are increasingly encouraging it. Researchers have attempted to determine the efficacy of joint custody and the effects of joint custody on children. Studies have been able to pinpoint several factors that support successful joint custody arrangements. However, the research on joint custody is plagued by studies with limited samples, lack of consensus on definition of terms, and in adequate measurements to determine the degree of hostility present between parents. In general, research does not suggest the superiority of joint custody over sole custody, but it does document those factors that are worth reviewing to determine the best interests of the child in either sole or joint family structures.

Parent Characteristics that Influence
Joint Custody Success

Researchers have reached a general consensus regarding the identification of parental characteristics that can influence a healthy adjustment to
joint physical custody arrangements. When discussing the viability of joint
custody, most of the professional literature has differentiated between parental behaviors that suggested successful joint physical custody options
from parental behaviors that suggested unsuccessful joint physical custody
arrangements.

In an attempt to assemble information highlighting parental behaviors
distinguishing successful and unsuccessful joint custody arrangements, the
following review of the professional literature is offered (Elkin, 1991;
Gardner, 1991; Saposnek, 1991; Steinman, Zemmelman, and Knoblauch,
1985; Taylor, 1991).

Positive Parental Behaviors

> Commitment to make joint custody work
> Capability to assume responsibility for child rearing
> Ability and willingness to negotiate differences
> Willingness to cooperate and communicate in child-rearing matters

In addition, other characteristics include high self-esteem, respect for
boundaries, tolerance for a wide range of feelings, and the effective management of feelings and emotions.

Negative Parental Behaviors

> Very low self-esteem
> Rigidity in thinking
> Ineffective problem solving
> Inability to test reality
> Difficulty differentiating between their needs and the needs of their
>   child
> Feelings of vulnerability and powerlessness in relation to former
>   spouse
> Deep mistrust
> Fixed belief that the former spouse is all bad
> Overwhelming anger and continued need to punish the former spouse

Tendency to blame the former spouse for the end of the marriage, the child's problems, and one's own difficulties

Intense, continued hostility and conflict that cannot be diverted from the child

Geographical factors making joint custody difficult

Frequent litigation for sole custody of the children

Child neglect

Family violence (child abuse, emotional, physical, and sexual abuse)

History of addiction by one or both parents

Significant character disorders

Researchers have pointed out that it is erroneous to assume that parents are willing and able to undertake a joint physical custody agreement simply because they have agreed to it through mutual consent or because it has been ordered by the court. The reasons behind parent choice of custody arrangements vary. Research suggests that the motivation underlying the decision for joint custody significantly influences the outcome for the family. For instance, in a study conducted by McKinnon and Wallerstein (1986) all parents acknowledged the need for children to maintain a relationship with both parents, but their commitment to this ideal varied. They concluded that parental motivations influence the quality of the parent-child relationship. They identified five main driving forces behind joint physical custody decisions:

1. Commitment to the child
2. Limited parental partnership
3. Response to the demands of work
4. Denial of the divorce
5. Need for restitution

Saposnek (1983) added that motives also include the desire to limit child-rearing responsibilities, reconciliation fantasies, revenge, retaliation, and control of the other parent. Joint physical custody may also be requested to avoid payment of child support or in an attempt to prevent a parent from relocating with the child.

The inquiry should focus not only on parental characteristics but also on the characteristics of the child. Steinman (1984, p. 117) stated,

It may be that a cooperative, smooth running coparenting relationship is necessary but not sufficient condition for children to do well. In other words, we need to consider not only which parents, but also which children make good candidates for joint custody.

Saposnek (1991) reported that children under the age of three were able to tolerate the transitions of a joint custody arrangement when parental conflicts were not witnessed by the children. In contrast, preschoolers generally coped less well even when the quality of parenting was sound. Difficulty adjusting to a joint custody structure at this age may have more to do with developmental milestones and situational factors.

In general, the professional must consider young children's need for predictability, their perceptions of time, and their sense of attachment to various family members. Professionals must also consider the importance of peer relationships and feelings about school and neighborhood when considering arrangements for latency-age children and adolescents. Studies continually (McKinnon and Wallerstein, 1986) suggest that young children raised in a joint physical custody situation fare best when their parents are highly committed to their children, sensitive to their children's needs, shield their children from parental conflict, and give their children permission to develop a quality relationship with both parents.

Research continually highlights the complex realities of divorce. Determining the structure of the binuclear family is a very complex task that involves consideration of multiple variables that are influenced by a variety of sources. Regardless of the family structure, children need parents who are dedicated to their well-being, who support each other, and who separate their own personal problems and conflicts from their role as parents (Maccoby and Mnookin, 1992; Williams, 1987). One home or two, children benefit most from two parents who love, nurture, and protect them from parental hostility (Blau, 1993; Block, Block, and Gjerde, 1986; Luepnitz, 1991; Marguilies, 1992; Wallerstein, 1991).

IS JOINT CUSTODY THE PANACEA?

Most researchers (McKinnon and Wallerstein, 1986; Kline et al., 1988; Wallerstein and Blakeslee, 1989) have discovered that the form of custody has little influence on the psychological outcome of children. The most significant factors include the parents' emotional functioning at the time of separation, their level of anxiety and depression, and the degree of conflict between parents one year postseparation. In addition, the age, sex, and temperaments of the children significantly influenced the outcome. Brotsky, Steinman, and Zemmelman (1991) support the notion that the quality of the family atmosphere influenced outcome more than the type of family structure. They stated that children raised in a joint custody arrangement coped better when parents protected their children from conflict, nurtured and supported their child, valued their child's relationship with the other parent, and were able to make mutual decisions for their child's well-being. Elkin (1991) added that a child's positive adjustment was also affected by continued involvement with both parents as well as easy access to each parent.

In highly conflicted circumstances, joint physical custody places youngsters right in the middle of the battlefield. When high-conflict cases involve frequent parent-to-parent transfers, children are more often caught between their parents' disputes and are passively used by their parents (Johnston and Campbell, 1988). Johnston, Kline, and Tschann (1991) reported that children living in highly conflicted joint custody arrangements were more depressed, withdrawn, aggressive, and otherwise disturbed than their counterparts living in sole custody arrangements. Moreover, they reported that parental conflict increased with frequent-access arrangements. Therefore, joint custody that requires frequent transitions is contraindicated when parents are engaged in high conflict. However, more time-sharing plans are incorporating neutral exchange sites such as schools and libraries as a means of easing transitions for children.

Contrary to some professional opinion, joint custody does not necessarily guarantee a reduction of parental hostility (Block, Block, and Gjerde, 1986; Luepnitz, 1991; Marguilies, 1992; Wallerstein, 1991). Felner and Terre's (1987) review of the literature suggests that joint custody did not decrease postdivorce conflict. In fact, they suggest that such an arrangement may instead invite parental warfare. They found that parents involved in a court-ordered joint custody arrangement or those encouraged to participate in joint custody arrangements were unable to create a family structure that nurtured and supported their children. Brotsky, Steinman, and Zemmelman (1991) stated that under these circumstances, joint custody arrangements were dysfunctional. Specifically, these parents were unremittingly hostile, did not appreciate and support the child's relationship with the other parent, could not effectively negotiate differences or coordinate child care responsibilities, and could not shield the children from parental warfare. Steinman (1984) concluded,

> We should not assume that parents are prepared to undertake joint custody simply because they have technically agreed or compromised through mandatory mediation. A legal agreement does not necessarily mean parents have steeled their disputes, or have the resources to implement joint legal custody . . . [it] is at greater risk of failure when . . . [court] ordered in the hope that it will end a battle and parents will learn to cooperate. (p. 119)

According to Garrity and Baris (1994), divorcing parents must learn to construct a cooperative relationship. Such a relationship rarely evolves on its own. Garrity and Baris maintain that only one-quarter of divorcing parents are fortunate enough to construct a cooperative relationship during the first year or two after the separation. Fifty percent of divorcing couples need to disengage and avoid each other for a time before they make any attempts at coparenting. Finally, the remaining quarter of all divorcing parents are unable to construct a shared parenting relationship without the assistance of a trained professional.

AUTHORS' VIEWS ON CUSTODY

Research literature does not clearly prove that one form of custody is better than another, yet it clearly enumerates the variables necessary for a child's and family's healthy outcome. Concentrating parental efforts on replicating those elements in each binuclear family becomes paramount. The PC should focus less on a specific custody arrangement and more on encouraging parents to engage in an ongoing cooperative relationship and continuous healthy involvement in their child's life.

Whenever possible parents should be given the executive power to create for themselves a binuclear family structure that is in their families' best interest without interference from adversarial procedures. It is important to assist parents in the development of cooperative parenting plans that reflect the unique needs of their family. When helping parents realign the family structure, the qualities of the parents, the characteristics and needs of the children, and the environmental factors influencing the family should be considered.

Because numerous mitigating factors influence a family's ability to establish a two-family home, it is naive to believe that all families are suited for a joint physical or legal custody arrangement. A mandated presumption for joint custody overlooks the needs of individual families. A one-size-fits-all approach to custody is a dangerous assumption. After all, joint physical custody is an ambiguous term that can be structured around variable time-sharing plans that meet the needs of the child. We are not discounting the noteworthy benefits that joint custody can offer families. Variations on joint physical custody can be a wonderful gift to children when parents are mature enough to make the necessary sacrifices for their child. However, when it is contraindicated it can be disastrous for the child. Hence, a child of a joint physical custody arrangement can reap the benefit or pay a very steep price.

In a similar fashion, joint legal custody also has its shortcomings. We do not recommend joint legal or physical custody in cases of domestic violence, abuse, harassment, or a serious imbalance of power. Realistically, in these situations the primary parent should not be held accountable to consult with the other parent on significant parenting matters. On the other hand, a parent granted sole custody is at risk of excluding the other parent because he or she has been granted the right to do so. This arrangement often gives sole custodial parents the right to think of themselves as the only parent. Since parents with sole custody may move anywhere they choose and make any decisions they want, the other parent is reduced to being a "visiting" parent with no rights and no assurance that he or she will be able to stay active in the child's life. Even when parents have the potential to be respectful coparents and one parent has been granted sole custody, they usually lose this ability and become highly exclusionary. Without the serious contraindications noted here, we encourage joint legal custody over sole custody so that both parents can be required to respectfully share the joint decisions of raising their child.

COOPERATION

Although custody is very important to parents, it is not as important to children. Children simply want to love both parents and have their parents cooperate. Therefore, the parents' ability to work together is far more important than the actual division of time. Parental characteristics promoting cooperation can be identified. Some are inherent and cannot be altered; others can be taught and therefore modified by the parents. The following characteristics are similar to those of successful joint custody. These characteristics have the potential for creating a cooperative relationship between coparents no matter what the final custody arrangement.

Personal Qualities and Emotional Stability

> Impulse control
> Responsibility for one's contribution to problems
> Adequate self-esteem
> Empathy for others
> Tolerance for differences and ambiguity
> Consideration for another's point of view
> Respect for boundaries
> Confidence in new roles (single, coparent)
> Effective problem solving
> Ability to focus on present versus focus on the past
> Acceptance of the end of the marriage

Emotional detachment from the marital relationship
Ability to realign relationship from former spouse to coparent
Adequate support gained through friends, family, and support groups

Separation of Parent and Child Needs

Empathy and sensitivity to child's needs
Capability to distinguish own needs from child's needs
Ability to sacrifice self-interest for the child's interest
Understanding of the impact of parental conflict on the child
Recognition and avoidance of loyalty binds

Appreciation of Child's Relationship with Both Parents

Support and appreciation of the bond between child and both parents
Flexibility regarding time-sharing opportunities
Recognition of the positive parental qualities of the coparent
Encouragement of contact with extended family members on both
  sides of the family

Parental Values and Attitudes Regarding Child Rearing

Personal differences between parents separated from child-rearing
  matters
Tolerance of and respect for differences in parenting styles
Support for appropriate child-rearing decisions across households
Acceptance of differences across households (rules, roles, structure)

Trust and Comfort in Parenting Abilities

Respect for each other as parents
Competence in providing adequate care that safeguards the children
Adherence to agreements regarding child-rearing matters

Communication Addressing Child-Rearing Matters

Focus on issues related to the child
Direct and appropriate communication between parents rather than
  through the child
Restrictions on conversations in front of the child
Courteous interaction in and out of the presence of the child

Ability to appropriately disengage from conflicted interactions

Exchange of information regarding the child's needs, concerns, successes, and schedules

Notification of important events and sharing of records in a timely manner

Establishment of Two Homes

Both homes referred to as the child's home regardless of how much time is spent in each home

Access to both parents and homes

Flexible, yet respectful boundaries between households

Tolerance for unexpected events that disrupt time-sharing arrangements

Similar family structures, rules, and responsibilities in both households

Continuity and predictability between homes

BARRIERS TO COOPERATIVE COPARENTING

Although some parents are capable of assuming a cooperative relationship on behalf of their children, some do not have the necessary knowledge or skills to practice new cooperative behaviors. Parents bring to the process of parent coordination their unfinished business from the marriage and their negative and destructive beliefs about the coparent. Until these beliefs and characteristics are identified and addressed, parents do not make the progress needed to create a healthy binuclear environment. However, even when coparents are taught communication and negotiation skills needed to assume a parenting partnership, they often do not make necessary changes. Remarriage or relocation can also significantly impact the coparenting relationship. Some parents report that they had a cooperative relationship prior to a remarriage or relocation. For additional information on the significance of the stepparent on the conflicted relationship see Chapter 8.

Many professionals working with high-conflict couples have identified behaviors that block or prevent parents from mediating their disputes. Johnston and Campbell (1988) refer to these barriers as a "divorce transition impasse." They maintain that the impasses families experience are determined by both psychological and social factors and are typically multileveled and multilayered. Johnston and Campbell believe that parents are entrenched in repetitive behaviors that are influenced by internal conflicts and external pressures. Their tri-level model (Figure 6.1) takes into

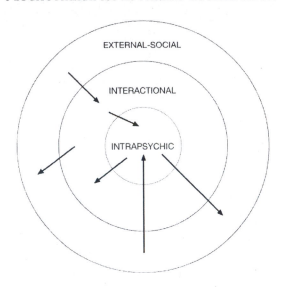

I. Intrapsychic level
   A. Vulnerability to loss
      1. Prior traumatic loss
      2. Separation-individuation conflicts (diffuse, counter-, and oscillating dependency)
   B. Vulnerability to humiliation/shame
      1. Mild—specific acknowledgment
      2. Moderate—projects total blame
      3. Severe—paranoia
II. Interactional level
   A. Legacy of a destructive marriage
   B. Ambivalent separation—shattered dreams
   C. Traumatic separation—negative reconstruction
III. External-social life
   A. Tribal warfare
   B. Role of mental health professionals/attorneys
   C. Role of court/judge

FIGURE 6.1. Sources of Divorce Impasses. (*Source:* From J. R. Johnston and L. E. G. Campbell, 1988, p. 67. Reprinted with permission. A full explanation of this table is available in Johnston and Campbell, 1988, *Impasses of Divorce: The Dynamics and Resolution of Family Conflict.* New York: Free Press/Macmillan.)

consideration influences of the social world which includes extended family members and significant others as well as the larger contextual network of the legal and mental health professions. At this level, others involved with the family may form coalitions or alliances with the parent, legitimize their negative beliefs, and consequently add to the adverse actions of the parents. At the interactional level, Johnston and Campbell identified the impasse as either a continuation of the marital conflict or the consequence of a traumatic or ambivalent separation between the couple. Impasses at this level can also be influenced by the child's emotional and behavior difficulties and the strategies used by the child to cope with the parental warfare. At the intrapsychic level, they view disputes between the parents as arising out of the need to manage intolerable feelings created by the divorce in psychologically vulnerable parents.

While working in their model, therapeutic family mediation, Irving and Benjamin (1995) identified the systemic processes that maintained an impasse which in turn impaired the parents' ability to engage in negotiation. Although they recognize that barriers to negotiation can occur over substantive issues, they maintain that underlying affective processes observed through dysfunctional patterns of interaction serve to impede the negotiation process. They suggest that impasses generally involve one or a combination of the following systemic elements:

- Individuals immobilized by distress stemming from the separation, thus reflecting individual differences in responsiveness or sensitivity
- Couple dysfunction characterized by a continual attachment to the former spouse or a pattern of interaction that hinders effective negotiation
- Parent-child relationships which generally lead to cross-generational coalitions that exclude the other parent
- An enmeshed family system characterized by poor boundaries between parental and child subsystem

Divorce involves not only the relationship between two parents as they restructure their family but also the larger social network. In adopting an ecosystemic view of the binuclear family, the system components constrain and are constrained by other system components. Although each level has its own internal organization, they operate within and/or in conjunction with the other levels.

PARALLEL PARENTING

As noted, some parents may not be able to sustain a collaborative relationship due to the complexity of the forces they encounter as they try to reorganize their lives. In situations of high conflict, parental interactions usually trigger conflicts. As a result, attempts to coparent heighten the children's distress rather than eliminate it. In highly conflicted relationships, when all else fails, it is better for coparents to parent separately rather than jointly. Some professionals in the field refer to this type of limited parenting as parallel parenting.

According to Stahl (1999b), in situations of parallel parenting parents care for their children at different times and have little or no direct interaction with each other. The aim of the system is to reduce the level of conflict in the family by significantly minimizing the parents' contact. Unfortunately, sometimes parallel parenting develops simply because one or both parents are unwilling to even attempt communication. For these parents, being mandated to work with a parent coordinator is beneficial because it forces the parents to cooperate for the sake of their child.

However, parallel parenting has its own significant disadvantages. Parents establish their own rules, routines, and discipline in each household. They do not exchange ideas. Due to the parents' inability to coordinate their efforts, the child must sacrifice in several ways: loss of continuity between households; increased likelihood that the child will manipulate both parents; inability to participate in extracurricular activities on the other parent's time; and living in a compartmentalized world.

Although the aim of parallel parenting is to reduce the level of conflict by significantly minimizing the parents' interactions, it should never be the parenting style of choice. Unfortunately, even with no risk factors, some parents and their attorneys will insist upon a parallel parenting arrangement. Many of these parents prefer such an arrangement simply to avoid the other parent. This type of thinking allows parents to take the easy way out and put their emotional needs before the needs of their child.

Currently, custody determination is predicated upon the child's individual needs. The best-interests-of-the-child presumption considers many factors, such as the child's developmental needs, the parents' ability to meet those needs, and the ability of the parents to work as a collaborative team. Researchers have been able to identify the elements that lead to the success or failure of joint custody arrangements. Similarly, scholars have explored the characteristics of parents that are essential to the creation of a cooperative partnership as well as parental characteristics that create barriers to cooperation. Regardless of the type of custody arrangement, the child's time-sharing arrangement has endless possibilities.

The CPI model encourages parents to determine a time-sharing option that will work best for their child. The professional familiar with a variety of time-sharing options for different ages will be able to assist parents to make informed decisions. When parents can resolve the time-sharing dilemma without the court's intervention, they are more likely to work in a cooperative manner.

Chapter 7

Time-Sharing Options

With the assistance of the parent coordinator, parents may develop a child-friendly and age-appropriate parenting plan. Therefore, it is important that the PC gain a comprehensive understanding of the developmental needs of children and how these needs influence living arrangements. This chapter offers a brief review of the current literature germane to developmental stages, attachment theory, and time sharing. As part of a parenting plan, the PC may assist parents in developing a living arrangement tailored to their family's unique needs. In most postdivorce cases parents may request assistance in modifying their current time-sharing arrangements. Although the division of time spent with each parent may indicate a custody arrangement, parent coordinators do not make any recommendations regarding custody.

Time-sharing arrangements are also known as access plans, visitation schedules, or parenting time. Each of these terms focuses less on custody and more on the child's schedule. Unfortunately, there is no universal approach to creating time-sharing plans appropriate for each age group. A multitude of factors must be considered when determining arrangements for the family. The parent coordinator should provide accurate information while highlighting the numerous factors that should be considered in designing a plan for the family.

CONSIDERATIONS

Historically, legal professionals have routinely used standard living arrangements regardless of the child's developmental needs. Until recently, many standard arrangements offered the noncustodial parent a visitation schedule that included alternating weekends and one evening during the week. As legal professionals and mental health professionals have blended their respective fields of expertise, living arrangements have become more reflective of the unique needs of the family rather than a one-size-fits-all approach.

Many factors must be considered when assisting parents with a time-sharing plan. The factors listed here will be addressed in greater detail later in this chapter.

Child Factors

1. Age and developmental stages
2. Temperament
3. Attachment
4. Sibling factor
5. Special needs

Adult Factors

1. Primary child care provider
2. Availability
3. Work and travel schedule
4. Personal limitations
5. Support system
6. Distance between homes
7. Parental experience and skills
8 Parental pathology and emotional stability

Coparent Factors

1. Degree of parental conflict and influence on transfers
2. Ability to communicate about the child
3. Ability to share in parenting decisions
4. Parallel parenting

AGE AND DEVELOPMENTAL STAGES

Determining what is in the best interest of the very young child creates professional debate and parental concern. This section offers a comprehensive view of the emotional needs of the very young child. This section discusses the following aspects:

1. An overview of "normal" childhood developmental stages and risks
2. The impact of temperament on the issue of appropriate time-sharing plans
3. Attachment theory

4. Separation anxiety
5. Contact versus continuity for the very young child
6. Differences in maternal and paternal parenting styles
7. Overnight outcome research
8. Phased plans for the very young

When examining normal child development it is important to consider the emotional risks associated with different time-sharing arrangements. The following stages of development (up to age five) are most likely to be affected by time-sharing arrangements.

Infants to Twenty-Four Months

Developmental Tasks

1. The child differentiates between primary caretakers and all others.
2. The child develops a secure attachment with at least one primary caretaker.
3. The child develops a sense of trust by developing primary relationships.
4. During toddler years they use relationships as a secure base from which to explore their world and return.

Developmental Risks Related to Time Sharing

1. The child's ability to establish a secure and trusting relationship may be interrupted by the loss of a caretaker's physical availability.
2. The development of trust can be inhibited by parental conflict and/or a lack of continuity of care.

General Recommendations

Very young children need stability, security, and predictability as well as a conflict-free environment. Parents must provide consistency and nurturance to their infant. It is generally agreed that until children are about three years old they require a stable environment including stable caretakers. This should take precedence in any living arrangement. Most experts will agree that infants should reside in one primary home. Generally, overnights are not recommended for infants. At age eighteen months, a child may be able to tolerate one or two overnights with the nonresidential parent if a meaningful relationship exists with that parent. If possible, parents of infants may establish a home base for the child; the parents should visit the child at the child's home base rather than have the child travel between their two homes. If the child is traveling between homes, continuity and stability between households should be established. This can be accomplished by parents duplicating items in both homes (blanket, crib, high chair) and by maintaining consistent routines for meals, bedtimes, and naps. Also, transitional objects such as stuffed animals and blankets should move between homes.

In predivorce families in which both parents participated in raising the child, the child will more than likely have a keen awareness of one parent being absent from the home. In these circumstances, it is important for the child to have frequent contact with both parents. Ideally, no more than two days should pass without contact with each parent. Parents should consider having the parent not living in the home base spend several hours two days per week and one full day on the weekend with their one-year-old. One-week absences of one parent are usually too long.

Toddlers (Twenty-Four to Thirty-Six Months)

Developmental Tasks

To develop increasing autonomy and sense of separateness.

Developmental Risks Related to Time Sharing

1. Separation anxiety stress
2. Parental conflict
3. Lack of continuity of care

All three risk factors may increase the child's home and behavioral problems, increase difficulty in formation of healthy relationships, and decrease capacity to be self-reliant.

Preschoolers (Three to Five Years)

Developmental Tasks

1. To learn initiative
2. To become more autonomous
3. To develop appropriate sexual identity
4. To develop peer relationships
5. To learn to share

6. To develop impulse control
7. To develop logical thinking rather than magical thinking

Developmental Risks Related to Time Sharing

Emotional chaos at home and in the surrounding environment undermines the child's ability to learn basic physical and intellectual skills necessary to master early school tasks and expectations. Besides the child's age, temperament should be a significant factor when selecting a time-sharing arrangement.

General Recommendations

Three-year-olds are usually able to tolerate change better than their younger counterparts. Preschoolers may have difficulty adjusting to transitions between parents. Children must be provided with very clear and concrete information regarding change. Living options at this stage can be quite varied. A child in this age range may be able to tolerate three days without seeing the absent parent. A very small percentage of five-year-olds may be able to spend a week with one parent and a week with the other parent with phone calls and/or visits in between. Predictable, frequent, and regularly scheduled time with both parents is important.

TEMPERAMENT AND ATTACHMENT

Temperament is defined as one's customary frame of mind or natural disposition, such as excitable, even tempered, sensitive, volatile, moody, or flexible. However, research has shown that a child's temperament can change classifications from secure to insecure due to the stress of divorce and/or the loss of a parent.

A child's temperament can be determined through several sources. Parents can provide the following information: (1) historical data that include achievement of developmental milestones, (2) description of the child's social skills and independent play, (3) ability to transition from one activity to another, (4) level of frustration tolerance, (5) reaction to change, (6) ability to maintain attention, and (7) perseverance. Teachers and caretakers can address the same elements through formal observations and checklists. Parents can also be asked to complete standardized checklists. The information collected may offer an indication of how the child will navigate the process of family separation. As a result, elements of the parenting plan, such as living arrangements, transportation between homes, and continuity and stability can be created to accommodate the child's unique temperament. Although the PC may assist the parents in determining the child's overall temperament, the PC should not spend an inordinate amount of time discussing temperament. It is not the role of the PC to determine custody.

Attachment is fundamental to psychological health. As defined by Bowlby ([1969] 1982), attachment is an enduring affective bond characterized by a tendency to seek and maintain proximity to a specific figure, particularly when under stress. It has been determined that attachment is especially important during the first two years of life. Children may successfully attach to more than one adult: "Although there may be hierarchies of relationships, most infants develop selective attachments simultaneously to a small number of people who provide regular contact and care" (Warshak, 2000, pp. 438-439).

According to Schaffer and Emerson (1964) young children have social attachments as follows:

1. The asocial state (birth to six weeks)
2. The state of indiscriminate attachments (six weeks to six to seven months)
3. The state of specific attachment (about seven to nine months)
4. The stage of multiple attachments (by eighteen months)

Crucial Components for Attachment

According to Whiteside (1998, p. 495) young children can develop secure attachments if the following criteria are met:

1. The caregivers are nurturing and predictable.
2. The caregivers have a management style that incorporates firm limits with both empathy and responsiveness.
3. The child has adequate time on a regular basis to develop a close bond.
4. The parenting styles are authoritative (i.e., firm with clear limit setting, while responsive and empathic) rather than authoritarian, punitive, indulgent, or neglectful.
5. One or more caregivers coordinate the different parts of the overall system.

Ludolph and Viro (1998) presented information based on Bowlby's attachment theory at the thirty-fifth annual conference of the Association of Family and Conciliation Courts in Washington, DC. The presenters enumerated the five components identified by Bowlby that are considered to be crucial in constituting an attachment bond:

1. Using the attachment figure as a safe haven in times of distress
2. Using the attachment figure as a secure base from which to venture out independently
3. Having a strong emotional tie with the person regardless of whether the tie is positive, negative, or mixed
4. Seeking to be in close proximity to the person
5. Mourning the loss of the absent person

Individual Differences in Quality of Attachment

Mary Ainsworth (1978) found that infants differ in the types (or qualities) of attachments that they establish with their caregivers.

1. *Secure attachment:* About 65 to 70 percent of one-year-old North American infants fall into this category. The securely attached infant actively explores while alone with the primary caregiver and is visibly upset by separation. The child is outgoing with strangers when the primary caregiver is present.
2. *Insecure attachment:* These children are anxious and resistant. About 10 to 15 percent of one-year-olds fall into this category. Although they appear anxious and are unlikely to explore while the primary caregiver is present, they become very distressed when the primary caregiver departs. When the primary caregiver returns, they are ambivalent. They will try to remain near primary caregiver but they will resent him or her for having left. Anxious/resistant infants are quite wary of strangers, even when the primary caregiver is present. A child that will not leave his or her primary caregiver has an insecure attachment style.
3. *Insecure/disorganized:* These children are anxious and avoidant. These infants (about 20 percent) seem uninterested in exploring when alone with their primary caretaker. They show little distress when separated from the primary caretaker and will often avoid contact when he or she returns. They are not particularly wary of strangers but may sometimes avoid or ignore them in the same way that they avoid or ignore their primary caretaker.
4. *Disorganized/disoriented:* Many infants who do not clearly fall into one of Ainsworth's three attachment categories show a curious mixture of the resistant and the avoidant patterns. In reunion episodes, these toddlers may act dazed and confused; or they may first seek

proximity and then abruptly move away as the primary caretaker draws near. These children may be drawn to their caregivers but may also be fearful due to neglect or physical abuse. Aggression in children may be related to disorganized attachment. Ninety percent of maltreated children show signs of disorganized/disoriented attachment.

Separation Anxiety

Separation anxiety is normal during the second year of life and should not be confused with separation anxiety disorder. Furthermore, the child must show signs of anxiety when left with different individuals, not just the other parent. In other words, the child would show signs of separation anxiety when dropped off at preschool and when left with a grandparent, not just when being transferred to the other parent.

It is not uncommon for divorced parents to claim that their preschooler has "separation anxiety" as a way to control the time-sharing arrangement or as a reflection of their own generalized anxiety. Some parents truly believe that their child has separation anxiety until the PC can help them differentiate between normal anxiety and pathological anxiety. Furthermore, it is not uncommon for separation anxiety to be induced by a visitation schedule or an anxious parent.

A child's ability to separate easily is related more to temperament, while reunion behaviors are related more to attachment. If the child demonstrates a sensitive temperament, then the young child may do best with one primary home rather than two.

Continuity versus Contact

It is often very difficult for parents to determine whether their child should live in one primary home or two. This is especially true for the young child. Parents must ask themselves, "Which is more important? The need for frequent contact with both parents or the need for continuity?" Depending on the child's temperament, he or she may require the continuity and stability that one primary home offers as opposed to frequent moves between two homes.

Special considerations must be made for the young child who is still breast-feeding. While breast-feeding is undoubtedly a sufficiently valuable form of supply nourishment to a child, some mothers may use extended breast-feeding as a way to receive and maintain primary custody. Breast-feeding is a temporary situation that should be respected, but not at the expense of the child's relationship with both parents.

Anxious parents and their attorneys can easily find quotes taken out of context and cited from partial research that will support their desired conclusions. It is imperative that the PC help parents to see the value in both continuity and contact so they can find solutions suited to their unique child. Usually the "primary parent" will declare that the child needs continuity more than contact while the "secondary parent" will claim that frequency is most important.

It appears that some professionals who are concerned about continuity for the young child will take a stand for a "primary home." On the other hand, some assert that to delay the overnight visitation may create the wrong message to the child and increase stress when the child finally begins overnights. Due to the conclusions drawn from attachment theory research, more professionals are choosing to err on the side of continuity. Other professionals promote the need for frequent contact, especially when the young child is bonded to both parents. They tend to recommend no more than three or four days without either parent unless they are traveling.

Conversely, some parents in the early process of the divorce may choose a shared physical custody arrangement for their young child. When this occurs, the parent coordinator may wish to gain an understanding of how the parents reached this outcome. By considering the answers to the following questions the PC may be able to uncover the parents' rationale:

1. Are the parents overfocused on avoiding court at the expense of their child?
2. Are they overconcerned with being "fair" to each other?
3. Are they simply looking at their work schedules and what is convenient to both of them?
4. Do the parents truly believe that a shared arrangement will benefit their child?

The PC can encourage parents to carefully think about the living arrangement through the eyes of their child. A discussion focusing on the advantages and disadvantages of the arrangement may provide the parents the insight necessary to make modifications that meet their child's needs.

According to Whiteside (1998), research data documented a wide variety of successful two-household parenting arrangements for children age five and younger. He noted that there is a serious impact on the child's development when caregivers are not working in a collaborative manner to meet the child's needs. Whiteside (1998, p. 495) reported:

Neither the shape of the care giving network nor the time-sharing schedule has the most potent effect on children's developmental; rather, it is the quality of the parental alliance and the parent's warmth, sensitivity, and discipline style that make the difference between a well-adjusted child and a child who is angry, scared, or limited in cognitive and social skills.

Young Children and Overnights

As noted, when dealing with time-sharing arrangements for the young child, the issue of primary home and contact versus continuity all lead back to the controversial issue of overnights for young children. If the young child is comfortable with both parents then frequent contact with both parents is recommended. However, the issue of overnights in both homes may or may not be advised depending upon other factors. Researchers Kelly and Lamb (2000) found through empirical research that overnights do not harm the young child. They noted that the greater harm is in losing contact with the noncustodial parent. Yet researchers Solomon and George (1999) concluded infants with regular overnights are more likely to be described as disorganized or unclassifiable.

Biringen and colleagues (2002) believe that in most cases the young child should spend every night with the same parent when the parents live apart. Many professionals refer to "restrictions" on overnights for young children. "Blanket restrictions" grew out of concern over separation anxiety in young children. The research addressed the following elements: concern for the primary attachment between parent and child, separation issues, and a belief that overnights with fathers will harm infant attachment with their mothers.

Many of these same professionals hold the opinion that the young child up to age two should have frequent shorter contact of two to three hours with the noncustodial parent while sleeping in the same home and same bed every night. Unfortunately, having frequent contact without overnights creates other problems. This arrangement increases the number of transfers for the child and, therefore, increases the potential for conflict and tension with the child present. Many will claim that the child twelve months of age with a secure attachment can handle one overnight with the noncustodial parent. Proponents of one primary home tend to believe that the child five years of age can spend one week with the noncustodial parent as long as he or she also has contact with the custodial parent during the week. In some situations children younger than five, especially if they have older siblings, may be able to extend this period of time away from the primary home.

Although some professionals feel strongly about one primary home, others do not agree that adequate empirical research has been conducted to support a blanket restriction. According to Warshak (2000, p. 423), "Only one study, published after blanket restrictions were promulgated, compared the attachment status of toddlers who spend the overnights with one versus both parents." The study conducted by Solomon and George (1999) compared infants in separated/divorce families with infants who live in homes with two married parents. Warshak (2000, p. 423) concluded that Solomon and George mislead their audience when they stated that "overnight visits did not improve the infant-father attachment and actually harmed the infant-mother attachment." Warshak, on the other hand, found no significant differences between these two groups on incidence of secure and insecure relationships.

Warshak (2000) also stated:

> The opinion that children can tolerate sleeping during the day in their father's presence, and in the presence of hired attendants in day care centers, but not at night with their fathers, cannot be said to express a scientific judgment. (p. 440)

Warshak advocated for professionals to consider overnights as an option, not necessarily that every infant and toddler should have overnights. According to Gould and Stahl (2001), the issue of overnights for young children should be made dependent upon several factors. They report that each child and each situation must be fully examined before determining the issue of overnights. Some custody evaluators favor delaying overnights for young children for a period of time, while others take a strong position stating that to delay overnight visitation until the child is four or five can actually increase the young child's anxiety by setting a precedent.

To maintain high-quality relationships with their children, parents need to have sufficiently extensive and regular interaction with them, but the amount of time involved is usually less important than the quality of the interaction it fosters:

> Time distribution arrangements that ensure the involvement of both parents in important aspects of the children's everyday lives and routines—including bedtime and waking rituals, transitions to and from school, extracurricular and recreational activities—are likely to keep nonresidential parents playing psychologically important and central roles in the lives of their children. (Lamb, Sternberg, and Thompson, 1997, p. 400)

Whiteside (1998) summarized the research into three different models. The first model is predicated on the assumption that very young children need a primary and stable attachment to their mother who performs the duties of the primary parent and provides the bed to sleep in. The relationship between mother and child is paramount. Thus the relationship between the father and the child is peripheral. This model focuses on the negative effects of regular separation from the mother. The second model places great importance on children having a father or father figure in the household. This research explores the positive effects of father visits and the negative effects of father absence. The third model focuses on a family systems perspective and looks at the full network of relationships surrounding the child.

Whiteside (1998) stated that research on the effect of overnights with the nonresidential parent for children under age five is extremely scarce. He wrote that Hodges (1991) and Kalter (1990) did not express concerns about overnights away from the primary caregiver when the children are age three or older. Yet they did make evident concerns about overnights for children under age three. Maccoby and Mnookin (1992) discovered that over 40 percent of children age three and younger do spend overnights with their fathers, and that children in this age range who do not have such overnights are highly likely to lose contact with their fathers within three years. Accordingly, continued efforts conducting empirical research on this subject is extremely important.

Pruett and colleagues (2004) argue that "it is not the amount of time that nonresidential parents and children spend together, but the kinds of interaction that accompany longer stays and overnights" (p. 40). They also believe the importance of father involvement outweighs any detriment to overnights. Their results indicated that "overnights play an important role in child adjustment in some limited respects and by illuminating a larger picture that indicates it is not overnights in and of themselves that are most important" (p. 53). They found that the context surrounding the parenting plan was crucial to the way it may be experienced by the young child.

The conflicting findings regarding appropriateness of overnights for young children suggest that careful consideration of each family's specific circumstances needs to be addressed when assisting parents with determining time-sharing arrangements. Additional research in this area may help parents make more informed decisions that have a higher probability of providing an environment suited for optimal growth and development of their children.

Maternal versus Paternal Parenting Styles

It is important to help parents value and appreciate the child's relationship with the other parent as well as his or her parenting style. Typical stereotypes regarding maternal and paternal parenting styles (Pruett, 2000) include the following:

1. Fathers have a preference for physical stimulation right from the beginning.
2. Mothers tend to prefer soothing their infant right from the beginning. (Children respond to stimulation and soothing styles. Their heart rates increase when they see their fathers and decrease when they see their mothers.)
3. By age two, fathers tend to play with their children more than mothers.
4. Fathers allow their children to crawl all over them.
5. Mothers tend to be more safety conscious and set more limits.
6. Fathers tend to give their child more room to explore.
7. Mothers tend to have more difficulty letting go of their children.
8. Fathers tend to encourage autonomy more than mothers.
9. Fathers tend to make more comments about misbehavior.
10. Mothers are more likely to rescue the child.
11. Fathers are more likely to tease and surprise.
12. Mothers are more likely to micromanage.
13. Mothers are more involved in the day-to-day details.

The parent who keeps up to date on the details in the child's life is often referred to as the gatekeeper. Since mothers typically tend to be more detail oriented and often more protective, they tend to be anxious about the father's ability to parent. For example, mothers are concerned about issues such as, Will father remember to RSVP for the birthday party? Will he require our child to wear a hat or provide adequate supervision? Fathers typically complain that the mother is overinvolved, is overprotective, and creates dependency, especially in their sons. Like all stereotypes, there are certainly exceptions to these parenting styles. Nonetheless, the gatekeeper may be resistant to trust the other parent with "their" child. Sharing these stereotypes can help parents see the value in both styles.

Besides encouraging parents to tolerate each other's parenting style, it is important to value and respect the "noncustodial parent" so that he or she will stay involved in the child's life. Fathers are still more likely to be the noncustodial parent. The greatest barriers to keeping fathers involved in their children's lives include the mother's attitude, access to their child, and the father's commitment to their child.

Child Outcomes of Involved Fathering

According to Pruett (2000), involved fathers (married or single) impact children in several ways.

Behavioral Impact

- Reduced contact with juvenile justice
- Delay in initial sexual activity, reduced teen pregnancy
- Reduced rate of divorce
- Less reliance on aggressive conflict resolution

Educational Impact

- Higher grade completion and income
- Math competence in girls
- Verbal strength in boys and girls

Emotional Impact

- Greater problem-solving competence and stress tolerance
- Greater empathy, greater moral sensitivity, and reduced gender stereotyping
- Increased frustration tolerance
- Fewer angry outbursts

Phased Plans for Young Children

When the child is an infant or preschooler, it is best to consider a phased parenting plan. Unfortunately, most family-law attorneys and judges do not understand the benefit of developing a plan that takes into consideration the changing needs of the child. It is not unusual to review a plan developed by the attorney or court for a young child that does not take into consideration the modifications needed for a school-age child. For example, a settlement agreement written for a three-year-old child indicated that the parents would pick up their son from school at 10:00 a.m. Once the child entered public school, the conflicted parents were unable to reach a mutually satisfying modification to the start of the time-share arrangement. To avoid unnecessary court involvement, both parents and their attorneys should be encouraged to consider the future needs of the family rather than focus only on the current family situation. In this way, the need to utilize court services in the future may be eliminated.

With the assistance of the parent coordinator, parents can be guided to consider both present and future needs of their family. To create a present- and future-focused plan, time-sharing arrangements can be delineated for each major developmental level, keeping in mind the time requirements for each of the different phases of school enrollment.

OTHER FAMILY FACTORS

The Sibling Factor

When a very young child has an older sibling, he or she may be able to tolerate longer periods of time away from one parent. Much like a security blanket, an older sibling becomes a comfort as well as a consistent factor that travels between homes. This information can be very reassuring to an anxious parent.

Same Home, Two Parents

Some temporary orders require the parents to rotate in and out of the marital home while the children remain in their familiar surroundings. In this situation, both parents must share a dwelling that functions as their residence when they are not living in the marital home. This arrangement requires a great deal of trust between parents, the consideration of each other's personal belongings, and mutual care of the residence. This arrangement is ideal for the very young child who may still require a crib and other infant equipment. However, parents should not spend overlapping time in the home during transfers. This may confuse the young child and increase the likelihood of parental conflict. Transfers at day care may work best in these situations. Less conflicted parents may even set this type of arrangement up on their own while they are working out the details of their divorce.

The Older Child (Six- to Twelve-Year-Olds)

As the child grows so do the options. Yet specific details need to be considered when developing a living arrangement for this age group. When establishing two homes, peer group affiliation, geographical proximity of both homes, and continuity of school and friendships are very important factors. Elementary age children may be able to tolerate a shared parenting arrangement. If travel between the two homes and the time-share arrangements becomes a hardship for the child and affects school performance, participation in extracurricular activities, and relationship with peers, parents will have to adjust the child's schedule to meet the child's needs, not their own.

Developmental Needs of the Adolescent

Just as the young child has his or her own set of special needs, so does the adolescent. Adolescents must take steps toward independence. Peer group affiliation becomes increasingly important. Although teens are making this shift, they still require adult supervision. They also need to know that their parents are still available to them and will accept them unconditionally. The teen's social, academic, and extracurricular needs may dictate the living arrangement. At this stage of development it is critical for parents to be flexible as long as the teen is not allowed to bounce between homes on a whim. Parents are advised to consult with their teens for ideas on how to schedule visits. As much as possible, the teen's ideas should be put into practice. The living arrangement can range from home base with one parent with flexible but consistent time with the other parent for activities, overnights, and dinners to a plan including school year with one parent and summer vacation with the other parent. With any arrangement, both parents should spend flexible and consistent time with their teenager. Also, strict adherence to time-share arrangements may not be possible. Flexibility and provisions for makeup time should be built into the parenting plan. For example, if the teen resides more with the father and his high school is having a homecoming game on the mother's weekend, the teen may not want to go to the mother's home if she resides in a different neighborhood. Parents of teens must learn to focus less on their own "rights" and more on their teen's emotional and social needs.

Families with Special Needs

Just as it is important to acknowledge the influence of culture on a family, it is equally important to acknowledge how a family member with a disability or special need impacts the family. Some factors to consider include (1) the home's accessibility for physical limitations, (2) parental ability to provide the structure needed for a child with ADHD, (3) parental ability to assist the child with a learning disability, and (4) parental ability to provide consistent limits for a child with an oppositional defiant disorder. Children diagnosed with attention difficulties generally should not move between homes during the school week. Likewise, any adult disabilities should be considered when developing parenting and time-sharing plans.

Degree of Parental Conflict

As noted in the previous chapters, parental conflict is a very important factor to consider when assisting parents with their time-sharing plans. If parents are unable to conduct themselves in a civilized fashion when in the presence of each other, the number of transfers should be kept to a minimum and occur at neutral locations such as school or day care. Schedules can be arranged to minimize the number of transitions children experience and the amount of contact parents must have with each other. However, to minimize transfers, a change in the "ideal" time-sharing arrangement may be necessary. For instance, a weekend time share may need to be extended from Friday after school to Monday morning at the start of school rather than evening exchanges on Friday and Sunday. Such a change would eliminate contact between parents by using the school facility as a neutral exchange site. Police stations should be avoided as much as possible unless there is a serious risk of physical harm. Transfers at police stations may communicate to the children that one or both of their parents may be dangerous. It may also imply that the child's parents are incapable or unwilling to resolve conflicts on their own. As a result, the children may not feel comfortable with their parents and will observe ineffectual conflict resolution skills.

It is essential that the time distribution fosters quality involvement of both parents in the children's day-to-day life unless there is a valid reason that this cannot occur safely. Ideally, both parents should be involved in morning and bedtime rituals, travel to and from school, homework and long-term assignments, car pools, extracurricular activities, religious ceremonies, and the supervision of household chores. Children need sufficiently extensive and regular interaction with their parents to maintain close, satisfying relationships. However, the quantity of time is generally less important than the quality of interaction it encourages.

PLANS BASED ON CHILD'S AGE AND LEVEL OF PARENTAL CONFLICT

Garrity and Baris (1994) created visitation schedules recommended for children in infancy through eighteen years of age who are exposed to various levels of parental conflict. Figures 7.1 through 7.5 highlight their recommendations.

Level of Conflict

Minimal	Mild	Moderate	Moderately Severe	Severe
Select primary residence based on caretaking history. Nonresidential parent has short, frequent visits—daily depending on availability and caretaking history. If dual primary residence, parents share daytime caretaking and establish one nighttime caretaker. Overnights are not recommended.		Daily visits possible if in neutral environment that infant is comfortable in (i.e., day care, trusted friend or relative, supervision service). Two home visits per week possible provided conflictual environment can be neutralized. If parents cannot adhere to minimal verbal exchange, neutral visiting environment is mandatory.	No visits at home. Visits twice a week in a supervised environment. Assessment mandatory before unsupervised visitation possible. Full assessment to consider each parent's capacity (1) for impulse control; (2) to change problem-solving style; (3) to empathize with child; (4) to create and maintain a safe environment.	Supervised or therapeutic visitation only.

FIGURE 7.1. Recommended Visitation Schedules, Infancy to Two and One-Half Years (*Source:* Reprinted with permission from C. Garrity and M. Baris, *Caught in the Middle: Protecting the Children of High-Conflict Divorce*, Table 5.1, p. 53, Copyright © 1994, Jossey-Bass, a subsidiary of John Wiley & Sons, Inc.)

		Level of Conflict		
Minimal	**Mild**	**Moderate**	**Moderately Severe**	**Severe**
Time initially distributed in proportion to parents' direct caretaking prior to divorce.	May introduce longer visitation periods for child gradually throughout this stage to a maximum of a split week.

Implement overnights for child—1 per week initially, extend to a maximum of 3 per week toward the end of this stage.

Long-weekend-short-weekend concept, preferably including a weekday visit, is a possibility if one parent works full time during the week and the other does not. | Minimize transitions. Eliminate midweek visit.

Move toward one lengthier visit per week—2 days/1 overnight toward the end of this stage.

Use neutral transition places whenever possible. | Supervised visits only until full assessment of parents and child obtained.

Frequency of supervised visitation determined on a case-by-case basis, taking into account the child's feelings (i.e., child is not expressing fear of visitation).

Full assessment to consider each parent's capacity (1) for impulse control; (2) to change problem-solving style; (3) to empathize with child; (4) to create and maintain a safe environment. | Supervised or therapeutic visitation only. |

FIGURE 7.2. Recommended Visitation Schedules, Two and One-Half to Five Years (*Source:* Reprinted with permission from C. Garrity and M. Baris, *Caught in the Middle: Protecting the Children of High-Conflict Divorce,* Table 5.2, p. 54, Copyright © 1994, Jossey-Bass, a subsidiary of John Wiley & Sons, Inc.)

Level of Conflict

Minimal	Mild	Moderate	Moderately Severe	Severe
Many children still require a home base. Child visits from 1 to 3 days weekly with nonresidential parent. OR Alternating half weeks at each parent's home if consistent contact with community, peer group, school, and extracurricular activities can be maintained. Child could have multiple overnights. Full week at each parent's home can be phased in toward older end of this stage.		Minimize transitions. Use neutral transition places—school, activities, day care. Distribute visitation into one time block per week.	Supervised visits only until full assessment of parents and child obtained. Frequency of supervised visitation determined on a case-by-case basis, taking into account the child's feelings (i.e., child is not expressing fear of visitation). Full assessment to consider each parent's capacity (1) for impulse control; (2) to change problem-solving style, (3) to empathize with child; (4) to create and maintain a safe environment.	Supervised or therapeutic visitation only.

FIGURE 7.3. Recommended Visitation Schedules, Six to Eight Years (*Source:* Reprinted with permission from C. Garrity and M. Baris, *Caught in the Middle: Protecting the Children of High-Conflict Divorce,* Table 5.3, p. 55, Copyright © 1994, Jossey-Bass, a subsidiary of John Wiley & Sons, Inc.)

Level of Conflict

Minimal	Mild	Moderate	Moderately Severe	Severe
One home base with specific evenings, weekends, and activities at the other home scheduled for regularity and predictability. OR Equal basis with each parent is possible, up to 2 weeks in each residence. Maintain accessibility to school, peers, and extracurricular and community involvements from both homes. "Nesting": Both parents moving in and out of same residence is another possibility. Presuming close relationship, summer may be split 50-50, approximately 4 to 6 weeks in one block.		Minimize transitions. Use neutral transition places—school, activities, day care. Distribute visitation into one time block per week.	Supervised visits only until full assessment of parents and child obtained. Frequency of supervised visitation determined on a case-by-case basis, taking into account the child's feelings (i.e., child is not expressing fear of visitation). Full assessment to consider each parent's capacity (1) for impulse control; (2) to change problem-solving style; (3) to empathize with child; (4) to create and maintain a safe environment.	Therapeutic visitation only.

FIGURE 7.4. Recommended Visitation Schedules, Nine to Twelve Years (*Source:* Reprinted with permission from C. Garrity and M. Baris, *Caught in the Middle: Protecting the Children of High-Conflict Divorce*, Table 5.4, p. 56, Copyright © 1994, Jossey-Bass, a subsidiary of John Wiley & Sons, Inc.)

	Level of Conflict			
Minimal	Mild	Moderate	Moderately Severe	Severe
One home base with specific evenings, weekends, and activities at the other home scheduled for regularity and predictability. OR Equal basis with each parent is possible, up to 2 weeks in each residence. OR "Nesting": Both parents moving in and out of same residence is another possibility. Establish "permanent schedule" with some flexibility built in. Adolescent input essential; adolescent cannot be forced into schedule he or she had no involvement in creating. Maintain child's accessibility to school, peers, and extracurricular and community involvements from both homes.		Minimize transitions. Distribute into one longer block—split week, alternating weeks, or up to 2 weeks in each residence. Transitions handled by child (bike, car, or public transportation),or an agreed-upon neutral place (school or activity) is selected. No nesting. Therapy considered if child refusing visitation or strongly taking sides.	Supervised visits only until full assessment of parents and adolescent obtained. When adolescent is aware of endangering situation, is capable of leaving independently, and is expressing a desire for unsupervised visitation, such visitation should be given consideration. Frequency of visitation determined on a case-by-case basis, taking into account the adolescent's feelings. Full assessment to consider each parent's capacity (1) for impulse control; (2) to change problem-solving style; (3) to empathize with adolescent; (4) to create and maintain a safe environment.	Therapeutic visitation only.

FIGURE 7.5. Recommended Visitation Schedules, Thirteen to Eighteen Years. (*Source:* Reprinted with permission from C. Garrity and M. Baris, *Caught in the Middle: Protecting the Children of High-Conflict Divorce,* Table 5.5, p. 57, Copyright © 1994, Jossey-Bass, a subsidiary of John Wiley & Sons, Inc.)

SPECIFIC TIME-SHARING PLANS

Many creative time-sharing options are available to parents when considering their child's living arrangement. When thinking about the new family structure, parents and professionals should consider the unique needs of the family rather than replicating a standard option commonly used in the court system. As already noted, a number of significant factors influence the success of any living arrangement.

The first section highlights options that are based on one primary home. However, this does not imply that one parent is "primary parent" and the other the "visiting" parent. It is possible for parents to choose one of the primary home options and identify the arrangement as joint physical custody. To avoid gender bias, the letters "A" and "B" are used to signify each parent. In addition, other elements involved in the development of a plan were taken under consideration and should be considered when brainstorming options for families. Each of the following samples consider the (1) number of overnights in each household, (2) length of time between contact with parent A and parent B, (3) number of parent-to-parent transfers, and (4) the number of transfers during the week.

Primary Home Options

Standard Visitation

Standard visitation generally refers to alternating weekends plus a midweek dinner or overnight. Standard visitation is also referred to as the "traditional court-imposed model." The child stays primarily with one parent and shares time with the other parent every other weekend from Friday through Sunday evening and every other Wednesday, usually for dinner. This schedule is implemented in situations of sole custody and joint legal custody, and it may even be identified as joint physical custody. In Figure 7.6, the child spends only four overnights with parent B and twenty-four overnights with parent A every four weeks. Weekends are alternated (Friday through Sunday) with an alternated dinner midweek.

Extended Weekend Plans

It is becoming more popular to extend the standard visitation by one or two days, especially when transfers need to occur at the child's school or day care center rather than at a parent's home. For example, instead of the standard Friday at 6:00 p.m. until Sunday at 6:00 p.m., which requires two parent-to-parent transfers, it is extended in combinations shown in Figures 7.7 through 7.10. See Figure 7.7 for the alternating Friday to Monday with alternating midweek dinner plan. Sunday drop off has been extended to Monday morning.

The option in Figure 7.8 is the same as in Figure 7.7 with the exception of an overnight midweek. Transfers occur on Friday at release of school until Monday morning at school plus alternating midweek from release of school until next morning.

The option in figure 7.9 is the same as Figure 7.7 with the exception that there is a dinner each week instead of on alternating weeks. Transfers occur

Mon.	Tues.	Wed.	Thurs.	Fri.	Sat.	Sun.
A	A	A	A	A/B	B	B/A
A	A	A/B/A	A	A	A	A
A	A	A	A	A/B	B	B/A
A	A	A/B/A	A	A	A	A

FIGURE 7.6. Standard Visitation Plan (twenty-four overnights with parent A, four overnights with parent B)

Mon.	Tues.	Wed.	Thurs.	Fri.	Sat.	Sun.
A	A	A	A	A/B	B	B
B/A	A	A	A/B/A	A	A	A
A	A	A	A	A/B	B	B
B/A	A	A	A/B/A	A	A	A

FIGURE 7.7. Extended Weekend Plan: Alternating Friday to Monday and Alternating Midweek Dinner (twenty-two overnights with parent A, six overnights with parent B; four parent-parent transfers)

Mon.	Tues.	Wed.	Thurs.	Fri.	Sat.	Sun.
A	A	A	A	A/B	B	B
B/A	A	A	A/B	B/A	A	A
A	A	A	A	A/B	B	B
B/A	A	A	A/B	B/A	A	A

FIGURE 7.8. Extended Weekend Plan: Alternating Friday to Monday and Alternating Midweek Overnight (twenty overnights with parent A, eight overnights with parent B; zero parent-parent transfers)

on Friday at release of school until Monday morning at school plus every midweek for dinner.

The plan in Figure 7.10 is the same as Figure 7.8 with the exception that there is an overnight each week instead of alternating weeks. This plan has the child transferring without parent contact but nonetheless shifting from one parent to the other a total of four times within a seven-day period.

Figure 7.11 shows alternating Thursdays at the release of school until Sunday at 6:00 p.m. Figure 7.12 is the same plan with the addition of a midweek dinner on off weeks. Figure 7.13 shows the same plan plus Thursday until Friday morning.

Mon.	Tues.	Wed.	Thurs.	Fri.	Sat.	Sun.
A	A/B/A	A	A	A/B	B	B
B/A	A	A	A/B/A	A	A	A
A	A/B/A	A	A	A/B	B	B
B/A	A	A	A/B/A	A	A	A

FIGURE 7.9. Extended Weekend Plan: Alternating Friday to Monday and One Night Every Week for Dinner (twenty-two overnights with parent A, six overnights with parent B; four parent-parent transfers)

Mon.	Tues.	Wed.	Thurs.	Fri.	Sat.	Sun.
A	A/B	B/A	A	A/B	B	B
B/A	A	A	A/B	B/A	A	A
A	A/B	B/A	A	A/B	B	B
B/A	A	A	A/B	B/A	A	A

FIGURE 7.10. Extended Weekend Plan: Alternating Friday Plus One Overnight Every Week (three overnights one week with parent A and four overnights with parent B, then six overnights with A and one overnight with B for a total of eighteen overnights with A and ten overnights with B; zero parent-parent transfers)

Mon.	Tues.	Wed.	Thurs.	Fri.	Sat.	Sun.
A	A	A	A/B	B	B	B/A
A	A	A	A	A	A	A
A	A	A	A/B	B	B	B/A
A	A	A	A	A	A	A

FIGURE 7.11. Alternating Weekend Plan: Alternating Thursday to Sunday (twenty-two overnights with parent A, six overnights with parent B; two parent-parent transfers)

Figure 7.14 shows alternating Thursday at the release of school until Monday morning at school, plus alternating Thursday from release of school for dinner. Figure 7.15 shows the same plan but Thursday is always an overnight.

Mon.	Tues.	Wed.	Thurs.	Fri.	Sat.	Sun.
A	A	A	A/B	B	B	B/A
A	A	A	A/B/A	A	A	A
A	A	A	A/B	B	B	B/A
A	A	A	A/B/A	A	A	A

FIGURE 7.12. Alternating Weekend Plan: Alternating Thursday to Sunday (twenty-two overnights with parent A, six overnights with parent B; two parent-parent transfers)

Mon.	Tues.	Wed.	Thurs.	Fri.	Sat.	Sun.
A	A	A	A/B	B	B	B/A
A	A	A	A/B	B/A	A	A
A	A	A	A/B	B	B	B/A
A	A	A	A/B	B/A	A	A

FIGURE 7.13. Alternating Weekend Plan: Alternating Thursday to Sunday with Alternating Thursday Overnight (twenty overnights with parent A, eight overnights with parent B; two parent-parent transfers)

Mon.	Tues.	Wed.	Thurs.	Fri.	Sat.	Sun.
A	A	A	A/B	B	B	B
B/A	A	A	A/B/A	A	A	A
A	A	A	A/B	B	B	B
B/A	A	A	A/B/A	A	A	A

FIGURE 7.14. Alternating Extended Weekend Plan: Alternating Thursday to Monday with Alternating Thursdays for Dinner (twenty overnights with parent A, eight overnights with parent B; two parent-parent transfers)

Mon.	Tues.	Wed.	Thurs.	Fri.	Sat.	Sun.
A	A	A	A/B	B	B	B
B/A	A	A	A/B	B/A	A	A
A	A	A	A/B	B	B	B
B/A	A	A	A/B	B/A	A	A

FIGURE 7.15. Alternating Extended Weekend Plan: Alternating Thursday to Monday with Thursday Overnight (eighteen overnights with parent A, ten overnights with parent B; zero parent-parent transfers)

Some professionals refer to the plan in Figure 7.15 as a 9/5 arrangement. In other words, every two weeks the primary parent has the child for nine days and the other parent has the child for five days. The 9/5 schedule minimizes the sense of a primary home for the noncustodial parent. Besides minimizing the number of transfers, the extended weekend is positive in that the noncustodial parent stays involved with the school and comes to know the teachers and the child's classmates. For psychological reasons, the 9/5 plan feels less like one parent is labeled as a "visiting parent." In addition, the parent with nine days is less likely to resent the other parent and refer to the coparent as a "Disney parent" because he or she is actively involved with homework and school rather than just enjoying the weekends. Another advantage is that the extended weekend, especially the 9/5 plan, feels fairly close to a 50/50 plan in both homes while still providing a primary home.

Since the extended weekend usually includes Thursday, we recommend that the next midweek period be on Thursday to keep continuity. The only possible disadvantage to having every Thursday evening is that Thursdays are very important study nights for the elementary age child, with tests scheduled routinely on Fridays.

Deciding between a midweek dinner versus an overnight should depend upon all the other factors such as the child's age, temperament, school needs, and parental relationship. The other important factor is how far one parent lives from the child's school due to the school drop offs each week.

The material in the remainder of this section is included by permission of the Arizona Supreme Court. The material is from the Arizona Supreme Court's 2001 publication "Model Parenting Time Plans for Parent/Child Access." The booklet was drafted by a statewide Arizona Supreme Court committee of judicial officers, mental health providers, and attorneys; the committee created the material after consulting with nationally known experts on child development and after reviewing current research and guidelines from other communities. The booklet is available on their Web site at <www.supreme.state.az.us>.

Options Depending Upon Age

Birth to Twelve Months

Infants learn at a rapid rate but they cannot retain experiences over time. Therefore, it is important to have frequent contact with both parents and a predicable schedule. The parents' schedule must work around the infant's routine.

Option A (1): Three periods of three to six hours spaced throughout each week.

Option A (2): Two six-hour periods spaced throughout each week.

Option B: Two three-hour periods and one eight-hour period spaced throughout each week.

Option C: Two periods of three to six hours and one overnight each week.

Twelve to Twenty-Four Months

The young toddler can attach to many caregivers. However, transitions between homes may become more difficult for children this age.

Option A (1): Three periods of three to six hours spaced throughout each week.

Option A (2): Two six-hour periods spaced throughout each week.

Option B: Two four-hour periods and one eight-hour period spaced throughout each week.

Option C: One daytime period of three to six hours and two non-consecutive overnights each week.

Twenty-Four to Thirty-Six Months

Although children this age are becoming more independent, they may still cling to their caregiver and resist separation. Predictable and regularly scheduled routines help children manage their fears and help them learn that the world is a safe place. It is very important that the transitions are stress free as possible. [See the section Transitions Between Homes for more specific transfer suggestions.]

Option A (1): Two three to four hour periods and one eight-hour period spaced throughout each week.

Option A (2): Two periods of three to six hours and one overnight each week.

Option B: One period of three to six hours and two non-consecutive overnights each week.

Option C: One period of three to six hours and two consecutive overnights each week.

Three to Five Years of Age

The three- to five-year-old is attached to their regular caregivers and separation may cause them to be uncomfortable and anxious. They may also be fearful about unfamiliar activities. This child may show increased discomfort when moving between parents' homes. They benefit from structured time with children their own age away from their parents. The child may be more likely to resist going to the other parent if the parents are tense, hostile, or argue with each other at the exchange.

> Option A (1): Two consecutive overnights every other week and an additional overnight or afternoon/evening period each week.
>
> Option A (2): Three consecutive overnights week one. Another overnight or afternoon/evening period of three to four hours may be added in week number two.
>
> Option B: Four consecutive overnights week one. Another overnight or afternoon/evening period of three to four hours may be added in week number two.

Six to Nine Years of Age

Six- to nine-year-old children may worry that one parent does not love them or that they will lose one parent. They may also experience intense longing for the absent parent. Some benefit from spending more time at one home, while others move back and forth on a regular basis with ease. All scheduling should maximize the parent's time off from work.

EQUAL TIME-SHARING PLANS

Rotations

Some parents prefer frequent rotations, especially for the young preschool child, because it does not require the child to be away from either parent for long periods of time and it works well for a 50/50 joint physical custody. Frequent interrupts during the school week are not well suited to the school-age child. Besides the typical one-week rotation, 2-2-3 and 2-5 rotations are also options for parents who want to have "equal" time with their children.

2-2-3 Rotation

The parents alternate the weekends and Monday/Tuesday. In other words, the parent with Monday and Tuesday also has the following weekend. The next week the other parent has Monday/Tuesday with the weekend. The advantages include fewer transfers, the week is more consistent, and the child is never gone for more than three days. The disadvantage is it may be difficult for parents to coordinate their work schedules differently each week so they can maximize time with their young child. The transfers can occur at day care or preschool so that there are no transfers parent to parent. A child with separation anxiety should never have both parents present at transfers because he or she will do much better dealing with only one parent at a time. See Figure 7.16 for an illustration of this plan.

2-5 Rotation

In this option, the parent with Monday/Tuesday always has Monday/Tuesday while the Wednesday/Thursday parent always has Wednesday/Thursday. In addition, they alternate weekends. The advantage of a 2-5 rotation is that parents can coordinate their work schedules better; the advantage for the child is fewer transfers and longer uninterrupted periods of time. This schedule can also benefit the young child if he or she has the same activity every week that includes only one parent. For example, the child is in a church choir every Wednesday at the father's church. The disadvantage for the young child is that there are five consecutive days away from one parent rather than three days. Figure 7.17 illustrates this plan.

One Week Rotations

The authors have found the one week on and one week off rotation works best for children approximately nine years of age and older. However, a child with an attention deficit problem tends to do best in a primary home during the school week. When using a one-week rotation, the transfer days should be done at school every Friday. This allows the child to bring home school papers and begin the next period at a more relaxed time. The disadvantage to this plan is that the child may feel shuttled back and forth. Some children also complain about having to carry an overnight bag every Friday.

Mon.	Tues.	Wed.	Thurs.	Fri.	Sat.	Sun.
A	A	B	B	A	A	A
B	B	A	A	B	B	B
A	A	B	B	A	A	A
B	B	A	A	B	B	B

FIGURE 7.16. Equal Time-Sharing Plan: 2-2-3 Rotation

Mon.	Tues.	Wed.	Thurs.	Fri.	Sat.	Sun.
A	A	B	B	A	A	A
A	A	B	B	B	B	B
A	A	B	B	A	A	A
A	A	B	B	B	B	B

FIGURE 7.17. Equal Time-Sharing Plan: 2-2-3 Rotation

Mon.	Tues.	Wed.	Thurs.	Fri.	Sat.	Sun.
B	B	B	B	B	B	B
A	A	A	A	A	A	A
B	B	B	B	B	B	B
A	A	A	A	A	A	A

FIGURE 7.18. Equal Time-Sharing Plan: One Week On, One Week Off

If the parents can work out an arrangement to transfer the weekly bag without the child, this system may work well. It is important to recognize that children may claim they want this type of arrangement but the reason may be based on a desire to be "fair" rather than on their own needs. The following example of a one-week rotation has a transfer on Monday morning at school. Figure 7.18 gives a visual representation of this plan.

LONG-DISTANCE PLANS

Long-distance living arrangements bring on new dilemmas. Once again, no magic formula or easy answers exist for arranging a long-distance plan. As with other living arrangements, the possibilities are endless. Parents must consider the unique demands of the family, the children's emotional, psychological, and developmental needs, as well as the distance the child will have to travel between homes. As children mature, long-distance planning must encompass the child's new focus on friends and school-related activities.

Moving very young children between distant homes is generally not recommended. Parents should do all the commuting when their children are under the age of three. The out-of-town parent can make arrangements to reunite with the child at the child's residence. Depending upon the child's age and the type of relationship between parent and child, the out-of-town parent may need to arrange for hotel accommodations nearby and visit the child at his or her home if possible. Older children may be able to room with the parent in the hotel or arrangements can be made to vacation out of the area. Regardless of the child's age, parents may decide that the out-of-town parent will do all the commuting between homes. Depending on their age, children may travel to see their parents for long weekends and extended holiday periods.

Travel arrangements should be child friendly and as stress free as possible when children travel to the distant parent's residence. If children are traveling by air, nonstop flights should be planned, and the airline should be asked to make suitable adjustments for the child. Parents can create a more comfortable environment on the plane by packing the child's favorite pillow, blanket, and stuffed animal. Also, coloring books, paper, crayons, markers, small activity books, as well as spill-proof drinks, snacks, wet wipes, and a change of clothes can be packed in children's backpacks to accompany them on the plane. Travel by bus may not provide a safe and secure environment for a child given the frequent stops, length of travel, and possibility of accidents. Children should not be required to travel on holidays for their parents' convenience or to reduce the amount of travel expenses. Long-distance relationships between parent and child may require some adjustments based on specific age groups.

Birth to two years: In order to maintain a close bond between the out-of-town parent and very young child, weekend visitation once per month at the out-of-town parent's residence is recommended when travel is limited to three or four hours. One additional weekend each month in the residential parent's community can be planned to maximize contact but minimize travel. Under these circumstances, the child can reside with the out-of-town parent at a hotel or a relative's home.

Two to six years: If the distance between parent and child is not too great, a two- to six-year-old child may be able to spend two weekends per month at the out-of-town parent's home. Alternating weekends may offer the best arrangement for maintaining a close relationship between parent and child. During those months that have five weekends, the fifth weekend may be taken by the out-of-town parent in the child's primary community.

Six to thirteen years: Older children can generally make the necessary adjustments to long travel between homes on an alternating weekend basis if the distance is not too far. Once again, during those months that have five weekends, the fifth weekend may be taken by the out-of-town parent in the child's primary community. Long-distance visitation can become complicated once a child is involved in extracurricular activities that require participation on the weekends. In these circumstances, the out-of-town parent may need to travel to the child's community and share the weekend with the child at a hotel or relative's house. The out-of-town parent should assume all the responsibility for the child's transportation and day-to-day needs.

TRANSITIONS BETWEEN HOMES

Transitions between households are potentially a very stressful time for both parents and children. During the transition time, children are required to detach from one parent and reconnect to the other parent in a relatively short period of time. Under the best of circumstances, transitions may also be uncomfortable for the parents. It may be the only time parents come in contact with each other. The parents must focus on assisting their child with the logistics of the physical change and deal with the child's feelings, while also preparing themselves for the adult encounter. The child's transfers can be greatly improved when parents can act civil and respectful at this time.

Parents need to learn and understand the demands placed on children during the transitions between households. Torn between two loving households, children may experience mixed feelings ranging from loneliness and sadness to anticipation and excitement. Normally, transitions require an adjustment period of a few minutes to an hour or longer.

The child may exhibit unusual behavior before or after moving from one home to another. A child may seem anxious, withdrawn, or act out. In most circumstances this is normal behavior. The child is reacting to the change. All children react differently as they depart from one parent and reacquaint themselves with another. It does not necessarily mean that one or the other parent is harming the child during the visit. Many conflicted parents are convinced that their child's transitional behaviors indicate a problem with the coparent or time-sharing arrangement rather than a normal reaction to the change.

The following general guidelines can offer parents the structure needed to reduce anxiety and reassure the child.

1. Prior to Transfers
   - Establish and maintain a routine that includes parent-child interaction such as reading a book or watching a short video.
   - Pack a comfort bag that includes some of the child's favorite possessions such as a blanket or stuffed animal if the child is young or a photo album if the child is older.
   - Pack medication, if needed, with adequate instructions on how it is to be administered.
2. At Transfers
   - Arrive on time to ensure prompt drop-offs and pickups.
   - Establish a "good-bye ritual" such as giving the child two kisses and a hug before transfers.

- Keep transfers brief and do not get into discussions with the coparent.
3. Upon the Child's Return
    - Start and continue a "hello ritual" once the child has unwound from his or her arrival.
    - Allow the child to spend quiet time in his or her room or other area of the home if he or she chooses.
    - Honor the child's preference to talk or not talk about the time spent with the other parent.

If the child is taking longer to adjust or displaying disruptive behaviors to a significant degree, some alternatives may need to be negotiated on a trial basis to alleviate the pressure on the child. For example, a father of an eight-year-old boy remarried a woman with a six-year-old son. Each Sunday when the eight-year-old returned to his father's home, he would intentionally annoy his stepbrother to the point of harassment. To alleviate the disruptive behavior, the father and stepmother implemented a new strategy on Sunday evenings. The mother and six-year-old left the home just before the eight-year-old returned home. The pair returned one hour later. This allowed the eight-year-old and his father to spend one-on-one time with each other and the child to reconnect with his surroundings. Once the stepmother and stepbrother returned home, the two boys generally cooperated. The eight-year-old was distressed because his stepbrother was able to spend time in the home with his father while he spent time with his mother on weekends. Although he enjoyed his time with his mother, he envied his stepbrother for being able to have his father's full attention.

Ideally, the child should return home a few hours before bedtime to allow the child to reconnect to his or her environment and family members. The time of transition may be disruptive to the child's lifestyle. For instance, a child may return home late on Wednesday evenings which delays her bedtime. As a consequence, she falls asleep every Thursday in class. The time of the transition should be changed to meet the child's need for sleep. The transition time on Wednesday evening may need to be moved to 7:00 p.m. instead of 8:00 p.m. To accommodate this change, it may be possible to start the time share one hour earlier on Wednesday afternoons.

In moderate to severe levels of parental conflict, transitions between homes should be minimized if parents engage in open warfare in front of their children. Openly hostile parents require specific guidelines regarding transfers of the children. To shield the children from the potential conflict, the procedures need to keep parents disengaged from each other. For example, parents may be prohibited from communicating with each other at transfers. The transitions may include one parent remaining in the residence while looking out a window to ensure the children's safe entrance into the home. The delivering parent either pulls up to the curb or in the driveway and remains in the car while the children depart. The parents should also be instructed not to honk the horn more than once, if necessary. They may also need to be told not to screech the car wheels as they speed away from the children's home.

Other parents may engage in "terror huddles" during the transition process or sabotage the exchange by delaying the good-bye or by making comments that upset the child. Terror huddles involve the parent holding onto the child in such a way as to communicate fear while waiting for the other parent to tear them away. The parent may make comments to the child which convey that the other parent is dangerous in some way. Similarly, parents may hide the child behind them to imply that the other parent is to be feared. While the child is being forced to leave the parent, this parent may make comments such as, "You can call me when your mother is mean to you." In these circumstances as well as others that provoke parental hostility, no parent-to-parent transfers should occur. If this is not practical, then neutral exchange sites should be used, such as the day care center, school, supervised exchange center, office of the parent coordinator, or public locations such as a fast-food parking lot.

In situations in which a school facility is used as a transition site, the receiving parent can pick the child up from school and return the child to school the following day or after the weekend. The use of the school as a neutral site may require an additional overnight stay with one parent. The strain of adding an additional overnight must be balanced against the strain of the child observing parental warfare. Although the time may be extended beyond what may be recommended for a particular age of child, the absence of feuding parents far out weighs any consequence of the extension.

Besides the transitional behaviors just noted, other circumstances may indicate the need for a neutral exchange. For instance, the child may exhibit the following:

- Problematic transfer behaviors
- Separation anxiety (not necessarily separation anxiety disorder)
- Difficulty leaving one or both parents
- Visitation refusal

Parents may also demonstrate behaviors that may negatively impact the child's ability to transfer between homes. For example, parents may

- disrespect the transfer time by arriving too early or too late;
- delay or create painful good-byes;

- carry a "walking" child into the arms of other parent;
- make alienating comments and/or engage in verbal abuse;
- use negative body language; and/or
- audio- or videotape transfers.

Violence or threats of violence during transitions may require very specific safety measures. Under these circumstances, school pickup or supervised exchanges may be necessary to ensure the child's and parent's physical and emotional safety and prevent parental conflict. If necessary, arrangements can be made for the transition to take place in the parent coordinator's office. The parent with custody can drop off the child at the office ten minutes before the exchange. The receiving parent can arrive at the coordinator's office ten minutes after the time of the exchange. This creates a stress-free environment and offers the parents a method to avoid contact. Obviously, if this method is used, the parent coordinator must be able to orchestrate the supervised exchange. This type of exchange is often used by professionals working at traditional supervised exchange facilities.

Another means of supervising the exchange at the coordinator's office is to request that a friend or relative bring the child to the office twenty minutes before the end of the parents' joint session. Ten minutes before the end of the session, the noncustodial parent can leave the building. Then the child can enter the meeting room to reunite with the receiving parent. After ten minutes, the parent and child may leave the building. In the meantime, the friend or relative can leave the area. This method also allows the parent coordinator to observe the interaction between parent and child.

As noted, creating neutral transitions may require the time-sharing arrangement to be modified in one form or another. Parents may object to the extension of time for developmental, personal, or financial reasons. Depending on the reason, alternatives may be explored. If an objection arises due to developmental reasons, an extra telephone contact between the absent parent and the child can be negotiated. Personal issues can be addressed by exploring the parent's motivation. Perhaps the parent is coming from a position of self-interest rather than a child focus. The parent believes he or she will be lonely and needs the child for companionship. The disadvantages of relying on the child for emotional and social needs can be discussed. The parent can be encouraged to fill the time without the child in a more constructive way such as attending a class or going out to the movies with a friend.

Financial motivation is more difficult to assess. In some areas, the number of overnights or percentage of time the child spends with each parent determines child support payments. Although most parents will not openly admit they do not want to pay any additional child support, the parent may be resisting a modification in the living arrangement to avoid increased support payments. Likewise, a parent may resist a change because the child support payments may decrease. The coordinator can tell a story about a similar situation in which one parent refused to accommodate the child's needs because it would result in a reduction in child support. The PC can highlight the negative consequences the child continued to experience because of the parent's selfishness and follow up by referring to the parents in the room as parents who would never put themselves before their child.

SUPERVISED AND THERAPEUTIC VISITATION

Supervised visitation is a service provided to parents and their children in which a third-party is present during the visit and under circumstances in which there is concern about the care the child will receive while in the presence of the parent. Supervised visitation is most often used in circumstances of (1) alleged or confirmed cases of physical abuse and sexual abuse, (2) alleged or confirmed substance abuse, (3) ineffectual, deficient, neglectful, and emotionally abusive parenting skills, (4) reunification of child with absent parent, and (5) threat of abduction.

Depending upon the nature and severity of the case, supervised visitation can be facilitated by a trained professional or, at times, by a family member or friend. Many supervised visitation services are offered across the nation. These facilities provide trained individuals who oversee the visitation and may offer feedback to the parent after each session. Some services may also provide written reports upon request and with proper releases. Some agencies provide only on-site supervision while others provide off-site supervision and will spend time with the parent and child in the community.

At times, the courts enlist the assistance of family members or friends for supervised visitation when the situation requires monitoring the interaction of the parent and child. Depending on the court's structure and personnel, the court may request feedback regarding the parent-child relationship. More often than not, the attorney of the supervised parent will advocate to move the visitation from supervised to unsupervised as soon as possible.

Whether supervised visitation is under the direction of a professional or family member, there should be a clear understanding of the goal(s) of the visitation with detailed objectives that improve the parent-child relationship. With such objectives in place, the courts can determine when supervised visitation can be eliminated. Such a plan also reassures the custodial

parent that provisions are set to determine the safety of the child when supervised visitation is no longer in place. From there, a transitional visitation
arrangement can be developed moving from a very structured environment
to a more natural setting conducive to the enhancement of parent-child relationships. For example, the supervised visitation can be changed to require
the parent and child to meet at the supervised site at the beginning and end
of the visitation schedule while spending time only in public places such as
malls, movie theaters, and child-oriented restaurants. At the end of the session, the professional working with the family can individually interview
both the parent and the child to evaluate the unsupervised visitation.

Parent coordinators working with families that are involved in supervised visitation can develop a detailed plan that outlines the movement from
supervised to unsupervised visitation. In addition, the coordinator can monitor the visitation to ensure that all parties are complying with the order and
guidelines. The following is a sample plan that was developed for a parent
abusing alcohol. The PC overseing this plan would request random alcohol
screes prior to moving to the next phase. The custodial parent would provide the child's transportation through phase three of the unsupervised plan.

From Supervised to Unsupervised Visitation

Parental Goals

1. The supervised parent will consistently arrive to the supervised visitation substance free.
2. The supervised parent will demonstrate the ability to build rapport with
   the child by (a) relating to the child at his or her developmental level,
   (b) validating the child's feelings, (c) demonstrating empathy for the
   child, and (d) exhibiting the absence of controlling and manipulative
   behaviors.
3. The supervised parent will appropriately set limits with the child and
   follow through on consequences if necessary.
4. In the event that the child inquires about the parent's behavior or spo-
   radic contact, the supervised parent will explain the reason for supervision to the child and take responsibility for his or her actions.
5. The supervised parent will respect any other guidelines created by the
   parent coordinator.
6. The supervised parent will continue in the outpatient treatment program and consult with his or her sponsor at least once per week.
7. The supervised parent will pass all random screens and requested by
   the PC or supervisor.

Supervised Visitation Plan

Phase One—Supervised

The custodial parent provides transportation to and from all supervised visits.

1. Two-hour visits once per week at the family center under the supervision of a trained professional for four consecutive weeks.

If goals are not met, continue previous phase.

Phase Two—Supervised

1. Four-hour visits once per week at the family center under the supervision of a trained professional for three consecutive weeks.

Phase Three—Supervised

1. Four-hour visits once per week at a public location such as a mall, playground, entertainment facility, or movie theater with supervisor for three consecutive weeks.
2. After three weeks, supervised parent and child meet with PC to discuss their visits.

Unsupervised Visitation Plan

Custodial parent provides transportation to noncustodial parent's home. If noncustodial parent is sober, the child will stay with this parent. If not, the child returns home with the custodial parent.

Phase One—Unsupervised

1. Three-hour visits once per week without a supervisor at a public location such as a mall, playground, or entertainment facility.
2. Child will call custodial parent after two hours of visitation.
3. After three weeks, previously supervised parent and child meet with PC to discuss their visits.

Phase Two—Unsupervised

1. Four-hour evening visits once per week at a public location such as a mall, playground, or entertainment facility.
2. Child calls custodial parent after two hours of visitation.

3. Overnight after four-hour evening visitation with a relative present until 10:00 a.m. the following morning.
4. After three weeks, previously supervised parent and child meet with PC to discuss their visits.

Phase Three—Unsupervised

1. Once per week, all-day visitation with overnight until 11:00 a.m. the following morning for three consecutive weeks.
2. Child will call custodial parent at 2:00 p.m.
3. Child contacts custodial parent for pickup if noncustodial parent breaks guidelines.
4. After three weeks, previously supervised parent and child meet with PC to discuss their visits.

If all phases are met, and after the PC has determined that the child is safe while under the care of the previously supervised parent, unsupervised visitation may continue. Periodic random screens may be required by the monitoring PC. A new time-sharing plan may need to be developed to accommodate the family's circumstances.

In situations in which the parent-child relationship has so extremely deteriorated or been too severely marred that a professional supervisor is not equipped to repair the relationship, therapeutic visitation would be the service of choice. It may be used in the circumstances noted previously as well as when allegations of poor management skills, lack of parental empathy, situations of delayed paternity, or visitation refusal. In cases of parental alienation, a therapist or PC trained in the dynamics of parental alienation should facilitate the visitation. In this situation, the focus of the visitation would be to reunify the parent and the child and undo the damage the custodial parent has inflicted upon the child and parent.

Therapeutic visitation is a type of supervised visitation facilitated by a psychotherapist with knowledge and experience in children's issues of divorce, developmental stages, and parent-child relationship building. Parent and child meet in the therapist's office while the therapist observes and offers feedback either during or after the session. The therapist teaches and models effective parenting practices. These behaviors are practiced by the parent under the guidance of the therapist. The overall emphasis of both therapeutic and standard supervised visitation is to provide a physically and emotionally safe environment for the child, while allowing parent-child access until the visits can be unsupervised and the time-sharing plan implemented.

Parental Access

Parents must consider numerous factors when developing a child-friendly schedule, including their child's development, age, and temperament, the degree of parental conflict, and their parenting styles. The correlation between these factors as well as others, including attachment theory and their influence on living arrangements, have been the subject of research for quite some time. In addition, researchers have concentrated their efforts on exploring issues germane to the time-sharing arrangements for the very young child. Time-sharing schedules, such as phased plans, should be tailored to the family's unique circumstance. In addition, plans can be created that take into consideration special needs, long-distance parenting, and supervised visitation. Regardless of the time-sharing plan, parents must learn how to minimize stress for their children when transitioning between homes, or limit the number of parent-to-parent transfers.

Throughout the first section of this text, the PC has been exposed to the fundamentals of setting up a parent coordination program based upon the CPI model. In addition, an inside view of the legal system along with custody and time-sharing arrangements offers the PC the basic knowledge he or she may need in order to implement a program. The final preparation covered in Chapter 8 reviews the different types of sessions and timing of each session as recommended in the CPI model. Chapters 9 through 11 focus on creative techniques and strategies to increase the likelihood of a positive outcome for families. These techniques also fortify and support the PC's efforts by providing a variety of options for dealing with difficult parents.

Chapter 8

The Intervention Phase

A thorough understanding of the different types of sessions utilized in the CPI model will greatly enhance the success of the process of parent coordination. The precise timing of each of these sessions will also influence the outcome.

INITIAL INTERVIEW

Initial interviews, also known as intake appointments, are held with each parent individually prior to the first joint session. These sessions are generally fifty minutes in length. The initial interview allows the parent coordinator to get an understanding of a variety of issues. Specifically, the initial interview allows the PC to clarify information on the intake paperwork, collect additional information, and explain how parent coordination works. This session also offers each parent the opportunity to share information about the coparent and to ask questions. Parents are generally not allowed to talk about old marital issues after this initial session. At the completion of each parent's intake appointment joint sessions should be scheduled.

In the intake appointment, a parent coordinator may be inundated with stories of family violence against one or both parents and/or claims of physical, emotional, or sexual abuse of the child. It is always prudent to take these allegations seriously and err on the side of safety. As the parent coordinator reviews the domestic violence assessment completed by each parent, a safety plan must be incorporated prior to beginning any joint sessions.

With regard to child abuse and neglect claims, the PC must be careful not to ignore warning signs or to assume that everything the parents report is accurate. As mandated reporters, PCs are expected to make a report as soon as possible. Ultimately, the PC may have to inform both parents that the PC must make a report to protective services. This can be done in a manner that educates parents to the mandated requirements without indicating that the PC believes the allegations are true or false. Parents must be reminded that the PC is not responsible to determine if the child was abused; the PC's responsibility is to collect data to assist the family and/or make a mandated report if needed.

It is important to recognize that high-conflict parents are at risk if they make their own report of suspected abuse. A parent-initiated report may appear to be vindictive rather than concerned. To reduce the likelihood that a legitimate case for abuse will be minimized based on the adversarial nature of the parents' relationship, parents can be advised to bring their child to the pediatrician, the parent coordinator, the child's therapist, or a hospital so that the professional can make the report. Keeping in mind that most of these parents are determined to prove the other parent is inadequate, the PC should also take claims of neglect seriously. Meeting with the child and speaking with a neighbor or the child's teacher can assist the PC to determine if a report should be made.

At the onset of the interview, the PC should offer each parent a general overview of the intake agenda. For example, the PC might say, "This session is an opportunity for you to ask questions regarding the program and an opportunity for me to ask you some additional questions. Would you like to ask questions, or would you prefer that I begin?" By knowing what to expect, the parent may be more at ease and relaxed. The following topics are usually discussed during the intake appointment.

1. Explain the difference between psychotherapy and parent coordination:
   - The process is not confidential.
   - The PC may be authoritative rather than empathic.
   - The focus is on the child's well-being rather than the individual needs of parents.
   - The focus is on parental interaction rather than individual personal issues or past relationship issues.
   - Relevant concerns are determined by the parent coordinator

Next, gather information regarding the following areas:

2. Perceptions of the marriage/divorce, including
   - A brief background focusing on past marital/partnership issues
   - The parent's perception of the reasons for the divorce/separation
   - Information to determine if the parent accepts any responsibility for the end of the marriage/relationship
   - A brief time line noting significant events in the couple's relationship

3. Risk factors
   • Determine risk factors that may influence the parent coordination process such as family violence, perceived harassment, etc.
4. Perception of how the child is coping
   • By questioning how each parent perceives their child's situation, the parent coordinator may gain an understanding about the extent to which each parent understands children's issues in divorce as well as their ability to separate their own needs from the needs of their children. Parents will either view their children as separate individuals with needs all their own, as an extension of themselves, or as a function of their adversarial needs. They will either offer an accurate report of their child's situation and behaviors or distort what they observe.
5. Potential goals of the program
6. Scheduling needs
   • Determine the parent's scheduling needs and limitations.
   • Emphasize the need to be flexible when scheduling joint sessions.
   • Remind parent of mandatory attendance if court ordered.
7. Provide a copy of *Cooperative Parenting and Divorce: A Parent Guide to Effective Co-Parenting* (optional).

Some parents may not be able to express everything that they believe is important during the fifty-minute intake session. Parents can be asked if they would like an additional session to discuss their individual issues. The PC should inform parents that there will be an additional charge for the extra session. At times, when limited to one intake session, the PC may need to gently shorten the parents' responses in order to keep them brief.

TYPES OF SESSIONS

Knowing how to structure the process of parent coordination is one of several critical components influencing a successful outcome. The number of sessions, the timing and pacing of these sessions, and who will attend each session should be based on the interactional nature of the system and the parent coordinator's clinical judgment.

Individual versus Joint Sessions

A systems approach primarily involves a conceptual framework. The CPI model of parent coordination is built on this theoretical framework. Since the primary concern is the interaction taking place between the parents and how this interaction affects the children, we highly recommend joint sessions unless there may be a threat of physical or emotional harm to one or both parents. Joint sessions offer the most accurate understanding of the family circumstances. Joint sessions may be contraindicated (1) when there is serious physical risk to either parent or the parent coordinator or (2) if the coordinator is unable to effectively manage the session or either parent's verbal aggression. Although parents may say that there is an emotional risk, this may be a maneuver to avoid cooperating with the coparent or to enlist the coordinator's support. The PC must determine if this is indeed the situation or if the parent is attempting to manipulate the parent coordinator. The anticipated danger associated with joint sessions tends to dissipate when it no longer serves the purpose of manipulation. The parent coordinator must assess the risk rather than let the parents or their attorneys determine the risk.

The PC may assume that joint sessions cannot occur if a protective order is in place. However, it is not unusual for the same judge that issued a protective order to also require the parents to meet in joint sessions. If this occurs it is best to send a memo asking for clarification. Just as visitation may be an exception to a protective order, parent coordination may be similarly designated. For example, a supplemental order may state, "Neither parent may come within 100 yards of the other with the exception of joint sessions under the direction of the parent coordinator."

It is not unusual for one or both parents to exhibit poor impulse control and anger management to the degree that it hampers the parent coordinator's maneuverability. When faced with significant conflict that cannot be contained by the management techniques employed in this text, the PC should meet separately until the parents are able to defuse their anger long enough to allow them to minimally collaborate on their child's behalf. Chapter 10 offers additional information on anger-management techniques. The PC must keep in close contact with the individual therapists to determine when joint sessions can be resumed. Individual sessions with the PC should be kept to a minimum to avoid discussions about the coparent. As soon as possible, joint sessions should recommence.

Initially, anger and animosity between some parents is so great that contact between them must be avoided. Staying in contact with each other can be so damaging that the PC may advise the parents to make a clean break from each other as a temporary measure. For these parents, other measures may include neutral exchange sites at natural times of the day, such as the end of the school day, in order to avoid contact between parents. A clean break means that parents do not see each other for a specified period of time and/or they are assigned not to communicate with each other. When parents must communicate information that involves the children, they are instructed to leave a nonemotional message on the person's answering machine when they know the other parent will not be at home. If, under these circumstances, parents are still unable to communicate appropriately, they are advised temporarily to call or fax the information to the parent coordinator to exchange between the parents.

A clean break may also mean temporarily removing all evidence of the person so as not to be reminded of him or her. However, the parent should never remove pictures of the coparent from the child's room. A temporary clean break can be damaging to the child if it is continued beyond a couple of months. But as a temporary measure, enabling a parent to avoid contact, to begin to disengage, and to decrease the level and degree of conflict between the parents can be valuable. In the best interest of the child, however, this must be temporary.

Although the CPI model discourages individual sessions after the first appointment, at times the parent coordinator may meet with each parent individually as part of a joint session. This type of meeting is referred to as a caucus. Traditionally, information gathered in a caucus during the course of standard mediation is considered confidential. In other words, the information shared by one parent in the absence of the other parent is not divulged to the second parent when the PC has both parents present. However, since parent coordination is not a confidential process, parents must be reminded of this when they meet separately after their intake appointment.

A caucus is used for various reasons. It is not uncommon for parents to reach an impasse over a child-rearing matter. Caucusing with each parent may assist the PC to gain a more comprehensive understanding of each parent's perspective as it relates to the matter at hand, and as a consequence be able to break through the impasse. In some situations only one parent is stalling the process over a specific issue. The PC should request a caucus with both parents even though only one parent is caught up in extraneous issues. It is necessary to meet with both parents under these circumstances because the process of parent coordination strives to create a neutral setting. Parents may become suspicious if the PC meets with only one parent. They may also feel left out of the process and believe that alliances are being formed between the PC and other parent. In addition, caucusing offers the PC the opportunity to decrease the tension and animosity in the room. Each parent can be helped to regain their composure, identify their inappropriate behavior, and identify their individual goal(s) for the session. The parent coordinator can coach the parents on the skills necessary to engage in constructive communication and conflict resolution.

JOINT SESSIONS

Isaacs, Montalvo, and Abelsohn (1986) maintain that joint sessions with high-conflict parents held prematurely are often counterproductive. They believe that such an encounter between high-conflict parents requires careful preparation and pacing. When these meetings first take place they should be brief, adhere to a predetermined amount of time, and maintain a focus on predetermined topics. During joint sessions, the parent coordinator creates a structured environment with clear guidelines and ground rules by using the "agreement and expectations" form located in the Appendix. The PC pays careful attention to the topics under discussion, selecting one at a time while placing limits on the topics that will and will not be discussed. The parent coordinator must work to avoid those topics that create volatile behaviors on the part of one or both parents until such time that the parents have acquired the skills to negotiate and problem solve in a businesslike manner. In essence, the parent coordinator will support controlled businesslike encounters while skillfully managing hostile eruptions.

As always, the PC must be sure to clarify behavioral expectations and consequences as well as tightly control the negotiation topics and be prepared to act as a referee if verbal fighting ensues. He or she must interrupt the interaction and refocus the parents' attempts to battle it out. If the confrontation escalates, the parent coordinator must step in and maintain order or, when necessary, end the session. The PC must be in control of all sessions at all times. In the beginning, it is better that the PC err on the side of too many limits than not enough.

As parents interact they generally respond to each other in patterned behavior that exacerbates their communication style. These patterns tend to take on a life of their own. As a result, it may be difficult for parents to act logically and rationally. Depending on the pattern of interaction, the PC must break down the behaviors needing to be changed into small, observable skills. Once these initial skills are accomplished, successive skills can be introduced.

Parents may present themselves as avoiders, habitual adversaries, or a combination of the two. If parents avoided conflict during the marriage, they are likely to continue to do so in the postdivorce relationship. The avoidant parent resists direct contact with the coparent. It is not uncommon for these parents to deny the presence of conflict. What they do not understand is that the absence of contact represents conflict. When there is contact, which there will always be, avoiders engage in cyclic fighting. That is, they will argue over unresolved issues with little or no successful resolution or give each other the silent treatment. As a result, they will do everything in their power to avoid the escalating warfare that has led to repeated failures.

Any attempt at direct communication carries the threat of more unsuccessful battles. Consequently, if they communicate at all, these parents will communicate through their children or attorneys. In addition, they will make unilateral decisions about their children's welfare which typically leads to further conflict. It is an important task for the parent coordinator to increase confidence in "avoiders" by identifying any simple success in their communication style and praising their efforts in session. Having coparents present in the sessions together will interrupt their avoidant style.

Unlike avoiders, habitual adversaries seem to relish the intensity and retaliation of their behaviors. They remain emotionally engaged with each other through their frequent disputes and attempt to win each battle at any cost. Their communication is direct and intense. They are intent on beating each other to the punch and inflicting pain before the other parent can attack. Each adversarial action triggers the next unproductive response. Both parents desire to control the other and demonstrate a strong need to dominate. They attempt to meet their own needs by denigrating the other parent. The focus is on proving their innocence and their belief that the other parent is inadequate. Winning dominates their thinking, but it should not dominate the sessions. Besides using other techniques described in this text, the PC may consider exaggerating their competitive aggression by keeping track of the "wins" on a dry board, labeling the score columns "Mom Wins/Dad Loses" and "Dad Wins/Mom Loses." Then, at the end of the session, ask, "How does your competitive nature impact on your child's adjustment?" And, "What will your child learn from watching you compete for power and control?"

Divorced parents also present themselves in a complementary rather than symmetrical fashion. As with many couples, one parent may demonstrate aggressive traits while the other engages in avoiding behaviors. The "aggressor's" desire to control and dominate is balanced by the "avoider's" withdrawal. The withdrawal may lead the aggressor to feel enraged and become even more determined to get a response from the avoider. In this sense, conflict escalates in a pattern of pursuit and retreat. The more the aggressor pursues, the more the avoider withdraws and vice versa. This pattern will serve only to exacerbate their negative beliefs about each other. Once the parent coordinator has a detailed understanding of the unsuccessful interactions, her or she can offer the parents an awareness of the problematic interaction. The interaction between parents should be explained in such a way that they can understand how the mother's response influences the father's response and vice versa. The value of reviewing their interactions on videotape together cannot be underestimated. The responsibility for change is placed upon both parents. For instance, one parent can be told to "turn down" behaviors while the other is told to "turn up" behaviors. If the aggressive parent was to feel heard, he or she might not be so quick to attack. Conversely, if the avoidant parent did not feel threatened, he or she might be willing to listen and consider the other parent's point of view. Ideally, the PC can balance the interaction by developing assertiveness without aggression in both parents.

Professionals working in the field of divorce have documented the patterns and interactions that typically characterize divorced parents. Therapists working as parent coordinators are highly encouraged to review contributions to the field by Ahrons (1979b, 1990, 1994), Garrity and Baris (1994, 2002; Baris et al., 2001), and Johnston (1992, 1997; Johnston and Campbell, 1988; Johnston, Campbell, and Tall, 1985; Johnston, Kline, Tschann, 1991; Johnston and Roseby, 1997). For additional information on techniques used in joint sessions see Chapters 10 through 13.

The First Joint Session

The first joint session must be highly structured. It is generally different from all the other joint sessions. It offers the parents the opportunity to ask any additional questions they may have regarding the process of parent coordination and how it is different from psychotherapy. The PC must assess:

1. safety issues,
2. the degree of hostility and aggression between the coparents, and
3. the extent this animosity will impair the coordinator's ability to orchestrate an effective session.

These observations coupled with the intake and prerelationship assessment offer the parent coordinator a starting point with the family.

After reviewing the expectations and signing the necessary releases, the parents should create mutual goals with the assistance of the parent coordinator. This activity requires parents to address the behaviors they wish to change. Furthermore, it gives the PC an outline for the direction the sessions will need to go while keeping the PC accountable for staying on task.

The PC needs to help parents understand that their goals are not necessarily "agreements"; they are simply goals about what they will be discussing over time. When hostile parents attempt to create mutual goals, their suggestions are often inappropriate. The PC should help them to word their goals in a manner that will encourage the coparent to agree upon the "mutual" goal. See Chapter 11 for additional information on creating mutual goals and reframing inappropriate goals.

As noted, when the parents' mutual goals are actually agreements, the PC can make this distinction. For example, during the first joint session, the father complained about the mother letting the children read legal documents. While developing goals, the father requests: "We will shield our children from all aspects of the legal process." If the mother agrees, then it does not need to be added to the mutual goals. It is an agreement and is added to the agreement sheet. When the final parenting plan is written, parents are less likely to change their mind about an agreement since they have already committed to the agreement.

Joint Session Procedures (Eighty-Minute Sessions)

After the first joint session, the CPI model uses a predictable and structured agenda for each session. However, the higher the conflict between parents the more important it is to adhere to tight limits and additional structure.

I. Business (approximately the first five minutes)
   A. Financial: Accept payment and notify the parent of any outstanding fees. Provide a statement at the end of each month. Discourage parents from using this time to discuss their financial issues with each other or to discuss changes to their schedules or other parenting matters.
   B. Schedule: Schedule several future appointments to reduce time spent coordinating schedules. Encourage parents to discuss their child's schedules (e.g., soccer game) in the waiting room before and after each session. Make this request only when the parents are able and willing to conduct themselves in a businesslike fashion. If the parents are not in a Cooperative Parenting and Divorce Group then section II is applicable.
II. Education (approximately fifteen to twenty minutes)
   A. Introduce new material: Focus on relevant concepts until parents grasp the information before moving ahead. Ask parents what they learned from each chapter.
   B. Homework: If parents experience difficultly comprehending concepts, try one or more of the following:
      1. Assign additional homework.
      2. Request that they seek assistance with the specific skill or concept from their individual therapist.
      3. As a last resort, arrange an individual coaching session with the parent.

III. Review agreements (approximately five minutes) (The CPI model uses an agreement sheet to keep track of all the parent agreements.)

    A. Agreements: Quickly review each of the previous agreements to determine if the parents are keeping their commitments. This process highlights loopholes that need to be clarified and demonstrates parental commitment. Mark in the margin which agreements have been kept or met. When parents are asked to report on how a plan or agreement worked, they tend to derail the session by discussing new complaints and other issues not related to the original request. When this occurs, the PC can redirect the parent to write a phrase down in the parent guide to help remember the issues he or she wants to address.

IV. Mediate (majority of the eighty minutes)

    A. Encourage each parent to identify in one brief sentence two parenting concerns to discuss in session. Record these concerns before beginning the mediation process. Any time-pressured issues should be addressed first. It is the parent coordinator's responsibility to determine the order in which the concerns will be discussed. Parents generally respond to this request in several ways. Parents may (1) attempt to address several issues at a time, (2) not be willing or able to identify a parenting concern, (3) be too anxious and unable to state a concern, or (d) recite their concern in very general terms. The PC can request that each parent prioritize their concerns and choose only one to address at a time. If they cannot think of an issue the PC can review their assessment form or mutual goals. When one issue is made up of several issues, the parent can be coached to narrow it down to one specific issue. On the other hand, the PC may want to actually enlarge the issue. For example, if a parent states, "I'd like to talk about how uncooperative he has been!", this is too general. Coach the parent to be specific: "I'd like to discuss what happened this past weekend when I made a reasonable request." Conversely, if a parent focuses too narrowly, e.g., "I'd like to discuss how rude her husband was at our daughter's baseball game!", coach this parent to uncover the larger issue. "I'd like to discuss reducing tension for our daughter whenever we are together at her activities."

    B. Display concerns on a flip chart or a dry board (optional): Whenever possible, the PC should help parents to break their concern into a behavioral request. For additional techniques, see Chapter 9.

    C. Record all issues and concerns in case notes.

D. Record agreements and temporary plans
- The PC should record all agreements, including temporary agreements, as they are made.
- At the end of the session both parents should sign the back of the agreement sheet. The PC is advised to make copies of each agreement sheet for the parents to take with them. This will reduce confusion and unnecessary calls to the PC later in the week.
- Agreements can be typed onto a disk each week. In this way the parenting plan will be much easier for the PC to develop.

E. Model a business meeting: The PC can structure each session similar to a business meeting as a way to model such an interaction for the conflicted parents. Of course, the parent coordinator should also model other elements of a business meeting such as effective communication skills, limiting the conversations, and focusing on the problem rather than the person. As a result, the parents will witness business skills in action. They will be applying the beginning steps to negotiation long before the skills are introduced. The parents will also experience how staying focused on one issue at a time will increase the likelihood of resolution.

EXTENDED FAMILY SESSIONS AND SIGNIFICANT OTHERS

Both parental cooperation and warfare can be endorsed by the extended family and other significant individuals involved with the family. Alliances can be formed across generations and among friends and significant others that can support the family in a healthy adjustment to a two-household structure. On the other hand, these same coalitions can encourage parental avoidance, legitimize illusions, and further distort and fuel the situation. With this outcome in mind, children run the risk of being estranged from a significant part of their family network. When this occurs, it is unlikely that the child will benefit from the richness of his or her heritage and time-honored traditions as well as the resources of emotional and physical support gained from close and meaningful relationships with extended family members. Therefore, every effort should be made to facilitate the contact between the child and his or her extended family.

Likewise, it is equally important to interrupt the extended family's attempts to create loyalty binds for the children. Part of the focus of the program should be on distinguishing the boundaries between generations, while at the same time outlining the support network of the family system.

First, parents should be required to educate their own parents and signifi-cant others on the adverse effects of divorce on children. They should be in-structed to avoid pulling these individuals into their warfare. If parents are unable or unwilling to persuade the extended family to assume a supportive relationship with their children, then intake sessions must be scheduled with family members. It becomes the role of the PC to meet with the ex-tended family members and align with their delicate position. At the same time the coordinator must explain the psychological danger of negative comments about either parent. After meeting with extended family mem-bers, the parent coordinator can determine if they need to be involved in joint sessions with the coparents.

The PC must determine how and when significant others in the life of the parents will be introduced to the parent coordination process. The degree of their involvement in the program can be determined by their level of in-volvement in the parent's life, their contact with the children, and the extent that their involvement in the system invites conflict. Each adult must be given the message that they need to work together toward promoting a posi-tive relationship between parents, between children and parents, between children and both sides of their extended family, as well as between children and other significant adults in their lives. Ultimately, each subsystem sepa-rately and together must promote an environment sensitive to the child's needs.

As a rule of thumb, significant others should not be brought into joint sessions until the parental subsystem has stabilized. Boundaries must be clarified among the adults. Each adult's role and responsibilities to the chil-dren must be determined. Relationships between children and stepparents or significant others are important, but they should not come at the expense of the biological parents. The biological parents should always be viewed as the primary parenting team.

THE STEPPARENT FACTOR

High-conflict families often include stepparents who may also bring their own children to the family unit. The struggles within a stepfamily in-crease when children are identified as "mine, yours, and ours." The child of divorce may go from being an only child into a stepfamily where they be-

---

The remainder of this chapter is adapted from Susan Boyan (2002), Stepparents and High-Conflict Divorce: Asset or Liability?, The Peaceful Co-Parent.

come instantly the oldest, the youngest, or the middle child, resulting in a tremendous shift in family role and position. In addition, the child living in a stepfamily may be placed into more loyalty binds, particularly if the mother and stepmother are competing for the child's affection. Likewise, if the father and stepfather both compete to take their son hunting for the first time, problems will naturally escalate.

Since fairy tales such as Snow White and the evil stepmother, the term *stepparent* has received a lot of negative press. Many parents find the term offensive. The fact remains, however, that a marriage proposal from a divorced parent means someone will soon become a stepparent. If the divorced parent already has a conflicted relationship with his or her former spouse, the stepparent may significantly impact upon the primary parental team.

There are as many different types of stepparents as there are people, yet they seem to fit within one of three types. Most stepparents appear to be either antagonistic to the binuclear family or a wonderful asset to the family. To parallel another fairy tale, the types of stepparents are like Goldilocks' response to the three different bowls of porridge. One bowl of porridge was way too hot, one was way too cold, and one was just right.

1. The overinvolved stepparent (way too hot)
2. The underinvolved stepparent (way too cold)
3. The complementary stepparent (just right)

The overinvolved stepparent tends to be antagonistic toward his or her spouse's coparent, while the complementary stepparent supports the coparent relationship. The underinvolved stepparent is fairly nonexistent.

The Overinvolved Stepparent

Overinvolved stepparents overstep their natural role by trying to function as a primary parent, which creates unnecessary problems for everyone. As noted in Figure 8.1 this type of stepparent tries to stand within the inner circle with the child and biological parent. They may believe that they are functioning from a position of love and involvement rather than overinvolvement. At times, overinvolved stepparents may attempt to bypass their spouse and speak directly to the coparent about parenting matters. They may insist on making primary parenting decisions or refuse to allow their spouse to contact the coparent without their direct involvement. The overinvolved stepparent is like an actor who attempts to steal the show, when the

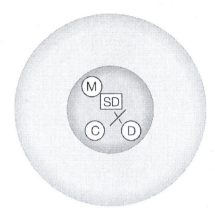

FIGURE 8.1. The Overinvolved Stepparent (One Step Ahead)

stepparent is actually employed as the parental understudy. The over-involved stepparent tends to have low self-esteem. He or she often falls into one of the following types:

1. Lacks confidence in spouse's ability to deal with the coparent
2. The spouse may play the victim and solicit the stepparent's involvement
3. Exhibits a need to micromanage all aspects of his or her new family
4. Feels threatened by or jealous of spouse's relationship with the coparent

The overinvolved stepparent attempts to handle the coparenting relationship directly rather than from behind the scenes. When they become overinvolved, they are then too involved in the parental team, which then results in becoming a major player in the parental conflict. Overinvolved stepparents may even find the conflict appealing in terms of joining with their spouse in a common cause. They are likely to believe all the horrible stories they hear about the coparent. As a result, they may spend sleepless nights thinking of ways to confront or change the coparent.

Overinvolved stepparents tend to cross parental boundaries without any apparent awareness that they have done so. For example, this type of stepparent may insist on being at each transfer to protect their spouse or simply out of principle. He or she actively joins in litigation with a real passion. Some may not allow their spouse to ever be alone with the other parent. The stepparent may even intercept a phone call and refuse to let the children speak to their parent until they have spoken to the stepparent first.

These stepparents may encourage or even insist that their stepchild call them "mommy" or "daddy." They may introduce themselves as the "parent" rather than "stepparent," or they may omit the coparent's name when registering the children for school. Stay-at-home stepmothers are at greatest risk for functioning as the primary parent since they are often responsible for the child. This increases tenfold if the overinvolved stepmother and her spouse have primary custody. An overinvolved stepfather may come into the new marriage in the role of "white knight" to help the woman deal with a miserable man. Nonetheless, male or female, the overinvolved stepparent usually becomes a liability to an already conflicted situation.

Involving the Overinvolved Stepparent

Families with an overinvolved stepparent (or two) generally need a parent coordinator. Therefore, it is necessary to recognize how an overinvolved stepparent may affect the process of parent coordination. One of the first indications that a stepparent may become a liability is usually an overreaction to being left out of the first joint session. The stepparent may even threaten the process by demanding to be present for his or spouse. When the stepparent is fueling the conflict, it is essential that only the biological parents are involved in the joint sessions for the first four or five appointments. This makes an important and difficult statement to any intrusive stepparent or grandparent. Only when the "primary team" has made some basic improvements can the overinvolved stepparent be invited to join the process.

The PC must recognize that leaving overinvolved stepparents out of the joint sessions may antagonize them even more because they tend to become threatened by having their spouse meet without them. The stepparent may also become anxious about not being able to control the outcome. On the other hand, the biological parent may distort session information to his or her spouse. Until the stepparents are included in the process, it is wise for the PC to videotape the sessions in anticipation of the likely distortions.

Initially, it is wise to meet alone with overinvolved stepparents a few times so that they can express their point of view and reduce their anxiety. It is also wise to coach him or her as to the constructive "position" of staying one step behind the biological parents. They do not fully understand the consequences their actions may have on each family member. For example, stepparents should not take the lead regarding school or medical appointments. Nor should they take an active role in discipline when the natural parents are available during the first few years. Many stepparents as well as biological parents may need to understand the importance of not requiring or even encouraging the stepchild to call the stepparent "mom" or "dad."

The PC may need to refer the stepparent for stepfamily treatment or psychoeducation with another professional.

In addition, the overinvolved stepparent requires gentle but clear directives from the PC regarding staying out of the primary parenting decisions and allowing the spouse to do the primary communication between homes. The only exception is if the spouse is out of town. The PC should be very concrete with directives such as "Do not send any letters or e-mail to the other parent. Do not come out of the house during transfers." Furthermore, the stepparent will also need to learn how to sit quietly in a joint session and speak only when asked for input. For many stepparents this is a difficult task because they are not used to respecting boundaries.

The PC must use empathy with this stepparent by keeping in mind that inappropriate behaviors are usually based in fear or anxiety. The PC should try to align with this stepparent prior to inclusion in the joint sessions. This will allow the PC to give the stepparent feedback that may be difficult to hear. Other characteristics of an overinvolved stepparent may include the following: poor boundaries/intrusive, competitive, tendency to view situations in black/white, easily threatened, controlling, low self-esteem, and possessive tendencies.

The Underinvolved Stepparent

The underinvolved stepparent is both underinvolved in the parenting role and coparenting relationship and often underattached to the stepchild. As noted in Figure 8.2, this stepfather stays several steps outside the child's family. On the surface such a stepparent may appear to be highly respectful

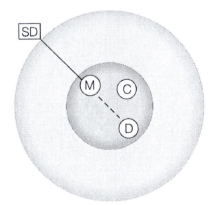

FIGURE 8.2. The Underinvolved Stepparent (Several Steps Behind)

of all the members of both households. However, he or she is generally invisible or detached from all relationships except for the relationship with the spouse. This type of stepparent is usually fairly passive and avoids conflict even at the expense of relationships. Some of these stepparents stay in the background (several steps behind) because they grew up as children with their own overinvolved stepparent. The underinvolved stepparent may stay in the shadows for fear of creating marital conflict. The young child living primarily with an underinvolved stepparent will experience an additional loss. On the other hand, adolescents who find themselves with an underinvolved stepparent may not experience such loss since their psychological goal is to detach from both families.

Involving the Underinvolved Stepparent

This stepparent will avoid being a part of joint sessions. He or she may even resist coming in for an intake appointment. More often than not, they will minimize their role or contribution in the two-home family. They will often claim that no issues remain with the coparent or the stepchild. They will state, "This has nothing to do with me." It is very difficult to get their involvement. If they are resistant, the PC should at least mandate an intake appointment before letting them off the hook.

Characteristics of the underinvolved stepparent may include the following:

- Distant
- Emotionally unavailable
- Overly conscious that he or she is "not the parent"

The Complementary Stepparent

The complementary stepparent understands and respects boundaries of the natural parents. They have no need to interject themselves between the parents. Ultimately, this stepparent remains "one step behind" the primary parents. As noted in Figure 8.3, this stepparent stands next to the spouse just outside the inner circle in a supportive role. He or she respects the child's relationship with both parents and does not try to undermine relationships. The complementary stepparent manages the children only when necessary while encouraging the parents to do the majority of the discipline. This parent tends to have high self-esteem and is not easily threatened by others. Staying one step behind does not mean that this stepparent is not connected to the stepchildren or that he or she does not get involved with parenting

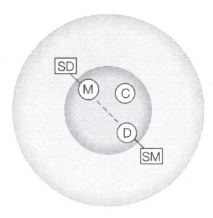

FIGURE 8.3. The Complementary Stepparent (One Step Behind)

matters. Complementary stepparents are a huge benefit to the children and to the parenting team. Complementary stepparents usually recognize their position as an important adult "parent" figure but as one that respects the boundaries of the biological parents. Generally they can see value in the coparent even when their spouse may not. Since their current spouse is in conflict with the coparent they are careful to walk the line between support and conflict. Complementary stepparents may even argue with their spouse when they witness inappropriate behaviors. The complementary stepparent tries to be supportive of both parents. This stepparent is mature enough to be willing to make sacrifices for his or her stepchildren.

In some situations the complementary stepparent can develop a friendly relationship with the coparent. A biological parent and stepparent may plan the child's birthday party together and enjoy each other's company. Yet the friendly stepparent cannot exist without a friendly coparent. When a positive stepparent–natural parent relationship exists, the child is the beneficiary. For example, when a father will be out of town for a father/daughter dance, he can call the child's stepfather and ask him to fill in. However, if the degree of conflict increases between coparents, it is difficult to retain the friendly stepparent and natural alignment.

Involving the Complementary Stepparent

This type of stepparent is a real asset; he or she complements the process. Sometimes the coparent has not recognized the supportive position and has misread motives. The child's positive relationship with this stepparent is often viewed as manipulative by the natural parent. It is refreshing when the biological parent learns that the stepparent supports the relationship with the child and that he or she will not be undermined.

The complementary stepparent can be easily included in joint sessions after participating in an intake appointment and one stepparent-parent session. His or her physical presence in joint sessions may significantly improve their spouse's behavior. This type of stepparent understands that *stepparent* is not an ugly word. He or she can embrace the position, love the children, and support the biological parents. He or she recognizes that to have a positive impact on the family system(s) he or she needs to take one respectful step back. Characteristics of the complementary stepparent may include the following:

- High self-esteem
- Confidence in the marriage
- Respect for parental boundaries

In certain situations the parent coordinator may need to request the assistance of a complementary stepparent. He or she may be more effective at communicating with the coparent than the spouse. In order for this process to run efficiently, ground rules and tight limits must be maintained, including instructing the biological parents not to request that the stepparent share any nonessential commentary with the coparent. Whenever possible, this strategy should be only a temporary arrangement. As soon as the stepparent can back out of this primary role he or she should do so.

The role of stepparent is very difficult and often underappreciated. No matter where he or she stands, the stepparent should always be kept in the loop by the spouse. However, when the coparenting team is conflicted, the wise stepparent should stand just one small step behind the parental team. In doing so, the stepparent demonstrates confidence in the spouse and love for the stepchild. He or she respectfully seeks to strengthen the parental bond without the fear of being left out. Furthermore, the child's other parent should try to value the fact that the child has a stepparent to love and care for him or her. The biological parent should be encouraged to see the stepparent as a valuable resource to everyone. The wise stepparent must work to respect all parties while stepping carefully to avoid trouble rather than create it. Ultimately, the stepparent who stays one step behind is an invaluable player in the parental team of raising children.

The descriptive categories for stepparents can also apply to significant others and even to grandparents. They may be supportive, invisible, complementary, or antagonistic. The same suggestions will also apply, especially if one of the biological parents is living with a grandparent or significant other.

Child Sessions

To gain firsthand knowledge of the child's perspective of the family and their adjustment to the separation, an individual session should be scheduled with each child. Before doing so, however, it is essential that parent coordinators understand their role, the purpose of the sessions, and their limitations when working with children. With this in mind, the parent coordinator must discern (1) the extent to which the child is handling family circumstance, (2) the nature and the severity of the child's stress, (3) the impact of parental behavior on the child, and (4) the personal, interpersonal, and environmental resources available to the child. Therapists can easily engage children by using puppets, role-playing activities, and creative play.

If the child has already established a relationship with a therapist, the PC should discuss the child's progress with this therapist before meeting with the child. The child's therapist may be able to provide the coordinator with information needed to work with the parents. Therefore, limited contact should be maintained with a child who has already established a relationship with a therapist.

When interviewing children it is essential to establish a relaxed atmosphere. Sessions should be fun and the PC should avoid interrogating the child. In order to elicit as much information as possible, the coordinator should gently encourage the child to provide examples and elaborations. If the coordinator is not experienced in or comfortable with working with very young children and the child is not in treatment, the PC should consider referring the child for treatment.

Because some children experience painful loyalty binds, they may not be forthcoming with information regarding their circumstances. For instance, some children may describe their parents and/or circumstances in equal terms while denying their true experience. In this way they can stay loyal to both parents. When this occurs, try using a prop such as building blocks to gain information from the child. The PC can give the child an uneven number of blocks or some other item. Then say, "You know that I am here to help both your parents. I need your help to do this. Can you show me with these blocks how much help your mom and dad need? Let's make a pile over here for Dad and a pile over here for Mom." If the child is unable to determine where the extra block should go, gently encourage him or her to place it in one pile by saying, "I guess this last one needs to go in Mom or Dad's pile, but I don't know where we should put it. Can you help?"

Children are sometimes more comfortable speaking with a sibling in the room. However, an accurate view of each child's perceptions may not be gained during sibling sessions. A younger child may parrot the ideas and thoughts of an older child. Also, one child may have bought into the alienation of a parent while the other child has not. Individual sessions with each child are recommended.

To determine the children's coping skills, gently collect information from children either through their play or from verbal feedback. Consider asking one or two of the following questions:

> What do you know about the divorce?
> What do you do when your parents argue?
> If I can help your parents to get along better, what would you want to happen?

Requests for information may include the following:

> Tell me about your time with your father/mother.
> Tell me what you like best about your father/mother (and stepparents).
> Tell me how your parents could change and become even better.

Finally, ask:

> Is there anything else I need to know?

Some children will ask for the chance to tell their parents their thoughts and feelings directly. Under these circumstances, the coordinator can invite the parents into the last portion of the session. The coordinator must structure the session carefully and require the parents to accept and respect the child's feedback without any negative consequences to the child. Let the parents know that their willingness to accept feedback from their child speaks to how much they love their child. Give the child a copy of the divorce rules. Then arrange a way for the child to respectfully tell parents when they are breaking a rule. Make sure that the parent approves of this plan before implementing it. Young children can be instructed to use nonverbal cues, such as a signal for time-out. Also, children can create a secret code word to draw a parent's attention to the behavior. This is particularly useful to alert parents to their inappropriate behaviors when friends are present or they are in public places. This empowers children to speak up and gives them hope that the situation may improve.

A report card designed for children to provide feedback on their parents' behavior has also been designed. When using a report card, the parent should not be in the room, as it will interfere with the child's answers. If the children are hoping that the PC will change their living situation they will usually be thrilled to fill out a confidential report card. Some will even ask to give it to the parent. Alienating children will want to give poor grades to the "hated" parent to increase the alienation. Resistance should be respected.

Many children are comforted by the knowledge that an adult figure is actively intervening in the family system to protect them from further discomfort. They are often relieved to know that someone can really help their parents, even if it is only a little help. They appreciate the benefit of their parents' improvement, and they are glad to know that the PC will try to hold their parents accountable. On the other hand, there will be children without hope who will appear to be distressed throughout the whole process.

When working with children who witness conflict between their parents and have been indoctrinated into the alienation of one or both parents, the PC must be aware of the child's attempts to manipulate the PC or distort the information. In situations of parental alienation, the child may attempt to form a coalition with the parent coordinator against one parent. While interviewing the child, the parent coordinator must get the child to provide elaborations and request examples of the allegations in order to elicit as much information as possible. In this way, a more accurate understanding of the family situation may be provided. When a child can identify only positive qualities in one parent and only negative qualities in another, it may indicate parental alienation. The child will use endearing terms to describe the "loved" parent and derogatory terms to describe the "hated" parent. See Chapter 13 for additional information regarding alienation.

Family Session or Relapse-Prevention Session

When the parent coordinator can be assured that the environment will be emotionally safe, the children should be invited to join their parents in a family session. This usually occurs after the parents have achieved their goals prior to moving to an as-needed basis. At times, it is useful to observe the family interact with one another as long as this does not create a loyalty bind or stress for the children. Before introducing children into the session, several issues should be considered: (1) the parents' ability to control their impulses, (2) the ability of the parents to interact with each other in a structured setting, (3) the degree to which the children may be experiencing loyalty binds, and (4) the presence of any alienation.

At the onset of the family session, the child should be brought into the room first. This will allow the child to choose a seat without having to choose between parents. Furthermore, the child can become comfortable prior to beginning the session. It is helpful to notice how the family positions themselves in the room and how they determine these positions. However, it is also important to simultaneously view the session from a child's perspective and to be alert to any loyalty issues. If parental alienation has occurred in the past, additional sessions with both parents will become a final intervention to assess progress. The relapse-prevention session should not occur unless the parents can be trusted to be appropriate. It is never advisable to conduct long interviews or conflicted discussions when the children are present with their parents.

When children have been involved in a relapse session and have had an opportunity to observe their parents' newfound ability to conduct themselves in a respectful manner, they are often very surprised. Most are pleased to see their parents in the same room without fighting. However, it may take a long time for the children to trust and feel comfortable with their parents' improved behaviors. Under the best of circumstances, having children in the session can be a great motivator to parents, especially when the children report fewer symptoms and an improvement in their situation. Children who have participated in the process are usually the first to recognize when parents need to return and generally encourage their parents to reestablish their relationship with the PC. Quite often, children thank the PC and/or their parents for creating a home environment free of unnecessary stress.

When the children are asked, "How will you know if your parents need to come back to see me?" the young child may say the following:

> "When my stomach starts hurting again."
> "When I start to worry about my daddy again."
> "When I hope that my stepdad and dad are not both going to be at my games."

The older child may say the following:

> "When I start avoiding being around any of them!"
> "When my grades start falling again."

Reunification Sessions

Reunification sessions may be helpful when the child:

1. refuses visitation with one parent,
2. reports being scared or anxious about being with one parent (unless the child has experienced or witnessed abuse),
3. does not know the parent,
4. experienced an interruption of visitation over an extensive period of time, or
5. has been alienated against one parent.

The parent coordinator should meet with the child prior to beginning reunification sessions to establish comfort between the child and the PC. When the first parent-child session occurs the child should enter the room without the parent. This allows the child time to get comfortable and to even discuss how he or she would like the session to proceed. Some families may require several reunification sessions. Unless the reason for the unification session is parental alienation, the PC may refer the parent and child to another therapist in order to keep appropriate boundaries.

In the case of alienation, the reunification sessions may take precedence over the parents' joint sessions. The PC should make this determination as soon as possible. In these cases, the alienating parent should not be allowed to remain in the building during the reunification sessions. The alienated parent is encouraged to bring photos of the child during past visitation periods to share in session with the child. The child can also be encouraged to bring a favorite toy or game to share with the parent. For children who are either anxious or resistant, bringing an item can ease them into the session.

As soon as improvements are made through the reunification sessions, parents will need to resume their joint sessions with increased regularity. Ideally, reunification sessions and joint coparenting sessions should initially be scheduled on a weekly basis. However, the financial situation of the family may prohibit this process.

TIMING AND PACING OF SESSIONS

One of the elements of a successful PC program is determining the type of session best suited for the family at any given point in the process. Although the process begins with intake appointments and subsequent joint sessions, the PC must assess the needs of the family on an ongoing basis. One aspect of the CPI model is determining when to include significant others and extended family members in the sessions. An expert coordinator uses his or her clinical judgment to determine the number of sessions, the timing and pacing of these sessions, and who will attend each session.

One of the topics discussed during the first joint session is the parents' method and style of communication. Coparent communication in high-conflict families will be impaired or nonexistent. Some parents ignore each other; some speak too often; while others have tried multiple ways of communicating without success. As soon as possible, the PC guides parents in the implementation of a communication model that fits their family circumstances. Chapter 9 examines the various types of communication methods and the skills necessary to improve the coparent relationship.

Chapter 9

Facilitating Effective Communication

Effective coparent communication is an essential element for preserving a cooperative relationship between former partners, but the parents may not have the luxury of waiting to communicate until they have mastered the skills of communication. First and foremost, parents need to be taught how to set up and maintain a communication system that fits their needs and abilities.

DESIGNING AN EFFECTIVE COMMUNICATION SYSTEM

Before teaching effective communication and negotiation skills, it is important to set up a system for regular communication between households. After learning what the parents have already tried, the parent coordinator should experiment with setting up a communication system for the parents to have weekly business meetings to discuss the children.

When designing a coparenting communication system, boundaries need to be clarified and ground rules should be determined. Coparent communication should focus on issues of child rearing, setting limits on unacceptable behavior that affects the children, and expressing opinions on matters that influence the children's well-being. Guidelines should also include scheduling the contact during time when the children cannot overhear the conversations, such as when they are asleep or are at school. Most parents choose to communicate with each other over the telephone or by e-mail at a designated time each week.

Ground rules reflect the appropriate communication skills taught to the parents during joint sessions while avoiding those behaviors that can ignite and add fuel to the conflict. Specific techniques are taught to appropriately disengage from verbal abuse. Topics that are off limits are delineated and adhered to. For instance, one mother was instructed not to mention her significant other. Although this may seem harmless, the mother would discuss the significant other in a manner which suggested that the she and the significant other were the major decision makers in their daughter's life. This type of behavior is disrespectful to the father and was a boundary issue addressed during joint sessions.

When designing a communication system, child-rearing topics are discussed in relationship to their complexity and potential to invite conflict. In the beginning, parents are requested to limit their discussions to changes in activity schedules, dates and times of medical/dental appointments, school activities, and illnesses. These topics generally require the parents to simply share factual information. The need to get into a lengthy, potentially heated conversation is limited. Once the parents have experienced success at this level, they may be challenged to take the next step and discuss topics that require a negotiated agreement such as change in time-sharing plans, the need for extra services (e.g., tutoring), and behavioral concerns. Furthermore, as parents become proficient in their ability to effectively communicate, they can use these opportunities to discuss situations in which agreements are not being kept or to address the inappropriate behaviors of a parent. For example, a father may be alerted by his child that his coparent is asking the child for information about the father's partner. Since this type of behavior causes the child to be put in a loyalty bind, the father has every right to discuss this situation with the mother in an appropriate manner.

The following are commonly used forms of coparent communication.

Weekly Conference Calls

The day, time, and the parent responsible for initiating the call must be determined and clarified in a written agreement. If necessary, the phone calls may be audiotaped for the coordinator's review with awareness of both parents.

Weekly E-Mail Communication

Parents who are working toward a cooperative relationship may choose to communicate by e-mail rather than by phone. The day and time of the e-mail message to be delivered and received must be determined. Although the parents will not be directly speaking to each other, they need to be reminded that written communication follows the same guidelines as verbal communication and ground rules still apply. If used appropriately, this type of communication is an excellent way to notify the other parent of school and extracurricular activities, dates and times of appointments, and to request schedule changes. However, e-mail has its limitations. When negotiating a mutually satisfying agreement, this form of communication can be cumbersome and may require multiple e-mails. Again, e-mails can be reviewed by the coordinator by copying the coordinator on the message or by bringing a printout of the message to the coordinator at the next joint session.

E-mail communication has the advantage of decreasing the likelihood of parental conflict because parents can think through the message before they send it. Some parents may be required to send their e-mail to the parent coordinator for review prior to sending it to their coparent. When this arrangement is used it is imperative that the parent coordinator charge for e-mail review to decrease the parents' dependence on the coordinator. The goal is for the parent coordinator to assist parents to rewrite or delete sections of their communication that may incite or fuel conflict. Parents should be weaned off this arrangement as soon as possible.

Another advantage besides impulse control is documentation. E-mail communication can be easily printed and placed in the parents' file. This may increase cooperation during the monitoring phase. Even though this may seem to set up an increased false sense of cooperation, the authors have found that when a parent learns new behaviors, even if it is for the wrong reasons, it increases the likelihood that the behaviors will remain. Furthermore, both parents are aware that their e-mail communications can be forwarded to the parent coordinator even during the as-needed phase. This too increases compliance.

E-mail communication does have a few drawbacks. First, we tend to read tone into written communication and base it upon negative beliefs from the past rather than on positive intent. With the help of the parent coordinator, parents can review an e-mail together in a joint session to determine if they are overreading tone into an appropriate comment or request. For example, "I hope you can meet us at the usual time on Friday" can be read in a neutral or even positive manner. It can also be read with sarcasm with the intent to fuel conflict. The parent coordinator can instruct the parents to assume the best from each other. Thus, they may not react to the statement, decreasing the likelihood that they will become irritated with the message and messenger. The parent coordinator may find that cognitive restructuring helps parents with their negative interpretations of written communication. Chapter 10 discusses cognitive restructuring. At the same time, the parent coordinator can coach parents to use care in communicating to each other. For example, they could rewrite the line to read: "Looking forward to seeing you Friday at 5:00."

Another disadvantage is that parents may overcommunicate with each other. The parent coordinator can set up guidelines to keep the communication to a minimum. For example:

Sarah will e-mail Jeff every Monday before 6:00 p.m. Jeff will respond by Tuesday at 6:00 p.m. If they have to respond to each other

they will not communicate by e-mail more than two days in a row unless there is an urgent message. In this event, the parents will use voice
mail. In addition, both parents will keep their communication strictly
about the children. Information shared that does not require a response shall begin with "FYI." Those communications that require a
response shall begin with "RR" for response requested. Each item
shall be numbered to minimize discussions and for ease of response.

Following is an example of concise e-mail communications.

Monday, August 23

Dear Bob,

FYI [no response requested]
- Kathy has another loose tooth to keep an eye on.
- Kathy and Frank have been getting along better this week.
- Frank's teacher said that tutoring is starting to pay off!

RR [response requested]

1. I will be out of town on the weekend of Sept. 12th. Can we exchange for the weekend before or after?
2. Did you get a copy of the revised soccer schedule?
3. Kathy says that the band teacher has to get a commitment form
from both of us. Is this true?

Mary

Tuesday, August 24

Dear Mary,

FYI
Nothing new to share

RR
1. That's fine. How about the weekend afterward?
2. No
3. Yes, we are both required to sign the commitment sheet. Kathy
should have it for you to sign.

Bob

At times a parent may not respond in a timely manner to an e-mail message that contains a request. To avoid unnecessary frustration, the message can be stated in a manner that implies an answer. For instance,

---

August 30

Dear Bob,

RR
I am going out of town from September 12 through September 16. Would you like to care for Kathy and Frank in my absence? If I do not hear from you by September 5, I will conclude that you are not able to take the children and I will make other arrangements.

Mary

A Communication Notebook

Customary standards for parental communication need to be altered in situations of high conflict or when protective orders limit the contact between parents. Parents in this category may keep a communication log or notebook instead of talking directly to each other or using their children to pass messages. This form of communication works very well with young children who have more frequent transfers and who are unable to read. The log is transferred in the child's bag as long as it does not create a stressful situation for the young child. With infants and toddlers, parents may note the child's eating habits and sleeping schedule along with the other parenting matters noted previously. Parents should not read the notebook when their child is present.

Specific guidelines and rules for the notebook need to be explained to parents. Information shared in this book should focus only on the children. At a minimum, parents may share information regarding medication, medical/dental appointments, recent illnesses, and nap and eating schedule. It should be made clear that emergency or time-sensitive information should be communicated through voice mail. The communication notebook should be brought to joint sessions by the parent currently in custody of the notebook in order for the PC to review its contents.

Weekly Faxes

Similar to e-mail messages, the use of weekly faxes, along with their advantages and disadvantages, should be discussed with the parents. A method for answering the faxes in a timely fashion needs to be addressed.

Parents who are self-employed will not be as concerned about having a personal fax show up at work. Some parents have purchased fax machines to use in their homes. An advantage to using a fax is that parents can also send copies of the children's report cards, activity schedules, and school newsletters. This is especially useful for parents living far apart or even out of the country. The disadvantages are similar to e-mail communication. Parents may provide too much information, irrelevant information, or use a writing style that invites conflict. Coparenting fax forms have been included in the back of the Cooperative Parenting and Divorce Parent Guide. Following is a list of some fax topics included in the guide:

- Request for a change
- Request for input on a parenting decision
- Offer of extra time
- Child management FYI
- Child medical FYI

Weekly Communication by Mail

Obviously, mail communication has its drawbacks and should not be used unless it is absolutely necessary. If parents do not have e-mail or fax capabilities, have older children who may get access to the log, and are unable to participate in a civil conversation, this may be the communication method of choice. However, with this, as well as the other forms of communication, the parents must take the necessary steps to prevent their children from having access to the communication process.

Other than greeting each other, communication at transfers should be eliminated. Delayed departures create stress for the child. In addition, parents should not combine parent-child phone calls with parent-parent calls. In other words, parents should not try to speak with the other parent before or after a call to their child. Again, this creates unnecessary stress.

ALTERNATIVE PARENT COMMUNICATION

Not all parents can communicate effectively by phone, e-mail, or in person. For those who have tried and even audiotaped their phone conferences for PC review, alternative systems may need to be implemented. No matter what system is used, parents should be reminded that they may call each other in an emergency or when an issue is urgent, such as not being able to pick up the child from school.

Voice Mail Communications

Some parents will not have access to alternative ways of communicating with each other. However, most parents do have answering machines and taped messages can be reviewed by the PC if necessary. Conflicted parents can be encouraged or even required to communicate by voice mail only while the other parent is at work. It is imperative that they recognize that the child may overhear a message. Nonetheless, parents have been able to effectively use the voice mail system as long as the PC considers all the loopholes. When new loopholes are discovered, the PC must not let either parent abandon the whole system until after modifications have been tried.

Web Communications

For those parents who are too highly conflicted to develop a cooperative relationship, <www.Our FamilyWizard.com> is a useful parent communication Web site. Parents who can afford to use this system communicate online to develop a calendar, trade days, store documents, share health information, list teachers' and coaches' names and numbers, and much more.

Communication Through the Parent Coordinator

At times, the parent coordinator will become the communication link between warring parents. When parents are unable to effectively communicate in one of the ways outlined earlier, the parent coordinator may provide the avenue for parental communication. Under these circumstances, clear ground rules will need to be established. For example, the mother leaves a voice message for the PC claiming that the coparent has not responded to her e-mail request. The PC may contact the father to request he e-mail the mother right away.

Besides sharing information with the parents, the parent coordinator's method of communication should reflect the skills utilized in session. In this way, the coordinator is not only attempting to reach a mutually satisfying resolution to the problem but also modeling effective communication skills. Parents can be encouraged when speaking to the parent coordinator to use these new skills. This communication approach can be used as a stepping stone to direct parent-parent communication in the future. Furthermore, the parent coordinator can teach parents to communicate messages that are child focused rather than self-focused.

PARENT-CHILD COMMUNICATION

Highly conflicted parents need instruction on how to talk to their children in a manner that will not cause the children additional stress. Telephone communication, similar to face-to-face contact between parent and child, can create loyalty binds for children. In situations in which a parent is engaging in inappropriate telephone conversations with the child, the parent coordinator might insist that all these conversations be audiotaped without the child's knowledge. These tapes are turned in to the coordinator by the problematic parent on a weekly basis for the coordinator's review. Depending on the content and quality of the conversations, the coordinator may schedule an individual session to review the tape and design detailed ground rules. The guidelines might include the following:

Acceptable Topics

- School
- Extracurricular activities
- Recent movies
- Dilemmas involving friends

Off-Limit Topics

- The other parent
- The other parent's significant other
- Child support
- Court matters
- Involvement of the other parent in the child's life

Other guidelines may include avoidance of discussions that result in stress for the child such as the use of guilt and interrogation, manipulation, or loyalty binds.

The parent coordinator will need to explore the advantages and disadvantages of any system and set a time period in which to reassess the effectiveness of the approach.

TEACHING COMMUNICATION SKILLS

Parent coordinators may choose to use a text as a resource for the parents. The CPI model of parent coordination uses the material highlighted in *Cooperative Parenting and Divorce: A Parent's Guide to Effective Coparenting.*

Fire Metaphor

A fire metaphor can be used to illustrate conflict and teach communication skills. A spark that is intended to hurt just a little can light the fuse to a huge explosion. Parents are told the more furious the arguments, the more difficult they are to stop and the more destruction they cause. However, on the other hand, the coordinator demonstrates how a spark without fuel quickly burns itself out. If the coparent does not add fuel to the fire, the initial spark from the critical comment or the sarcastic tone quickly extinguishes itself and no argument develops. Without the defensiveness or attack found in a coparent's response, no fire will burn and the tiny flame will go out. The coordinator explains that both parents provide something to make the fire burn and it takes only one parent to extinguish the flame.

It is advantageous for the parent coordinator to teach parents how three elements—tone of voice, body language, and words—are like the matches that light a fire. Any one of these elements can elicit a negative response. The coparent, slightly singed from the lighted match, quickly fuels the fire with one of the three common responses: defensiveness, counterattack, or withdrawal. For example, the defensive response, "I am not weak," is all that is needed to show one's hot button has been successfully ignited and to become caught in the fire. "Maybe I am what you say, but you're worse," is the counterattack that adds fuel to the fire. Abruptly hanging up the phone without warning or leaving the area can fuel the argument through withdrawal. Attack, counterattack, and withdrawal provide the needed oxygen for the flame. The bigger the fire, the more difficult it becomes to extinguish. This is the same with conflict.

Although parents may think that it is reasonable to fight fire with fire, the coordinator must emphasize that both parents can get burned. By engaging in the conflict, parents are harmed by vengeful comments and can be scarred from the legal battles that often follow. More important, the coordinator highlights that the victim who gets hurt the most is the child caught in the middle. The child neither lights the match nor fuels the fire, yet the child is the innocent victim asleep upstairs while the building burns. The child feels the heat from the argument but is powerless to control its destructiveness and helpless to extinguish it.

The parent coordinator can develop the parents' communication skills by pointing out specific ways in which they can both light the fuse and fuel the fire.

Tone of Voice

An argument, like a fire, can start small. A few words, a tone of voice, or the rolling of eyes can light the match that gets the fire going between the parents. For instance, the use of sarcasm, threats, or whining will likely push the coparent's hot buttons. Parents must learn that sarcasm is not wit; it belittles a person as severely as hurtful words. Tone of voice can illicit anger by drawing the other person in with its pleading sound. It is important to remind parents that a demanding tone usually begets a response that is just as demanding. Parents can start a fight with their tone of voice even when their words are not the problem. When a PC allows parents to use a negative tone of voice it will direct the focus to the coparent relationship and away from the problem at hand. It prevents any focus from staying on the child.

Body Language

Body language, too, can be the match that sets the argument burning. Body language can be threatening even when one does not push, shove, or prevent another person's free movement. When parents point a finger while speaking to the coparent or sit forward in an aggressive manner, their body language has contributed to failed communication efforts. The subtle ways we use our body to express our emotions can be just as likely to start a fight as verbal language and can be even more provocative.

Words That Light Fires

The PC must watch carefully for use of words that impair verbal and written coparent communication. The following are all problematic communication styles: blaming, accusing, demanding, commanding, giving advice with statements that start "You should," name-calling, and playing psychologist.

Hot Buttons

Hot buttons are the issues, the voice tone, or the body language that increase the likelihood for each individual to be drawn into an argument. Some hot buttons are universal, while others may be based upon the history of the parental team. When hot buttons are pushed, the person responds with defensiveness, counterattack, or withdrawal. Only when the parents become aware of their personal hot buttons can they prepare themselves to change their response. The parent coordinator must diligently watch and identify each parent's hot buttons so that he or she can coach the parents to disengage.

Fire Prevention Techniques

A parent coordinator can take the fire analogy farther. For example, parents can be taught that either one of them can prevent an argument; either one can put the fire out. The parents can be taught techniques for preventing conflicts and ending the fight. The first way to limit the damage of a fire's destruction is to prevent it before it starts. This does not mean that parents will never say the wrong thing or look the wrong way. It does mean that they can learn to minimize danger by not lighting matches in drought-stricken forests. The following fire prevention techniques maybe useful.

The Three Ws

When. Parents are instructed that conflict can often be prevented by carefully choosing when to talk. They should call to make an appointment. Then both parents can choose a time that is convenient and when distractions can be limited. It is important that parents select a time when children are not within earshot so that the parents may discuss issues freely. Transfers are not the time for discussion of coparenting issues.

Where. Next, parents are encouraged to choose a location conducive to good discussion. They might choose to speak by phone while the children are in school or in a public place that encourages rational discussion and brings out businesslike behavior. Parents need to choose a place where children cannot overhear their conversation.

What. Selecting the topic is the parents' next decision. Some topics are out of bounds; some are within limits.

The Three Ps

To enhance the parents' discussions, a parent coordinator may use the following descriptions to teach the parents about the 3 Ps.

Focus on the present, not the past. Parents should eliminate any discussion of the past unless the matter may affect the child in the future.

Focus on the problem, not on the person. Topics should focus on solving problems rather than pointing fingers. Parents must learn how to talk about problems such as "safety issues" or "homework conditions" rather than "the things you allow at your house." Parents should be encouraged to use language that continually stresses what is good for the child rather than what they do not like about the coparent. The problem is the problem.

Focus on the problem at hand, not the whole universe. Parents need lots of structure so they do not bring up too many issues at one time. The PC can assist parents to focus on one topic and discuss only that topic until a resolution has been made. When the conversation moves away from the topic, the PC may say, "That's important, but right now let's just finish discussing the problem at hand."

Use of I-Statements

The parent coordinator must help parents refrain from using blaming "you-statements." Parents can be shown by example how to use "I-statements" to share their opinions. For example, a blaming statement may sound like this: "You let our son ride in the front seat with an air bag! What is the matter with you? Don't you have any sense whatsoever?" By using the format shown in Box 9.1 parents can learn to express themselves in a more constructive manner: "I felt concerned and very annoyed when our son told me he rode in the front seat of your car, and what I'd like is for us to discuss the issue of air bags with his pediatrician."

I-statements help the communication process in several ways:

- They honestly describe how a person feels about a situation. Since feelings are always acceptable (even when actions are not), the statements themselves are more likely to be acceptably received.
- Full I-statements quickly relate a person's thoughts about the situation and the possible effects on the child. They can be child focused. Therefore the discussion is more likely to focus on what is best for the child.
- They do not invite defensiveness or counterattack. Instead, they allow a respectful difference of opinion and a sharing of ideas. By not forcing someone to take an opposing position, they open the door to possible agreement.
- They make a brief and clear request.

Full I-Statement. At times, the parent coordinator will want to encourage parents to use a full I-statement to give a more complete picture that includes the negative impact the problem has on the child. Full I-statements follow the format shown in Box 9.1. The following is a specific example of a parent-to-parent full I-statement.

> "I feel worried when Alex is home alone after nine p.m. because he's unprotected and something could happen to him. I would like him to have a sitter if he's going to be alone after nine p.m. Can you agree to that?"

BOX 9.1. Formats for I-Statements

I-Statements

I feel/felt _____ (insert feeling word)
when _____ (this happens)
and what I'd like is _____ (insert your request).

Full I-Statements

I feel _____ (insert feeling word)
when _____ (insert what happens that concerns you)
because _____ (the negative effect it has on the child).
And what I'd like is _____ (your requested change in the behavior).

The full I-statement format keeps the problem focused on the child and the benefit of the coparent's changed behavior to the child. It clearly changes the focus from what "I" want to what the parent believes is good for the child. The last phrase of the I-statement requests a response from the other parent. Since parents may not be able to answer immediately, the coordinator can teach parents not to press for an answer right after they have delivered the I-statement. Likewise, they can be coached to respond to the request by saying, "I will think about it and get back to you by _____."

The parent coordinator should use every reasonable opportunity to encourage parents to use the I-statements. At times, parents become frustrated with the coordinator's request to use an I-statement in its appropriate form. The coordinator must praise the parents' efforts at being concise. When parents divert from the format, the PC can instruct them to start over and create one sentence that includes the basic parts of an I-statement. Parents should be told that this technique may at first feel strange or even silly, but it will begin to pay off as they master this skill. The parent coordinator should also model the use of I-statements whenever it is appropriate, particularly when the coordinator is becoming frustrated with the parents' behavior. For example, the following is a PC-to-parents I-statement:

> "I feel frustrated when you both repeatedly forget to protect your child from conflict at transfers, because your son is very anxious about your fighting. What I'd like is for both of you to say goodbye to your son before the other parent arrives so you can avoid getting into a negative conversation. Can you agree to that?"

Reflective Listening

Conflicted coparents tend to speak over each other rather than listen. Reflective listening is a powerful fire-prevention skill that the parent coordinator will need to teach, coach, and model. In order to assist parents to use the technique, the parent coordinator should point out the following elements:

1. Reflective listening is an active skill. It is the first step in respectful communication. Before the listener shares thoughts and opinions, he or she must reflect the speaker's thoughts. Once the speaker feels understood by the listener, then the roles can switch and the listener becomes the speaker. Otherwise, the speaker may feel misunderstood, and the listener may not fully comprehend the speaker's thoughts. Thus the communication process may be undermined before it begins.
2. Reflective listening does not indicate agreement with the person's thoughts or feelings. For example, one parent may state that vegetarian foods are healthier for the child. The other parent can reflect the content of the message by saying, "You believe that a vegetarian diet is a healthy diet for our child," and still be a meat eater.
3. Reflecting the coparents' opinions requires that parents put aside their own opinions and emotions temporarily. They need to actively listen to the coparent's thoughts and feelings, then put the person's opinions into their own words. The parent coordinator can teach parents to avoid adding to or subtracting from the message delivered by their coparent. The more accurate their description, the better the chances are that they will solve the problem. Reflective listening does not include any personal comments.

   Example #1: The mother addresses the parent coordinator, "You don't ever let me talk as much as him! I want another parent coordinator." The parent coordinator responds, "So, you're really feeling annoyed with me because it seems that I don't let you speak as much as your coparent. And you'd like another parent coordinator. Is that right?"

   Example #2: If a parent tends to be too long-winded the coordinator might say, "Excuse me, but I really want to make sure I am understanding what you are saying before you go on." Then the coordinator reflects the parent's partial comments before allowing him or her to continue.

It is imperative that the coordinator explain to parents that reflective listening will not immediately end a confrontation. Reflective listening does, however, reduce the level of the conflict because it indicates that the other parent is carefully listening to the speaker's underlying concerns. If parents can help identify their coparent's concerns, they may be able to extinguish the flame. Because everyone appreciates being listened to and understood, reflective listening should be taught as one of the first fire-prevention skills.

Defusing with Limit Setting

The parent coordinator can coach parents how to remove themselves from conflict. The coordinator can illuminate that neither parent is solely to blame; both of them are equally responsible for every argument. Conflict cannot happen without the two of them, yet it takes only one parent to extinguish the flame. Parents can learn how to defuse any argument and take control of conflict.

Many high-conflict couples have a difficult time setting appropriate limits. The parent coordinator can help parents recognize the situations in which limits should be set and then instruct them on how to set these limits in the following circumstances:

- To protect their child from experiencing parental conflict or tension
- To protect themselves from an uncomfortable or unsafe situation
- To end a discussion that is deteriorating or continually off the topic

Limit-setting skills include:

1. The parent will use an I-statement to request a change in the offensive or inappropriate behavior.
   For example: "I feel discouraged when you continue to interrupt me when I am speaking. What I would like is for you to let me finish my statements." The parent coordinator should inform parents to alert the coparent prior to ending a conversation. Withdrawing in a respectful manner is very different from the type of withdrawal that escalates conflict. Abruptly leaving the room or forcefully hanging up the telephone are inappropriate ways to disengage from a heated conversation. Parents should be taught this difference and encouraged to make a specific comment indicating that they are ending the conversation. If a behavioral request does not resolve the unproductive communication or inappropriate behavior, then the parent should move to steps 2 and 3.

2. The parent postpones the conversation until another date and time. With the calmest voice possible, parents can be coached to say, "This isn't doing us much good. I'm hanging up now and I will call you tomorrow." In face-to-face interactions, parents might say, "I can see we are not getting anywhere. I am going to go now. I will call you tomorrow evening after our child is in bed."

3. Next, the parent gently hangs up or leaves the conversation. It is essential for parents to stand behind their words and remove themselves from the situation if the behaviors of the coparent do not change. After parents are able to use I-statements and reflective listening with minimal coaching, the parent coordinator can teach the seven steps to negotiation.

Negotiation Skills

Parents should master negotiation skills both in session and out of session before they finish the program. Because parents may develop a dependency on the coordinator, it is important to emphasize that one of the coordinator's responsibilities is to prepare the parents to work out issues on their own.

During the negotiation process, parents must be taught to remain child focused. Effective parents will make sure their child's basic needs come first. Parenting issues must not get focused on one parent "winning" and one "losing." When this happens the child loses. Each time either parent tries to win at the other's expense, they are winning the battle but losing the war. The battle is the immediate parental disagreement; the war is the long-term development of their child. The long-term goal, raising a happy and well-adjusted child, is the sole reason that the two adults continue their relationship. With their common goal in mind, they can execute the negotiation process in a manner that results in finding the best solution for the child. This process must be repeated in joint sessions as often as needed.

When parents get caught up in power struggles and lose sight of their child's welfare, the coordinator can interrupt these behaviors by tossing a coin in the air and requesting the parents to choose their position by calling "heads" or "tails." This simple technique catches parents off guard and interrupts their destructive behaviors. After the parents have identified their position (heads or tails), the parent coordinator might say, "It's heads. I guess Mom is the winner! It appears that both of you are willing to gamble when it comes to your child's well-being."

Many of the topics that create conflict for parents are value laden and may have deeper meaning attached than the surface issue. For example, the scheduling of a child's bedtime may have more to do with the parents' own time management, rigidity with rules, and comfort with routines than with the child's need for sleep. It may be difficult for coparents to realize that they each may have different values and concerns. The parent coordinator can point out that different is not necessarily wrong; it is just different.

Prior to teaching the parents negotiation skills, the parent coordinator can assess the parents' ability to resolve child-rearing matters. By assigning parents a sample problem to negotiate, the coordinator can observe their strengths and weaknesses. This same assessment can be used to evaluate the parents' progress throughout the program.

TEACHING NEGOTIATING SKILLS

If the parents reach an impasse in their communication, they can follow a seven-step method for finding the best solution and putting it into effect.

Step 1: Name the Problem

One parent will notice or perceive that a problem is interfering with the well-being of the child. For example, Judy believes that their daughter may need tutoring during the summer months. She uses the 3 Ws to coordinate a time and place to discuss her concern with Dan. She names the problem: " I would like to discuss Jamie's struggle with math this year."

Step 2: Give Opinion, Reflect Opinion

Step 2 is perhaps the most critical step in moving from the problem to the solution. When this step is not handled carefully, the conversation becomes refocused on the relationship between the coparents rather than staying focused on solving the problem that affects the child. The parent coordinator must coach the coparents to take turns giving their opinions using I-statements. In the previous example, Judy would share her I-statement first and then Dan would reflect these concerns.

1. Judy gives her opinion; Dan reflects Judy's opinion.

   Judy's full I-statement: "I am concerned that Jamie still has not mastered math skills from fourth grade and may need tutoring this summer because she may fall even farther behind next year since they build on math skills. What I'd like is for us to agree upon someone to tutor her once a week during the summer and to share the costs."

Dan reflects Judy: "You're concerned about Jamie's math because you think she will have trouble in fifth grade and you want to share the cost of weekly tutoring this summer."

2. Now, if Dan cannot agree right away, he gives his own opinion. Then Judy reflects Dan's opinion.

Dan's I-statement: "I feel annoyed when you get so negative about Jamie. Just because math isn't her best subject does not mean she needs tutoring. What I'd like is for you to back off and let her have fun this summer without you micromanaging her time."

Judy reflects Dan: "So you get ticked off with me when I make too much of things. You think Jamie does not need math tutoring and you want me to let it go. Is that right?"

The purpose of step 2 is for each side to have the opportunity to explain their own thinking on the subject fully. When it becomes clear that they are opposed in their positions, they move to step 3.

Step 3: Brainstorm Solutions

During this step, parents propose alternative solutions other than their original request. Parents must be told not to judge or evaluate solutions at the same time they are brainstorming potential options. Instead, parents are instructed to suggest as many ideas as they can think of to solve the problem. The coordinator can encourage parents to dig deep and come up with wild ideas just to get their creative juices flowing. When one idea is suggested, try suggesting the opposite idea. By opening their minds to all kinds of creative solutions, parents might come up with an outlandish idea that works better than all the simple solutions they thought of at first.

To assist parents with the skill of brainstorming, the parent coordinator can create a nondivorce situation that does not reflect the parents' current situation. Parents can be told to suggest four or five possible solutions. This will reduce tension and build confidence. When the parents are successful with a nondivorce issue, the parent coordinator can request that they resolve a "real" divorce situation that does not currently apply to their family. Then the parents select an issue that they are facing using the steps of negotiation with coaching from the parent coordinator.

BRAINSTORM OPTIONS TO JAMIE'S TUTORING

Mom's original request: Judy makes an appointment with a tutor for Jamie, and Dan pays one-half.

Dad's original request: Judy drops the issue of tutoring and lets Jamie have unstructured fun during the summer.

1. Dan agrees to tutoring, but Judy pays the fees.
2. They will speak with Jamie's teacher and if the teacher states that Jamie needs the service they will share the costs.
3. Dan agrees to have Jamie tested and then decide.
4. Judy consults with a teenager that Jamie likes to see if she could provide tutoring during the summer.

Step 4: "Choose a Solution"

The parent coordinator reminds parents that they are trying to answer the key question, "What is the best solution for our child?" Through the process of choosing a solution, parents might find that they can even combine some of the proposed solutions and propose a solution that is even better.

As part of the brainstorming process, parents may find that they need more information in order to determine the best solution. The parent coordinator can direct the parents to consider what they need to know or do to resolve the matter. Then plan how this step will be accomplished by completing steps 4, 5, and 6. For instance, a father believes their son should not be allowed to go to rock concerts at the age of thirteen, and the mother believes there would be no harm in allowing him to attend with friends. They may end up agreeing that their child can attend select concerts as long as a parent is present. When this is determined, the parents decide which concert he may attend and who will supervise him.

At times, parents may have difficulty agreeing to a solution if they believe that the solution will lock them into a long-term commitment. When this happens, the parent coordinator can encourage the parents to propose a time-limited option. The time limit might be a few days, a few weeks, or a few months, depending on the situation. The parents need to make the specified time period long enough to give the solution a chance to work.

For instance, the parents are in conflict over where their daughter should take ballet classes. The father wants her to remain in her old dance school indefinitely, while the mother wants to transfer immediately to a ballet school in her new neighborhood. The parents end up deciding that she will complete the ballet classes for the year offered in her father's neighborhood.

After the spring recital she will take any future ballet lessons near her mother's new home.

By setting a designated period for trying out the solution, parents do not have to put all their eggs in one basket. If the parents designate a specific time for evaluating the solution in action, they are free to return to the drawing board and renegotiate if the solution is not working for either them or their child. They do not have to choose the perfect solution the first time; they only have to find a solution that they are willing to try for a limited time. The coordinator can teach them to ask themselves, "Can I live with this for three weeks?" If the answer is yes, then it is a great solution. The parents have something to try, and it just might work out for the long term.

Step 5: Review: Who Does What by When?

In the previous example Judy and Dan agreed to have Jamie tested before they decided about her need for tutoring. Step 5 means summarizing the agreement in their own words and indicating who is responsible for taking which actions. It is a good idea to also name the time when these actions should be completed. This step holds parents accountable and may prevent future problems.

By reviewing these guidelines before the parents end the conversation, they can prevent the frustration that can occur when there is not clarity regarding everyone's responsibilities.

Step 6: Put the Solution into Action

All the previous steps have occurred during the same conversation. Now parents end the conversation and put their agreement into action. However, when problems occur, it is usually due to one of the following reasons:

1. A parent is not committed to the solution
2. The parents did not cover all the necessary details to adequately and smoothly put the solutions into action
3. A parent forgets about the long-term commitment to his or her child and falls back on the short-term desire to win.

Commitment is crucial to the long-term goal of a healthy upbringing for the child. If a coparent loses faith in the other parent's willingness to carry out agreements, both the coparent relationship and the child's well-being are in jeopardy. A sense of mistrust is extremely damaging to the long-term effectiveness of coparenting.

Step 7: Reevaluate

As part of step 5, a date is selected to reevaluate the effectiveness of the solution. In order to teach the parents to evaluate their solution, the parent coordinator can instruct them to ask, "What worked? What didn't? What needs to be changed? Was it a one-time situation or does the situation recur and the solution need to continue on a regular basis? Who benefits from the solution?"

Before the parents terminate their work with the coordinator, they can be assigned a small issue to be negotiated (1) in the waiting room before their joint session, (2) in the waiting room after a joint session, (3) by phone between sessions (children asleep), or (4) over coffee (no children present). Then suggest addressing a more significant issue to be negotiated in a manner of their choice.

COMMUNICATION METAPHORS

A creative PC can develop a multitude of metaphors to assist parents to grasp the concepts of effective communication. For instance, if the parents enjoy their child's softball games, the coordinator may use playing catch as a metaphor for effective communication. The game of catch shares many similar elements with the process of communication. A discussion of the game of catch can be used as a way to introduce the skills of communication. For example, when individuals play catch they usually play with the intention of throwing the ball in a manner in which it will be caught rather than throwing the ball in a wild fashion. Likewise, when the speaker communicates a message, the goal is for the other person to catch the message as easily as possible. The speaker wants to be heard and understood. Therefore, it benefits parents to speak in a fashion that will increase the probability that the listener will grasp the meaning. Other possible parallels include the following:

> It takes two individuals.
> It takes cooperation and attention from the other player.
> Practice improves skills.
> Respect and fair play are important when playing catch.

Metaphors can be used in many different ways and can also be used by the PC to assist angry parents. For example, some classic images for an explosive parent might be an erupting volcano or a broken dam. It is impossible to stop the lava when a volcano erupts and just as impossible to stop the flow of water on command when the dam breaks. Visual images such as these may help parents to understand why they cannot expect themselves to use skills such as I-statements if they stuff their anger rather than deal with issues as they arise. As one might accurately assume, many of the parents who participate in parent coordination have anger difficulties.

Regardless of the degree of anger, an effective coparent communication system is essential to the establishment and maintenance of a cooperative relationship between parents. A workable system identifies the mode of communication, clarifies the ground rules, outlines the topics of discussion, and determines the frequency of the discussions. Once the system has been established, parents learn effective communication and negotiation skills designed to reduce conflict and encourage mutual problem solving. In order to effectively teach communication skills, the parent coordinator must simultaneously address any issues of anger and impulse control. Chapter 10 explains the origins of anger and provides various techniques to manage this specific emotion.

Chapter 10

Managing Angry Parents

Anger in divorce is inevitable. Divorcing spouses, at some point in the grief process, will find themselves angry at each other. The PC will encounter parents with varying degrees of anger. High-conflict couples have an usually difficult time managing their anger. Some just cannot or will not let go of their anger. For some parents, this state becomes a permanent one. Divorcing parents are often reacting to pain, betrayal, loss, and grief. Continued hostility between divorced parents may indicate that the losses associated with a divorce have not been fully accepted. Under these conditions, divorced parents use their anger and rage as an emotional buffer to protect themselves from experiencing their hurt and to stay victimized. Those parents with significant anger problems are the least likely to change during the process.

The first part of this chapter highlights general information about anger that will provide the PC with a foundation of knowledge for working with conflicted parents. The final portion includes many of the CPI techniques used with angry parents. A brief section on domestic violence is also provided within this chapter.

THE ANGRY PARENT

Angry people are typically individuals who do not have a script or model for dealing with anger in a productive manner. They do not have effective emotional resources and are therefore not good at problem solving. Many of these parents also exhibit problems with impulse control, may be diagnosed with personality disorders, and/or experience substance abuse problems. The angry person believes that as soon as the fuse is lit, it must blow. He or she does not recognize that the fuse can be lengthened to provide time to find more effective options for dealing with feelings.

The angry parent is often basically just an angry person. A history of violence is not necessarily the problem; anger is. Many of these parents are easily agitated, may experience road rage, and can become verbally abusive with those closest to them. The angry person believes that the other parent does everything intentionally just to get to him or her. Angry parents simply prefer to blame others and demand that their coparents change. Thus they often project their anger onto others.

Angry parents often use hostile body language that they are generally unaware of. For instance, they point fingers, raise their voice, interrupt, use rapid-fire questioning, and/or sit forward in their seats. By viewing themselves on videotape, parents can be alerted to their hostile behaviors and then taught new and more effective techniques.

Rapid escalation of parental conflict is quite common during joint sessions. High-conflict parents have so many unresolved grievances that an argument can erupt at any time with little provocation. Some parents have had a long-standing feud with their former spouse and may have been involved in years of litigation. Others are easily provoked and may not respect authority figures. Many are coping with numerous challenges associated with the divorce process. While parents are in the midst of their intense animosity, they focus all their efforts on defending themselves or on attacking the other parent.

Some parents have a very difficult time recognizing and acknowledging that their anger, resentment, and bitterness may be a cover for the hurt they have experienced with regard to the separation. To avoid their vulnerability, angry parents may find reasons to stay angry. Prior to the separation, a parent may harbor anger for the following reasons:

> The partner would not communicate in the marriage.
> The partner would not show affection in the marriage.
> The partner showed greater loyalty to his or her own family of origin.
> The partner would not seek marital treatment in the marriage.
> He or she feels abandoned.
> Dishonesty, broken promises, and/or an affair occurred.

After the separation, a parent may continue to nurture anger for the following reasons:

> Feeling betrayed/abandoned by the partner or children
> Feeling disrespected
> Experiencing financial issues
> Feeling frustrated over the lack of commitment to agreements
> Being on the receiving end of alienation and visitation refusal
> Experiencing harassment behaviors
> Feeling left behind by a new relationship or stepparent
> Ongoing litigation

Anger is an attempt to manage frustration and take control of one's environment. Many factors can contribute to anger, such as childhood abuse, attentional or learning difficulties, physical pain, depression, sleep deprivation, poor nutrition, and other diagnoses. Anger is often a cover for deep emotional pain and loss.

The higher the person's self-esteem, the less angry he or she becomes in any given situation. The parent with low self-esteem is at risk of feeling vulnerable. In general, when an individual has low self-esteem his or her ego is in charge.

> When someone is rude or disrespectful, it causes us to question our own self-worth and lash out with anger. This is why a person with low self-esteem is highly sensitive—because his opinion of himself fluctuates with his ability to impress others. Self-esteem and ego are inversely related—when one goes up, the other goes down. (Lieberman, 2002, pp. 6-7)

When someone gets angry, it is because he or she is, to some extent, fearful. The fear comes from losing control of some part of one's life or self-esteem. "Anger is the impulse response to this fear, which sparks the conflict" (Lieberman, 2002, p. 9). Angry parents with low self-esteem will direct anger at the coparent, believing that this person is responsible for robbing them of power or control. If the coparent does not respond respectfully, the angry parent will project the anger onto this person because his or her sense of self has been damaged. They require approval from others to feel good about themselves. When we experience hurt, we react defensively. In turn, this anger inflates our ego and provides us with the sense of identity, control, and permanence that we believe was taken from us.

According to Meichenbaum (2002), eight situations make people angry. Meichenbaum's eight provocations have been expanded upon in Box 10.1 to illustrate their relevance to divorce situations.

ANGER VERSUS AGGRESSION AND DOMESTIC VIOLENCE

A distinction must be made between anger and aggression. Anger is an emotion, an affective response. Aggression is an act toward another with the intent to hurt or harm. Verbal insults can therefore be aggressive. Hostility is the long-term or chronic result of anger and aggression. However, only a small percentage of angry feelings result in aggression or hostility. When people have poor impulse control or poor social judgment they may "look"

BOX 10.1.
Eight Situations That Cause Anger

Provocation

1. Interruption of plans or goals
   a. Your picnic plans are ruined by a thunderstorm.
   b. You cannot reach your child by phone as agreed.

2. Implications of noncompliance
   a. Child does not turn off TV when asked.
   b. Your coparent did not consult you before registering your child for ballet.

3. Concern about injury
   a. The car in front of you cuts you off.
   b. Your coparent does not require your child to use a bike helmet.

4. Expectations
   a. You expect your boss to promote you, but he does not do so.
   b. You expect your coparent to help care for your child when you go out of town, but she is unwilling.

5. History repeating itself
   a. You have requested that your spouse call you when he or she is running late for dinner, but your spouse continues to "forget" to do so.
   b. You have confronted your coparent because she "forgot" to tell you about a parent-teacher conference again.

6. Overload
   a. You are not sleeping well, your job is on the line, and the kids are fighting.
   b. All of the three previous problems are going on, plus your coparent cannot be reached.

7. Personal peeve/violation of rules/values
   a. You hear about a married friend having an affair.
   b. Your child tells you that Dad has a girlfriend spending the night.

8. Embarrassment
   a. Your child is disrespectful to you in public.
   b. Your coparent is drunk at your child's baseball game.

aggressive. However, there is a difference between the demonstration of poor impulse control and poor judgment and aggressive behaviors. The difference is tied to the intent of the behavior. Behaviors that are intended to hurt are considered aggressive, while other behaviors may be simply an expression of anger.

Many coparents arrive deeply entrenched in their adversarial roles. They demonstrate behaviors such as hostile comments and body language, tense tone of voice, angry outbursts, and rage directed toward the parent coordinator or other parent. Other parents become visibly agitated, interrupt, rise from their chair, pace about the room, or slam books. Some make subtle and not so subtle threats to the PC such as, "What would your ethical board think?" or "You're just looking out for him." The intent of the aggressive act is often to win a power struggle with the parent coordinator, coparent, or the legal system. If aggressive behaviors are allowed, then parents displaying these behaviors will validate the belief that they have control over the PC and the coparent. Needless to say, this is a dangerous belief. Similar to an acting-out child, without limits and consequences their behaviors will become worse.

The purpose of this section is to offer some basic facts about domestic violence in order to assist parent coordinators to become sensitive to the dynamics in this area.

This brief text does not adequately address the complex and important issues associated with domestic violence; thus, the PC is encouraged to study this topic in further detail. At one time domestic violence referred only to forms of physical assault. Over time this definition has expanded. According to Johnston (1993), domestic violence is

> the use of physical force, restraints or threats of force to compel one to do something against their will or do bodily harm to self, cohabitant, or family members, or the mother or father of one's child. It includes but is not limited to: assault (pushing, slapping, choking, hitting, biting, etc.), use of or threat with a weapon, sexual assault, unlawful entry, destruction of property, keeping someone prisoner or kidnapping, theft of personal property, and infliction of physical injury or murder. Psychological intimidation or control may also be maintained through such means as stalking, harassment, threats against children or others, violence against pets, or destruction of property. (p. 3)

Even with this broadened definition, it is not unusual for victims of abuse and violence to minimize their experience because the results did not place them in a life-threatening position or result in hospitalization, a broken bone, or a bruise. Some individuals naively believe that they desired the abuse or that they are not a victim of "real abuse" because their partner did not close his or her fist or may not have touched them at all. Some do not understand or believe that men can be abused or battered by women.

Due to the many forms of aggression, some domestic violence experts have suggested that the term domestic violence should be replaced with the term domestic abuse. Others argue that terms such as conflict, abuse, and domestic violence have become blurred, dangerously complicating matters. Although physical assaults may result in serious injury or even death, particularly during a family separation, physical assaults are not always the most damaging form of maltreatment. Psychological and economic assaults, sexual coercion, harassment, and all forms of threat are serious boundary violations. Abuse is a form of power and manipulation intended to shame, degrade, and control. The role of substance abuse, especially alcohol, interferes with developing alternatives to aggression. When domestic violence is present, the degree of physical and sexual abuse of children is also greater.

In particular, the coordinator should be familiar with Johnston and Campbell's (1993) five types of violence and partner abuse:

> Type 1: Ongoing or episodic male battering
> Type 2: Female-initiated violence
> Type 3. Male-controlled interactive violence
> Type 4: Separation and postdivorce violence
> Type 5: Psychotic and paranoid reactions

See the appendix at the end of Chapter 3 for additional resources.

DOMESTIC VIOLENCE AND CUSTODY DISPUTES

With regard to custody and visitation, it is generally assumed that children should have contact with both parents. Unfortunately, in situations of divorce, abusive relationships are often mislabeled as conflicted rather than abusive. As a result, specialists in partner abuse fear family courts are confusing the two and ignoring the serious consequences of abuse and violence both for parents and for their children. Parent coordinators must understand the difference and use every opportunity to protect each member of the family while educating the legal professional.

To make matters worse, it is not uncommon for a divorcing parent to resist a shared-parenting arrangement when the marital relationship had been abusive or violent. Unless claims of domestic violence have been adequately documented by police reports, medical reports, audio or video tapes, or a third-party witness, the court system may not take the victim's concerns seriously. The parent claiming either undocumented physical violence or other forms of abuse may not be believed. Unfortunately, their resistance to a shared-parenting arrangement may then be viewed as bitterness or alienating behavior rather than a reflection of genuine anxiety for their and their children's safety.

Nonetheless, in custody disputes it is common to recommend primary custody to the parent who is most likely to communicate with the coparent and the parent most likely to share the child with the other parent. This can be very misleading. For example, if an abusive male manipulates the system so that he can use their child to increase access to the former spouse, he may create the illusion that he is the preferred parent for primary custody. If this parent attempts to communicate with a resistant coparent, he may also appear cooperative. When an abusive parent is granted primary custody, he or she becomes empowered by the courts to continue the campaign to control, manipulate, and intimidate. Ironically, a parent's concern about an abusive partner may ultimately have a negative influence on being granted custody.

IMPACT OF DOMESTIC VIOLENCE ON CHILDREN

Domestic violence, observed by a child of divorce, may negatively impact the child's development and sense of attachment in a similar way as those who experience direct physical and sexual abuse. The child's developmental mind is damaged and stunted by domestic violence. However, children do not have to see the violence or be the recipients of it to be seriously harmed. Children experience fear and isolation. They heal only after the nonoffending parent completes his or her own healing.

Experiences of Children of Domestic Violence

Neglect

Feelings of anger, helplessness, vulnerability, and confusion

Loss of childhood

Self-esteem damage

Increased behavioral and/or academic problems

Increased number of physical complaints

Lack of trust in parental figures

Overall higher levels of anxiety

Anticipatory anxiety over the next attack

Fear and insecurity

Increased separation anxiety in the young

Increased nighttime fears

Visitation refusal

Lack of confidence

May feel responsible for the violence

May identify with the batterer (believe violence is acceptable)

May bully children or animals

May identify with the victim

May develop suicidal/homicidal ideation

ANGER AND EMOTIONAL ABUSE

The tongue has the power of life and death.

Proverbs 18:21

As stated, abusive relationships are not always physical in nature. Abuse is any behavior that is focused on power and control. Therefore, abuse can be physical, sexual, and emotional. Anyone can become verbally abusive once in awhile. The angry person does so with much greater frequency. Some people are chronically involved in verbal abuse. Although these behaviors are less dangerous than physical abuse, they are nonetheless still inappropriately aggressive and must be addressed quickly by the PC in order to maintain an emotionally safe environment. The verbally abusive parent may exhibit behaviors in the following ways. He or she may

- Use sarcasm, ridicule, open insults, toxic language
- Attempt to manipulate by getting into the other person's face or standing too close
- Attempt to manipulate by blocking the other person from leaving
- Attempt to control and micromanage in an aggressive manner
- Not accept limits and will call back ten times if the other parent does not say what the abusive parent wants to hear
- Make demands rather than requests
- Use name-calling
- Withhold money as a form of economic abuse

According to Suzette Haden Elgin (1995, p. 36), "Verbal abusers are not interested in the answers to their questions or responses to their statements that would be expected in other circumstances. They are not interested, other than coincidentally, in the issues they raise." Elgin reported that verbal abusers are interested in only one of two outcomes:

1. A demonstration of their power to get and keep the attention of the person they are speaking to
2. An emotional reaction

Elgin also declared that verbal abusers may not be consciously aware of these goals and they may not be intending to inflict pain on other people. The verbal abuser falls into one of three groups. In order to help both the verbally abusive parent and the coparent, the parent coordinator should be able to understand the differences in each of the three groups in order to orchestrate the most appropriate intervention.

1. Those who are attempting to achieve one of the two goals just cited
2. Those who are unaware of any other way to deal with tension and conflict
3. Those who abuse verbally due to a psychological problem or unresolved trauma in their past

Stress placed on particular words by the speaker can create hostility. For example, the angry parent asks: "Why is your new husband coming to our son's game?" If the word "why" is stressed it may imply sarcasm. If the phrase "our son's game" is stressed, the message may sound possessive and exclusionary toward the stepfather. This is why some parents will read hostility into an e-mail in which hostility was not intended. The PC must be alert to these distinctions so that angry parents may come to understand the problematic nature of their style of communication rather than their choice of words.

SAFETY MEASURES

Whether or not a parent displays mild anger or has a history of domestic violence, the PC should be very careful to ensure the parents' physical and emotional safety in sessions and when they leave the building. Safety measures must be considered and addressed prior to the first joint session. Some safety options may include a combination of the following:

- Caucus or shuttle sessions
- Videotaped sessions
- Bringing someone to wait in the waiting room
- Bringing someone to sit in the session with them (not participating)
- Having the anxious parent sit with free access to the door or sit closer to the PC
- Having the anxious parent arrive and leave before the angry/aggressive parent

As the PC comes to know both parents and their behavioral patterns, safety measures may be relaxed over time. For example, some parents make false allegations against the coparent during the marriage and even during the divorce. Some coparents become highly anxious in situations that do not warrant their anxiety.

The easy task is to recognize angry parents; knowing how to manage their pain and their inappropriate behaviors is the more difficult task. In additon to setting limits, the experienced coordinator will take the techniques outlined in the next section and expand on their own repertoire.

ANGER-MANAGEMENT TECHNIQUES

Due to the number of conflicted parents with anger and substance abuse problems as well as Axis II diagnoses, parent coordination can be enhanced by an extensive repertoire of clinical skills, including the ability to step outside the box when necessary. The techniques highlighted in this section are suited for mild and moderate forms or anger, while others are designed for more severe forms of parental conflict. Furthermore, some techniques were created to be used in joint sessions while others are better suited for coaching sessions. The easiest and least intrusive techniques should be used first to avoid an escalation of anger.

Anger-Awareness Techniques

Cost of Anger

Although anger may work to coerce others to comply with our demands, it carries a very high price tag. The PC can help the angry parent to see that using anger to control others breeds more anger and/or passive-aggressive responses. The following common parenting problems demonstrate this dynamic and can be introduced by the PC.

> If you yelled at your young daughter to get into the tub, what would she do? Sure she would most likely run to get into the tub, but she might also be anxious or fearful of you. That is a high price for both of you.

> What would your teenager do if you lectured and threatened him about poor grades? Yes, he might not study at all just to get back at you. So, you see, sometimes our anger can make matters worse. The same applies when adults unfairly express their anger at each other. If you are interested in learning how to communicate without unnecessary anger I can coach you in a separate session.

Cost-Cost Activity

The cost-cost activity encourages parental cooperation and commitment by requiring parents to focus on the detrimental effects of parental hostility on their child by comparing and contrasting the costs and benefits of conflict and cooperation. In addition, this activity helps parents recognize any secondary gain when they remain in conflict. They tend to think that it would cost them or their child nothing to cooperate (the other parent is just the problem). Using the information outlined here, different possibilities can be explored with the parents as the eight headings are completed. The PC can create a chart on a piece of paper or duplicate one on a dry-erase board for the parents to complete during the session. This activity can also be done as a homework assignment. See Figures 10.1 and 10.2 for examples of completed charts.

Cost-Cost Parental Conflict	
What is the cost to the child?	**What is the cost to the parent?**
Loss of self-esteem/confidence	Always on your guard
Poor academic performance	Stress/anxiety/health problems
Stress/anxiety	Loss of sleep
Increased anger	Tension
Frustration/despair/depression	Frustration/despair
Lack of parental protection	Impact on spiritual life
Loyalty binds	Expense of ongoing litigation
Tension at parent transfers	Decline in work performance
Headaches/stomachaches	Stress on a new relationship/marriage
Responsibility for the break-up	
Inability to concentrate	Poor modeling of anger management
What is the benefit to the child?	**What is the benefit to the parent?**
Power	Rush of adrenaline
Ability to manipulate	Sense of power
	Fun of competition
	Satisfaction of revenge
	Satisfaction of "being right"
	Pleasure in blaming other parent
	Reward of being "victim"
	Negative attachment to former spouse

FIGURE 10.1. Cost-Cost Analysis of Parental Conflict

Cost-Cost Parental Cooperation	
What is the cost to the child? Give up inappropriate power Give up being a victim Give up negative attention Give up manipulation of parents	**What's the cost to the parent?** Give up the blame game Give up anger Give up being right Give up revenge Give up being a victim
What is the benefit to the child? Improved chance for happiness Self-esteem/confidence Security and protection Normal personality development Peaceful existence Reduced anger/tension Improved coping skills Improved relationships	**What's the benefit to the parent?** Improved chance for happiness Self-esteem/confidence Safety Decreased stress levels Peaceful existence Reduced anger/tension

FIGURE 10.2. Cost-Cost Analysis of Parental Cooperation

Many parents also find it difficult to identify the cost of cooperation for the child. When parents cooperate, some children may have to give up negative attention, manipulation, being spoiled, or power over others. If parents are struggling to complete this task, either give them additional time or complete it together.

Anger-As-a-Choice Activity

Some people do not recognize that anger is a choice. The PC can ask the parents to each identify something they believe they cannot do. Once they have identified these traits about themselves, the PC can ask the parents to recite the same sentence changing the word "can't" to "won't." This technique can be modeled by the PC by providing the following example: "I can't cook" to "I won't cook."

Next, the PC can encourage parents to use divorce/coparent examples. The parents write down two sentences that they often say about their relationship with their coparent starting with the words *I can't,* such as "I can't seem to talk civilly with my former partner." Then, the parents substitute the word *won't* for the word *can't.* Parents are asked how they reacted to this activity. Some parents will choke on their own words when they realize that it is really a decision that they can make. Parents can recognize that if the choice is theirs, then they are free to choose the result they want. They can come to understand that they are not controlled by their coparent or anyone else. They can choose their own direction.

Constructive versus Destructive Anger

Parents may not be able to distinguish between constructive and destructive uses of anger. More often than not, parents may believe that anger is associated with only negative consequences. This is especially true for the parent that believes all anger is dangerous in one way or another. Parents with strong religious beliefs are also at risk of fearing their own anger. To help parents recognize the positive consequences of anger, they may be asked the following questions:

> "What percentage of the time would you say your anger gets in the way?"
> "How will using your anger constructively influence your child's emotional well-being?"
> "Is your anger reactive or proactive?"

In addition, storytelling can be used to provide parents with examples of how anger can be used constructively. For instance, the PC might say, "I know a woman who was in a crippling car accident. She remained a prisoner in her own home for the first year following the accident before she allowed herself to experience her anger. She used her anger constructively, enrolled in school, and became a rehabilitation counselor."

Reframing and Rating Anger

Reframing can be a successful technique as long as the PC gently acknowledges the parent's pain without minimizing his or her defense mechanism. For example, instead of saying, "You're really not angry; you're just hurt that she left you," the PC can say, "I can see how angry and hurt you are about the divorce."

Identifying and rating core emotions is a simple intervention that can assist angry parents to manage their emotions and label their negative emotions into smaller "less angry" descriptions such as disappointed, irritated, annoyed, frustrated, angry, or explosive. They seem more comfortable covering their hurt with anger and indignation. Since anger is harder to soften than sadness, fear, and disappointment, the PC should work to transfer anger to a less intense emotion that may be easier for the parent to acknowledge (Figure 10.3).

Anger Metaphors

As identified in the previous chapter there are numerous examples of useful metaphors. This is especially true for anger metaphors, such as a pot that is boiling over. If the top is left on the pot and the pressure is held in, it will explode. Parents may be asked, "How would you best manage the boiling pot?" The PC can help the angry parent recognize that constructive options are available such as, "I'd turn down the heat." Containment activities can help parents avoid holding their anger in or letting it out. The PC can watch for indications of the angry parent's patience, tolerance, impulse control, or any other sign of "attempting to turn down the heat." Parents will benefit from encouragement and praise for any signs of improvement. For instance, the parent coordinator might say, "I noticed that you did not interrupt this time. I really appreciate how you are trying to hold back. I could see you breathing instead of interrupting."

FIGURE 10.3. Scale Used to Translate Anger into a Less Intense Emotion

Additional metaphors typically used to portray anger include dormant volcanoes, underground minefields, explosives, fireworks, containers under pressure, short fuses, flooding, thunderstorms, hurricanes, tornadoes, and a brewing storm.

Other metaphors more suited to the parents' experience can be used to describe their pain. Also, a more subtle anger metaphor can become a form of coaching that signals the angry parent in the presence of the coparent.

Impulse-Control Techniques

Anger problems usually involve impulse-control problems. Therefore, developing a variety of impulse-control techniques will assist the PC working with this population.

The STPA Technique

The PC can teach the parents jointly or in a coaching session how to use the STPA technique as follows.

Step 1. Stop: "When a situation suddenly occurs, such as your coparent leaving a last-minute message about a change in schedule, the first thing to do is to *stop* yourself from reacting immediately."

Step 2. Think: "Now is the time to start thinking. *Think* about the long-term goal for your child. Think about how you'd behave in a business relationship. Picture how you'd act if you were both in business suits in the middle of a group of businesspeople. Now double check your thinking by asking yourself, Am I trying to get something for myself here or can I put my interests aside temporarily to put my child's interests first?"

Step 3. Pause: "Now take another breath while you *pause*. Let it out slowly. Keep yourself from reacting. A fast comeback is not useful. Act as if you are almost in slow motion. The pause will seem longer than it really is. Clear your head by exhaling your emotions."

Step 4. Act: "Now you are ready to act. If you are unclear on how to respond, you may want to ask for time to consider the situation. If in doubt ask for time. Request an appointment to discuss the matter. If you choose to respond, just remember to use nonblaming I-statements. Consider alternative actions and problem-solving techniques. Then when you've decided what is truly in your child's best interest, take action."

Anger-Containment Techniques

In order to be successful in developing a cooperative relationship during and after the separation, former partners need to manage their anger in constructive ways. They must learn to identify it, contain it, defuse it, and use it productively. Once this occurs, their anger will diminish over time and their need to lash out at each other will decrease. Some techniques to contain anger include the following:

> Request that the parents record their issues on a piece of paper. The parent coordinator might say, "That sounds important and I want you to stop and write it down so you won't forget it. We will come back to it. For now, just take a moment and write a key word to remind yourself of your concern."
>
> If the anger is focused on past pain, it is important to identify this immediately and empathically instruct the parent to record (contain) the issue on an index card or on the last page of his or her parent guide. The PC should acknowledge the parent's pain while encouraging him or her to contain it in the session. The PC can also suggest that the parents participate separately in a ritual of some kind between sessions. The PC can assist the parent to visualize a safe container. For instance, the PC can begin by saying, "I realize that you are very upset, and I can see how your style seems to get in the way of being heard by your coparent. Would you be willing to try something different?" At this point, the coordinator has several options:
>
> - If any containers are present in the room the PC can ask the parent to imagine putting all the anger into one. Or, the parent coordinator can ask the parents to visualize one of their own containers. The parents can be advised to place or imagine themselves placing all their strong feelings into the container while they calm themselves.
> - The parent coordinator might say, "Can you sit on that feeling for just a minute? Okay, take a breath; now another one; that's good. Don't worry; you still have the right to your feeling and it is okay to calm yourself." The PC can suggest that they place their anger in their left hand while they focus on their child's photo.
>
> The angry parent can be asked to make a note of what he or she is feeling. In a coaching session, the PC can ask this parent to write a one-page letter to the other parent expressing these feelings. However, the parent coordinator must instruct the angry parent to mail the letter to the PC's office and not to the coparent. This should be done in

an empathic manner so the angry parent will not feel shamed or rejected by the parent coordinator.

Although old marital issues are not to be addressed in parent coordination, sometimes they resurface and impede the process of building collaboration. If both parents agree to use a session to address a specific past issue, consider allowing it. Make sure that they have mastered some of the communication skills before addressing an unresolved issue. The scope of the session should be clarified before they meet. Both parents need to be aware of exactly what will be discussed. To prepare for the session, both parents should be instructed to design an I-statement to be used at the beginning of the session. Clearly state to the parents that the goal of the session is to increase understanding.

Limit Setting

Expressions of anger and the threat of physical violence can jeopardize sessions and interfere with the coordinator's judgment, influencing his or her ability to remain objective and neutral throughout the process. In order to circumvent the adverse effects of these behaviors, the PC must immediately step in and firmly interrupt this pattern. Likewise, the parent coordinator should avoid getting into power struggles with one parent. Clear and specific limits should be administered. Often the best approach is to begin with positive interventions and intertwine them with increasing limits. Ground rules and limits should be discussed at the beginning of the first joint session.

> Step 1. Acknowledge the feelings: "It seems that you are having to struggle to contain your anger. Knowing that this is not the place for you to express your anger, can you think of anything that will help you control your reactions? Would it help if you left the room to get a drink of water?"

Whenever possible, the parent coordinator should both attempt to help the parent modify the aggressive behavior and consider referring him or her to community programs dealing with cognitive restructuring, grief work, or impulse control.

> Step 2. Clarify expectations: "I know that the circumstances can tempt you to react, but one of the goals of this process is to practice impulse control and manage your anger. I expect you to practice

these skills during our sessions as well as outside this room. When you start to yell or use obscenities it undermines your relationship with your child's other parent and therefore hurts your child. I need you to try the STPA technique (Stop, Think, Pause, and Act)."

If the behavior continues, the PC should describe the effect of the behavior on others. It is likely that the coparent will react to the aggressive behaviors. By calling attention to the behaviors the parent coordinator is letting the coparent know that the PC understands the dynamics occurring in the room and the effect they have on others. This is especially powerful for the coparent to witness, particularly if he or she has been intimidated by the aggressive parent's anger. This is generally a new experience for the aggressive parent who has become accustomed to defensive reactions from others. Now he or she is faced with someone calmly asserting a position.

Step 3. Set clear limits: "I feel concerned when you sit forward, point your finger, and raise your voice because it interferes with your attempts to be heard. I need you to sit back, take a deep breath, or leave the room for a short break."

If this is not successful, then the PC would move to the final step to manage the behaviors by firmly communicating that such behaviors will not be tolerated.

Step 4. Final limits with consequences: "If you can't calm down immediately, I will end the session. If that happens I will let the coparent leave while you stay here and calm down. You will be responsible for paying the full fee for the session. You decide."

If the angry coparent does not leave or calm down, the parent coordinator should stand up and say, "It looks like I need to call security."

Step 5. Termination: Although step five is rarely necessary, it is important to follow through and appear calm.

The parent coordinator should not assume that each step must be used with every acting-out parent. Depending upon the parent's internal anger management, the parent coordinator may need to move to step 4 or 5 and eliminate the request for cooperation. The PC must know the unique needs of each parent and be aware of their reactive styles and limitations. The PC should intervene as soon as possible rather than wait for the anger to erupt. Through early intervention, the PC can model the ability to identify the parents' early frustration signs prior to their actions. When dealing with aggressive parents do not schedule joint sessions after work hours. In addition, coparents should not walk out of the office and building together.

Relaxation Techniques

A referral to another provider may help an agitated parent learn relaxation and stress-management techniques. However, the PC can always teach basic deep-breathing techniques jointly or in a coaching session. Parents may be told that deep breathing and anxiety cannot coexist. Deep breathing can trick the body into believing that there is no state of alarm.

Parents can also be taught to give themselves permission to take a "time-out" whenever necessary. A "time-out" can even be encouraged during the session. The PC informs the parents that either one may step out of the room if they need a break for any reason, including to manage their anger. However, parents must learn to verbalize their intent to return to the room.

Cognitive Restructuring Techniques

"The driving force behind hostility is a cynical mistrust of others. Expecting that others will mistreat you, we are on the lookout for their bad behavior—and we can usually find it" (Williams, 1989, p. 26). The most effective intervention for anger or impulse problems is a cognitive-behavioral approach. Albert Ellis's rational emotive therapy, the basic framework for cognitive restructuring, is an essential element to assist parents manage their anger and develop effective conflict resolution skills. It emphasizes the role of the irrational belief system as the root of the problem. Through cognitive restructuring, parents are taught to change their negative beliefs to help them manage their anger and other emotions. As a result, they are in a better position to develop and use effective conflict-resolution skills.

More often than not, high-conflict divorcing couples accept self-indoctrinated beliefs that perpetuate the animosity between them. Johnston and Campbell (1988) stated that the extremely negative views of divorcing couples become fixed, confirmed by society, and validated by years of conflictual interactions with each other. Recently, Gottman (1994a) stipulated that divorcing couples experience an increase in aversive interactions by the time they have reached separation. Negative interaction outweighs positive exchanges. Hence, negative attributions about each other become generalized, exaggerated, and fixed. Thus, by the time they divorce, couples do not expect to be able to work cooperatively. It seems hopeless, impossible, and contradictory to their decisions to divorce. Until the parents are able to change their belief systems they will not be able to make necessary communication changes.

It is important that parents feel thoroughly understood, but it is equally important not to promote and reinforce distorted views. To do so places the PC in a compromising position. The coordinator runs the risk of misleading the parent and reifying polarized positions. With gentle persuasion and lots of support, parents are challenged to identify their distorted beliefs and replace them with constructive realistic thoughts. Parents are taught that the situations they encounter, particularly their coparent's behavior, are not what causes them distress, but rather how they interpret the event and behaviors. With the assistance of the PC, parents learn to identify distorted beliefs, replace them with realistic thoughts, and recognize how their own actions trigger the other parent's response.

Common Irrational Beliefs

Several common beliefs or themes generally emerge among separating or separated parents. These themes tend to center around trust, power, and control and include the language of always and never:

> "I can never trust her!"
> "He is always going to control me."
> "He can never be a good parent."
> "I am right and she is wrong."
> "He never ever loved me."
> "She does not consider the needs of our child."

As themes evolve, the PC should openly identify them and challenge the parents to replace their distorted beliefs and illusions with realistic thoughts. In the early stages of the process parents may exhibit significant resistance and even shock when they are asked to consider a different set of beliefs. Even so, the PC continues to interject new information or interpretations that challenge the parents' unrealistic views. For example, the parent may believe the coparent will always be controlling. The coparent could be asked to restate this belief, while changing the word "always" to "sometimes." Although the parent will debate the revised belief, the coordinator must keep pointing out that the parents have nothing to lose and everything to gain from shifting their position.

In many instances of high-conflict divorce, parents have a difficult time separating their reality of the divorce from the other parent's relationship with the child. For instance, if the father walked out on the mother, then the mother may believe that the father will abandon the child. Consequently, an essential element is to separate the world of the parents from that of their child. Cognitive restructuring is also helpful under these circumstances.

To introduce cognitive restructuring it is useful to present examples in the following order:

Example 1. Begin with a nondivorce-related example.
- *Activating trigger:* Son leaves book bag at the front door even after being told not to do so.
- *Beliefs:* "He is so defiant!"/"He doesn't care about what I say."/"He is going to grow up to be a slob and it will be a reflection on me!"
- *Emotional consequences:* Irritation, frustration, anger, hurt
- *Action:* Parent yells at the child.

Using the same trigger, the PC then suggests the following change in belief:

- *Beliefs:* "He is in such a hurry to take the dog out that he forgets. This doesn't mean anything."
- *Emotional consequences:* Only slight irritation.
- *Action:* Talks to son and asks him to offer a solution that will work for him.

Example 2. The PC selects a trigger that has occurred while working with the parents. Using themselves to demonstrate, the PC might identify an example similar to the following:
- *Activating trigger:* Mother consistently comes late to our joint sessions.
- *Beliefs:* "She doesn't really want to be here."/"She is not going to comply with this program."/"She is testing limits."
- *Emotional consequences:* Irritation, frustration, concern
- *Action:* Confront the parent or hold it against her.

Next, the PC demonstrates what would happen if he or she could erase the negative beliefs, thus changing the outcome.

- *Same activating trigger:* Mother consistently comes late to sessions.
- *Modified belief:* "The mother is working too hard and handling more than her share of the parenting responsibilities."

- *Emotional consequences:* Compassion, understanding, mild irritation
- *Action:* Gently ask what can be done to get her to the appointments on time.

If the parents are mildly conflicted, all four examples can be completed with both parents in a joint session. If they are highly reactive, only Examples 1 and 2 should be done together. Personal examples involving the coparent should be completed in a coaching session or with another provider.

> Example 3. The PC then asks the parents to select an example from something that has happened in their joint sessions.
> Example 4. The PC then allows the parents to select issues from those that have occurred between sessions.

While following this progression, with each negative belief presented, parents are asked to create one positive or neutral response.

To benefit from all the techniques and strategies, parents must continually challenge their beliefs about their coparent. Otherwise, they will become conditioned only to react. They will watch for every opportunity to "prove" that their negative assumptions are accurate while ignoring behaviors that could refute their negative beliefs. In addition, parents will watch carefully to guard against a perceived attack. As this happens, distorted and distress-maintaining thoughts become the rule.

Negative Beliefs

Parents can be asked to record their negative beliefs on a piece of paper to bring to the next joint session. The PC helps them recognize how other situations trigger the familiar, yet negative, beliefs they harbor about each other. Parents are asked to create a belief that leads to less intense feelings. For example: "He wants to control my life" can be changed to "He is concerned about our child and it comes out sounding controlling." Also, "She is a liar" can be changed to "I am having difficulty trusting my coparent." Any improvement should be noted as progress. Encourage small steps, but expect strong resistance.

The parents' negative beliefs generally become their primary resistance and, therefore, the primary focus of attention. The parent coordinator can continue to uncover the parents' negative beliefs and attempt to move each parent to a more realistic view of the situation.

At times, a parent's belief may be reality based and not exaggerated. Also, at times it may be physically dangerous to change a belief such as in situations of physical abuse ("He will try to physically hurt me again") or neglect ("She always got drunk on the weekends even when she had our child"). Therefore, be sure to explore all potential risks. For instance, refer parents for alcohol assessment, request periodic drug screening, set up therapeutic visitation, make outside referrals, or conduct unscheduled home visits. If in doubt, thoroughly investigate the situation.

According to Gottman (1994b), the most destructive aspect of a troubled marriage is when "partners seize on powerful thoughts and beliefs about their spouse that cement their negativity" (p. 102). He also stated that the couple's inner thoughts must be challenged or else the marriage will collapse. In the same manner, the conflicted postdivorce relationship will not improve until the parents are willing to chip away at the cement that holds their negative beliefs together. Gottman also concluded that during conflict couples tend to use thoughts that are either "self-soothing" or "distress maintaining." He used the term *flooding* to describe the physiological response that occurs when a person experiences "system overload." Negative inner thoughts are the basis of flooding. Flooding will cause a reactive response, generally hostile, intended to counterattack, defend, or withdraw. Gottman (1994b) stated, "If your inner script is dominated by thoughts that exacerbate your negative feelings, rather than soothe, you are likely to become flooded in response to defensiveness, anger and stonewalling" (p. 120). This is particularly true for parents in high-conflict divorce. The hallmark of success is the ability to challenge their own distorted beliefs.

Distorted Beliefs

The majority of negative beliefs that upset us are distorted. When parents maintain rigid negative beliefs about the other parent they rarely pay attention to their own contribution to the conflict. Instead they are locked into endless fights over who is to blame for the conflict and ultimately the distress of their child. The way they perceive the problem determines the way they believe it should be solved. Consequently, neither parent is doing anything to solve the problem other than suggesting that the other parent should change. It is imperative that parents understand that as long as they continue to blame the coparent and maintain negative beliefs, they will never be successful. The PC must challenge their damaging thoughts while highlighting any attempts the parents make to focus on their own solutions.

Escalating Triggers

In some circumstances, it may be helpful to point out the reciprocal nature of the parents' interactions that may escalate conflict. Generally, the interaction between two individuals can be viewed in one of two ways. Parents may be involved in behaviors that invite conflict because they try to outdo each other. For instance, the more one parent attacks, the more the other counterattacks. On the other hand, parents may be engaged in behaviors that are in opposition to each other. For example, the mother may overly exaggerate her concerns regarding the father's child-rearing practices because she perceives him to be insensitive to their child's needs. The father may be more relaxed about child-rearing matters because he believes that the mother is too uptight about such matters and exaggerates each event. In essence, each parent tries to make up for the supposed inappropriate behaviors of the other by doing more of the opposite, resulting in a polarized stance. As in many other situations, parents need to recognize that it is not an either/or proposition, but rather that both parents are contributing to the event.

Once parents have grasped a general understanding of cognitive restructuring, they are shown how their actions trigger the other parent's negative belief system. The concept of "escalating triggers" is used to show how parental actions are reciprocal and interactive. Each action triggers a reaction. By examining how each parent's action triggers the coparent's negative belief system, the interplay between the parents can be interrupted.

Reframing Activity

The PC will find that one or both parents may hold on to negative expectations about the coparent. This creates unnecessary difficulties for the whole family. For example, angry parents are more likely to believe that everything their child might tell them is the truth. This allows the angry parents to feed their own negative beliefs. Rather than become frustrated with this common occurrence, the PC can draw a simple picture frame similar to the one illustrated in Figure 10.4.

Parents visualize the other parent's face inside the frame along with their thoughts and expectations. The PC places negative (–) signs around the picture frame with a couple of positive (+) signs. Next, the PC asks the parents to consider the outcome of harboring a negative view of the coparent: "If you expect the worst, what do you think will be the outcome? When we expect something negative to happen, it usually does. If parents believe their child will never amount to anything they usually end up being correct."

The PC then changes most of the negative symbols to positive ones, similar to the frame in Figure 10.5. The parents are asked to consider the following: "If you expect the best, what do you think will be the outcome? When we expect the best, we may be right or we may end up wrong, but at least we have a *chance* of getting what we want."

Coaching Techniques

If a parent needs only one or two coaching sessions (mild to moderate versus historical anger problems), then the PC can proceed as long as the

FIGURE 10.4. Negative Expectation Frame

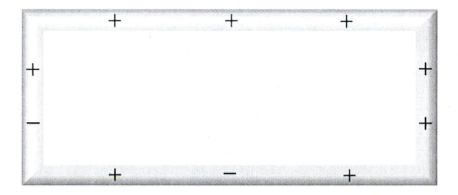

FIGURE 10.5. Positive Expectation Frame

coparent feels comfortable with the private coaching session. Otherwise, the same goals or issues could be shared with the angry parent's individual therapist.

Role-Play

During the coaching sessions, angry parents can practice changing their negative responses to more constructive reactions. The PC can use the parents' typical triggers and set up a situation in a role-play. Role-play of this nature should be done after parents have learned how to change their beliefs through cognitive restructuring exercises. For more on coaching techniques see Chapter 11.

Modeling Techniques

Modeling is one of the most powerful techniques available to the PC. Modeling can be used in many different ways. The PC is in an ideal position to teach through his or her own behaviors in coaching and joint sessions alike. Specifically the PC can model impulse control, humility, maturity, and the effective use of I-statements and reflective listening.

Similarly, the parent coordinator can intervene and offer assistance to the angry parent who has not yet learned to use effective communication skills. Both modeling and coaching can be done with the parent individually or in a joint session. For example, the parent coordinator may say,

> "Tom, I noticed that you become easily agitated and raise your voice when Judy does not seem to be listening to you. I can imagine how frustrating that must be for you. However, the way you react may interfere with your ability to be heard by Judy. Would it be okay if I stop you and help you to learn a new way to express yourself that may lead to a better outcome? May I pretend to be you just for a minute? I will try to communicate to Judy what I think you are trying to say. I want you to notice what I do differently. For instance, I am not going to point my finger at Judy. I am going to speak calmly rather than forcefully. Are you ready?"
>
> [Parent coordinator to Judy] "Let me try to say this in a different way for Tom. 'I feel really annoyed when I ask for a change in the schedule and you immediately say no without hearing me out. This is especially annoying when I have been trying to be a little more flexible with you. What I would like is for you to hear me out before you respond to my request.'"

The modeling of I-statements and reflective listening are always the first place to start with the mild to moderately angry client.

Bibliotherapy

Although parent coordination is not therapy, bibliotherapy can be useful to the process. Anger-related books to refer parents to include but are not limited to Carter and Minirth (1993), Burns (1999), Sapolsky (1998), Potter-Efron and Potter-Efron (1995), and Cullen (1992).

Anger Log

The PC may encourage the angry parent to keep a log or journal of angry feelings to practice rating and using cognitive-restructuring techniques during the week. Angry parents, much like anxious clients, want to run away from their uncomfortable feelings rather than wade through the feeling. They must learn to tolerate the emotion without acting upon it. However, the PC should never adopt the role of the parent's therapist. If intensive treatment is needed, the parent should be referred to a competent professional.

Some other coaching goals for the angry parent might include the following:

1. Inoculate the parent by practicing role-play situations that "light their fuse."
2. Practice using communication skills with the PC playing the role of the coparent.
3. Teach them that problems are issues to be solved rather than some type of provocation.
4. Coach them to use other words such as *hurt, abandoned, anxious, lonely, annoyed, irritated, disappointed,* or *frustrated.*
5. Coach them to recognize that they have choices.
6. Coach them to imagine their anger at 100 percent and then lower it to a 75 percent intensity.
7. Teach that taking a time-out is a manner of exerting control.
8. Coach with cognitive-restructuring skills to change their internal scripts.
9. Teach them how to analyze the chain of reaction. For example, "Help me see how you went from _____ to _____."
10. Identify their "should" or "ought" but do not dispute it. Help them to see how they can shift from a rigid rule to live by to a preference to live by.

11. Teach them the difference between request versus demand:
    Preference/request: "I would like it this way."
    Demand: "It has to be this way."
12. Incorporating the parents' sessions on videotape to be used as a re-
    view of the parents' actions and to determine how successful they
    were in accomplishing what they wanted.
13. Practicing "exit lines." Teach the parents to value time-out rather
    than to see it as hostile or avoidant behavior.

Other Techniques for Managing Anger

Validating Anger with Reflective Listening

It is helpful to validate the angry parent's indignation even though he or
she may overreact to a transgression. For instance, the PC might say, "I can
see how upsetting it is for you when she neglects to call when you have
asked this before" or "You're annoyed when he does not have your son return your call as planned."

Interrupting the Blame Game

The PC can frame the parents' resistance to taking responsibility for their
anger by using some of the following phrases to interrupt their pattern of
blaming the coparent: "I can see how upset you are. However, I hate to see
you give all your power away to your coparent" or "I can see how much
power she has over you. That must be very frustrating."

The PC may also want to "tell" parents through storytelling the importance of acknowledging our part of interpersonal conflict. A story can be
told about a man who was married four times. Each time he got a divorce he
claimed it was never his fault. The only thing he felt responsible for was
"picking really poorly." The PC ends by saying this man was not very mature and that if the parents start dating they had better be able to tell the next
romantic interest what was their part of the failed marriage or they should
run for the hills!

Cognitive Dissonance

It is very difficult to dislike someone who not only likes us but also respects us. If someone you do not like gives you a real compliment it causes
you to reevaluate your feelings. We tend to admire, respect, and like someone once we are told that they have some positive feelings for us. This is

called reciprocal affection. When a parent asks the coparent for help this can also create a shift in attitude. Asking for help to solve a computer problem increases self-esteem, reduces anger (at least temporarily), and may result in an improved coparent relationship. However, this does not apply when asking the coparent for additional time with their child. The PC can coach parents to compliment and request assistance in a manner that will create this shift.

Reshaping the Parent's Self-Esteem

If the PC wants the parent to be less tense and reactive, the PC can say, "I admire how well you handled yourself just then." If the PC wants a parent to become more flexible with the coparent, the PC can notice a small sign of flexibility and say, "I appreciate how flexible and child focused you can be." The parents will be compelled to act in line with the PC's image of them.

Permission to Reject a Suggestion

The PC can give parents the permission to not do something. Instead of saying, "I want you to be more flexible," say, "You don't need to be flexible if you don't want to." This gives the parents the power to cooperate rather than having to comply. A request puts a person in charge. That is why a flight attendant says "take your seat" rather than sit down, which would put her in charge. However, it is essential that the PC recognize that this is only a technique to encourage behavioral change. If it does not, then the PC must not hesitate to be more direct.

Praise and Encouragement

The key is to give angry parents what they crave at times when they are not upset. In this way, the PC becomes the angry parent's source of psychological nourishment. Therefore, they are unable to bite the proverbial hand that feeds their psyche. The PC can also teach the other parent in a coaching session how to manage this skill with the angry coparent.

The mild to moderately angry parent may respond positively to praise from the PC. It is important that the PC praise in a manner that does not seem condescending. For instance, "I noticed you wanted to sit forward and interrupt her again, but you didn't. I want you to know I appreciate your catching yourself."

Indirect Criticism

The angry parent is often a fragile individual. Therefore, criticism is likely to increase his or her anger. PCs can use themselves or another client to illustrate a particular problem. For example, instead of "You really made a big mistake with your teenager," the PC can say, "When my own teenager tells me I am embarrassing her it seems so ridiculous, but I have to work to be sensitive to her feelings. Unfortunately, sometimes I forget and I really feel badly." Or "I had a family that I worked with in which the teenage child refused to be seen with her father because he wore his work uniform when he picked her up from school. He had to learn how to take this into consideration rather than be mad at her reaction." The PC can use an I-statement to acknowledge the inappropriate behavior. This will allow the PC to be supportive and not hypercritical.

Education

Both parents can be taught the definition of insanity: "Insanity is doing the same thing over and over expecting different results." Some parents will identify with this expression from the frustration of being a parent and also from their former marriage. Parents can be taught to apply this concept to the coparenting relationship. For example, if the parent has a pattern of interrupting the coparent and it does not result in success, why should they continue this behavior? If the parent has a pattern of running late and the coparent complains unsuccessfully, why continue to complain? This type of education can point out to parents their unproductive patterns.

In a coaching session, the PC can educate the angry parent on the physical damage that anger can have on their body. Information about hypertension, heart disease, ulcers, and cancer can be a real wake-up call for the angry parent. Using the child's picture, the PC can ask the angry parent how the child would react if the angry parent died prematurely. This may seem like shock therapy, but sometimes fear is necessary.

Communication Skills

Teaching parents how to use effective communication can be a very important skill for reducing anger. Teaching parents to use the 3 Ps and other communication skills found in Chapter 9 can be reinforced during coaching and joint sessions.

Use of Forgiveness

Some parents choose to carry their anger and bitterness like a badge. Unless a parent has serious emotional problems, the PC can assist parents to defuse their anger by considering the concept of forgiveness. Some parents will be open to the idea of forgiveness because they have become aware of the negative impact their anger has on their child. If the parents are resistant to this concept then the PC should not continue in this vein. However, if a parent requires ongoing treatment to assist in the process of forgiveness, a referral to a qualified professional for this service is in order.

Everett Worthington (2001) uncovered significant information focusing on forgiveness that may be helpful to the parent coordinator assisting the angry client. In his book *Five Steps to Forgiveness: The Art and Science of Forgiving,* Worthington reported:

1. Anger-prone people are three times more likely to have a heart attack or bypass surgery.
2. Men who are better at diffusing anger had half as many strokes as angrier men.
3. Women who harbor feelings of anger are four times more likely to have unhealthy cholesterol levels and higher body mass index, which are both linked to heart disease.

Parents need to be reminded that forgiveness

1. does not mean that you condone the coparent's behavior.
2. does not mean your pain is not real or not justified.
3. does not mean you have to receive an apology.
4. does not mean reconciliation.

Humor

> Humor is the great thing, the saving thing after all. The minute it crops up, all our hardnesses yield, all our irritations and resentments flit away, and a sunny spirit takes their place.
>
> Mark Twain

Humor has a therapeutic effect. Although the use of humor may be viewed as an easy way to decrease tension, a therapist and parent coordinator must be careful not to use humor too soon or in a way that will insult either parent. Humor should never be used to join with either parent at the expense of the other. Some parents may actually relax in the first joint session with a little humor in the form of playfulness. For example:

> Did the two of you speak in the waiting room? You did. That's great. You are already ahead of some parents who won't even look at each other (or even grunt when spoken to!).

If this type of comment does not reduce tension, then this technique should not be used for several more sessions, if at all.

Parental Feedback

Throughout the program, the PC offers feedback to parents. This feedback can be especially helpful with impulse-control problems. Feedback forms may highlight parental interactions as well as each parent's strengths and weaknesses. Usually, this feedback is offered at the end of the session. By offering the information at the end of the session parents cannot qualify the observations and thereby dilute the parent coordinator's message or become distracted during the session. Parents are given the opportunity to discuss feedback sheets by arranging an individual session. Time during joint sessions is not used to address the feedback. Likewise, a requested feedback appointment cannot involve any discussion about the coparent or sharing of secrets.

Not all parents respond favorably to or comprehend this type of feedback. When parents are involved in individual therapy it is useful to send the feedback sheets directly to the therapist with the permission of the parent. Some parents benefit from video examples of their behavior.

Referrals for Treatment

When the parent's anger is such that outside treatment will be necessary, the PC should make a referral privately so as not to embarrass the angry parent in front of the coparent. However, if the parent is unwilling to comply with the parent coordinator's recommendation, then a memo should be sent to both attorneys indicating the parent's lack of compliance. Whenever possible the PC should make the recommendation for "impulse control" treatment rather than "anger management." The PC should avoid using the term *abusive* and use the terms *healthy versus unhealthy anger* when appropriate.

Dealing with Noncompliance and Angry Parents

In dealing with chronic noncompliance on the part of one or both parents, the PC must gain the support of the guardian and/or attorneys. The parent coordinator may also adopt the following statement when trying to encourage cooperation:

> It is important for you to know that I have recorded in my notes the behaviors that are interfering with your ability to cooperate and comply with the program requirements. It is my job to bring these to the attention of the judge/guardian. I wonder if there is anything I can do to help you?

Before notifying the judge, the PC must be sure to read the court order or settlement agreement carefully in order to clarify whether the judge is to receive information regarding the case. In some situations, it will not be stipulated, meaning the PC must not send any memos to the court. To do so under these circumstances will only antagonize the situation. If a guardian has been assigned to the family, and the guardian has ordered the parents to participate in parent coordination, reports should be addressed to the guardian and copied to each attorney. Likewise, when parents are participating in the program because it was mandated in the final settlement agreement, the PC will need to clarify with the parents' attorneys the degree to which the attorneys will still be involved in the case and if they want to receive memos. Once a final settlement has been reached, the attorneys may no longer be involved in the case.

Keep in mind that any time attorneys receive memos and updates, the PC runs the risk of involving them in an adversarial process. The CPI model of parent coordination asks parents to agree not to become involved in adversarial proceedings while they are working with a PC. The PC can remind the attorneys that their clients have made this agreement. This reminder can be in the form of a brief comment during a telephone conversation, a sentence in a cover letter, or a short memo.

In general, when dealing with chronic noncompliance and/or inappropriate behaviors, the PC may consider the following options:

Consult with the guardian if one has been appointed to the case. Explore alternatives and brainstorm solutions. Invite the guardian to sit in on a conjoint session. A guardian can be your best ally.

Recommend a temporary break in the program while one parent becomes involved in individual therapy to address specific time-limited issues. Design the treatment goals for the individual therapy and send copies of the goals to each attorney. Contact the individual therapist on weekly or biweekly basis in order to monitor the treatment. During consultations with the therapist discuss the focus of treatment and explore the therapist's ability to view the problem from a systems perspective versus aligning with the client's worldview. At times, a therapist may accept and heighten a parent's distorted reality. Also, explore the therapist's willingness to coordinate treatment goals and make arrangements for periodic consultations. It may be necessary to exchange sessions notes after a release has been obtained from both parents. If the therapist is compromising the treatment of the parent and adversely affecting the parent coordination process, it may be necessary, assuming you have authority from the court to do so, to make a referral to a different therapist. Offer the parent three names of reputable systems-oriented therapists that the PC has worked with in the past.

Audio- or videotape a session to document noncompliance. The noncompliant parent will usually declare that the parent coordinator is biased and favors the other parent. A videotaped session may help the parent objectively observe his or her behaviors. Furthermore, the noncompliant parent can also be advised to watch for supportive behaviors directed toward him or her from the coordinator. More often than not, the parent has not acknowledged these behaviors during the sessions. Never allow either parent to leave the office with a video- or audiotape. The tapes should always remain with the parent coordinator. If it would be useful for the individual therapist to view the tape, this should be arranged between the two professionals with the permission of both parents. If the parents are required to view the tape as part of a homework assignment, require them to schedule a time to view it in the office. Another reason to videotape sessions is to protect the PC from hostile parents who may threaten to complain to the licensing board or the judge. Acquire the parents' consent for videotaping at the first joint session.

Close the case and notify all parties of this action. When a parent is in contempt of court and refusing to follow the judge's order, the judge cannot act on the contempt unless charges are filed by the opposing attorney and brought before the judge. However, in some jurisdictions, the court will track compliance and initiate their own contempt actions. It is essential to become very familiar with the law and policies of the courts. Even though the PC may temporarily close a case, he or she still may become involved in the future.

Use of Consequences

Consequences are structural interventions designed to alter behavior. Consequences are not punishment. The intent is not harm but rather to motivate a person to make better choices. The legal system refers to consequences as sanctions. It is imperative that the parent coordinator record all other previous attempts to change behaviors and to interrupt patterns that adversely affect the children. Consequences should, whenever possible, consider the child's needs and not be used to punish a parent. Some consequences to consider are the following:

> *Inconvenience:* When the parents meet halfway and one is chronically late, the tardy parent could be made responsible for transporting the child both ways for several weekends.
>
> *Time Modifications:* If a pattern has developed in which one parent transitions the child thirty minutes to an hour later than agreed upon, the parent coordinator can design a temporary time-sharing plan that would require the tardy parent to transition the child thirty minutes to an hour earlier the following transition. As with any consequence, it is important to frame it positively rather than imply punishment. It is equally important to state it in concrete terms and to reflect a child focus. For instance, the parent coordinator might say, "Frank, it looks like you are having difficulty being on time when you return your child to his other home. This seems to upset your child and his mother. You know by now that this can cause stress for your child. What I think would be helpful is to delay your pickup time by thirty minutes whenever you run late thirty minutes or more at the previous visit. This arrangement will start this weekend and occur for the next four weeks. If you are late, equal time will be deducted on Sunday."
>
> *Restricted Time-Sharing Arrangements:* Parents who choose not to comply with agreements that protect their children's emotional and physical needs can be assigned to supervised visitation. For instance, temporary supervised visitation can be recommended for a parent who chooses to use alcohol while sharing time with his or her child.
>
> *Continued Negative Comments About the Other Parent:* This parent could be assigned to come to a session early to review videotapes of older children speaking about how similar behaviors created stress for them while growing up and how they eventually turned against the parent that made these comments.

Fees for Services: Chronically late parents can be responsible for paying the majority of the session fee instead of splitting the fee equally between parents as outlined in the program expectations form. For instance, the tardy parent can pay 60 percent of the session while the other parent pays 40 percent.

Scheduling Alternatives: Parents who do not comply with orders stipulating that they must provide the other parent with a vacation schedule by a designated date can forfeit their right to select the vacation time. The other parent can designate the noncompliant parent's vacation time.

Written Updates: Noncompliance as well as disruptive behaviors can be recorded on feedback sheets and then sent to the guardian or attorneys.

Assignment Completion: Incomplete assignments can be reassigned until they are satisfactory. Individual sessions to complete assignments may have to be arranged, which will also result in an added expense for the noncompliant parent.

Limit Setting: Parents demonstrating disruptive behaviors can be asked to leave the session and required to pay the full fee for the joint session.

Defusing Anger

At some point in the separation process, parents will experience various degrees of anger. High-conflict couples generally experience greater difficulty dealing with this emotion. More often than not, parents going through a divorce respond with grief, hurt, and fear associated with the end of the partnership. Others are retriggered years postdivorce by new situations such as remarriage or relocation.

During joint sessions, hostile interactions are likely to erupt and require skilled management by the coordinator. Techniques designed specifically for the angry parent may also be used to assist parents exhibiting other difficulties. Chapter 11 highlights general techniques and strategies utilized in the CPI model.

Chapter 11

General Techniques and Strategies

To enhance the process of parent coordination, active interventions based on systems theory and behavioral, cognitive, and experiential techniques have been provided. While working with high-conflict separating parents, parent coordinators must adopt an active and directive approach with strong limit setting. Baris and colleagues (2001, p. 147) recommended,

> The parent coordinator should think of him/herself as a good parent—
> one who is caring; sets appropriate limits and expectations; motivates,
> model empathy, honesty, and integrity; handles conflict fairly; and
> confronts with compassion the pain that underlies the "bad" behavior.

The overall focus of parent coordination is to unsettle the family system to allow for change rather than focus on restructuring the whole family system. Parent coordination focuses on minimizing conflict between parents for the protection of the children.

Although it is recognized by most systems therapists that change in one part of the system will produce change in other parts of the system, parent coordinators are faced with the question of determining where they should focus their inquiry and influence change in a multilevel and very complex system. The coordinator must weave together relatively general and opposing views which may or may not be useful in integrating the information in a systemic and comprehensive way. A focus on the immediate family, namely the parents, would be a logical starting point. Any small change in the interaction of the problem, strategically directed, may in fact lead to beneficial change.

When dealing with the divorcing population it is necessary to carefully structure interventions. Most therapies involve some means for providing the therapist direction over treatment outcome. Although parent coordination is not therapy, it must also provide a structure to effectively generate change. This chapter provides a multitude of techniques to assist the parent coordinator in this endeavor. However, under no circumstance should a parent coordinator persist in using a technique or approach that is not working.

To do so may invite resistance, reduce credibility, and negatively influence the process. Ultimately, the PC should be constantly assessing the process to determine if the parents are accepting and assimilating new information as well as new skills. The techniques and strategies utilized by the parent coordinator must be designed to meet the needs of the particular family system.

In some cases, the parent coordinator must look for the least detrimental solution rather then the best possible solution. In situations of parental alienation and high-conflict divorce, sometimes the intervention suited for the best interests of the child is the one that will produce the fewest adverse effects for the family, particularly the child. Due to the complexity of the family system, the issues associated with divorce, limited research, and the developmental needs of children, it is difficult to identify a "perfect solution."

Behavioral expectations assist the PC structure the environment, maintain order, create a sense of safety, and provide a model for constructive interaction. By explicitly establishing ground rules, the PC creates an atmosphere that builds on positive collaboration and minimizes negative interaction. The parent coordinator must communicate that he or she is in charge of each session. Therefore, it is necessary to set limits on behaviors as well as topics of discussion in order to curb impulses, encourage parents to take responsibility for their behaviors, and develop skills that lead to parental cooperation. The parent coordinator must be willing to direct and manage each session by

> Consistently reinforcing behavioral expectations
> Combining firmness with empathy
> Ending destructive sessions or interactions
> Holding parents accountable for their behavior
> Providing feedback that will lead to behavioral change

Behavioral expectations are presented to parents in the form of verbal and written communication at the beginning of the first joint session. Providing a written expectation form for the parents at the beginning of the first joint session will minimize confusion and clarify parental responsibilities.

General Program Expectations

Expectations regarding program requirements may include

> Clarification that parent coordination is not therapy
> Payment for services and cancellation policies

Procedures for contacting the parent coordinator
Confidentiality issues
Emergency procedures
Involvement of the legal system
Temporary changes to the court order

Parental Expectations

Parents are expected to do the following:

1. *Maintain a child focus:* Parents are expected to view each situation from a child's perspective. They are encouraged to focus on the needs of their children rather than their personal needs.
2. *Maintain a present focus:* Discussions regarding past marital issues are discouraged if they have no bearing on the present relationship between parents or the relationships between children and parents.
3. *Demonstrate impulse control:* Parents are required to practice the anger-management techniques highlighted in the model as soon as possible.
4. *Show courteous and respectful behaviors:* A business relationship is modeled in each session. Parents are encouraged to conduct themselves in a businesslike manner by practicing courteous behaviors. They are asked not to interrupt another person or dominate the time.
5. *Treat each other as partners in parenting:* While maintaining a child focus, parents are encouraged to view each other with equal importance in the life of their child. Although the time the child spends with each parent may be different, parents learn to view their parenting responsibilities as having equal value.
6. *Work on new behaviors between sessions:* Parents are required to complete homework assignments between sessions to reinforce concepts learned in the session. They are also instructed to use the new skills when interacting with their coparent outside the sessions.
7. *Remain focused on one issue at a time:* In order to reach mutual decisions on their child's behalf, parents are taught to focus on one issue at a time before moving on to another issue.
8. *Separate the issue from the person:* Parents are expected to focus on an issue rather than attacking their coparent.
9. *Honor the divorce rules:* Parents are strongly encouraged to review them with their children, and post them in their home. The divorce rules are listed on page 17 of the *Cooperative Parenting and Divorce* workbook.

As parents learn new behaviors, control their impulses, and begin mastering effective communication and negotiation skills, the parent coordinator may not need to rigidly reinforce these ground rules. Yet the coordinator must recognize that the topics of discussion might increase the probability that parents may not always be able to control and manage their behavior.

ENCOURAGING COOPERATION
AND FOSTERING COMMITMENT

Judges, attorneys, and guardians ad litem have typically referred resistant families for mandated treatment. Consequently, parents may or may not be personally invested in making changes to improve the family circumstances, particularly the parent-parent relationship. Some parents will participate with minimal expectations of success while others come in with high expectations. The PC must determine (1) the parents' motivation to change and whether their level of motivation can be increased, (2) how much the parents are impacted by their hostile circumstances, and (3) the distress of their children.

If it is determined that a parent does not see any value in the program, the PC can tailor the program to meet the specific needs of that parent. For example, the parent coordinator, during the first individual intake session, may begin by saying to the resistant parent,

> "Let me see if I understand your dilemma. In the past you have tried to make decisions about your child with your coparent, but he refuses to cooperate. In your frustration you sought legal representation to make sure your child is being cared for properly. You believe that you have already done everything in your power to establish a cooperative relationship with your child's other parent. Therefore, you do not see any value in your participation in the program but believe that your coparent should receive individual assistance to straighten him out. So, if it wasn't for the judge ordering you to participate you wouldn't be here. Is that how you see it?"

Depending on the parent's response, the parent coordinator may reply by saying,

> "I can understand your frustration regarding your coparent's lack of commitment to a parenting relationship and your resentment at being ordered to participate when you have already given it a shot. Yet you seem able to see that there would be a benefit to a cooperative rela-

tionship between yourself and your child's other parent. Since you must be here, is there any parenting issue that you would like to resolve on your child's behalf in this setting rather than continuing to seek modification through the court?"

The parent coordinator should not only attempt to join the parent regarding his or her unfortunate circumstance but also offer the parent an opportunity to voice a more personal and hopefully relevant complaint about the same general problem. As a result, the parent may be more willing to enter an agreement with the parent coordinator since the coordinator has given the parent some power to make such a decision for himself or herself without the mandate of the judge. However, the parent may not be willing to enter any agreement even though he or she has included the program in the divorce settlement or been ordered by the court to meet all the requirements of the program. Under these conditions, the PC may suggest an alternative by pointing out the parent's dilemma. Since the parent has been ordered by the court to attend, there really is no choice in the matter. Some experts (Goldstein, Freud, and Solnet, 1979) believe that the legal system may actually foster positive change in a small measure by acting as a controlling agent. The parent coordinator can attempt to gain the cooperation of the parent by saying,

> "Since in the past you didn't have any influence over your coparent, and the court system has provided you with the only means of gaining some satisfaction, you see litigation as the only way to go. However, that very same court system has ordered you to participate in the program. So, how are you going to satisfy the judge and keep yourself in his good graces?"

The PC could also say,

> "Since you have been ordered to participate in this program and I am expected to work with you and update the court, we might as well work together. Let's see what we can do."

It is not unusual for one or both parents to negatively shift their positions between sessions. This generally happens if a parent contacts his or her attorney, extended family members, spouse, or a friend to discuss the session and agreements reached during the session. The attorney, unknowingly or sometimes intentionally, will undermine the progress made by the parents. This shift may also be due to defensiveness and resistance toward the parent coordinator if the coordinator is viewed as aligning with the other parent.

The parent coordinator should explore what caused the shift and then create an appropriate intervention directed at the source. If the resistance increases, the parent coordinator may want to invite the guardian into the next joint session to observe the process. In general, the other parent, who has been less resistant, is willing to have the GAL present in hopes of moving the resistant parent forward.

MUTUAL GOAL SETTING

As noted in Chapter 8, during the first joint session, parents create their mutual goals for the program. It may be necessary to ask the parents to clarify their goals:

> If you look back after the completion of this program and you feel it has been well worth your time and money, what would change between you and the other parent?

The PC might instead ask, "What do you think you will be doing differently when you are parenting as a team?" Being aware of the issues noted on the parents' assessment forms will help the PC frame each goal to focus on the parental team in a manner that will lead to behavior change. As the process unfolds, the PC may describe goals in very specific behavioral terms. To help parents define their goals in observable terms, the PC may ask the following: "What would be one small thing that you could begin doing that would indicate that _____ is happening?"

The parents are informed that some of their mutual goals may be focused specifically on their child while others may be focused on their coparenting relationship. The parent coordinator must communicate to the parents that coparenting improvements directly benefit their child. Both types of goals should be encouraged.

Sample Mutual Goals

Between Coparents

1. To learn how to communicate and negotiate effectively
2. To avoid future court proceedings
3. To learn how to work together regarding management of our child
4. To learn to be flexible with the other parent
5. To increase trust between parents and stepparents

6. To learn when our child might be manipulating us and to give the parent the benefit of the doubt
7. To share parenting information in a more timely manner
8. To acknowledge each other and act appropriately at joint-attendance activities
9. To ensure parental access by phone on a daily basis
10. To consult on all major, nonemergency parenting decisions

For the Child

1. To shield our child from parental conflict and tension
2. To shield our child from negative comments made about either parent
3. To allow our child to love both parents and his or her extended family
4. To reduce stress for our child at transfers

Once parents have identified general goals, the PC should check for mutual agreement and expand upon each of the goals so that they are concrete, observable, and realistic. Goals that may lead to beneficial results for the family should be actively supported. Written goals will help both the PC and the parents determine the following:

- How they are doing midway through the process as well as indicate the completion of the process
- Which parenting issues need to be resolved and mediated for the parenting plan

Reframing Negative Goals

At times, parents may create a mutual goal that is adversarial or an attack against the other parent. The parent coordinator can reframe these goals. For instance, a parent might say, "She will stop trying to control everything I do with the children." This could be reworded as one of the following: "Both parents would work as a respectful team when discussing parenting issues" or "Both parents would respect the other parent's input before making important parenting decisions" or "Both parents will be respectful of each other's boundaries and not interfere with each other's parenting when the children are with them." Additional examples are shown in Box 11.1.

Parents may agree to a goal that is better suited as a parenting agreement. When this happens, the PC should place the agreement onto a separate agreement form for the parents to initial rather than place it onto their goal

---

BOX 11.1. Examples of Reframing Negative Goals

Parent's Inappropriate Goal

"She would stop lying to me!"

Reframe

"Both parents will work to increase trust by communicating openly and honestly about situations concerning the children."

Parent's Inappropriate Goal

"He will stop using alcohol when he is driving and he would watch our child better."

Reframe

"We would discuss safety issues."

---

sheet. Parents should sign the goal sheet and agreements they make, even if the agreement is only a temporary one.

At times, parents may create a goal or an agreement that is either too general or too specific.

> *Parent's initial goal:* "I'd like to discuss how rude her stepdad was at the baseball game!" (too specific)
> *Revised goal:* "I'd like to discuss reducing tension for the children whenever we are together at their activities." (larger issue)

FACILITATING PARENTAL RESPONSIBILITY FOR BEHAVIORS

The overall emphasis of parent coordination is to help the parents take responsibility for their own behaviors as these behaviors relate to their co-parenting relationship as well as their relationship with the child. The most obvious way to do this during the session is to teach parents effective techniques, offer feedback, and point out how these behaviors may influence their child's development. Parents should be encouraged to take this step and objectively identify and change their negative behaviors during and especially outside the sessions.

Hopes and Dreams Activity

With the help of the parent coordinator, parents can identify their hopes and dreams for their child in the first joint session. Parents may complete this activity before or during the first joint session. This activity is also found in *Cooperative Parenting and Divorce.* If the parents do not have the book, the PC can direct the parents to list their hopes and dreams for their child on a piece of paper prior to the first joint session. The coordinator can start the activity by pointing out the obvious qualities or characteristics most parents want for their children, such as positive self-esteem, self-confidence, educational success, and physical and emotional health. The purpose of this activity is to (1) join the parents in an activity that focuses on their child in an area that they can probably agree upon (this may be the first time in a long time that the parents have jointly agreed), (2) focus on qualities that promote a healthy child, (3) foster movement toward behavior change, and (4) help parents to identify their contribution to the problems. The PC combines the parents' ideas on a flip chart or dry-erase board, taking one idea at a time from each parent. The PC encourages them to identify valuable and mature qualities by asking:

> "When you child is faced with a difficult task, what quality might help him?" (Encourage words such as perseverance, frustration tolerance)
>
> "What qualities will ensure that your child has a healthy adult relationship in the future?" (Encourage words such as communication skills, tolerance for differences, negotiation skills)
>
> "What qualities will your child need in the future to be able to stand up to peer pressure to use drugs?" (Encourage words such as impulse control, frustration tolerance)
>
> "When your child is tempted to do something potentially dangerous, what quality can assist her to resist the temptation?" (Encourage words such as high self-esteem, integrity, impulse control)

By knowing each parent's problem areas, the PC can help them to include hopes and dreams that represent their own personal issues. For example, if the parents cannot control their desire to yell at each other, guide the activity by asking questions that will encourage them to identify the child's growing need for "impulse control." If parents are highly critical, they can be prompted to include "tolerance" in this activity.

After they have completed this task and when the PC is sure that some of the parents' most important deficits are included in the activity, then the second part of the activity can be completed. This part is more difficult for parents to complete, especially in front of each other.

The second important goal of this activity is to encourage parents to honestly identify one or two negative behaviors they have practiced that are interfering with their child's ability to reach their hopes and dreams. The parent coordinator invites the parents to objectively look at their hopes and dreams and find at least one quality that their current behavior may be interfering with. The PC may need to be gentle and say something such as, "I know this is difficult to do, especially in front of your coparent. I guess I am asking you to 'own up' to things you may not want to say. This is a task in honesty and maturity." The PC can prompt the parent by asking, "What are you doing in your own life that is interfering with what you want for your child?" For example, if the parents have identified conflict resolution as a skill they want their child to develop, ask them if they are successfully modeling conflict resolution. The PC will need to remind the parents frequently that they are powerful role models for their children.

As parents admit to any shortcomings, the PC must be quick to acknowledge the difficulty of the task and thank them for their honesty and commitment to their child. Parents need to be reminded that they are not expected to be perfect since there is no perfect parent. If this activity is completed at the beginning of the program, more than likely this will be the first activity in which the coordinator may have to gently confront the parents directly. The parents must be confronted with the painful reality of how their behaviors affect their children. They cannot have it both ways. If they want their child to have impulse control they must model their own impulse control. If they want their child to be able to get along with others, they will need to model those cooperative behaviors. In most circumstances, it is also important for the coordinator to be very direct and sometimes even confrontational right from the start. The coordinator can point out to the parent the consequences of his or her behavior, and whenever possible deliver it with compassion.

Although parent coordination is not therapy, it is not unusual to observe parents seeking approval from the PC. If parents respect the coordinator, they may want to "earn points" from the coordinator. The experience may feel similar to dealing with sibling rivalry. When this happens, it often resembles sibling rivalry with each parent trying to prove that they are the "preferred child." This reaction may be the parents' attempt to align themselves with the parent coordinator and/or be acknowledged by the parent coordinator for their efforts.

It is vital that parents understand that their hostility will strongly influence their child's adjustment. For instance, their negative comments or acts of hostility toward each other will greatly interfere with their child's self-esteem. Most parents will include positive self-esteem on the hopes and dreams activity sheet; yet few parents fully understand that children gain a positive sense of identity from both parents. A child's ability to develop healthy self-esteem is hampered if one or both parents are criticized. Consequently, parents who routinely say negative comments about the other parent in the child's presence are not modeling respect and are tearing down their child's own self-esteem.

Create an Action Plan

This next activity requires parents to reflect upon each of the hopes and dreams that they identified as negatively influencing their child's well-being. The parents write out an action plan that lists the hope, their inappropriate behavior, and an alternative positive behavior. See Box 11.2 for an example of a written action plan.

Divorce Rules

The divorce rules are available in *Cooperative Parenting and Divorce: A Parent Guide to Effective Co-Parenting* and on the Web site <www. cooperativeparenting.com>. These rules should be reviewed with both parents during a joint session. This activity is designed to facilitate parental responsibility for their own behaviors and foster commitment to these rules. The PC can require the parents to take a copy of the rules home to review with their child and post in each of their homes in a location chosen by the child. The parents can invite their child to give them feedback if they forget one of the rules. Parents must make a commitment not to become upset with their child when their child offers them feedback. If they cannot ensure that they can appropriately handle their child's feedback, then they should not ask their child for this information. Otherwise, it would create a mixed mes-

---

BOX 11.2. Action Plan Example

Goal/Dream	My Damaging Behavior	Alternative Positive Behavior
My child will have positive self-esteem.	I make negative comments about the other parent when my child can overhear.	I will stop making negative comments in front of my child.

sage by indicating that they were open to feedback yet unwilling to take their child seriously and make the necessary changes to enhance the relationship with their child. In addition, it negatively influences the level of trust between parent and child and creates an unstable environment for the child. If parents are able to make this significant step, they can sign the page as a commitment that they will keep the agreements implied in the divorce rules.

MAINTAINING A CHILD FOCUS

During each parent's intake session, it is common for parents to attempt to form a coalition with the parent coordinator against the other parent. They will attempt to persuade the parent coordinator to take their side and support their position as if they were still pleading their case to the court. The PC should empathize with the parent's situation but begin to plant the seed that the primary concern is for the children. Slowly, the parent coordinator can shift to the child's perspective. The parent coordinator must be very clear in explaining to the parents at the very beginning of the program that the coordinator functions not only as a neutral third party but also as an advocate for the children, not the parents. Furthermore, the PC must articulate that at times he or she may appear to take sides with one parent over the other, but in actual practice, the parent coordinator is considering only the best interest of the child. It is recommended that the PC communicate the following to the parents: "Since you love your children and want what is best for them, their well-being will be my priority. I will be very adamant about your children's needs and make suggestions on their behalf."

During the initial appointment, the parent coordinator must balance empathy for the parents with concern for the plight of their children. As soon as parents begin meeting in joint sessions, the focus will shift more and more toward the child, even at the cost to the parent. This is an important progression. Note the following progression from parent empathy, to a child focus, to very direct child-focused statements and ultimately directives:

> I realize that this is very difficult for you as parent. However, I am very concerned about how the conflict and tension impacts on your child.

> I have said this before, but I am going to say it again. This is not about you or the other parent. This is about your child. So, I am going to insist that you put your emotions and needs to the side and focus on your child. Stop talking for a moment and look at this picture of your child and let's get back on track.

As you know, my job is to safeguard your child's needs. We are not here to focus on your personal issues. You need to address them with your therapist. We are here only for your child. We will not discuss that issue.

When parents are engaged in open warfare, the parent coordinator must firmly reinforce the ground rules and, if necessary, actively intervene and interrupt the negative communication exchange taking place between parents. This is accomplished by refocusing the discussion on the needs of the children. The parent coordinator may ask very specific questions regarding the child's adjustment to the divorce. The parent coordinator can ask the parents to consider the child's reactions to their interchange by requiring them to perceive the situation from their child's point of view. The parent coordinator might say,

As I was sitting here observing the interaction between the two of you, I put myself in your child's shoes. My stomach began to ache, and I became tense. If I were a kid I'd desperately want to run and hide. What might be your child's experience when she observes your behaviors and what are you willing to do differently?

When parents are enraged at each other to the detriment of the child, it is very easy to withdraw from the interaction and emotional reactivity of the parents. However, the coordinator must remain active. Once the coordinator can appeal to their parental instincts and their desire to provide a healthy experience for their child, parents seem to be able to empathize and become sensitive to their child's dilemma. By carefully choosing their words, PCs can create an atmosphere of collaboration by giving the parents credit for knowing what their children need and calling on their expertise to help solve problems. The emotional outbursts the parent coordinator endure reduce the child's exposure (Baris et al., 2001).

Johnston and Campbell (1988) maintain that a strong child-advocacy approach is needed in certain circumstances. If efforts to describe the children's experiences do not persuade the parents to act on behalf of their child, they advise therapists to confront parents with specific examples of their child's distress. At the same time, however, they recommend that the therapist avoid blaming the parents but stress the compromising position that their children are in.

Photo Technique

To emphasize the importance of maintaining a child focus during the sessions, parents are requested to bring in an eight-by-ten photograph of the child or children to their intake session. The PC can put the photograph in a clear plastic frame/sign holder and place it in an area of the room where both parents can easily view it. The photograph will serve as (1) a focal point when parents are evaluating their decisions, (2) a touchstone when finding their direction and getting back on track, and (3) a reminder when choosing behaviors.

If necessary, dramatic techniques may be used whenever one or both parents have lost focus on their child. For example, the PC may turn over the child's photograph when the parents try to pick fights. In addition, the PC may want to make black-and-white copies of the photograph to tear up as a means of getting the parents' attention. Finally, to demonstrate the damage they create for their child, the PC can ask the parents to place a bandage over the clear frame to illustrate the wounds they inflicted on their children. These techniques increase parental cooperation by emphasizing a focus on the detrimental effects of conflict on their child's adjustment.

Three Rings

To illustrate the interrelationship between the divorced parents and their child, a diagram using three rings is drawn on a dry-erase board. As illustrated in Figure 11.1, the two larger rings represent the divorced parents and the smaller ring connecting the two parent rings represents the child. This illustration can be used to make the following points:

1. Even divorcing parents should try to stay close together in a metaphoric way to assist their child. Parents can do this and even live across town or across the country from each other.
2. The child is the only reason divorced parents are still connected. The child is the most important part of their new relationship rather than in a marriage where the marital relationship should come first.
3. Children are not complete and their identity overlaps with both parents.
4. If one parent is absent the child will have a chunk missing from his or her self-esteem

Figure 11.1 also demonstrates the importance of maintaining contact with each other for the sake of their child. In other words, the parents work

FIGURE 11.1. A Two-Home Family

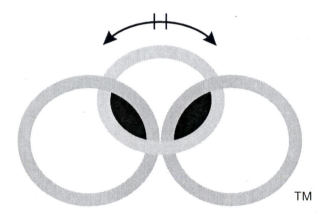

FIGURE 11.2. Parental Conflict: Damage to Self-Esteem

together to support their child by increasing the child's level of happiness, enhancing the child's self-esteem, and decreasing the level of tension and conflict between the two households.

A similar diagram can be used to indicate how a child's self-esteem can be negatively affected by parental conflict and loyalty binds (see Figure 11.2). Children sense that they are somehow connected to their parents. Thus if someone criticizes the parent, the child feels criticized too. The parent coordinator can explain that this is the reason a child will be hurt and defensive if another child says something mean about his or her parent. Criticisms, put-downs, and name-calling directed at the other parent are experienced by the child as a direct hit. Although it is not physical, but rather psychological, it results in the child's loss of self-esteem.

Taking a Position Rather than an Interest

Parents lose sight of their child easily when they are emotionally charged. Therefore, the PC can help parents recognize when they are taking a position rather than an interest in their child. A story works best for explaining the difference. For example, tell a story about a father who believed that he had his sons' (ages two and seven) best interest foremost in his mind. He maintained a rigid belief that the mother was objecting to their vacation to deny him access to his children. The father informed his coparent that he would be taking advantage of his vacation with his children as stipulated in the divorce settlement. However, the father overlooked the fact that the divorce settlement indicated that the father's two-week vacation was to be split into two separate weeks. He stated that he was taking the children to Disney World in February for ten days. He further added that the arrangements had already been made by his current wife's parents.

The father declared that the mother was being unreasonable. He was unwilling to consider that a lengthy vacation in Disney World would probably be troublesome to a two-year-old who had never been away from his primary caretaker for more than two to three nights. He was also unwilling to consider the older son's absence from school and the consequences of such an extended absence on his school performance. In order to help the father see that he was focusing on his own needs rather on his sons' needs, the PC had to gently soothe the father while challenging him to comprehend the motivation for his behaviors.

The next example illustrates how parents can become child focused or self-focused.

> *Situation:* The parents are determining the educational placement of their daughter. They decide to visit the public school and two private schools before reaching a decision.
>
> *Child focus:* The father decides that the public school placement is adequate and allows him to take advantage of his tax dollars and save for her college education. The mother determines that the private school would offer the added benefit of religious education. In addition, attendance in the private school would not make it necessary for their daughter to attend religious training on Sunday mornings.

Self-focus: Since the divorce, the father believes that the mother controls most if not all of the parenting decisions. As a result, the father engages in a competition to dictate the educational placement of their daughter. He insists that the daughter attend the public school even though the mother is willing to pay the private school tuition.

Final decison: The parents mutually agree that their daughter may attend the private school at the mother's expense, but they also agree to review the placement at the end of the first year to determine if it meets their daughter's educational, social, and emotional needs.

Acoustic Activity

The PC can write the word *conflict* vertically on a flip chart or dry-erase board. Parents are asked to brainstorm words that fit with each letter and summarize the characteristics of conflict. Next, the parents are requested to generate words that represent feelings children may have when caught in the middle of their parents' battles. The PC may ask the parents to do this activity together if they are agreeable. The parents can then list the feeling words to the right of the parental behavior:

Parental Behaviors Characteristic of Conflict			Children's Feelings		
C	=	Critical, controlling	C	=	Confused, crushed
O	=	Obsessive (rigid thinking)	O	=	Overwhelmed
N	=	Negative, name-calling	N	=	Numb, nervous
F	=	Fight to win, flight, fuel	F	=	Frustrated, furious, frightened
L	=	Loss of control, litigate, legal battles	L	=	Lonely, lifeless
I	=	Ignore, insult, initiate	I	=	Irritated, insecure
C	=	Command, compete	C	=	Cautious
T	=	Threaten	T	=	Tearful, tense, timid

EQUALIZING POWER

One of the goals of parent coordination is to promote effective communication and conflict-resolution skills between separating parents. One element that adds to the success of resolving conflict is to equalize the bargaining power of each parent. To determine each parent's negotiating power, the parent coordinator can consider substantive resources such as education, occupation, and income. Other resources to consider are personal characteristics such as intelligence, emotional states, status, attitudes toward risk, beliefs or ideologies, coping mechanisms, and relationship patterns (Bryan, 1994).

Just as in standard mediation, it is dangerous to assume that the couple has equal bargaining power or an equal capacity to assert themselves and negotiate effectively. For instance, a weak or fearful parent may not be able or willing to enter the joint sessions with his or her coparent. The PC should attempt to boost this parent's confidence in meeting new challenges, particularly apprehension at being with the former partner. After joint sessions are reconvened, it is important to secure the trust of the parents, particularly the weaker parent. The parent coordinator must be sensitive to power imbalances in the relationship of the parents, convey that he or she will be in control of the session, and protect the parents from any adverse actions.

When signs of intimidation erupt in the session, the PC must either interrupt the interaction or side with the weaker parent. This can be done by sitting slightly closer to the weaker parent or by emphasizing a concept this parent shared through the use of reflective listening. Isaacs, Montalvo, Abelsohn (1986) stipulated that the therapist should become an advocate of the parent most under pressure. They believe that when working with highly conflictual couples, the therapist must be ready to openly support the weaker parent until that parent is able and willing to be assertive when dealing with the more forceful parent. Specifically, they have found success with the therapist actively blocking the impaired communication process taking place between the parents and asking the forceful parent to talk directly to the therapist. When responding, the therapist matches the parent's magnitude and emotion while modeling an appropriate response. However, if this occurs to a significant degree the PC should recommend that one or both parents seek individual treatment until such time that they can effectively participate in joint sessions.

The parent coordinator can assist the anxious or weaker parent in other ways. The PC may allow the parent to decide where he or she would prefer to sit during the sessions. In the case of past family violence, anxious parents may bring a neutral party to sit with them in the waiting room. In addition, the anxious parent should be encouraged to express specific anxieties to the parent coordinator in an individual session. During this session, the anxious parent, with the help of the PC, can create a plan of action for dealing with aggressive or intimidating behaviors of the other parent during joint sessions. For example, anxious parents might agree to step out for a drink of water whenever they perceive themselves to be out of control or overly anxious. If they do not feel safe, even if their reality seems distorted, the parent coordinator must work toward improving the situation rather than allowing the anxious parent to avoid joint sessions.

INCREASING PARENTAL RESPECT

As noted in Figure 11.1, the three-rings logo, used in *Cooperative Parenting and Divorce,* can be used to demonstrate the necessity of both parents working together for the sake of their child. Using the illustration, the PC can help parents empathize with their child. By erasing the circle they can recognize the loss a child would experience without both parents.

Parents who are angry or hateful are often resistant to acting respectful of the other parent. The PC must stress that no one can ask them to feel respect, but they can be expected to act respectfully. The parent coordinator can reflect back on the hopes and dreams activity when working with a resistant parent. If either parent refuses to act respectful because it feels dishonest, the PC can share the following story:

> Let's say that your child does not like her classroom teacher one bit. She is angry with something the teacher did or did not do. She comes to you and says that she hates the teacher. What would you advise your child to do? Would you tell her she did not have to act respectful because she did not feel respectful? Would you tell her she could ignore the teacher or call her names? Of course not; you would give advice that would help your child to learn to cope with stress effectively. Since you are the most important model, you will need to demonstrate respect and impulse control no matter how you feel.

Positive Parenting Qualities Activity

Parents need to learn that each parent offers something special to their child. One parent might be particularly patient or a good listener. One might be skillful with computers and math. Since each parent brings his or her own special gifts to the parent-child relationship, having two parents involved in the child's life doubles the chance that the child will acquire these skills. A parent coordinator can ask the parents to name two or three positive parenting qualities or characteristics in their coparent. After they are able to complete this task, the coordinator can ask them to do it again, but this time from their child's point of view: "What characteristics, qualities, and skills do you see that your child might enjoy or admire?" or "Does your child's other parent like to laugh and play silly games?" or "What things would your child enjoy about the other when the child is in a different stage in life?"

Although this may be difficult for some, it is essential that parents identify positive qualities in each other. Some parents are determined to forget why they married the coparent in the first place. Parents may struggle to separate the former spouse from the coparent. Due to their pain and bitterness, they may refuse to acknowledge anything positive about the other parent. The PC can point out that a negative marital quality is not necessarily a negative parenting quality. For example, just because the former husband lied about a marital affair does not mean that he cannot be trusted to be honest about his children. According to Baris and colleagues (2001, p. 60),

> The artistry of being a PC is to simultaneously understand why a client will see the other parent in a certain way but also to say, "I see it differently," and not make it sound like a challenge to the defenses of the client.

If a parent is experiencing difficulty completing this task, it is likely that he or she harbors intense negative beliefs about the coparent. The goal of this exercise is to help the parent recognize that every person has both positive and negative qualities and the presence of the negative qualities does not negate positive ones. The parent who is still emotionally engaged will have significant difficulty with this exercise. Likewise, the parent with a personality disorder will struggle with the "all or nothing" dilemma of this activity.

If necessary, the PC can create additional assignments to assist parents with this concept. For example, the parent can be requested to make two separate lists as homework. One list should note five negative qualities and the other name five positive qualities. The PC should not require the parents to share any of the negative qualities in the joint session. However, the PC may ask the parent to read only the positive qualities to the coparent. It is not unusual for the resistant parent to use negative body language as well as attempt to negate the positive qualities. For example, the parent might say, "He is a good provider . . . even though the child support checks are always running late." The PC must hold firm to limits and consider charging the resistant parent the full session fee until he or she is able to complete this activity. A referral for individual therapy may also be warranted.

Positive Memories Activity

Parents can still treasure positive memories of their relationship and family. Even if parents have been divorced for years, recalling positive memories (preferably prechildren) can assist with the grief process while also increasing parental respect. To assist parents with this concept, the PC requests that the parents write down one or two positive memories they want to treasure that include their former partner and one or two positive memories that include their former partner as well as their children. Before they share these memories, the PC can point out the benefit of this activity by asking the following questions: "How will recognizing positive memories of your past relationship help you?" "How will recalling these memories help you establish a collaborative relationship with your coparent?" "How will your children benefit from being told about these positive memories?"

Similar to the positive qualities activity, this activity may generate resistance from angry parents. Parents may try to deny the existence of any positive memories. They must understand that their children will also benefit from their ability to recall and share these memories. If they become tearful they may need some additional support from a therapist, a support group, or some additional reading on the concept of letting go. After parents have successfully identified a positive memory, they may be asked to share the memory with their child as long as it is age appropriate and the coordinator can trust in their ability to complete the task.

John Gottman (1994b) maintained that if couples put a negative spin on their past memories together it is an early warning sign that the marriage is in serious trouble. Similarly, divorced parents who are able to recall the positive sides of the marriage are better able to move toward a healthier coparenting relationship.

Focus on Parental Values

Using the hopes and dreams activity, the PC can assist parents to recognize their mutual goals for their child. When parents reach an impasse, the PC may use the hopes and dreams information to move parents beyond their position of self-interest to one of a child focus. The parent coordinator can point out to parents that they share the same goal for their child. For example, one parent brings up the fact that their ten-year-old daughter has been lying. They want to connect this to the other parent in a blaming way. The PC can see this coming and is ready to interrupt. Instead the parent coordinator may say, "I remember how both of you said in the hopes and dreams activity that you wanted your daughter to grow up to be honest and follow rules. This is an opportunity to work together toward the same goal. Are you willing to help her with this or would you rather just attack and blame each other?" Before either parent can say anything negative, the PC quickly adds, "I know you both love her very much. She needs your help, so let's talk about what both homes could do to reinforce the rules relevant to lying."

The next step is to brainstorm ways that they can assist their child to establish and maintain this value. After the brainstorming stage, parents can be guided to a mutual agreement even if it is a temporary one that will be re-evaluated in one month. Prior to the evaluation the parents must establish some neutral criteria for assessment to decrease the possibility of them falling into the trap of promoting their own agendas.

For instance, a set of parents reached an impasse when discussing the educational needs of their fifth-grade son. The father reported that their son received his report card just prior to the joint session. Without any warning to the parents, the report card documented a 65 percent average in math. While reporting this information, the father became quite distressed and began to accuse the mother of a lack of interest in their son's education. The PC immediately interrupted this pattern and requested that the parents refer back to the hopes and dreams activity. The PC asked the parents to look for anything that they had written down regarding their son's education. The mother responded, "To achieve academic success necessary to go to college." The parent coordinator highlighted the fact that education was important for both parents and asked if a 65 percent average in math was acceptable to both of them. In unison, the parents said no. Thus, the parents shared a mutual value involving their son's education. At this point the PC coached the parents through the seven steps of negotiation until they had reached a mutually acceptable resolution to their son's academic failure. For further information on the seven steps of negotiation, see Chapter 9.

GUIDING THE PROBLEM-SOLVING PROCESS

Divorcing parents inevitably face many situations in which they perceive the need for immediate answers. In their distress and desperation, they often become dramatic or create an atmosphere that tempts the parent coordinator to respond. Empathizing with the child's predicament and stressful situation, at times the PC may be compelled to do just that—intervene without planning and considering the long- and short-term consequences of his or her suggestions. Premature actions on the part of the parent coordinator will decrease effectiveness, question competence, and hamper maneuverability. It also limits the parents' ability to problem solve in a respectful manner. Part of the goal of the program is for parents to assume responsibility for the decisions regarding their children and to become aware of and practice successful problem solving without the continued guidance of a neutral third party. Parents must learn that they need to work together for the sake of their children and rely on each other to provide the best answers to their family difficulties. The only time the PC should react immediately to a parenting situation is when the child is in imminent danger of physical or emotional abuse. However, sometimes it is necessary to provide information to parents in order to normalize the process, offer developmental information, or assist with the process of negotiation. In this capacity, the parent coordinator also functions as an expert in the field of child development. It is not uncommon for parents to want to discuss behavior-management problems, including how to get their young child out of bed, or how to know when a teenager is ready to date. In order to handle these issues, a seasoned therapist with a strong child therapy practice or experience in providing parent education classes is best suited for the work of a parent coordinator.

During the initial sessions, before parents have learned skills for negotiating, the parent coordinator tends to direct the conversations. As coparents begin to use I-statements and the seven steps to negotiating, the coordinator becomes less and less directive. The goal is for the coparents to work successfully in the session while the PC observes the interaction. Then parents are challenged to use these skills outside the sessions without the presence of the parent coordinator.

Besides pressuring the PC to take sides, divorcing parents typically tempt the coordinator to prematurely take a position. For instance, a parent may ask, "Don't you think Katherine should be home with me during spring break since all her relatives from out of town will be here to see her?" If the parent coordinator agrees with the parent he or she runs the risk of entering into a coalition with one parent against the other. (However, sometimes it is necessary to give an opinion, especially when safety or developmental issues are at risk.) The parent coordinator must assist parents in the process of negotiation and avoid the temptation to jump in and fix every problem. In response to the above example the parent coordinator might say,

> Based on the information you shared, I can see why you believe your child should spend spring break with you. In my work with parents I have learned that it is essential to consider all parties' points of view before reaching a decision. Let's hear from your coparent.

The parent coordinator reframes the issue in terms that are not inflammatory and creates an atmosphere for the generation of solutions (Gold, 1992). Whenever possible, words are chosen carefully in order to remove bias, positions, and judgments. Ultimately, the aim is to use neutral language that objectively states the problem in a way that does not endorse either of the parents (Moore, 1996).

The parent coordinator must demonstrate to the parents through reflective listening that he or she heard what was said and understood the message, while maintaining a neutral stance and guiding parental negotiations. See Chapter 9 for discussion on teaching the use of I-statements, reflective listening skills, and negotiation skill, as well as the 3Ps.

ENCOURAGING EXCEPTIONS AND AMPLIFYING CHANGE

As parents make changes necessary to promote a positive relationship on behalf of their child, it is important for them to view themselves as having control over their own behaviors and interactions. With this in mind, the parent coordinator should emphasize exceptions to the problems or difficulties as they occur. Questions that amplify change include the following:

> "How were you able to do that?"
> "How were you able to remain child focused?'
> "How did you overcome the desire to make a demand?"
> "What difference has this made to your child?"
> "What are you doing differently?"

Parents can be asked to identify something that went well or at least better since the last session. To assist parents, the PC can ask them to recall a specific behavior that was positive or a inappropriate behavior they could have acted upon but chose not to.

Parents can also be encouraged to recognize exceptions by asking them to notice the positive behaviors demonstrated by the other parent between sessions. As noted throughout this text, parents often focus on negative behaviors exhibited by the other parent which reinforce their negative beliefs and interfere with their ability to see any positive changes that are occurring. When parents expect the worst they usually find it. The following activity not only encourages parents to look for positive changes but challenges the negative beliefs of conflicted parents. Depending on the atmosphere in the room and the dispositions of the parents, this activity can be presented in a positive and playful manner. However, this activity may not suit all parents.

Expect the Unexpected

1. At the beginning of the session, the PC briefly explains the activity and offers information regarding the purpose of the activity. The PC must be sure to ask parents if they would be willing to try something different.
2. The PC gives each parent a piece of paper or index card and pencil and asks the parents to identify a specific behavior that they can demonstrate during the session that would promote cooperation. The PC stresses that this behavior must be easily observed by the other parent.

Parents are requested to write down the behavior on a piece of paper to give to the PC. The behavior must be observable. If not, the PC returns the paper to the parent and requests that he or she refine it. At first, the PC should refrain from offering examples to the parents. If they are struggling to identify a behavior, the PC can guide them. The PC should keep in mind the parents' strengths and weaknesses as well as behaviors that would encourage change. Some examples might include the following:

- When my coparent is speaking to me I will maintain eye contact (at least three out of four times).
- I will use I-statements without coaching.
- I will use reflective listening skills as least twice.
- I will not interrupt as much as usual.

3. The parents should not share the target behavior with their coparent. Each parent will be responsible for recognizing the other parent's chosen behavior at the end of the session.

This technique is a playful way to use the parents' competitive nature to impact changes in their behavior. The PC may note that parents

- will work harder to use effective skills.
- will expect the coparent to perform in a positive manner which will result in noticing improvements and exceptions, as well as challenge their negative beliefs about the other parent.
- will not only identify behaviors that the other parent was practicing but also name behaviors that were not listed on the coparent's card.

This activity can also draw attention to behaviors that are incongruent with their negative beliefs.

Motivational Assignments

At times it may be necessary to motivate parents to practice new behaviors on a weekly or session-by-session basis. In order to push them toward an improved coparent relationship in a relatively short period of time, specific "motivational assignments" encourage parents to practice new behaviors. These techniques are designed to persuade parents to "act as if" they are engaging in a courteous businesslike relationship. Most parents, if not challenged, will resist changing their behaviors. Through assigning these motivational tasks, the parents' resistance may be deceased by lowering their defenses and pushing them out of their comfort zone. They can save face without feeling vulnerable. Over time the new behaviors may become more natural. If the PC is persistent, he or she may be surprised at the movement parents can make when challenged to take a risk.

The PC may want to consider adding any of the following assignments to the parents' homework lists. If neither parent volunteers to go first, the PC can flip a coin.

Assignments for the Waiting Room

Week 1. Assign one parent to say hello to the coparent in the waiting room.
Week 2. Assign the other parent the next appointment to initiate hello.
Week 3. Assign one parent to share something positive about their child with the coparent.

Once parents acknowledge each other in a courteous fashion in the waiting room, they may enter the office.

Assignments for Encouraging Parent-Child Contact

1. Parents with caller ID may insist that their children answer the phone when the call is from the other parent. In this situation, parents may be requested to intentionally answer the other parent's call once per week. The parent is encouraged to use a pleasant voice when answering the phone and, with a smile, say to their child, "It's your mother/father calling to speak to you." Parents are instructed not to engage in a parental discussion of any kind. The PC should offer them very specific instructions and attempt to anticipate problems so they can be addressed prior to completing the assignment.

2. Parents can encourage their child(ren) to call the absent parent by saying, "You haven't talked to your mother in a while. Would you like to call her?" Parents can also be assigned to request that their children share information with the absent parent. For instance, they might say, "I am sure your father would like to know about the A on your math test. Why don't you give him a call?" Parents must be reminded that their tone of voice and body language should match what they are saying to their children.

Assignments to Encourage Courteous Transitions

1. As a first step, parents may be required to make eye contact and nod to each other.
2. The arriving parent may pull in the driveway and honk the horn. If this is already occurring, the arriving parent can be encouraged to go to the door and knock or ring the doorbell one time and wait for his or her child. If no one answers, the parent should return to the car and beep the horn as usual. This assignment should not be used if the parents are at risk of serious conflict at transfers.
3. In the event that a parent does not normally answer the door when the coparent comes for the children, the PC can assign a specific day that this parent will intentionally go to the front door.
4. As a follow-up assignment, the parents can be challenged to take the next step. If appropriate, the receiving parent can offer the arriving parent to step just inside the door. Parents must greet each other with a pleasant "hello." If the parents are still unable to communicate with each other in an appropriate manner, they should be warned not to engage in any conversation other than the greeting. This exercise may not apply to every family situation, so caution must be employed.
5. In addition to greeting each other, parents can also say good-bye to each other while their child is present.

Assignments to Encourage Acceptance of the Coparent

1. As noted in the positive qualities technique, the parents can be asked to share one of the qualities with their child that reflects on the coparent. For example, they might say, "You know your way around the computer just like your mother." Parents can also be assigned to make similar comments to their children about extended family members on both sides of the child's family.
2. Parents can be requested to add the other parent's birthday to the family calendar.
3. Parents may be assigned to assist their child to make or purchase a gift for their other parent for birthdays, Mother's/Father's Day, and other special occasions.
4. Prior to vacations, parents can be instructed to help their child purchase and send a postcard to the absent parent.

Assignments to Foster Joint Attendance at Child's Activities

1. The custodial parent can be assigned to encourage his or her child to go over to say "hello" to the other parent, or

2. Once both parents arrive at the event, the PC may request that they make eye contact and greet each other in the presence of their child.
3. The PC may designate specific seating at the event. The aim is to encourage parents to sit in close proximity to make it easier for their child to keep track of the parents. Gradually the parents can work toward sitting one to two rows apart and, if possible, to sitting in the same row with a chair between them for coats and belongings.
4. Parents can be informed of the benefits of hosting one birthday or graduation party for their child that includes friends and relatives from both sides of the child's family. Ultimately, parents should determine if this is a good choice for their family.

Assignments During the Sessions

1. After the first few sessions, parents should be expected to speak directly to each other rather than to the parent coordinator.
2. Request that the parents notice a positive behavior that was demonstrated by the coparent between sessions during times of transition or during the weekly phone conference.
3. Solicit (but do not demand) an apology for disrespectful behavior. Assist the parents with both the apology and the response to the apology.
4. When one parent is flexible or cooperative with a request, encourage the other parent to say thank you. It benefits both parents.

THE POWER OF METAPHORS

Metaphors can prove extremely useful, particularly if they are similar to the family's day-to-day experience. When working with a conflicted couple the parent coordinator can use the fire metaphor described earlier to show how arguments get started and the consequences of such arguments for all family members. Skilled parent coordinators can create other metaphors from information they learn about the parents. For example, if the parents are both avid spots fans, the coordinator can use sports analogies to teach skills and motivate change. If either parent runs a company or is in sales, this can also work well as a possible metaphor. Chapters 9 and 10 contain additional metaphors.

APPLICATION OF EFFECTIVE STORYTELLING

The use of brief storytelling can be effective at addressing an issue in a less direct or confrontational manner. Stories can also be used to help parents recognize new options or normalize their situation. This is similar to Richard Gardner's famous mutual storytelling. The parents' real-life situation or their negative beliefs about the situation is "their story." The PC relates to the parents a "real story" or one created from different stories. (Be sure to protect the identities of former clients.) Do not point out the moral of the story, just as with young children.

Situation: One or both parents feel that their situation is hopeless.

Story: Several months ago a family was referred to me who was told by the judge that he would put their seven-year-old son into foster care if they continued their never-ending battle over their child. They were directed to make some immediate changes in their behavior. A review conference was scheduled for two months later at which time the judge wanted to see concrete results that the parents had indeed taken him seriously and changed their behavior. These two parents took the judge at his word and were afraid they would lose their son. They started taking the program seriously, identified their contributions to the conflict, and began to make some important changes. They finally stopped focusing on each other and worked on themselves. At the review conference, they presented themselves to the judge in a cooperative manner. They were able to provide the judge with evidence that they could make sacrifices for their son. I am happy to report that these parents are still putting forth the effort that is necessary but not always easy to make the situation better for their son. He is really doing well now!

Situation: One or both parents believe that their teenage daughter did not care if they fought because she was with her friends and had already disengaged from both parents. They believed that it was too late to make changes in their coparenting relationship.

Story: I worked with a conflicted family with a teenager. It was evident to me that the teenage boy was very agitated by having to come to see me for an individual intake session. The young man was adamant that his parents could never make any improvements in their behavior because they were too immature. He reluctantly took a copy of our divorce rules, rolled his eyes, and left the room. After his parents began working with each other, his mother indicated that every Saturday she found a copy of the divorce rules folded up tightly in the back pocket of his jeans.

COACHING TECHNIQUES

Coaching has become a very popular approach among therapists and other professionals. At times, the parent coordinator can function as a coach and yield positive results. According to Baris and colleagues (2001), coaching as an intervention is individually supportive and acknowledges the strengths of the coached parent. Coaching can be explained by the following sports analogy.

A group of young children are participating on a basketball team. Their coach works with them during practice. The coach teaches specific skills and attempts to improve their game. During the games the coach is unable to stop the activity to teach a new technique. Instead, the coach must instruct the team members from the sidelines. The coach might use techniques of encouragement, praise, or even raise his or her voice over the noise if necessary. In addition, the coach may use signals to instruct players. Although the coach is prohibited from going on the court, he or she is very involved in the game. An effective coach does not passively watch from the bench.

Likewise, the parent coordinator remains very active while parents learn how to communicate and negotiate in a constructive manner. Like a coach, a PC may remove players from the game if they refuse to play by the rules. If a member of the team needs some additional skill development, the coach might meet with the player one-on-one a few times to reinforce a skill.

Another way to visualize coaching during a joint session is to imagine a split screen with the mother on one side of the screen and the father on the other side. During a joint session, the parent coordinator can speak to one side of the screen as if the other parent is not present. This has to be done briefly so as to avoid insulting either parent. The idea is simply that the parent coordinator may speak to one parent while shutting out the other parent briefly. By using split-screen coaching, the PC may encourage a parent to practice appropriate behaviors by saying: "Just ignore what she just said and stay focused. That's it, just keep telling me what happened," or "Don't let him derail you; just stay focused."

In joint sessions, coaching may include use of hand signals through the split-screen concept. For instance, the parent coordinator may respectfully introduce a signal for "too much" when the parent provides too much information at one time. The parent coordinator might indicate with his or her hands that the parent needs to shorten what he or she is saying. The parent coordinator can act as if he or she is "reeling in a big fish." This usually gets a laugh while also reminding parents not to react or defend themselves.

When one parent interrupts the other parent, the coordinator can use a simple quiet signal often used by teachers and parents. The creative PC can work with parents to develop effective signals that are easy to respond to without derailing the focus of the conversation or being demeaning to the parent.

Hand signals may include pointing to the child's picture in the room. Other signals might draw attention to the fact that parents need to take a deep breath or stop talking. Creative ideas will come to the PC who is interested in helping to coach without words.

Coaching can focus on any number of skills associated with the process of parent coordination. For instance, communication and negotiation skills, anger management and impulse control, and written correspondence. The PC can interrupt ineffective communication and coach the parents on how to rephrase their request using an I-statement. Parents often react to the same triggers that occurred within their marital relationship. The coordinator can block this interaction through the use of coaching. In this situation, both parents can be coached. As mentioned in Chapter 9, the coordinator can help parents write appropriate fax and e-mail messages by pointing out the destructive language and replacing it with constructive language that will increase the likelihood that the parents will get what they want.

Caucus

A caucus is often used during the process of mediation. A caucus is a brief meeting with each parent individually that focuses on a very specific issue. A caucus is generally used to

C = Coach a parent on a specific skill
A = Act as agent of reality
U = Understand the process or dynamics occurring between the parents
C = Confront inappropriate behaviors
U = Undo negative interactions
S = Separate and stabilize the parents when tension mounts

Ultimately, a PC should work with parents with the goal of assisting them to become independent of the coordinator's coaching as soon as possible. The aim is to help parents communicate and negotiate effectively without the assistance of any third party. The parent coordinator's role decreases over time as the parents demonstrate effective skills.

Training for Self-Talk

Self-talk is a coaching technique used by each parent rather than a third party. It is the internalized voice of the person. Parents can learn to coach themselves with the use of self-talk:

"This won't get me anywhere."
"I can do this for our child. I love her more than I dislike *him*."
"I want to be heard by her, so I need to stay calm and reflect what she is saying."

"LETTING GO" AND DETACHMENT TECHNIQUES

Parents learn to let go of the old marital relationship. This is especially true for parents in the predivorce process. However, some postdivorce parents benefit from working on these techniques as well. If the postdivorce parents have emotionally moved on, this activity may not be necessary.

Grief Activity

Parents need to be educated regarding how the grief process applies to divorce. The PC can ask parents to briefly describe their own grieving process or to mention one of the Kübler-Ross stages that they have had particular difficulty navigating. The stages are included in *Cooperative Parenting and Divorce: A Parent Guide to Effective Co-Parenting*. If one or both parents are still in significant distress, the PC may recommend that they seek additional therapeutic assistance. Depending on the level of distress, the parent coordinator may need to temporarily postpone additional joint sessions. Parents who are still hurting need to be reminded that grief is an individual experience. They may repeat some stages more than once or get stuck in one stage for a time. Their children may have similar experiences.

Also, parents must understand that all people respond to grief in their own way and at their own pace. It is not unusual for the parent who left the relationship to be further along in the grief process than the one that was left behind. More than likely the parent that left began the grieving process during the partnership while making the decision to leave. The parent who resisted the divorce may not begin the grief process until the announcement of the separation. Often the parent who is in the most pain is surprised to learn that the other parent is not insensitive but rather just much farther ahead in the grief process.

Rituals

One reason that divorce is so difficult is because no symbolic ceremony or ritual marks the transition point from the old to the new. Rituals help parents let go of pain from the past as well as interrupt their negative behaviors. Creating a ritual or ceremony can be helpful for letting go of the marital relationship and beginning a new relationship as coparents. Since a divorce tends to feel strangely anticlimactic, rituals can be very helpful to parents and children. They offer a concrete visual representation of the transition from one to two homes. Four rituals are outlined in Chapter 3 of *Cooperative Parenting and Divorce: A Parent Guide to Effective Co-Parenting.* If requested, the PC can consider performing one of these rituals during one of the joint sessions with parents. For additional ideas on rituals refer to Imber-Black and Roberts's (1992) suggestions in *Rituals for Our Times.*

Forgiveness

Parents who recognize the importance of a spiritual or religious life are more likely to consider the benefits of forgiveness. If in doubt, the PC can ask parents what they think about the concept of forgiveness. Their response will let the PC know if forgiveness will be useful to a particular couple.

Forgiveness can free a person from the power another person has over them. Parents can learn that forgiveness is always under their control. In order to help their child, parents must give up their need to be a victim to the event or to hold on to the action of their coparent. In order to do this, the parent who feels injured needs to recognize that seeking revenge is not productive. Forgiveness results in giving up the right to retaliate. Through forgiveness, the forgiver can regain control over his or her life while letting go of the resentments buried in the past. The result is a release of energy and a sense of freedom. A parent coordinator can educate parents to the personal benefits of forgiveness, not to mention the benefits to their child's adjustment.

Since parent coordination is not therapy, it is important that parents not focus on their former marriage. However, in the process of exploring forgiveness, some parents may choose to devote one session to work on forgiveness. For more information on forgiveness refer to Chapter 10.

Detachment Activity

"Detachment" is a difficult concept for some parents to grasp. Parents must understand that they can be attached to someone they do not like. Parents naively believe that if they do not want the person back this stance automatically means that they are detached from that person. This is especially true for the parent who has remarried. It is essential that parents recognize that the opposite of love is not hate; it is indifference (Potter-Efron and Potter-Effron, 1995). Therefore, if they hate their coparent they are still firmly attached to the past relationship. Although parents are not pleased to hear this, they will need to take an honest assessment of how they are attached to the coparent through strong negative (or positive) feelings.

Using a dry-erase board or chart, the PC can draw a scale or a continuum from 1 to 10. The PC asks the parents to picture someone they are happy to be "attached" to. Then ask them to come up with words to describe what it means to be attached to this person:

> "How often do you think about the person you are attached to?"
> "How strong are your feelings for the person you are attached to?"

Parents can be asked to rate their level of attachment to the other parent using the same scale. A 1 represents detachment and 10 represents significant attachment. Parents should rate their level of attachment when issues are not related to their child. For instance:

> Seeing the coparent's telephone number on the caller ID
> Your e-mail being ignored by the coparent
> Observing the coparent walking on the street with a significant other
> The coparent asking to speak to you

Many parents resist but sooner or later realize they are attached through bitterness, anger, hate, and pain. When they reassess their attachment they rate themselves more attached to their former spouse than they did at the outset. If they seem discouraged, the PC can support them by reminding them that one of the goals of the program is to help them disengage from their former spouse and marital relationship. The coordinator can remind them that if they act as if they are disengaged they will eventually get there.

EXTERNALIZING THE PROBLEM

By externalizing the problem, the PC models how to separate the person from the problem and/or the impasse that is maintaining the conflict. In essence, the problem or impasse is located outside the parent or parental team. The intent is to provoke problem resolution by promoting personal empowerment. Parents recognize that they can choose to make it better or they can choose to keep it bitter.

Creating a United Parental Team

In an effort to create a united parental team, the PC can externalize the situation by emphasizing that their coparenting relationship and the degree of conflict determine their child's adjustment to the family's separation. What matters most is the solution to the problem rather than focusing on who is right and who is wrong. Parents can be encouraged to join together to fight the adverse effects of the divorce on their family. In this situation, the parent coordinator emphasizes the urgency of the children's situation. Their situation is framed in such a way that the parents have no other choice but to work together for the sake of their children. For example, during a joint session the parent coordinator asked, "Was there a time when the two of you presented a united front and stood up to your child's attempts to get the two of you angry at each other?" Mother quickly chimed in, "Our fifteen-year-old daughter asked me if she could go to the movies with a mixed-gender group of friends. The movie she was planning on viewing was rated R. I told her that she couldn't go. Our daughter yelled, 'If I was at Daddy's he would let me go! He thinks you are an old fuddy duddy anyway and way too over-protective.' In response, I reminded her of the rule that both her father and I agreed upon. She is not allowed to see R-rated movies until she is seventeen and only after one of us has previewed the movie first. I allowed her to blow off steam. Later that evening I called Joe to explain the incident exactly how it happened, without accusing him of any wrongdoing. He assured me that he did not call me an 'old fuddy duddy' or 'overprotective' and agreed to speak to her about our rule the next time he saw her."

Externalizing the problem also helps parents challenge negative beliefs and behavior patterns that influence outcomes. It is a very compelling perceptual shift. The parent coordinator reframes the problem from negative to neutral and from blaming to future desired behaviors (Baris et al., 2001). Additional information on negative beliefs is located in Chapter 10.

A View from Above

When parents are having difficulty maintaining a successful discussion or promoting problem resolution, the PC can ask one or both of them to take "a view from above." Similar to the concept of "putting on a sociologist's hat," parents learn to observe themselves rather than becoming a part of the interaction. This technique requires parents to dissociate on command. Parents can be instructed to pause and look at themselves as if they were an impartial third party looking down at the interaction.

While they detach themselves from the current dynamic, they are asked to observe the words they are using, their tone of voice, and body language that may get in the way of effective communication. They may also notice a behavior of the other parent that triggered their negative response. Afterward, parents can be requested to name at least one of their own behaviors that was interfering with the process. The PC can follow up by encouraging them to state a behavior that could replace the ineffectual one or prevent them from reacting negatively to the behavior that triggered their response. Essentially, parents learn to externalize their interaction by locating it outside of themselves. As a result, it may be easier for them to slow down their negative impulses, neutralize their emotional response, be more objective about their behaviors, encourage accountability for their actions, and detach themselves from their own agenda while promoting what may be in the best interest of their child.

MODIFYING TECHNIQUES

Many of the techniques offered in this chapter are essential to the implementation of the program, such as reviewing expectations, fostering commitment, setting goals, and using effective problem-solving strategies. Other techniques are designed to encourage parents to be child focused while taking responsibility for their contribution to the problems as well as the solutions. Storytelling can be used to help parents normalize their situation while introducing new options to solve their difficulties. Metaphors are also useful in introducing new skills. In addition, teaching parents to externalize an interaction increases impulse control while promoting more effective problem solving.

Although numerous strategies are at the coordinator's disposal, the impaired parent will challenge even the most skilled coordinator. The following chapter describes the problematic parent commonly associated with high-conflict divorce. Having the knowledge and experience to work with the impaired parent increases the likelihood of successfully implementing the techniques offered within the model.

Chapter 12

The Impaired Parent

As parent coordinators begin working with high-conflict divorced parents they quickly become aware of the range of impaired parents. Cases are few and far between in which parents have their child's interest foremost at heart. Those parents respond quickly to the educational component of the process. As they learn how their behaviors have damaged their child, they get their priorities in line. Many of these parents have the capacity to cooperate, but the external influence of litigation, their grief process, and the impact of outside influences temporarily impair their ability and/or willingness to work cooperatively with their coparent. These are the parents who can make improvements postsettlement. However, the majority of parents seen by a parent coordinator have serious limitations and many are emotionally impaired. In highly conflicted circumstances, some parents demonstrate personality traits or disorders that significantly interfere with their ability to successfully coparent.

FAMILY SYSTEMS VERSUS DIAGNOSIS

Although the CPI model is a systems model, it is important to have an adequate understanding of the current diagnostic and statistical model of mental disorders. Whenever possible, the CPI model focuses more on parental style and issues of safety, and less on actual diagnosis. At times, however, an accurate diagnosis may be very helpful to the PC. Those times include the following:

1. When the impaired parent needs to be referred out for additional services
2. When the family had a custody evaluation that included diagnostic results
3. When the PC process breaks down and the PC is asked to testify regarding the parents' ability to work respectfully and effectively with each other
4. When the PC senses that the impaired parent may file a licensing complaint

The majority of the parents referred into parent coordination fall into one of the following categories or combination of categories:

1. Parents with anger problems
2. Parents who are narcissistically vulnerable
3. Parents with an Axis II diagnosis
4. Parents with a bipolar diagnosis
5. Parents with substance abuse or other addictions

Narcissistically Vulnerable Parents

Self-esteem is related to the regard one has for the dignity of one's own character. Therefore, self-esteem is related to a sense of worth. "Narcissism is not self-esteem or self-love per se, but the actions a person engages in to be able to hold oneself in high regard" (Baris et al., 2001, p. 20). It enables individuals to monitor and self-adjust their perception of self.

Narcissism can be defined as a normal or abnormal regulation of self-esteem. As Stolorow and Lachman (1980) noted:

> Narcissism embodies those mental operations whose function is to regulate self-esteem . . . and to maintain the cohesion and stability of the self representation. . . .The relation of narcissism to self-esteem is analogous to the relation between a thermostat and room temperature. A thermostat is not equivalent to room temperature, nor is it the only determinant of room temperature. It is the function of a thermostat to regulate and stabilize room temperature in the face of a multitude of forces which threaten to raise or lower it. . . . When self-esteem is threatened, significantly lowered, or destroyed, then narcissistic activities are called into play in an effort to protect, restore, repair and stabilize it. (Stolorow and Lachman, 1980, as cited in Baris et al., 2001, p. 20)

The narcissistically vulnerable parent is one with some narcissistic traits without fitting the diagnosis of narcissistic personality disorder. Since self-esteem is vital to happiness, narcissistic thinking becomes problematic only when the person must significantly distort reality to regain a sense of equilibrium. It is not unusual to find at least one parent in a high-conflict family that cannot empathize with the other parent.

The way in which the wounded parent responds to the wound will become problematic to the success of the joint sessions. Some parents must overidentify with their child to a point of enmeshment. The wounded parent who was abused as a child may believe that his or her own child has also been abused. The parent's reality becomes the reality of the child. For example, "If my husband lied to me, then he will lie to my child!" Therefore, one response to the narcissistic wound of divorce is to become totally enmeshed with the child. The parent's goal is to identify with the child in such a manner as to push the other parent out. One sign of enmeshment between parent and child is when the parent refers to the other parent in the third person or with formal titles, such as "Dr. Smith."

Johnston and Campbell (1988) describe three different levels of handling narcissistic wounds. Level one includes using others to confirm one's value by simply listening to them. The second-level narcissistic wound goes one step further. These individuals require more than just feeling listened to by others. They must have the listener agree with them. In the case of divorce, this would mean that the listener would agree that the other parent is "no good." The third and most pathological level is when they require more than agreement and support. The individual needs the listener to believe that revenge is justified. They project their own anger onto the coparent and then see the anger as being directed at them. When parents reach the third level of narcissistic injury, their ability to tolerate an opinion that is different from their own deteriorates. They see those who disagree with them as stupid or in denial. They view others as "for them" or "against them." They often see themselves as victims of the coparent, the parent coordinator, and the legal system. "The more the maintenance of self-esteem is externally placed, the more vulnerable an individual is to narcissistic wounds" (Baris et al., 2001, p. 42).

Most vulnerable parents are motivated by the fear that the other parent will "win" if they do not keep up their defenses. Stahl (1999b) reported that for the more disturbed of these parents, giving in may represent a fear of annihilation or loss of self. He added that winning or losing is linked to the parents' self-esteem. Parents with a borderline personality disorder attempt to win in order to soothe their internal pain and fear of abandonment. Narcissistic parents also fear abandonment as well as the loss of control. "While losing might mean different things to each parent (e.g., shame, loss, abandonment, rage, etc.) the key ingredient is how **unbearable** such a loss is to each parent" (Stahl, 1999b, p. 39). This parent may resist the parent coordinator's efforts out of general fear that the other parent may take advantage of them. This process of resistance not only guarantees conflict but also can take a toll on the PC unless he or she works diligently to keep an empathic perspective.

Indicators of Narcissistically Vulnerable Parents

The failure of divorce increases the chances of finding narcissistically wounded individuals in a high-conflict divorce case. According to Kopetski (1991) the following are indicators of a narcissistically vulnerable parent:

1. The other parent is seen as having a serious potential to harm the children, but these fears are unfounded.
2. The wounded parent gives the children a distorted, negative perception of the other parent.
3. The wounded parent talks to and treats the children as if the children were peers.
4. The wounded parent directly expresses a desire to limit or exclude contact with the other parent.
5. The wounded parent claims an entitlement or some other method of redressing an injustice.

Three Defensive Styles

Garrity and Baris (1994) identified the three defensive styles used to regain self-esteem:

1. "I am always right!" or "I am perfect!"
2. "My spouse is always wrong!" (Externalize and project blame)
3. "Maybe I will, maybe I won't." (Anger close to the surface)

Parents employing one of these defensive styles have a significantly difficult time working in a cooperative manner. Confronting any one of these three styles exacerbates the parent's ability to focus on their behaviors in order to evoke change. Their heightened emotional reaction leads to either a flight-or-fight response. The parent will want to either flee from the process or block the PC's attempts to efficiently maneuver within the system.

PERSONALITY-DISORDERED PARENTS

Several authors in the field have suggested that personality disorders are frequent among high-conflict parents, affecting one or both parents in approximately 60 percent of the families (Johnston and Campbell, 1988; Lund, 1995; Siegel and Langford, 1998;). According to the DSM-IV a personality disorder is an enduring pattern of inner experience and behavior that deviates markedly from the expectation of the individual's culture, is pervasive and inflexible, is stable over time, and leads to distress or impairment in interpersonal relationships. (Reprinted with permission from the *Diagnostic and Statistical Manual of Mental Disorders,* Text Revision, Copyright 2000. American Psychiatric Association)

Stahl (1999b) noted that Theodore Millon studied the personality traits of individuals diagnosed with personality disorders in order to gain an understanding of how personality traits influence relationships.

According to Stahl (1999b):

> most high-conflict families have one or both parents who exhibit either narcissistic, obsessive-compulsive, histrionic, paranoid or borderline features. They may have parents who become rigid in their perception of the other and tend to deal with things in their extremes. Many parents are polarized, viewing themselves as all good and the other as all bad. These parents experience chronic externalization of blame, possessing little insight into their role in the conflicts. They usually have little empathy for the impact of this conflict on their children. They routinely feel self-justified, believing that their actions are best for their children. No matter how much the helping professionals try to keep the focus on the child, these parents remain focused on the conflict. (p. 39)

According to Gregory W. Lester (1999) in his course titled Personality Disorders in Social Work and Healthcare, personality disorders are rapidly increasing in prevalence and "are responsible for many, if not most, treatment and case management failures." They are often distrusting, unreasonable, demanding, resistant, blaming, and avoidant. When they experience strong emotions, they either escalate or shut down. They also create drama and distress for individuals around them. Part of Lester's approach to personality disorders focuses on a shift from personality disorders to personality styles. The following information is adapted from sections of Lester's course materials and clinical observations made by Boyan.

Personality Disorder Patterns

According to Lester (1999), the personality-disordered individual has a pattern that involves two or more important areas of functioning:

1. *Thinking:* Ways of perceiving or interpreting self, others, and events
2. *Feeling:* Emotional range, intensity, stability, or appropriateness
3. *Interpersonal functioning:* The style and nature of their relationships
4. *Impulse control:* The ability to restrain, delay, or manage impulses

General Tips for Working with the Personality-Disordered Parent

The PC should lower his or her own expectations and aim at achieving only one goal at a time, trying to ignore the rest of the impaired parent's problems. The PC's goal is to increase the impaired parent's functioning and decrease his or her destructive behaviors. PCs should plan on coaching both in and out of sessions. PCs should always be intentional about what they are doing in the joint sessions; they should not wade in. The PC should also avoid becoming part of the drama; instead, the coordinator should make comments from "outside the drama." The parents will want to focus on the content of their problems, but it is more important to help them focus on their style while getting quick agreements about the content. Ultimately it is imperative that the PC convinces impaired parents that they can learn better ways to get what they want.

The coordinator should make sure all parental agreements are clear and very specific and must deal promptly with all broken agreements. The PC must pick battles carefully and not get sidetracked by irrelevant issues. In addition, PCs must set and maintain firm, reasonable, conscious limits, while managing their own energy. PCs should (1) avoid matching their affect (anger with anger), (2) be aware of their own countertransferences, (3) not get caught in the need to be right, (4) think de-escalate, (5) diminish intensity, and (6) avoid any exceptions to rules. If the PC begins to feel crazy it just means that he or she has become caught in the parents' drama.

Drama Patterns

Lester maintains that personality-disordered individuals experiencing conflict react in a survival-based pattern of distraction called "drama." Their drama prevents effective problem solving. Impaired parents switch between the role of victim, persecutor, and rescuer.

Although professionals would benefit from a comprehensive understanding of all ten personality disorders, the greatest number of parents involved in parent coordination will exhibit the characteristics of the immature type of personality disorders. For this reason, only the immature cluster of personality disorders are addressed. The chapter will focus on borderline, histrionic, and narcissistic disorders. For additional information, the practitioner should consult the *Diagnostic and Statistical Manual of Mental Disorders,* Fourth Edition, Text Revision, published in 2000 by the American Psychiatric Assoctiation.

Histrionic Personality Disorder

General Description

Histrionic individuals have a pervasive pattern of excessive emotionality and attention-seeking behaviors. They may be shallow, theatrical, and use their appearance and seductiveness to draw attention to themselves. They may appear childlike, superficial, and believe their relationships are more intimate than they actually are. Their speech is dramatic and lacking in detail.

Parent Coordinator Tips

Coordinators often feel irritated and impatient with the distracting behaviors of these parents. The PC should push them to use distinct and descriptive terms. They need to be structured so that they do not sidetrack the sessions or dominate the time. The PC should assist in focusing on alternative ways to get their needs met and should not challenge them too quickly. When in doubt, the coordinator should ask for clarification. The parent's behaviors should be observed while the content of the message is acknowledged. The histrionic parent has difficulty offering or following through with details. The PC can also focus on training them to be more socially appropriate as it applies to coparenting.

Narcissistic Personality Disorder (NPD)

General Description

Narcissistic individuals have a pervasive pattern of grandiosity in their behavior. They are arrogant, require admiration, and lack empathy. Their grandiose sense of self-importance results in exaggerated achievements and talents. They expect to be recognized as superior and are preoccupied with fantasies of unlimited success, power, beauty, and/or brilliance. They are envious of others, self-righteous, and have a strong sense of entitlement. They often exploit, manipulate, and demean others.

Parent Coordinator Tips

When working with the NPD parent, PCs may find themselves feeling angry, defensive, and working too hard. They should not confront the NPD's view of self as special. It is helpful if the PC brainstorms solutions with these parents with the intention of helping them to get what they want. The PC needs to be self-assured and friendly but not overly solicitous or nurturing. PCs should never defend themselves. During the intake session, the PC should use open-ended questions in order to encourage the parent to expound on his or her experiences. The PC should use mirroring/reflecting and soothing prior to confrontations. The PC can feed them "rightness" until their neediness calms down, so that the PC can then ask, suggest, recommend, or make a request.

Borderline Personality Disorder (BPD)

Because the parent coordinator frequently encounters parents exhibiting the characteristics of borderline personality disorder, more extensive information has been devoted to this personality disorder.

General Description

This individual has a pervasive pattern of instability of mood, interpersonal relationships, and self-image. The BPD exhibits frantic efforts to avoid real or imagined abandonment. They alternate between overidealization and devaluation of others (splitting). They can be very charming and childlike and then quickly shift to demanding or raging when they do not get what they want. They may be highly critical and hostile while also being dependent, overly intense, dramatic, thin-skinned, and blaming. Most distort what they hear, and some make untrue accusations. They set others up for a no- win situation and create facts to fit their feelings. They lack object constancy, may have narcissistic tendencies, and use all-or-nothing thinking. Their shifts in mood rarely last more than a few hours. Some individuals experiencing this disorder may also exhibit inappropriate anger, outbursts, stress-related paranoid ideation, vague threats, manipulation, and self-loathing.

Additional Information

According to Mason and Kreger (1998) more than 6 million people in the United States have BPD disorder, and these people greatly affect the lives of at least 30 million others: "Although the BPD individual feels the same feelings as everyone else, they feel them more intensely, act in ways that are more extreme and have a significantly difficult time monitoring their emotions and their behaviors" (p. 16). BPD is linked to high conflict, divorce, suicide, substance abuse, child abuse, physical, sexual, and emotional abuse, eating disorders, estrangement from family members, and much more.

In general, emotionally healthy people base their feelings on facts. People with BPD, however, may do the opposite. When their feelings do not fit the facts, they may unconsciously revise the facts to fit their feelings. This may be one reason why their perception of events during the sessions will be so different from those of the PC. Research indicates that most alienating parents demonstrate the characteristics of BPD. Yet it is not uncommon for a parent to look like a BPD during a very stressful and emotional divorce. It is imperative to recognize the BPD parent as soon as possible so that the PC can videotape joint sessions. Most BPD parents may benefit from viewing themselves on a videotape.

As with any disorder or disability, people experiencing BPD may not necessarily exhibit all the qualities discussed in this section. Each parent, as with any individual, is unique in his or her own way. The following is intended to offer a broad range of professional suggestions.

High Functioning, Low Functioning

People with BPD vary in their ability to function in the world. The high-functioning BPD individual acts perfectly normal most of the time. Successful, outgoing, well liked, and respected outside the home, they show their dysfunctional side only to people who know them very well. It is in intimate relationships that their problems create drama. High-functioning BPDs will appear normal until they are emotionally triggered. Although they may feel the same emptiness on the inside as the low-functioning BPD, they cover it up very well. Low-functioning BPDs have problems in most relationships rather than just the intimate ones. They often find themselves living from crisis to crisis.

Assumptions Held by BPD Sufferers

According to Borderline Central (www.bpdcentral.com), when interacting with BPD individuals, it is crucial to understand that their unconscious assumptions may be very different from those of others. They may include the following:

"I must be loved by all the important people in my life at all times or else I am worthless. I must be completely competent in all ways to be a worthwhile person."

"Some people are good and everything about them is perfect. Other people are thoroughly bad and should be severely blamed and punished for it."

"Nobody cares about me as much as I care about them, so I always lose everyone I care about—despite the desperate things I try to do to stop them from leaving me."

"I will be happy only when I can find an all-giving, perfect person to love me and take care of me no matter what."

"I can't stand the frustration that I feel when I need something from someone and I can't get it. I've got to do something to make this feeling go away."

Defense Mechanisms

The BPD uses all the same defense mechanisms as the average person. However, they use these mechanisms more frequently and with greater intensely. Some may dissociate as a way to run away from their pain. However, the primary mechanisms used frequently by the BPD individual include splitting and projection.

Splitting. The BPD parent has a difficult time seeing gray areas. To them, people and situations are all black and white, wonderful or evil. For people with BPD it is easier to understand the world if they put it into all-or-nothing categories. It is difficult for the PC to compliment the other parent without BPD parents thinking the PC does not like them because they believe only one parent can be "good."

Primarily, BPD individuals are desperately looking for someone to take care of them who will never leave, who will love them no matter what, who will never cross them, and who will ultimately make them feel whole and therefore erase their emptiness. When the PC is appearing to meet all their needs, the PC becomes their hero. However, as soon as BPD individuals perceive that the PC has failed them in some way, the PC instantly becomes the villain. BPD individuals form an opinion based upon the most recent interaction with that person. Their opinion of themselves also depends upon their most recent accomplishment or lack of accomplishment.

Projection. Projection is defined as the denial of one's own unpleasant traits, behaviors or feelings by attributing them to someone else. BPD individuals use projection as another defense mechanism to reduce their own anxiety, pain, or feelings of shame. They lack a clear sense of who they are and feel empty and inherently defective. Their goal is not to be difficult but rather to minimize their internal pain and shame. Following are examples of typical situations that reflect BPD projection:

COPARENT: You were late again at transfer!
BPD PARENT: It's your fault because you should have called to remind me! [I can't stand myself when I forget stuff.]

PARENT COORDINATOR: We need to let your coparent share his concern now.
BPD PARENT TO PC: You never let me talk so I can't get my issues heard. [I talk too much and dominate the time.]

Another way BPD parents may use this defense mechanism is to project their own feelings onto the coparent or the parent coordinator. They must deny their own flaws because they cannot tolerate anything less than perfection. Unless they are perfect they are worthless. A common theme is "If one thing is wrong with me, then everything is wrong with me. There cannot be anything wrong with me or I will be unlovable."

BPD PARENT TO CHILD: I know you like your dad more than me! [I'm unloveable.]
BPD PARENT TO PC: You don't have an available appointment because you don't want to have a coaching session with me. [I don't like being with me so why would you?]

Narcissistic Demands

Most BPDs have narcissistic qualities. They will consistently bring the focus back onto themselves. This is especially difficult in joint sessions in which the focus is on someone else—the child. Some BPDs will have extensive physical complaints and illnesses that they may use to get their way.

Lack of Object Constancy

Most adults can soothe themselves when they are upset. Part of this soothing process is the ability to remember those who love us even if they are unavailable or even deceased. This ability is referred to as object constancy. For the BPD individual it is difficult to hold onto this knowledge unless the person is present and available. If the loved one is not present he or she does not exist. For this reason BPD parents are often the most likely to attempt to alienate their child from the other parent. In addition, they are unable to "remember" the past in positive terms because it no longer exists. The PC can assist more severe BPD parents by providing them with a transitional object as long as this is done indirectly. Handing the BPD parent a business card or lending something to the parent such as a book can aid in this process. Offering coaching sessions can also be experienced as a reminder that the PC is available to them.

Feelings Determine Facts

Most people create their feelings based upon facts, but BPD individuals function as if their feelings should determine the facts. Facts are altered to confirm their feelings; they unconsciously make revisions to history. This process usually leaves those around the BPD individual feeling confused and even crazy. This is especially problematic for the child of a BPD individual. The PC who does not use videotaping with this population will soon get caught up in the BPD's version of reality. It is not unusual for the distortions to be the first sign that the PC is working with a BPD parent.

Divorcing BPDs

Most divorcing BPDs engage in a distortion campaign due to their feelings of abandonment and anger. According to Johnston and Roseby (1997), loss evokes powerful feelings of anxiety, sadness, and fear of being abandoned. Some individuals cover their grief with anger and try to postpone the abandonment of divorce by keeping their spouse in unending conflict. By fighting and arguing they can maintain contact and postpone the lack of contact. Furthermore, the authors maintain that the BPD experiences a fragile self-esteem that requires all sense of failure outside the self. This individual often demonstrates a self-righteous air of angry superiority and entitlement and accuses the ex-spouse of being psychologically and morally inferior. More often than not, the BPD rewrites the marital history to portray the former partner as intentionally plotting and planning from the beginning to exploit and cast the BPD parent off. He or she feels justified in seeking retaliation. Many divorcing BPDs will take a proactive stance and attack before they are attacked.

Countermoves

Countermoves are actions designed to restore the balance. BPDs use countermoves to justify their actions, to both themselves and others. Countermoves should be expected from the BPD, which means any intervention used by the PC will be asking them to do something differently. Their discomfort will increase and they will look for immediate relief, frustrating the overall process.

Manipulation versus Desperation

Mason and Kreger (1998) reported that the BPD's behavior is not intentionally manipulative but rather a desperate attempt to cope with painful feelings. They often act impulsively out of fear, anxiety, and desperation as a way to soothe their panic. Nonetheless, those impacted by these behaviors will undoubtedly feel manipulated.

It is not usual for BPD parents to threaten suicide if their partner asks for a divorce. During the divorce process and postdivorce they may continue to threaten others when they do not get their way. The threats may include telling marital secrets, moving the children away, kidnapping the children, or preventing visitation in some way. They may also threaten to call the police, make false allegations, or even alienate the children. It is important to recognize that this is not only a means of punishment but also a desperate attempt to relieve their pain by whatever means available. When BPD parents feel threatened they will request a new parent coordinator and sometimes threaten (or follow through with) a licensing complaint or a lawsuit against the PC. They may also threaten to write the judge or to refuse to comply with the order. It is important to recognize that BPD parents are not trying to hurt their coparent but are trying only to protect themselves. Nonetheless, their behaviors feel like emotional blackmail to those who deal with them.

According to Forward and Frazier (1997), emotional blackmail is a direct or indirect threat by someone to punish someone else for not doing what the person expects. Since most BPDs are attempting to protect themselves, emotional blackmail or manipulation are not necessarily useful terms to describe the BPD's motive. Yet their behaviors may "feel" like blackmail or manipulation to the other parent, their children, or the parent coordinator. Their pain results in impulsive acting out with the goal of self-soothing.

Acting In or Acting Out

Acting in refers to taking out anger on oneself, while acting out refers to using the other person to relieve the pain. Mason and Kreger (1998) reported that the BPD's pain is expressed by either acting in or acting out. Acting-in behaviors mostly hurt the BPD. They may feel extremely guilty about imagined transgressions. They may mutilate themselves, try to hold in their anger, and blame themselves for problems that are not their fault. Some BPDs will act in and act out. Acting-out behaviors are attempts to alleviate pain by dumping it onto someone else by projecting, blaming, criticizing, making accusations, using aggression, verbal abuse, and raging.

Typical BPD Triggers

It is important to understand the BPD parent's buttons are easily pushed. Therefore, it is beneficial to understand the reasons why the parent may be triggered by a certain action or word. In this way, it is more likely that the trigger can be avoided. Hot buttons or triggers, according to Mason and Kreger (1998, p. 111), are "stored-up resentments, regrets, insecurities, angers, and fear that hurt when touched and cause automatic emotional responses." Typical BPD trigger themes include the following:

> "Others are not predictable!"
> "The PC likes him more!" (I am all alone!)
> "My attorney is minimizing my feelings!"(I am not worthy!)
> "Her stepmom is critical of me as the real parent!"
> "They are taking the spotlight away from me!"
> "They want to label me!"

Borderline Rage

The BPD's natural intensity, impulsivity, and high level of anxiety over perceived abandonment often results in rage. According to Mason and Kreger (1998, p. 40), "Borderline rage is usually intense, unpredictable, and unaffected by logical argument." However, according to Linehan (1993), some BPDs underexpress their anger out of fear of losing control.

The BPD parent will attempt to engage the PC to debate what is right or wrong. The PC must avoid this. For instance, the PC might say, "I understand you believe this is all your coparent's fault. However, I see it differently and I cannot allow you to scream at him. Let's take a break so I can help you learn how to express your thoughts in a more productive manner."

BPD Parenting

People with BPD are emotionally and developmentally similar to children. They have difficulty putting their needs aside for others. This creates additional problems for BPD parents when the PC tries to teach them how to stay child focused. They may even resent their children's emotional needs and the attention they receive. On the other hand, the child is often seen as an extension of the parent. If BPD parents are feeling sad, they may become upset if their child is not upset with them. They see their child's separateness as disloyalty and abandonment. This is even more problematic when their child becomes more independent during adolescence. The BPD parent may create guilt for the child who is not attending to their emotional needs. They are likely to lean on their child and have difficulty separating their own needs from those of their child.

In a similar manner as the narcissistic personality-disordered parent, BPD parents may have trouble understanding when their child has feelings or opinions that are different from theirs. If the child is feeling emotionally dependent on the personality-disordered parent, then he or she may learn to accommodate the parent's needs rather than experience the parent's rage, rejection, or conditional love. If BPD parents have made efforts to alienate the child and the child is refusing visitation, the child may unconsciously choose the unstable and dependent BPD parent over the healthier parent. It is as if the child understands that rejecting the healthier parent will allow the child to retain two parents to love him or her. If they side against the BPD parent they will lose their love and end up with only one parent.

According to Dr. Janet Johnston of the Judith Wallerstein Center for the Family in Transition, the impact of the BPD parent on the child depends upon the types of behaviors exhibited by the BPD and the child's temperament. If the BPD "acts in" and has a caretaking child, then the child will most likely end up feeling overly responsible for the parent. If the BPD "acts out" and has a cooperative child, the child will most likely grow up to be very anxious. If the acting-out parent has a healthy and assertive child, the parent and child will most likely come to blows. Some BPD parents can become emotionally and/or physically abusive.

Parent Coordinator Tips

While working with this population, PCs will feel damned if they do and damned if they don't. Most BPD individuals are bright and can learn skills, but they rarely use them when they are upset. It is imperative that the PC set firm and consistent limits and use consequences for unacceptable behavior. The PC must expect distortions and rejection by the BPD as he or she will likely experience limits as rejection. The PC must give the parents copies of each agreement and tape session because the BPD will distort what was really said. The BPD must be taught the difference between a request and a demand. The PC should confront the BPD's self-defeating behaviors and ignore provocations. The PC is advised to help the BPD make self-destructive behaviors ungratifying. Reflecting and reframing are important skills to use with the BPD.

It is beneficial for the PC to schedule periodic coaching sessions or use caucuses to connect with BPD parents' "raw deal" instead of battling with their rage. When meeting separately do not allow them to discuss the coparent. Although this is wise for any coaching session, it is very important to hold the BPD gently but firmly to this expectation. Due to their strong tendency to split, careful consideration should be used if considering the use of two PCs in one session.

Setting limits with the BPD parent. Limits and boundaries allow us to know where we end and where others begin. Limits can be physical and/or emotional in nature. Limits protect like an outer shell; they bring order to our lives. Without limits the BPD parent will become dramatically out of control. According to Mason and Kreger (1998), healthy limits are somewhat flexible. If the limits are overly flexible then the BPD will violate the limits and intrusions can occur. Limits are not about control. The PC must ensure that the limits are the same with both parents and that no room exists for manipulation of these limits. This is not always easy to accomplish.

For example, the PC has a rule that neither parent can contact the PC unless there is a "child-focused emergency." A non-BPD parent calls the PC when his or her eight-year-old son is left to baby-sit a one-year-old sibling. The PC contacts the BPD parent to inquire about this. No matter how the PC asks, the BPD parent is likely to hear judgment. Very soon after this intervention the BPD parent tests the PC's limits by calling the PC to ask him or her to intervene because the son left his favorite baseball bat at the other parent's home. The PC leaves a message that this is not a child-focused emergency because the child has other bats he can use. The BPD parent becomes outraged at the PC's response, demanding that his or her concern is child focused. The BPD parent views the outcome of this situation as confirmation of his or her fear that the PC prefers the other parent.

Along with other forms of limits, the PC must charge both parents for phone calls, faxes, and e-mail communication because the BPD will push limits without clear consequences. The PC must be supportive while enforcing clear boundaries that make it clear which behaviors will not be tolerated.

Defusing techniques. When working with BPD parents, it is helpful to agree with some part of their statements. If not, the PC will get pulled into the BPD drama. For instance, consider the following dialogue:

BPD PARENT: I see you are going to start with his issue first again. [said in a disapproving way]

PC RESPONSE: Yes, I am. [not "His issue is more time sensitive" (defending)]

In addition, at times, it may be advantageous to agree that the BPD may be right.

BPD PARENT: I think it is ridiculous for our son to go to therapy. Everyone knows it would mean we failed as parents.

PC RESPONSE: You are right; some people might think that. [not "I have lots of clients and I can assure you that it does not mean that the parent's are always to blame" (trying to change her mind)]

Finally, validate their opinion.

BPD MOTHER: Mothers always get custody in this county. Judges understand the importance of having children with their mothers.

PC RESPONSE: I can see you have strong feelings about being the primary parent. The judge may or may not see it the same way. I guess we will have to see." [not "That is not always true. I know for a fact . . ."]

To avoid the BPD parent feeling abandoned by the PC, never

Defend your position
Deny his or her feelings
Counterattack
Withdraw

Additional Tips for Dealing with the BPD Parent

When conducting the intake, watch for a history of feeling victimized.
Treat the BPD with respect, empathy, and dignity.
Give positive feedback.
Ask questions.
Request alternative solutions.
Keep your message simple.
Watch your voice inflection and nonverbal communication.
Develop a noncombative style of communicating.
Watch for a distortion campaign against the former attorney or the PC.
Give copies of the session agreements.
Do not reward acting-out behavior.
Always insist upon taping the joint sessions.
Appeal to the BPD's desire to want the best for his or her child.
Emphasize the areas in which you and the BPD parent agree.
Find out how he or she prefers to receive your feedback.

Do not expect to be able to speak with BPD parents when they are raging.

Never match BPD rage with your own.

Never tell them to calm down when raging.

Do not take the BPD rage personally.

Do not try to convince the BPD parent of your view of the world.

Do not attempt to prove their accusations are false.

Do not be seduced by their idealization, because the devaluation is just around the corner.

Always remember that BPD parents' behaviors are more about them than about you.

Avoid words such as *always* and *never* (splitting).

Expect the unexpected.

Pick your battles.

For more information on BPD, read *Stop Walking on Eggshells: Taking Your Life Back When Someone You Care About Has Borderline Personality Disorder* by Paul T. Mason and Randi Kreger (1998) and *I Hate You—Don't Ever Leave Me: Understanding the Borderline Personality* by Jerold J. Kriesman and Hal Straus (1991).

ADDITIONAL PROBLEMATIC FACTORS

In addition, parent coordinators may be dealing with other factors or multiple problems. Some other issues/problems include the following:

The Bipolar Parent

Bipolar parents, particularly without effective medication, can be highly agitated, irrational, and out of control when they are in a manic phase. These parents can be very difficult to manage due to their lack of impulse control. They tend to dominate, interrupt, push limits, and become highly emotional. These parents need frequent coaching both in joint sessions and in separate coaching sessions. Having them view their videotapes in sessions with the parent coordinator can assist them in learning new behaviors. However, before this can happen they must understand that the parent coordinator is there to help them learn a more effective means of attaining their personal goals. Without this they will not be motivated to improve or to accept coaching.

*Distinguishing Borderline Personality Disorder
from Bipolar Parents*

At times, it may be difficult to distinguish the personality characteristics of the borderline personality disorder from those exhibited by the bipolar individual. The following outline offers some information that helps differentiate the two disorders.

Mood swings	The bipolar individual has a neurological reason for mood swings.
	The BPD individual's moods are always triggered by an event.
Impulsiveness	The bipolar individual is impulsive only when in a manic phase.
	The BPD individual is always impulsive.
Dichotomy	The bipolar individual does not dichotomize.
	The BPD individual always splits.

ADD Problems of All Types

Parents with attention problems often have impulse-control problems and organizational difficulties, run late for appointments, forget appointments, and may have self-esteem problems. These parents are often an annoyance to their coparent for all these reasons. They often marry very organized spouses. It is not unusual for parents with attentional problems to be blamed for more than their share of the marital problems and the coparenting problems. Their coparents need to learn to be tolerant and to see the positive qualities rather than focus on their coparent's weaknesses. For additional information read Hallowell and Ratey's (1995) *Driven to Distraction: Recognizing and Coping with Attention Deficit Disorder from Childhood to Adulthood.*

Obsessive Tendencies

The parent with obsessive-compulsive tendencies will be seen as highly rigid and controlling. It is important to see these tendencies as a coping mechanism for anxiety. Over time the coparent can begin to recognize this with the PC's help. Otherwise, the parent's controlling behaviors will be viewed as intentional and aggressive.

Alcohol and Substance Problems

The scope of this chapter cannot begin to address the issue of alcohol and substance abuse. However, the PC should be aware that parents may make allegations regarding the other parent drinking and driving, or having a substance or prescription drug abuse problem. Some families will report that physical abuse occurred in the past when the other parent was "using."

The substance-abusing parent must be required to seek an assessment if the PC believes that he or she may be using. If the parent coordinator is unsure if substances are being used and has heard about this only from the other parent, then the PC should encourage the potentially using parent to allow random screens. If parents are not using they are usually very quick to agree to three screens. The parent requesting the screen may agree to pay for those that are negative.

If agreeing to random screens, the parent should locate a laboratory that will not require a medical referral. After locating a lab close to the parent's home and work site, then the PC can make the first random call during a visit with the child. The next screen can occur a few hours after a visit. The last random call should be when the parent does not have the child. It is important that the coordinator have a consultant who can indicate how much time should be allowed between the random call and the parent's response time for different substances.

If the parent is unwilling to have a random screen the PC should consider one of two options. The PC can write in his or her notes during the joint session while reading each word out loud: "Even though father denies using illegal drugs, he refuses to allow the PC to call three random screens even with mother's agreement to pay for any negative results." When parents listen to the words as they are written, they often change their minds, realizing that their resistance looks like evidence. When this fails to provide motivation, a memo to both attorneys may. The last resort would be for the PC to advise the parent to expect a random call from the PC, or an emergency hearing may be requested.

It is also important to have the results faxed directly to the parent coordinator's office and make sure that the parent show photo ID at the lab. Otherwise, parents may send someone else to take the test.

The PC may also require an alcohol and drug (A&D) assessment or require involvement in a twelve-step program. Children's safety should be the most important factor for the PC to consider. Relapse plans should also be addressed if the parent is in recovery.

Sexual Factors

The PC may be assigned to a family based solely on either an allegation or a reality of sexual problems. It is essential that the PC accepting such a case is both comfortable and experienced working with sexual issues.

Sexual Addictions

With such easy access to pornography on the Internet, it is not surprising how many marriages have been destructively affected by this powerful form of addiction and betrayal. From pornography to sexual acting out, the PC may receive referrals for families dealing with sexual addictions. The PC should be informed about the impact of sexual addictions on the family and should also be aware of referral sources within the community such as a Sex Addicts Anonymous (SAA) twelve-step program. The PC will need to help the family develop guidelines to protect the children from access to pornography of all types. The PC may need to require the abusing parent to have a separate computer so that the children cannot accidentally access his or her "habit."

Sexual Allegations

This brief discussion cannot begin to address the issues of sexual allegations or sexual abuse in divorce. Parent coordinators should read Gardner's (1992) *The Parental Alienation Syndrome* to learn more about the prevalence of sexual allegations in conflicted divorce. If there is a serious concern the PC may want to discuss the value of a sexual deviance evaluation to alleviate concerns. Sexual deviance evaluations and assessments may be a service referral made by the PC. In addition, sexual abuse or poor-boundary allegations may require the PC to initiate a referral for the child to be seen by an expert in the field of sex abuse.

Other Factors

To provide the best possible services, parent coordinators are strongly advised to learn more about the following issues:

Family violence with or without protective orders
Families with special-needs adults (e.g., traumatic head injury)
Families with cultural differences
Families with religious differences

Allegations of abuse
Relocation issues
Affect disorders
Unemployment, bankruptcy

PROTECTING THE PARENT COORDINATOR

Due to the difficulty of working with these parents, it is imperative that the PC have adequate supervision/consultation support, professional insurance, and detailed and documented session notes. Furthermore, the PC must attempt to remain vigilant to his or her personal issues through therapy and consultation. This is particularly true for the PC working with high-conflict parents. With any form of competent service we must take responsibility for adequately exploring our own issues so that they are not inadvertently placed upon an already difficult situation. Videotaping of joint sessions can be extremely helpful in providing feedback both to the parents and to the PC. For example, if a coordinator experienced an abusive relationship in his or her family of origin, then this PC may be at risk of either overreacting or underreacting to an angry parent. Keeping perspective is vital to remain neutral and provide ethical and constructive services to high-conflict families. When working with this population, particularly those parents who are characterologically impaired, self-awareness is essential. Axis II parents often distort what happens in the sessions and then report inaccurate information against the PC to their attorney and even to the licensing board. The CPI model recommends using detailed intake forms that clearly outline the role and responsibility of the coordinator in order to protect the professional. Another method of protection is the use of videotaping the Axis II parent in a joint session. In addition, if an impaired parent leaves a voice message on the coordinator's machine, a copy of this message can be recorded onto an audiocassette. These messages often highlight the impaired parent's irrational beliefs and rage. Precautionary measures should be taken with the Axis II parent since the majority of complaints are made by this population.

Vulnerable Parent, Vulnerable PC

Typically high-conflict divorce is associated with vulnerable parents. The most skilled coordinator will be exposed to a variety of problematic parents which will increase their own vulnerability. Not only does the PC need to remain focused in his or her approach while working with this population, he or she must also take measures for protection from false allegations made by the impaired parent. In addition, the coordinator must set realistic behavioral goals that, at the very least, minimize the child's exposure to parental behaviors and limit the amount of parental interaction. Parents diagnosed with personality disorders engage in behaviors that may influence their child's willingness to share time with the other parent. As a result, the parent coordinator is faced with developing interventions intended to discourage visitation refusal. It is imperative that the PC be able to recognize and intervene when parental alienation truly exists. Chapter 13 defines normal visitation refusal and outlines the criteria for recognizing parental alienation.

Chapter 13

Extreme Circumstances:
Parental Alienation

Since the 1980s, alienation of a child from a parent following separation and divorce has attracted significant attention in custody disputes and in recent years has produced extensive legal, psychological, and media-based controversy (Kelly and Johnston, 2001). Most practitioners agree that alienation occurs on a continuum from loyalty binds to visitation refusal and includes any conscious or unconscious attempt to align a child against the other parent. Visitation refusal is a state in which a child is unwilling to spend time with the noncustodial parent.

It is essential to recognize that parental alienation is not the only situation that results in visitation refusal. Other normative factors may influence a child's refusal to visit the noncustodial parent. Some reasonable explanations for refusing visitation include activity conflicts and developmental factors such as an adolescent's growing social life. In addition, children of all ages may resist visitation for the following reasons: (a) the noncustodial parent's rigid or insensitive parenting style, (2) stepfamily conflicts, or (3) the child's alignment with a new "intact" (step)family. Obviously, some children may resist visitation due to safety concerns such as physical, emotional, and sexual abuse.

Therefore, visitation refusal can result from multiple factors: (1) the child's developmental issues, (2) the noncustodial parent's inappropriate parenting, and/or (3) the alienating efforts on the part of the custodial parent. The degree of all these factors must be considered prior to determining the primary problem contributing to the child's resistance. Those children who refuse contact with a parent based primarily upon a negative and intense campaign conducted by the custodial parent have been exposed to the emotional abuse of alienation.

To determine the level of alienation, the practitioner must consider the intensity of the behaviors, the frequency of one or more behaviors, the parent's motivation for the alienation, and the impact on the child's relationship with both parents. In cases of severe alienation the child becomes a participant in the alienation. Whether this is identified as a syndrome, visitation resistance, or severe child alienation, it does not seem to alter the devastating results.

PROFESSIONAL DEBATE

Professionals in the field of divorce have used various terms and definitions to describe situations in which children resist seeing a parent. In 1976, Judith Wallerstein and Joan Kelly coined the term *visitation refusal.* They defined this behavior as a pathological alignment between an angry parent and child. In keeping with a pathological focus, Richard Gardner (1987, 1992) identified visitation refusal as *parental alienation syndrome* (PAS). According to Gardner, this syndrome occurs primarily in the context of child-custody disputes. PAS refers to a situation in which a parent's conscious attempt to program a child to dislike the other parent is combined with the child's own negative view of the so-called hated parent. Gardner maintained that to be classified as a syndrome the child must contribute to the alienation of a parent. In situations in which the hated parent has actually abused the child in some manner, the syndrome does not apply. In some situations, alienation of the parent is justified. Parental alienation syndrome is applicable only when the targeted parent has not exhibited severe enough behaviors to warrant the child's rejection or hostility. The exaggeration of the hated parent's flaws is the hallmark of parental alienation syndrome.

More recently Kelly and Johnston (2001) shifted the focus from the parent to the child and created the term *child alienation.* Their model focuses on a family systems approach while considering the multiple contributing factors involved in visitation resistance. Kelly and Johnston (2001, p. 251) defined an alienated child "as one who expresses, freely and persistently, unreasonable negative feelings and beliefs (such as anger, hatred, rejection and/or fear) toward a parent that are significantly disproportionate to the child's actual experience with that parent." They described the rejected noncustodial parent as falling within the broad range of marginal to good enough and sometimes better parents, who have no history of physical or emotional abuse of a child.

Kelly and Johnston (2001) cited several reasons for a child's resistance to visitation: (1) high-conflict marriage, (2) opposition to a parent's style of parenting (e.g., rigidity), (3) parental anger, (4) a parent's insensitivity to children, and (5) a child's concern for an emotionally fragile custody parent. However, they added that no single factor creates the alienated child.

Additional professionals have continued to address situations in which a child may resist seeing a parent. Stoltz and Ney (2002, p. 220) defined visitation resistance as "any set of behaviors on the part of the child, parents, and others involved in the conflict that leads to the cessation of or significantly impedes visitation with the non custodial parent." They maintained that the problem does not rest with the custodial parent as Gardner (1987) claims, or with the child as Kelly and Johnston (2001) suggest, but rather with the dynamic created out of the unique social context. This focus on the interaction in the social context places the problem outside of any one particular individual. This nonblaming approach has the potential of creating numerous options for successful interventions. Stoltz and Ney have replaced the term *alienation* with *resistance*.

According to Ward and Harvey (1993), severe alienation occurs when the child is fully enmeshed with the alienating parent. This frequently develops with that parent because a child possesses few internal or external resources with which to resist the adult's influence. As a result, the enmeshed child embraces as his or her own the alienating parent's hatred, emotions, and outcome for the targeted parent. Thus it often becomes difficult to discern the source of the denigration.

Douglas Darnell (2001) identified three types of alienators: the naive alienator, the active alienator, and the obsessed alienator.

The naive alienator is a parent who means well and recognizes the importance of a child's healthy and satisfying relationship with both parents and extended family members. However, every so often this parent unintentionally makes a derogatory comment about the other parent or divorce matters. Fortunately, they recognize the inappropriateness of their behavior and feel guilty when their behavior negatively affects the relationship between their child and other parent. As a result, they take responsibility for their actions and correct their behavior.

Active alienators attack the other parent in the presence of the child. This behavior is the result of poor impulse control rather than a conscious attempt to denigrate the other parent. Once they calm down, they acknowledge that their behavior was inappropriate and attempt to repair the damage to their child. Similar to naive alienators, they encourage their children to have a satisfying relationship with the other parent. They are very concerned about their child's adjustment to the separation. At times, they can be very rigid and uncooperative with the other parent. However, they generally respect the court's authority and comply with court orders.

The obsessed alienator is intent on destroying the relationship between the child and his or her other parent. This alienator can be a parent, a grandparent, or both. They attempt to form an alliance with the child and generally succeed in enmeshing the child's personality and beliefs about the other parent with their own. They believe that their actions to protect their child from the other parent are justified and believe that they have been victimized by the other parent. They try to enlist the court's support in punishing the other parent with orders that interfere with the child seeing the other parent, yet they do not respect the court's authority.

It is the authors' belief that each of the views on visitation resistance have value and merit. As pointed out by Stoltz and Ney, the adversarial social context has been seriously overlooked. However, by overstressing the social context, Stoltz and Ney may oversimplify the phenomenon by attempting to avoid blame or pathology. The authors have found the custodial parent's psychological health to be a significant factor to be reckoned with along with several other factors, including the adversarial players and the social context.

Heated disputes as to the theoretical framework for the phenomenon known as parental alienation syndrome continue. Some professionals believe that Gardner's concept of parental alienation syndrome focuses on pathology. More specifically, the use of the term *syndrome* implies that the problem is something that resides within an individual and is not necessarily viewed in the broader context of the social network. However, Gardner (2002) defined parental alienation syndrome as just one subtype of parental alienation. This specific subtype includes an alienating parent's programming of a child into a crusade of denigration against the other parent, who is generally loving and devoted to the child. The primary etiological factor in PAS is the brainwashing parent. If there is no brainwashing parent, there is no PAS. Still, he maintained that some alienated children are not influenced by a brainwashing parent. Gardner stated that PAS has the advantage of directing attention to the programmer, and, when it is the primary cause, it is useful to label it as PAS. He added that the identification of this subtype makes the court's job easier.

Holman and Irvine (2002) alleged that the term *alienation* has become a catchall phrase attributed to a whole range of issues and behaviors. In an attempt to describe visitation resistance in very observable and workable terms, Holman and Irvine have identified two separate dynamics that may occur in a family that can be related to but are separate from alienation: undermining and obstruction. They argued that chronic interference with parenting time and undermining of the other parent creates a unique set of complex issues.

They defined an "undermining parent" as an individual who either overtly or covertly conveys to the child that the other parent is not good enough or may even be dangerous. For example, the undermining parent may say, "I am not surprised that your father wouldn't let you buy that shirt. He just doesn't understand the importance of being in style," or "Your weekend with your mother will probably be okay, but just remember to stay out of her way if she starts yelling." The undermining parent focuses on the personal qualities of the other parent and uses these characteristics to communicate to the child that the other parent just does not have what it takes to be a good parent.

While undermining focuses on the personality characteristics of the parent, obstruction focuses on the time the child spends with the other parent. The "obstructive parent" arranges circumstances so that the other parent does not have the opportunity to exercise all of his or her time with the child. For instance, the obstructive parent may always have a reason why makeup time cannot be arranged for a lost day, why it is impossible to have the child ready on time for the pickup, or why the child's activities should come before the other parent's time. Obstruction and undermining do not necessarily coincide with each other. Although parents may obstruct the time their child has with the other parent, they might never make a derogatory comment about each other.

CHARACTERISTICS OF ALIENATING PARENTS

It has been the authors' experience that parents who consciously alienate their children exhibit some of the following characteristics:

- Emotionally impaired (primarily borderline personality disordered)
- Sensitive to narcissistic injuries
- Need for control and power
- Enmeshed with their child (sleeps with or breast-feeds beyond the normal period)
- Overfocused on right and wrong, win and lose
- Revengeful, bitter
- Often mothers who are overinvolved with their own mothers
- May be female who did not have contact with her own father
- May employ the use of homeschooling as a way to block access to the other parent

Ward and Harvey (1993) identified many motivational factors that could lead a parent to alienate a child from the other parent by focusing on the interrelationship between the alienating parent and the child. They noted that an alienating parent may have strong underlying feelings and emotions experienced from earlier unresolved emotional issues which have resurfaced and become exasperated by the distress of the divorce. In order to avoid these unwanted feelings, the parent develops behavioral maneuvers that involve the child. Consequently, one way to deal with the pain and anger is to sue for sole custody of the child and exclude the other parent from the child's life. Ward and Harvey maintained that the motivating factors could either be unconscious or subconscious, and therefore the parent may not be aware of the feelings or emotions that drive these behaviors. As a result, these parents may deny any inappropriate behavior, but they continue the alienating behavior.

Other motivating factors may include the parent's conscious desire to protect the child from the other parent. However, despite their conscious desire they may unintentionally engage in alienating behavior. Typically this behavior results in milder forms of alienation, but, according to Ward, it should not be overlooked.

In severe cases, parents who are attempting to alienate their child from the other parent tend to be openly hostile and conscious of what they are doing to undermine the parent-child relationship. Often these parents are motivated by anger, bitterness, and revenge. They are often controlling, vindictive, immature, and have an "all or nothing" view. They isolate their child from further contact with the other parent. Allowing their child to remain neutral and love both parents is viewed as disloyalty. They deny that they are doing anything wrong. Instead they claim that they are only telling their child the "truth" about the other parent. These parents generally practice various forms of exclusionary behaviors and can be quite creative in their maneuvers. Some parents will go so far as to coach their child to accuse the other parent of sexual wrongdoings. Their ultimate goal is to permanently sever the relationship between parent and child. Unfortunately, in many of the severe cases, the "targeted parent" becomes frustrated and withdraws, confirming the child's negative beliefs.

Not all parents will demonstrate the intensity and frequency of behaviors characterized as severe parental alienation. Some parents will exhibit the same behaviors to a lesser degree. Many of these parents alienate their child from the other parent without conscious intent. These parents do not realize that they are forcing their child to take sides and therefore asking their child to reject the other parent. Some are simply heartbroken parents who are bitter and hurt because their former spouse has abandoned them. In their panic, they scramble to retain their child's affection. The fear of losing their child's love is so intense that they become overinvolved, overindulgent, and encourage their child to become dependent upon them. They will do just about anything, including denying their child the right to a satisfying relationship with the other parent, to protect themselves from additional emotional pain, rejection, and abandonment. Since many divorcing parents engaged in mild forms of alienation are unaware of what they are doing, some will respond favorably to feedback regarding the impact of their behavior on their child's well-being. In addition, these parents are generally not emotionally impaired and respond well to educational programs.

A few empirical studies have been conducted to identify the degree of pathology in alienating/aligned parents. Siegel and Langford (1998) concluded that the Minnesota Multiphasic Personality Inventory (MMPI)-2 could assist custody evaluators in identifying the defensive distortion associated with parental alienation. This study demonstrated that alienating parents were more likely to utilize the psychological defenses of denial and projection. These defenses are typically associated with people exhibiting externalizing personality disorders such as histrionic, borderline, narcissistic, and paranoid styles. As an example, the participants responded to questions in a

> defensive manner, striving to appear as flawless as possible, tried to appear highly virtuous and without emotional problems or difficulties, had tendencies to see themselves as "all good," and were in denial of any personal responsibility for the divorce or subsequent conflict. (Siegel and Langford, 1998, p. 7)

Unfortunately, many parents with personality disorders are not identified clearly by the MMPI-2 or other custody evaluation tools.

Limited research has been conducted to determine the characteristics of the noncustodial parent whom the child refuses to visit. Clinical observations revealed that these parents tend to (1) adopt a distant, rigid, authoritarian style (Lund, 1995); (2) be excessively rigid, insensitive to their child's needs, inept, and lacking empathy (Johnston, 1997); and (3) demonstrate passive or dependent behaviors (Ross and Blush, 1990). Alternatively, other clinicians described the "target" parent as "relatively healthy" and "contributing minimally" to the alienation (Turkat, 1994, 1995), as well as being the more emotionally and financially stable of the parents (Sanders, 1993). Stahl (1999a) also reported that the target parent may be the "healthier parent."

As more and more professionals study visitation resistance, Gardner's position has been replaced by perceptions that view alienation more as a process that takes place within the larger social context. Theorists have expanded their focus to include not only the interaction between family members and social agencies but also the legal system. Similar to allegations of child abuse, alienation is becoming a common element in custody litigation.

AUTHORS' VIEW OF THE ALIENATION CONTINUUM

As noted in Figure 13.1, the authors have identified a continuum of parental and child behaviors ranging from mild to severe that differentiate be-

(Child refuses to choose)   *(Child chooses)*

Mild	Moderate	/ Visitation refusal Severe
Naive (mild loyalty binds)	Active (parental alienation)	Obsessed (pathological aliention)

FIGURE 13.1. Alienation Continuum

tween visitation refusal and parental alienation. The left side of the continuum identifies parents who make infrequent yet inappropriate comments
about the other parent in front of their child. As a result, these behaviors
may create mild loyalty binds for the child. Parents demonstrating the behaviors on the left side of the continuum are not necessarily emotionally impaired, nor are they necessarily enmeshed with their child.

As the continuum moves to the right, the parent's attempts at interfering
with visitation become more problematic. Although the child may become
symptomatic under the pressure of the parent's maneuvers, the child continues to withstand the custodial parent's efforts to negatively impact the relationship between the child and the other parent. At this point, the child refuses to choose between the parents. However, once children reach the
vertical marker, they begin to give in to the pressure placed upon them by
the parent. In order to survive emotionally, the child generally chooses the
alienating parent and refuses to visit the targeted parent. Gardner focused
on this point of the continuum when he diagnosed parental alienation syndrome. It is our view that the larger picture focuses on the overall alienation
process which may or may not result in visitation refusal.

PARENTAL BEHAVIORS
CONTRIBUTING TO ALIENATION

Following is a list of behaviors demonstrated by parents who interfere
with visitation. Depending on the number and frequency of the behaviors,
the parent may be attempting to align with their child against the other parent. When it is severe it will result in visitation refusal and an estranged
relationship.

The alienating parent may do the following:

1. Promote a belief that he or she is "good" while the other parent is "bad." This parent teaches the child that the other parent is "totally unacceptable." For instance, the other parent is prohibited from entering the home and children are not allowed to bring home items from the other parent's home.
2. Repeat negative comments about the other parent in the presence of the child that may be believed over time.
3. Claim that their child experiences "separation anxiety." However, the anxiety occurs only prior to visitation.
4. Adhere to rigid time-sharing plans. Is resistant to an increase in time sharing by stating, "You're pushing things too quickly."
5. Use the child's illness as a way to block time-sharing plans. Claim the other parent cannot adequately care for the child during an illness.
6. Interrupt the child's visits in many different ways. The parent may call frequently to check on the child. This behavior increases the child's anxiety about the other parent. It may also make the child feel guilty about visiting the other parent and may significantly interfere with a meaningful visit.
7. Sabotage the child's visits. For example, the parent may delay the child's bedtime the evening prior to the visit in an attempt to negatively influence the visit. May schedule activities for the child during the other parent's time.
8. Magnify the other parent's flaws. For example, a parent who drinks occasionally may be referred to as an alcoholic.
9. Use negative names such as "adulterous," "abandoner," or "liar" to describe the other parent. Some distort the truth or provide factual information without considering the impact or inappropriateness of sharing adult information with the child.
10. Openly blame the other parent for the separation of the family. Neglects to take responsibility for his or her contribution to the problems.
11. Destroy all physical reminders of the other parent including pictures of the parent and child and the child's extended family.
12. Use "us" language with regard to the divorce, such as, "Your mother is divorcing us!"
13. Make loaded comments prior to their reluctant child leaving for visitation. Comments such as, "I'm sorry you have to go. I wish I could change things, but the judge said you have to go. Try to have fun. It will be okay. Just call me if you need me." Some parents claim they encourage their child to have fun with their other parent while at the same time

demonstrating strong conflicting messages. One parent went so far as to bless her children with holy water prior to a transfer.

14. Assume a neutral role with regard to time sharing. Insist that the child makes his or her own decisions. However, the child senses that the parent does not support a decision to share time with the other parent.

15. Employ guilt and manipulation to force the child into picking sides. Makes statements such as, "I miss you so much when you're with your father. I hate being alone." The parent may play the role of victim to gain the child's affection and pity. The messages often imply "poor me."

16. Utilize the answering machine to screen calls. Phone calls from the other parent are rarely communicated to the child, implying that the other parent is showing a lack of interest in the child's life. He or she may label normal attempts to contact the child as harassment. These parents often use call blocking as a way to deny access to the child.

17. Neglect to give the child letters, postcards, and packages sent from the "hated" parent.

18. Make it known, directly or indirectly, that to defend or love the other parent may cost the child the parent's affection. They assume an "all or nothing" attitude. Essentially, the parent uses fear to force the child to be loyal. The child believes that he or she can only love one parent and lose the other. They point out how they are the only "devoted," "trustworthy," and "dependable" parent.

19. Imply that the other parent is dangerous in some way. For instance, a mother may insist that her daughter wear pajamas rather than a nightgown when sleeping at her dad's house. In extreme cases, the parent may inform the child that the other parent will kidnap him or her one day. Some parents employ "terror huddles" at transfer implying that he or she may never see the child again.

20. Use religious beliefs and racial differences to discourage the parent-child relationship. For instance, a parent might say, "Your mother is filled with the devil because she wants a divorce" or "You're really black—you're not white like your father."

21. May encourage the child to use the mother's maiden name.

CHILDREN ALIENATED FROM A PARENT

A child's reaction to the alienation process is determined by numerous factors. Although the alienating behaviors of others involved with the child may be considered severe, the child may not be significantly distressed by these behaviors. Conversely, other children may demonstrate significant manifestations to relatively mild forms of alienation. Children who have been successfully alienated from a parent demonstrate many of the following behaviors:

1. Preoccupation with an overwhelming sense of "hatred" of a parent. They may relentlessly denigrate the parent's character without remorse. However, the children may still experience private affection for the "hated" parent.

2. View the "hated" parent as all bad and the "loved" parent as all good. They may identify numerous shortcomings and negative qualities in the "hated" parent. In contrast, they refer to the "loved" parent in idealized terms.

3. Maintains a clear distinction between the two households. They may avoid contaminating the "loved" parent's home with possessions from the "hated" parent's home. They may refuse to take gifts received from the "hated" parent to the "loved" parent's home.

4. Adamantly profess that their decision to renounce a parent is their own choice. They may deny any contributions provided by the "loved" parent.

5. A rehearsed quality to the child's allegations that usually include phrases that are not generally used by children. Without understanding, the children merely parrot the words used by the "loved" parent. They are unable to accurately define the terms they use and are frequently unable to provide concrete examples supporting their allegations.

6. Provides illogical and exaggerated reasons for their hatred of a parent. Distorts minor disputes occurring in the past.

7. Unquestionably accepts the allegations of the "loved" parent against the "hated" parent as the absolute truth.

8. Sense of moral outrage directed toward the "hated" parent. Strong belief that this rage is justified.

9. Disregards the feelings of the "hated" parent without remorse or shame; lacks empathy.

10. Lacks appreciation for gifts and other signs of affection received from the "hated" parent.

11. Refuses or tries to refuse visitation with the "hated" parent.

12. Uses "us" language with regard to the divorce. For instance, "Dad is taking us to court."

13. Frequently claims that the "hated" parent continually breaks promises. When promises are broken for practical reasons, the parent's behavior is viewed in a hostile manner. At times, they may falsify information to fit their needs.

14. Demonstrates selective amnesia regarding fun activities shared with the "hated" parent.

15. Ignores or rejects the "hated" parent when in the company of the "loved" parent.
16. When alone with the "hated" parent, experiences emotions ranging from animosity to subdued affection. They may begin to enjoy the company of the parent, then realize it is forbidden. They quickly withdraw or become hostile toward the parent.
17. Manipulates the "loved" parent to meet their own needs. They may use the threat of withdrawal of love to get what they want (adolescence and pre-adolescence).
18. Professes hatred for the extended family members of the "hated" parent.

IMPACT OF PARENTAL ALIENATION

On the Child

Some children knowingly participate in the alienation of one parent. However, some children are totally unaware of attempts to distance them from the other parent. In either case, consequences for the children are profound.

First, children will begin to doubt their own judgment or perceptions of reality if they are told what they perceive is not consistent with their own reality. A child becomes less able to identify and trust his or her own feelings about a situation because what one is told contradicts experience. In turn, continuing to accept the reality of only one parent may lead the child to conform to that parent's desires while neglecting his or her own needs. As a result, the child may consciously attempt to assume the role of "pleaser" or "caretaker" in order to stay in the good graces of the "alienating" parent.

Second, the child is caught in a loyalty bind. When a child makes false statements about one parent to please the other, the child is essentially aligning with one parent. This may precipitate guilt because of a perceived betrayal. However, over time, the child may accept the alienating parent's thoughts as the absolute truth. Under these circumstances, the child will no longer consider the parents' statements to be false but may incorporate them as his or her own.

Third, the child is being taught by a significant adult in his or her life that it is acceptable to lie or distort the truth to achieve a desired result. In this case, lying may result in the alienation of a parent.

Fourth, the child may turn against the alienating parent once it is discovered that he or she has been manipulated. The child may withhold love and express anger. Finally, and most important, alienation affects a child's sense of self. After all, a child is the product of both parents.

On the Coparenting Relationship

Obviously, severe manifestations of parental alienation significantly hinder the parents' ability to initiate and maintain a collaborative relationship on behalf of their child. When anger and revenge sever the ties that bind divorced parents, it is difficult to make progress in realigning the parent-parent relationship. In situations of parental alienation, parents rarely share equal status and power. Since the alienating parent has gained the child's allegiance, he or she tends to control the child's access to the other parent and plays a dominant role in parenting practices and decision making.

Parental alienation places the targeted parent in a vulnerable position. In most cases, the targeted parent is at the mercy of the alienating parent when it comes to sharing time with the child and having an influence on the child's welfare. In essence, the alienating parent has the upper hand. Even when the targeted parent turns to the legal system for assistance, the efforts are generally frustrated by the court's inability to evoke positive change. When courts do not put sanctions on the alienating parent it only reinforces the unequal power distribution and the targeted parent's helplessness.

However, it would be unfair to paint a picture that depicts the targeted parent as a passive participant in the conflict. At times, the targeted parent initiates his or her own campaign to denigrate the other parent during those times he or she has access to the children. Although, under these circumstances, the child frequently resists the targeted parent's attempt to engage him or her in a coalition against the alienating parent; the child has already pledged loyalty to the alienating parent. Nonetheless, it would still cause the child stress and has the potential of escalating the disruption of the parenting relationship.

On the Family

As the family realigns under conditions of alienation and high conflict, its ability to establish new roles is seriously disrupted. The likelihood of future contempt charges and litigation costs stimulated by the targeted parent shortchanges the family emotionally and financially. In addition, healthy parent-child relationships are jeopardized. In forming a coalition between one parent and child against the other parent, the parents' protective and executive functions are severely altered. The alienating parent and child are in danger of becoming enmeshed, forming strong, impermeable, rigid boundaries between parent and child. In addition, it is not uncommon for the alienating parent and child to develop a hostile-dependent relationship. Furthermore, children who have been alienated may assume adult roles or be used by their parents for emotional support.

During those times that the targeted parent is with the child, he or she may spend significant energy demonstrating love, which can create resentment for the new spouse, stepchild, or half siblings. In most cases, the parent is trying to make a significant impact on a child who demonstrates open hostility and demands to return to the "loved" parent. In response to the "targeted" parent's attempts to equal the playing field, alienated children fight to preserve the status quo and resist change.

When alienation becomes more intense, it is likely that the targeted parent will walk out of the child's life. Fueled by the loss of easy access to the child and the frustration associated with trying to build a loving relationship, the parent discontinues the fight, walks away from the situation, and essentially leaves the relationship with the child. Walking away may confirm the child's belief that the parent does not love him or her. On the other hand, if the targeted parent continues to fight for access, this will also be used as proof that he or she does not care. Either way it can be a no-win situation.

CASE STUDY CONTINUUM

Highlighted next are case studies that describe various levels of alienation. They were first introduced at a presentation titled "Creative Solutions for Parental Alienation" offered to family court professionals at the National Judicial Conference held in Tampa, Florida, in March 2001. These case studies are intended to assist professionals in understanding the dynamics of alienation and identifying creative solutions to meet the unique needs of the family from a family systems perspective.

Mild Parental Alienation: The Garcia Family

Alienating parent: Mother
Targeted parent: Father
Children: nine-year-old son and four-year-old daughter
Temporary physical custody: Mother

History

Three months ago, father filed for a divorce from his wife of eleven years. He has been openly dating an employee named Eva. Eva has one child.

Mother is angry and bitter. She is overconnected to the four-year-old daughter, while the son is close to his father. Mother attempts to alienate both children from their father.

Alienating Behaviors

Mother demands that father transport the children to activities that she has scheduled for them. While the children are with their father, mother calls them several times per day and keeps them on the phone for an extended period of time. She asks them questions about their father and Eva. She openly blames the father for the separation and makes comments such as, "Your father is divorcing us for that slut Eva." Mother generally cries when speaking of their father. She also makes statements such as, "He only has time for Eva and her daughter!" and "The worst thing I ever did was to marry your father!"

External Factors

Whenever father hears about the comments mother has made to the children, he has refrained from any negative statements about their mother. His friends and attorney have been encouraging him to defend himself. Mother's family has actively contributed to the situation. Maternal grandparents openly denigrate the father in front of the children.

Children's Response

Neither child has resisted scheduled time with their father. They love both parents. However, the son has returned to nocturnal encopresis and the daughter has become anxious and clings to both parents.

Moderate Parental Alienation: The Jackson Family

Alienating parent: Father
Targeted parent: Mother
Children: Daughter, age thirteen
Custody: Joint physical and joint legal

History

The Jacksons divorced one year ago. Mother is a high-powered executive who accepted a promotion three years ago. This promotion significantly increased her salary and her time away from the family. Mother and daughter have had a strained relationship for the past few years. Mother is better at setting limits with the child than the father.

Father teaches math at his daughter's middle school and coaches her soccer team. On the surface, he appears to be an attentive and devoted father. He is still focused on his pain and the divorce. He does not believe that the custody arrangement is in his daughter's best interest since he sees himself as the primary parent due to mother's travel schedule. He is also angry with the significant discrepancy between parental income and the limited amount of child support he receives.

Alienating Behaviors

Father uses guilt to encourage his daughter to align with him against her mother. His life revolves around his daughter and her activities. He makes sure that his daughter sees this as devotion. He also encourages her to be dependent upon him and to call him frequently. He is inappropriate at transfers, telling the daughter repeatedly how much he will miss her while she is with her mother. Both the father and the daughter attempt to sabotage the mother's weekend by making excuses. Father joins with his daughter whenever she complains about her mother. He demonstrates hostile body language whenever mother is present. Father calls his daughter after hours and makes comments such as "Your mother is more interested in money than in being a parent" and "If your mother really loved you, she would not make you go to her home" and "Your mother is being rigid and controlling!" and "Don't worry, honey, soon you will be able to determine your own schedule."

External Factors

The daughter's schoolteachers and other soccer parents contribute to the alienation against the mother. Father communicated to both teachers and coaches that the courts stated that all written and verbal information was to be shared only with him. As a result, the mother does not receive any information regarding school or soccer activities. Team parents socialize with father and ignore mother.

Child's Response

Daughter loves her mother but prefers her father because he is more of a friend than a parent. Although she often has a good time with her mother, it is not uncommon for her to call father to complain about mother as well as obtain his sympathy. She continually comments about her mother's negative qualities. She has become fairly manipulative. Her conduct at school has declined; she was suspended two days for smoking. Father kept this secret from the mother.

Severe Parental Alienation: The Brighton Family

Alienating parent: Mother
Targeted parent: Father
Children: Two sons, ages eleven and sixteen
Custody: Mother has physical custody of the children. The parents were awarded joint legal custody. However, mother has the legal right to make decisions when the parents are in dispute.

History

Father divorced mother six years ago after he entered treatment for alcohol abuse. He has been clean for six years. Prior to his recovery, father was involved with Internet pornography. He remarried three years ago to a woman he met in AA. For the past four and one-half years, the boys have refused to spend the night at their father's home. They limit their time to an occasional dinner without the stepmother. Since father remarried the situation has deteriorated. He has not shared a holiday with his sons since his second marriage. Mother lives with grandmother and they are overinvolved with each other. The children are homeschooled by the mother. Mother does not date and has no social life other than church activities and interaction with her children. Immediately after the separation she destroyed all items that reminded her of her former spouse.

Alienating Behaviors

Mother openly blames father for the divorce and for her financial situation. She has refused to allow the children to take anything to their father's home. Mother will not allow the boys to bring any gifts into the home that they receive from father. She will not answer any calls from father and "forgets" to give the boys any messages from him. She will not attend any activity that the father might attend. She will not copy report cards or give him parental information as required by the court order. Mother refuses to enforce visitation and believes that the children should be able to decide when to see their father. Although father was awarded visitation over spring break, mother denies father this time because she claims the boys are attending school at home. She has hired two different therapists for the children in an attempt to "prove" the boys should not see their father.

She is in contempt with regard to derogatory remarks, blocking access, and not contacting father for first right of refusal. Mother was found in contempt of court and, as a result, the judge sentenced her to jail for one day and night. Mother used this event as a way to further undermine the relationship between the children and their father and stepmother.

Mother refers to the father as an alcoholic and implies that he is dangerous. She sees things in black and white. For instance, she believes that she is the "good" parent and father is the "bad" parent. Mother refuses to speak to father and will not discuss any parenting matters with him. She calls the father's home in order to hang up on the stepmother. Since they reside in a state which allows the sixteen-year-old the right to refuse visitation, mother has increased her alienating efforts. She has encouraged the youngest son to be dependent on her and has attempted to keep him from growing up. Since the father remarried the situation has become more impaired, with the oldest son claiming that his father has been sexually inappropriate. Mother has made comments such as: "Your father is a drunk. He does not love you. He has everything and we have nothing. He spends all his money on his new wife and on taking us to court. He has threatened to have me thrown in jail!"

Targeted Parent's Behaviors

Father has attempted to force the boys to visit him. He has allowed them to determine the schedule. Neither of these efforts has proven useful. There- fore, father did not contact his children for eighteen months. Currently, his primary contact with his children has been by occasional phone call or din- ner. Recently, he has attempted defending himself and his wife from mother's negative comments. Due to the alienation, father did not invite the boys to his wedding for fear it might create a situation. Mother has used this against him.

Children's Response

The boys have refused visitation since the oldest son turned fourteen (now sixteen) and elected not to see his father. The oldest son has threat- ened to attack his father if he attempts to force his brother to visit with him. The youngest son does not believe that he should have to visit father on his own. Both boys claim that their decision to refuse visitation was their own choice and deny mother's involvement. Although they had a positve relation- ship with their father prior to the separation, they share their mother's out- rage and deny all positive memories of their father. The youngest son's grades have fallen, and the sixteen-year-old has begun sneaking out to smoke pot. Both boys have written to the judge in an attempt to avoid visita- tion with their father.

External Factors

Mother's attorney supports the children's decision to terminate contact with their father. This attorney encouraged the boys to write a letter to the judge and prepared them to testify prior to the court hearing. Maternal grandmother is very protective of her daughter and grandsons. She blamed the divorce on the father and speaks negatively about him as much as possi- ble even if the children can overhear her conversation. Father's attorney con- tinually initiates contempt proceedings against mother.

Creative Solutions to the Case Studies

Highlighted in this section are creative solutions that correspond to the case studies that describe the various levels of alienation.

Mild Alienation

 I. Comprehensive divorce parent education
 II. Detailed parenting plans
   A. Specifics details regarding time share, transfers, phone contact, etc.
   B. Specific details regarding parental conduct that is prohibited
III. Psychotherapy: individual, family, and play therapy with professionals who have experience in parental alienation

When mild forms of alienation have occurred for an extended period of time resulting in anxious children who may be demonstrating signs of distress, moderate interventions may be implemented.

Moderate and Severe Parental Alienation

 I. Detailed parenting plans with very specific details regarding
   A. Time-share schedule to minimize interference with the targeted parent's time
      1. Rigid schedules that do not require negotiations
      2. Guidelines for when the child is too ill to be transferred
      3. Longer and uninterrupted periods of time between child and targeted parent
   B. Transfers. Determine:
      1. Parental behaviors of both parents at transfer
      2. Nonparent to parent transfers
      3. Neutral exchange sites (such as library, restaurants, school)
      4. Use of a neutral third party for transfers
   C. Phone contact. Details:
      1. Frequency and duration of calls
      2. Child- versus parent-initiated calls
      3. Privacy for the child
      4. Temporary elimination of phone contact
   D. Guidelines for shared parenting decisions
 II. Enhancement of "targeted" parent-child relationship
   A. Child with the assistance of alienating parent sends targeted parent pictures, drawings, or stories in the mail with a positive note once per week

   B. Child describes a positive experience that he or she enjoyed with the targeted parent to the alienating parent

   C. Child keeps a journal or picture book highlighting positive experiences between child and targeted parent

   D. Child with the assistance of the alienating parent bakes a special treat for the targeted parent that is transferred at transition

   E. Child with the assistance of the alienating parent sends a postcard to targeted parent while on vacation

III. Psychotherapy: individual, family, play therapy with professionals experienced in parental alienation

IV. Appoint trained parent coordinator to

   A. Monitor parent-child relationships

   B. Monitor compliance with time-share arrangements and other aspects of court order

   C. Recommend sanctions to court

   D. Provide therapeutic visitation for child and targeted parent

   E. Provide case management and consultation

   F. Educate parents: communications skills, anger management, conflict resolution, children's issues in divorce, and danger of damage to the child's self-esteem

   G. Facilitate contact between targeted parent and child (phone, letters, gifts)

   H. Refer to other professionals with experience in parental alienation, i.e. filial therapy (parent-child relationship training) for child and targeted parent

V. Specific court sanctions for ongoing attempts to alienate

   A. Monetary fines

      1. Attorney fees

      2. Therapy, parent coordinator, or evaluation fees

      3. Contribution to college fund in the targeted parent's name

      4. Payment for child's personal phone line and purchase of phone

   B. Jail time (one weekend per interrupted weekend)

Severe Parental Alienation: All of the Same Interventions Plus

I. Therapeutic visitation for the child and targeted parent (reunification)

   A. Relationship-building sessions with professional present

   B. Videotaped sessions

   C. Alienating parent should not drop off the child for the visitation in professional's office

    D. Desensitization plan should be created for the child and targeted parent

    E. Phone contact

       1. Limit contact between child and alienating parent

       2. Use of speaker phone or audiotaped calls between the child and alienating parent

    F. Parallel parenting

II. Referral for psychological evaluation of the alienating parent and or child

III. Change in custody

    A. Temporary foster care

    B. Physical custody awarded to the targeted parent

    C. Supervised visitation and phone calls for the alienating parent for an extended period of time

IV. Specific sanctions for ongoing attempts to alienate child from parent

    A. Credit for additional weekend whenever targeted parent or child report that their time together was not successful

    B. Community service

    C. Public apology

    D. Increased time for the child and targeted parent

    E. Double time for targeted parent (three hours interference = six hours credit)

    F. Limit the child's favorite activity to targeted parent only

Parental alienation cannot be effectively defined without considering the family system and the social setting within which divorce is embedded. Identification of alienation must involve a multifaceted approach. Therefore, as noted in the case examples, extended family members are often actively involved in the alienating process and must also be involved in interventions. In severe cases of parental alienation, parent coordination may not be effective without the use of sanctions or consequences enforced by the courts. For further information regarding the use of strong sanctions for parental alienation, contact the Cooperative Parenting Institute.

Unfortunately, parent coordinators are faced with the extreme challenges associated with visitation refusal and parental alienation. To make matters worse, professional debate continues to erupt as practitioners attempt to define this phenomenon and identify the factors that influence a child's refusal to visit the noncustodial parent. Children may resist visitation due to normative factors or in response to safety issues. However, the most troublesome cases for the courts and coordinators are those children who refuse contact with a parent based primarily upon a negative and intense campaign conducted by the custodial parent against the noncustodial parent.

Depending upon the severity, various solutions can be implemented in an attempt to minimize the devastating results. These cases are the most likely to return to court and require the most detailed parenting plans. Thus the PC must become comfortable and proficient at creating parenting plans. Without highly specific plans, conflicted parents leave the PC's office with one problem solved but several new problems to stumble upon. Whether it is a pre- or postdivorce case, creating parenting plans will be a indispensable skill. In the final phase of the program, the PC incorporates the parents' agreements into a final parenting plan. Samples of both pre- and postdivorce parenting plans have been included in Chapter 14. However, since not all cases have a happy ending, Chapter 14 also examines variations on program outcomes.

Chapter 14

The Final Phase

VARIATIONS ON SUCCESS

Parent coordination is a very challenging, multifaceted, yet gratifying profession designed to enhance the lives of children in two-household families. The primary avenue to achieve this goal is to improve the coparent relationship. The challenges posed by high-conflict families vary in their severity; therefore, the degree of success varies with each family. Success is also defined by the limitations and strengths of each family member, their willingness to change, as well as the influence of outside sources, including the behaviors of the PC, on the family system. While attempting to maximize parental collaboration and minimize parental conflict, the PC must maintain realistic expectations. A parent coordinator will be at risk of becoming discouraged unless he or she revises expectations based upon the needs or limitations of the family. To avoid potential burnout, a parent coordinator must recognize that some parents will simply refuse to change.

Since each family is unique, the outcome of the parent-coordination process will reflect some variation of success. For instance, parents may not be willing or able to construct a collaborative relationship, but they have learned the importance of shielding their child from the adverse effects of parental warfare by developing a parallel-parenting arrangement. Even if parents continue to harbor negative feelings for each other, their child may still benefit from the outcome of the parent-coordination process.

Success includes any *one* of the following:

Improved parental communication
Increased parental cooperation
Improved relationship within the family system
Reduction in parental conflict
Reduction in loyalty binds
Reduction of child manipulation
Avoidance of court
Avoidance of police involvement

Clarifying loopholes in the parenting plan
Providing testimony

As the natural result of an improved coparent relationship, many parents are able to avoid the emotional and financial cost of utilizing the legal arena to resolve child-rearing matters. However, no matter how much the PC discourages litigation, some parents will return to court for one reason or another. At the very least, parents may use the services of the legal system in order to resolve parenting issues that were not resolved through the parent-coordination process. In more acrimonious cases, a parent may seek court intervention as a means of restitution. Furthermore, the presiding judge may require the family to return to the courtroom as a way to both hold the parents accountable for their behaviors and assess the family's compliance and progress. In these circumstances, the PC may be required to submit a report or provide testimony.

In situations of noncompliance by one or both parents, it may be necessary for the PC to share the family's progress with the court through testimony (Figure 14.1). Although this is not the preferred outcome, it is important for the PC to recognize that this is another form of success. Unlike any other professional, the PC has a unique opportunity to observe the family system. The testimony provided by the PC sheds light on the family and provides the court with information that is necessary to make an informed decision on behalf of the family.

CREATING PARENTING PLANS

In most cases, the parent coordinator assists the parents in the creation or modification of a workable parenting plan that considers the unique needs of the family. This document outlines parental expectations, agreements, and the degree of cooperation the parents are willing to assume. Ultimately, the parenting plan reflects the outcome of the parent-coordination process.

The remainder of this chapter discusses the components of a parenting plan, the limitations of court orders, and the differences between pre- and postdivorce parenting plans. In predivorce cases, finalizing the parenting plan to submit to the coparents' attorneys may indicate successful completion of the program. An incomplete parenting plan with an improved parent-child relationship may also indicate success. In postdivorce cases, success may result in revisions to their original court order or settlement agreement as a way to reduce the likelihood of parental conflict.

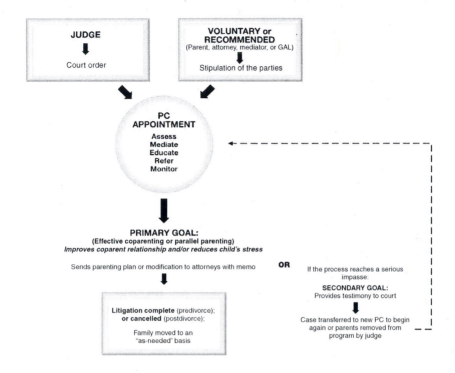

FIGURE 14.1. Parent Coordination Outcome Flowchart

Scope and Nature of Parenting Plans

The scope and nature of the parenting plan is dependent upon several factors:

- The extent of the divorce decree and/or settlement agreement
- The number of changes taking place in the family
- The stage of the divorce process
- The unique needs of the family

Each parenting plan should represent a unique understanding of the parents' responsibilities to the child and to each other. A parenting plan enables parents to define the limits of their partnership. It clarifies expectations in specific terms in order to minimize conflict and confusion. In situations in which custody is not being altered, the plan should focus primarily on agreements that will reduce parental conflict and loyalty binds and clarify specific parenting agreements. Some parents may have just entered the process of divorce and have not had the opportunity to clarify the terms of a parenting plan. The parent coordinator may or may not have to address all the components of a parenting plan. The components of a parenting plan are outlined in the Appendix. An important rule of thumb to remember is the greater the conflict, the more detail necessary in the final plan.

A parenting plan becomes the instrument that establishes roles, rules, and boundaries in clear and specific terms. The comprehensiveness of the plan depends on the type of relationship the parents share and their ability to work as a cooperative team. A detailed plan provides continuity and stability, necessary prerequisites to the healthy development of children. Detailed parenting plans enable the family to adjust to its new structure as boundaries are reestablished across households.

Parental expectations for their child's behavior are often value-laden. These expectations may carry a deeper meaning than the surface issue. For instance, the issue of an adolescent's curfew may have more to do with a parent's own rigidity and anxiety over the lack of supervision than the adolescent's need for sleep. When both parents agree on any of these expectations, it may be included in their parenting plan. If parents feel strongly about not exposing their child to R-rated movies, for example, they may choose to include language such as, "We agree that our child will not view R-rated movies until he turns sixteen or unless one parent has seen the movie and we agree it can be viewed by our child." However, when parents are unable to agree on specific points, then they will have to agree to disagree. At times the PC must use his or her own judgment to determine when an issue should no longer be discussed. Otherwise, the parents will be at risk of micromanaging each other and thereby increasing parental conflict.

In considering a parenting plan, the parents must be flexible and take into consideration the changing circumstances of the family and the developmental needs of the children. As the developmental needs of the children change and as families reorganize to stepfamilies, parents must understand that the parenting plan may need to be altered. Coparents should also recognize the need to remain flexible and open to several options when first establishing a plan. It is difficult for parents as well as the PC to foresee what may transpire as a result of a decision. Some parents may agree to incorporate a clause indicating that they will return to the parent-coordination process every other year to reevaluate their plan. Other parents will not be willing to do so.

The involvement of stepparents and significant others in the life of the child may be addressed in the parenting plan either pre- or postdivorce. In predivorce situations, most parents consider it premature to discuss the involvement of others in the child's life. The PC can assist parents to understand the value of taking this preventive measure. Issues to be considered that involve adult figures either pre- or postdivorce may include first right of refusal, management of the children, and transportation of the children. Parents may also stipulate that communication about the children will take place only between the biological parents unless an emergency situation necessitates the communication between parent and stepparent. Establishing boundaries between the biological parents and the stepparents will function as a preventive measure to reduce conflict between all parenting figures.

Occasionally, the PC may encounter situations in which the parents insist on a parenting plan that is not child friendly and could actually be detrimental to the child. The court may even legitimize their plan. In these situations, the PC may need to play devil's advocate by pointing out how the specific agreements in the document may indeed result in negative consequences for the child. For instance, the parents may decide on a time-sharing arrangement that requires a child exhibiting attention deficit disorder to move between homes twice a week by splitting the week in half. To call attention to this potentially harmful arrangement, the PC can generate questions regarding the child's organization skills, homework habits, and need for structure and routine, as well as how the living arrangement may impact on the special needs of the child. Storytelling can also be used to highlight detrimental elements of a parenting plan. The PC can create a story using characteristics similar to those of the child, the specific harmful elements, and the outcome for the child and family.

In addition, the parent coordinator can direct the parents to another professional with expertise in the area in question. For example, a neurologist can be consulted to gain better understanding of a child's attention-deficit needs. A psychotherapist who specializes in children's developmental needs can be consulted to determine if the living arrangement makes the necessary provisions for contact with both parents. If the PC is unable to nudge the parents to reconsider a plan, the professional can prepare the plan with a disclaimer indicating that the specific agreement was not recommended by the coordinator.

Writing a Parenting Plan: Predivorce

Those parents who are in the midst of navigating their divorce will come into the parent coordination process without a parenting plan or settlement agreement. Some of these predivorce parents have a temporary order that addresses temporary custody, time sharing, and basic financial matters. Under these circumstances, the parent coordinator may have to assume responsibility for assisting the parents in the development of a plan based on the needs of the family.

Generally, parents who are fairly cooperative during the divorce process do not see the value of including preventive language in the parenting plan. As a result, they tend to be resistant to developing very specific details in their plans. They may naively believe that they will never engage in significant conflict. It is important to discuss the value of backup plans in the event that the parenting relationship becomes conflicted in the future. The PC may use the metaphor of a tightrope walker to illustrate the value of working with a net. Although the net may never be necessary, one unforeseen move could become quite costly. This "net" is the detailed plan. If the parents never need their "net," then no harm will be done. Parents must be encouraged to clarify any and all problem areas as a preventive measure. For example, the plan may indicate, "Although parents agree to communicate on an as-needed basis, they will shift to Sunday-evening e-mails if either parent makes this request."

Prior to signing their parenting plan, parents should be encouraged to review the plan with their attorneys within a specified period of time. Once both parents, in the presence of the PC, sign it, parents may request that their attorneys enter the plan as an amendment to their original divorce or settlement agreement after it is signed.

In situations in which the parents are unable to agree upon all child-rearing matters, the parenting plan can outline the issues that the parents were able to mutually agree upon. In predivorce situations, most parent coordinators do not address financial issues. Parents will need to resolve the outstanding issues, including financial matters, with a mediator, with their attorneys, or through the court system. Once the parenting plan has been reviewed and agreed upon by both parents, the parent coordinator should contact both attorneys to stress the importance of having the parenting plan incorporated into a final settlement agreement or court order. In postdivorce cases, parents often require clarification or revisions to their original divorce document.

Predivorce Case Study

Mary and John Smith had been married for ten years. They have one son, Michael, age eight. During their last year of marriage and throughout the initial stages of the separation process, their interactions were highly conflicted. Their impaired communication style added to the intensity of the conflict. Michael was constantly put in the middle of his parents' negative interactions and frequently became a messenger. The parents have agreed that Mary would be the primary custodial parent during the school year and John would be primary custodian during the summer months. The parents agreed to a joint legal custody arrangement.

Coparents: Mary Smith and John Smith
Child: Michael Smith

Mary and John agree to incorporate all points of this parenting plan into their final divorce agreement. If any points of this plan are removed, all other points shall remain incorporated in the final divorce agreement.

Living Arrangement: Mary and John shall share joint custody of their son Michael Smith. He shall reside primarily with his mother during the school year and primarily with his father in the summer months. While Michael resides with his mother, he shall spend time with his father every Wednesday from 5:30 p.m. until 8:00 p.m. and alternating weekends from Friday at 5:30 p.m. until Monday at 8:00 a.m. at school. If school is not is session on Monday, he shall be returned to school on Tuesday morning. Father shall ensure that Michael is fed and his homework completed prior to returning him to his other residence. Father shall provide the transportation both ways during the midweek visit and the coparents shall share the transportation for all other visitation periods.

During the summer months, Michael shall spend time with his mother in the same fashion as the arrangement for his father during the school year. However, the mother shall return Michael to his father's home on Monday mornings at 8:00 a.m.

Holiday Schedule: The holiday schedule shall have priority over the regularly scheduled living arrangement, with no makeup time expected. However, when the holiday schedule creates more than two weekends in a row, the third weekend shall be adjusted unless they agree otherwise.

Holiday	Defined	Mother	Father
Spring Break	Release of school until Sunday 6:00 p.m. the night prior to the return to school	Odd	Even
Easter Weekend	Friday at release of school to Sunday at 6:00 p.m.	Odd	Even
Memorial Weekend	Friday at release of school to Monday at 6:00 p.m.	Even	Odd
Independence Day	6:00 p.m. July 3 to 6:00 p.m. July 5, or full weekend	Odd	Even
Labor Day Weekend	Friday at release of school to Monday at 6:00 p.m.	Even	Odd
Thanksgiving	Release of school until Sunday at 6:00 p.m.	Odd	Even

Holiday	Defined	Mother	Father
First Half of Winter Break	Release of school until the mid-point* of break at 6:00 p.m.	Odd	Even
Second Half of Winter Break	Midpoint of break at 6:00 p.m. to the evening prior to the return to school at 6:00 p.m.	Odd	Even
Mother's Day	Saturday at 6:00 p.m. to Sunday at 6:00 p.m.	All	N/A
Father's Day	Saturday at 6:00 p.m. to Sunday at 6:00 p.m.	N/A	All
Michael's Birthday	5:00 p.m. to 8:00 p.m.	Even	Odd
Parent's Birthday	5:00 p.m. to 8:00 p.m.	Own	Own
Halloween	Noncustodial parent will take Michael trick-or-treating until he no longer requires supervision	N/A	N/A

*Midpoint is an equal division of the winter holiday. If the actual number of overnights is not even, then the parents shall adjust the drop off/pickup time.

Teacher work days and holidays not outlined on the holiday schedule shall be considered part of the previous weekend.

Right of First Refusal: John and Mary agree to offer the other parent the right to care for Michael for any child care of eight (8) hours or more. A future stepparent shall be considered an extension of the custodial parent unless the time includes an overnight. This will allow Michael to remain in his home during the day with a stepparent. If the parent offered extra time is unable to care for Michael then it shall be the responsibility of the custodial parent to make and pay for any additional child care. If the offer is accepted no exchange or credit will be expected.

Summer Vacation: Each parent has the right to exercise a vacation period with Michael of ten consecutive overnights. Each parent shall notify the other in writing of his or her summer vacation schedule by March 15 so that Michael's vacation time can be coordinated between his parents. If there is a conflict in their requested dates, mother's dates shall take precedence in odd years and father's dates in even years. The vacation period shall take priority over regular living arrangements, and the holiday schedule shall take precedence over the summer schedule. Two weeks prior to the vacation, both parents shall notify the other regarding the specifics of the vacation. This notification shall outline the dates and location of the vacation, telephone numbers, as well as the type of transportation that will be used to travel to and from the vacation site.

During vacations, Michael will be given the opportunity to call the absent parent. In turn, the absent parent may initiate a telephone call to Michael, no more than once a day. In case of emergency, the vacationing parent will notify the absent parent as soon as possible.

Special Occasions: Each parent shall inform the coparent of the following special occasions at least seventy-two (72) hours in advance of each: religious events of significance, graduations, school open houses, parent-teacher conferences, birthday parties of friends/relatives, demonstrations of acquired skills (e.g., athletic events), and award ceremonies. However, each parent agrees that every attempt will be made to share written information regarding special occasions with the other by sending a copy of information outlining school, sports, and other events within one week. However, if the information is time sensitive, the parents agree to leave a voice-mail message the same day. Each parent shall have the same rights as the other to attend and participate in any such special occasions. During joint attendance, the parents agree to conduct themselves in a courteous fashion. The parent with whom Michael resides will be responsible for making sure that Michael is prepared with the appropriate clothing, uniforms, items, gifts for friends/relatives, etc., for the special event.

Telephone Arrangements: Michael shall be allowed to contact the absent parent at any time during reasonable waking hours. The absent parent may call Michael once per day between the hours of 8 a.m. and 8 p.m. on school days and 9 a.m. to 9 p.m. on weekend days. Both parents agree to respond positively to these calls, to give Michael privacy during the calls, and to ensure that Michael gets all phone messages.

Medical and Professional Appointments: Mother shall make routine medical/dental appointments. Transportation to medical/dental appointments shall be the responsibility of Mother. Mother shall inform Father of routine visits at least five days in advance. Father shall attend these visits with the mother provided that both parents are respectful and cooperative. If Father is not present, Mother will inform Father of the information shared during the routine visits, as well as prescriptions and any treatment recommendations. Mother agrees to notify Father within twenty-four (24) hours of the office visit.

In case of an emergency or illness requiring prompt medical/dental attention, either parent shall initiate treatment without prior notification to the coparent. Each parent shall immediately contact the absent parent in emergency situations.

The parents shall mutually agree upon any nonemergency medical, dental, psychological, and/or school-related assistance for Michael. If the parents are unable to mutually agree to such assistance, then they agree to consult a neutral professional that they mutually agree upon. If they are still unable to create a workable plan, they agree to work with the assistance of their parent coordinator to reach a mutual decision.

The parents agree that Father will maintain insurance coverage for Michael in the form of hospitalization and major medical through his employment. In the event that such insurance is not available through his employment, Father shall provide and pay for the premium associated with health and major medical insurance (comparable to the previous coverage). Father agrees to be responsible for any reasonable and necessary medical, hospitalization, dental, or other health-related costs not covered by insurance. Mother agrees to give Father medical receipts within one week of any treatment.

Health and School Records: The parents agree that each shall have free access to all schools, teachers, counselors, physicians, psychologists, psychiatrists, and dentists of Michael. Each parent shall provide the coparent with copies of all school records and report cards. If there is a fee to access records, the parent requesting the records shall be responsible for payment of these fees.

Extracurricular Activities: The parents agree that participation in extracurricular activities is important. The activities shall be mutually agreed upon and based on the abilities and interests of Michael. If they are unable to agree, Father may have the tiebreaker on any activity dispute. Michael shall be transported to these activities by the residing parent unless the parent's schedule interferes with his or her ability to transport Michael. Both parents shall work together to ensure Michael's participation in activities. Michael shall be involved in only one activity at a time. Each parent shall have the same right as the other to attend activities. During joint attendance the parents agree to conduct themselves in a courteous fashion. All fees associated with extracurricular activities shall be shared equally between the parents.

Toys and Clothing: Toys and clothing will be considered as belonging to Michael. If Michael wishes to take clothing or toys out of either home, he may do so with the exception of bicycles, video equipment, computer and Nintendo games, and any other expensive or fragile item deemed inappropriate to transport by the parent who purchased it. However, Michael's preferences shall be recognized and honored as much as possible assuming that he can carry and be responsible for the item. Any clothes that are sent with Michael will be washed and returned the following visit. Each parent shall provide clothing for Michael at his or her own expense.

Parent-to-Parent Communication Plan: The parent with which Michael resides shall initiate weekly telephone calls to the coparent every Thursday at 10:00 p.m. The focus of such telephone calls shall be topics related to parenting, such as highlights of Michael's activities, positive developments, recent illnesses, problems, change in eating and sleeping habits, etc. During emergency situations, the parents agree to contact each other by cellular phone regardless of time and location.

The parents agree to conduct themselves in a cordial, businesslike fashion during telephone contacts and transitions. The parents agree not to exchange information in Michael's presence. Information shall be shared during the weekly scheduled telephone contacts. The only exception would be time-sensitive information or to exchange medication and provide instructions for administering the medication.

Parental Behavior: The parents agree to encourage a direct child-parent bond. Each parent shall respect the coparent's right to develop his or her relationship with Michael. The parents agree that when Michael is under their direct supervision, he or she is totally responsible for their son during that time. Furthermore, the parents agree to encourage Michael to discuss grievances with the parent in question.

The parents agree not to interfere with the coparent's style of parenting or household rules. However, the parents agree to maintain similar bedtime and other basic household rules whenever possible. The parents also agree to eliminate corporal punishment in favor of consequences and restrictions.

The parents agree to work toward a more cooperative relationship. The parents agree not to badmouth or belittle the coparent or any significant other in the life of their child in the presence or earshot of Michael. Each parent shall refrain from negative behavior or body language.

Safety Expectations: Michael shall be required to wear a helmet while riding a bike, scooter, or skateboard, while skating, or while horseback riding. Any guns in the home shall be kept securely locked and out of reach at all times. Both parents shall ensure that Michael has Internet protection and has supervision when accessing the Internet.

We agree to discuss the parenting plan on a yearly basis to modify this plan if needed and to take into consideration Michaels's developmental needs.

We have read this eight-page Parenting Plan and agree to all points. However, this document shall not become binding for two weeks so that our attorneys may have time to review this plan and make any necessary changes.

In the future, before we seek modification through the courts, we shall schedule and share the costs of three meetings with the parent coordinator to act as an objective third party.

Mother's Signature/Date   Father's Signature/Date

Witness Signature/Date

Revisiting a Postdivorce Plan

Postdivorce parents appointed a parent coordinator will bring at least one, if not several, orders to the process. It is not unusual for these documents to confuse the parents. Although parents may have previously created a divorce settlement and/or parenting plan, it is not unusual for problems to surface as they implement their agreement. At times, plans prepared by attorneys and mediators may include loopholes and lead to differences of interpretation. A parent coordinator must predict and then prevent future misunderstandings by encouraging parents to consider even the minute details. Some typical problems characteristic of legal documents include the following:

- A lack of details created confusion and conflict among family members.
- Ambiguous terms led to different interpretations of stipulations of the court.
- There was inadequate consideration of the child's developmental, social, emotional, and physical needs.
- It lacked provisions for changes when new circumstances arise such as remarriage or relocation of a parent.
- No contingency plan was in place in the event parents cannot reach a mutual agreement. For instance, an agreement can include a contingency plan such as, "If parents are unable to agree on the shared cost of summer camp, the parents agree not to spend more than the cost of a one-week YMCA camp, or either parent may cover the additional costs to send their child to the camp of the parent's choice given it is agreeable to both parents."

An experienced PC should be very familiar with reading divorce papers and parenting plans and be able to recognize problems and loopholes quickly. The excerpt in Box 14.1 shows the typical language of an order developed by the court and/or the attorneys. This sample order illustrates typical loopholes and ambiguity often left in high-conflict orders. The language corrections made in Box 14.2 demonstrate significant improvements made to the original order.

Although parents may already have a divorce settlement that includes some or most of the elements in a parenting plan, these settlements may not cover the more subtle parenting practices generally outlined in a comprehensive parenting plan. Parents who enter the parent coordination process with a written order or settlement agreement already in place may report to

---

BOX 14.1. Original Court Order

[6]

Husband shall have visitation of the children on first and third weekends from Friday at 6:00 p.m. until Sunday at 6:00 p.m. The Husband shall also have access to the children for one evening per week until 7:30 p.m. The parties shall transfer the children at a mutually agreed upon location.

[7]

The parties shall have the right to communicate with the children daily at any reasonable hour when the children are with the other party.

BOX 14.2. Revised Parenting Plan

[6]

Father shall have custody of the children on the first and third weekend of each month from Friday at 6:00 p.m. until Sunday at 6:00 p.m. In the event that the first day of the month falls on a Saturday or Sunday, it shall be considered the first weekend of the month. Father shall have the right to exercise additional time with the children one evening per week. If the parents are unable to agree upon the day of the week, then it shall be every Wednesday from the release of school until 7:30 p.m.

The parents shall transfer the children at a mutually agreed upon location halfway between both homes. In the event that the parents are unable to agree upon the location, they shall transfer the children in the McDonald's parking lot at the corner of Telegraph and Grove Road. The parent with the children shall wait at least thirty minutes before leaving the drop-off location. They shall return home and the other parent shall pick up the children at the coparent's home. However, before picking up the children at the coparent's home, the traveling parent will call the coparent to notify him or her of the traveling parent's arrival.

[7]

Either parent may contact their children when they are with the other parent no more than once per day unless it is an emergency. In addition, the children may call their parent once per day unless it is an emergency. The calls shall be made prior to 8:00 p.m. on school nights and prior to 10:00 p.m. on non-school nights. If the absent parent calls the home and the call is not answered, the absent parent shall leave one friendly, but brief, message for their child. It shall be the responsibility of the custodial parent to ensure that the call is returned prior to bedtime.

the PC that certain aspects of their agreement are not working well. For example, the existing plan may indicate that the father spends time with the children the "first" and "third" weekend of the month, yet the parents are in significant conflict about what constitutes the "first" weekend. This must be clearly defined. Furthermore, the parents may find that they prefer Mother's Day and Father's Day to be designated as Sunday rather than the weekend. As long as both parents agree, these changes can be made.

Once the parent coordinator receives the court documents, he or she should review any previous agreements pertaining to parenting of the children. As the process unfolds, the parent coordinator should monitor the existing agreements to ensure that they are meeting the needs of the family while reducing the level of conflict between parents. If the original agreements are unaltered, then parents need not include them in the plan, unless they choose to have all of their parenting agreements contained in one document. Otherwise, the parenting plan can make reference to the court document outlining the agreement. In either case, the parenting plan should reflect any mediated modifications of the original agreement. For instance, the order states that the father shall (1) pick up the children on Fridays at 6:00 p.m. and return them to their mother's home Sundays at 6:00 p.m. and (2) pick them up on Wednesdays at 5:00 p.m. and return them at 7:30 p.m. However, to reduce the number of transitions for the children, the father shall now pickup the children on Thursdays at 6:00 p.m. and return them on Sundays at 6:00 p.m.

The following case study illustrates a parenting plan that was created postdivorce. It notes that it is a modification of their original settlement agreement and features the parents' revisions.

Postdivorce Case Study

Sam and Kim divorced four years ago. When Sam remarried last year it caused increased conflict between the parents and the two children. Prior to Sam's marriage he and Kim had been flexible and fairly cooperative with each other. Since Sam's marriage their conflict has increased and both parents have become rigid with regard to following the court order to the letter. His wife Kathryn is a stay-at-home mother who spends a significant amount of time with the two children. Kathryn has involved herself as a primary parent and as an adversary to Kim. Mother and stepmother have engaged in several unfortunate and intense conflicts. They returned to court when Kim filed a motion against Sam for a change in custody. The following is the final result of the development of a revised plan.

Parents: Sam and Kim Katz
Children: Allie and Thomas Katz
Case No. 1999-CV-3684-02
Date: June 13, 2001

Sam and Kim are choosing to modify their original settlement agreement dated December 21, 1998. The agreements below reflect the modifications. Any issues not addressed in this parenting plan shall remain intact.

Joint Legal Custody (page 1, #1): Neither party shall make a significant nonemergency parenting decision without first consulting the coparent at least twice. In the event that they are unable to agree on a parenting issue after two discussions, then Mother shall have final say on medical and educational disputes and Father on activities and religious disputes.

Time Sharing (page 2, #1b,c,d): As of the signing of this parenting plan, the six floating days shall no longer apply as outlined in the December 1998 settlement agreement. Instead the following time-share plan shall begin at the start of 2004/2005 school year. During the children's school year Father shall have physical custody of the children on alternating weeks from after school on Thursday until Monday morning at school. If school is not is session on Monday, then the return time shall be 9:00 a.m. The following week, Father shall have the children every Thursday from after school until Friday morning at school or 9:00 a.m. Father may choose two additional days per month as long as he gives mother four (4) weeks notice and as long as his choice is connected to his usual time. Mother shall attempt to accommodate Father's request; however, if she is unable to grant his request he shall be allowed to select a different date.

Summer Time Share: Each year prior to January 15th both parents shall indicate any special requests for the following summer. Beginning the summer of 2005, the summer shall be divided equally one week at a time. The summer rotation shall begin and end on Sundays at 5:00 p.m.

Transfer Location: The children shall be transferred at their school. However, when they are not in school the transfer shall always be made at their mother's home.

Holidays (page 17): The holidays listed on page 17 of the original order shall be defined and clarified as follows:

- MLK Day shall be defined as Friday after school until Monday at 6:00 p.m. as long as the children are out of school. If for some reason the school does not honor this holiday, then the weekend shall be treated as a usual weekend.

- Child's Birthday: The parent without the child on the child's birthday shall have that child for up to two hours on a school day and up to four hours on the birthday if it falls on a non-school day.
- Mother's Day and Father's Day shall commence at 6:00 p.m. Saturday and end Sunday at 6:00 p.m.

Parent-to-Parent Communication (page 3, #1h): Sam and Kim shall be the primary communicators regarding the children unless they are out of town or there is an emergency. Under these circumstances the stepparents shall be the primary communicators. Both parents shall communicate on a weekly basis through phone calls from work on Fridays between 12:00 noon and 12:15 p.m. If they are not communicating well, as determined by either parent, they shall use their backup plan, with Kim using his Sam's e-mail and Sam using Kim's cellular voice mail on a weekly basis. Emergency communication shall occur whenever needed.

Future Issues: Neither parent shall take any adversarial action against the coparent without first returning to address and mediate the issue at up to two appointments with their parent coordinator or any other agreed upon professional.

_____   _____
      Mother's Signature/Date   Father's Signature/Date

      _____
          Witness Signature/Date

A FINAL NOTE TO PARENT COORDINATORS

In an ideal world, divorced parents would separate their own challenges from their child's well-being and put their child's needs first. However, this task requires strength, maturity, commitment, and a willingness to give up the "fight to be right." It also demands that parents acknowledge their contributions to the conflict while developing new and unfamiliar skills. It is a task so difficult that it often requires the support and guidance of a trained professional—a parent coordinator—in order to reach maximum results.

As a parent coordinator you influence the lives of children by helping divorced parents provide the healthiest environment possible for their child's growth. To succeed you must believe that the potential for change resides deep within each and every parent and it is your responsibility to help them find it. Your task is seldom easy. You may even be criticized and your role unappreciated. Yet no matter how difficult the journey, you must maintain commitment to realistic change while advocating for children.

Improving the quality of children's lives is a noble purpose and you should be commended for the part you play in the process. The real reward comes when children's lives benefit as a result of your—and their parents'—hard work.

Appendix

Parent coordination is a relatively new professional field. Consequently, standards for the profession are minimal at best, and those that have been developed are not universally accepted. Enlightened professionals are spearheading focus groups such as the AFCC and the NPCA to discuss and create a standard code of conduct. Following are the professional standards created by the authors and used in the CPI model of parent coordination. Unfortunately, there are no national standards for the profession. It is hoped that as the field grows, each jurisdiction will develop a standard of practice leading to a national adoption of standards that define and refine the profession of parent coordination.

STANDARDS OF PRACTICE
FOR PARENT COORDINATION

Standard I. Ethical Services

A parent coordinator shall provide ethical and professional services to families in transition. He or she shall uphold this commitment by maintaining practices that reduce parental conflict, minimize stress for the children, and encourage families, whenever possible, to resolve their own parenting issues without litigation. The parent coordinator shall also clarify his or her role and responsibilities by obtaining a copy of the court order or settlement agreement prior to offering any services to the family.

Standard II. Clarification of Role

A parent coordinator must clarify and explain the difference between the role and responsibilities of a parent coordinator and other overlapping professions such as psychotherapist, mediator, and guardian ad litem. A parent coordinator shall ensure that parents understand, prior to each joint session, that parent coordination is not considered psychotherapy.

A parent coordinator shall strictly adhere to the role and responsibilities of a parent coordinator as outlined in the order or stipulation of the parties. They shall protect the family's rights and not overstep any authority granted through a court order, stipulation, or settlement agreement. In addition, a parent coordinator shall never make any permanent change to a court order or settlement agreement without written permission from both parents. Any written change agreed upon by both parents shall be forwarded to the attorneys and guardian ad litem as soon as possible.

Standard III. Child Advocate

A parent coordinator shall remain "child focused" and encourage both parents to do the same. He or she shall, to the greatest extent possible, ensure that the children are shielded from parental conflict, loyalty binds, and any other unnecessary stress. Whenever possible, a coordinator shall promote the active participation of both parents in the life of their child.

A parent coordinator shall assist parents to make informed decisions to promote the best interests of their children. A parent coordinator shall utilize effective mediation skills and creative problem-solving skills. All mutually agreed upon changes shall be initialed by both parents and included in a final parenting plan.

Standard IV: Impartiality

A parent coordinator shall remain impartial and stay aware of any biases, values, and/or professional issues that may interfere with his or her ability to perform the responsibilities of an effective parent coordinator. If the coordinator is unable to remain impartial, for any reason, he or she shall take the necessary steps to assign a new parent coordinator. In order to provide continuity of care, the coordinator shall provide a consultation with the new coordinator prior to transferring the case.

Standard V: Conflict of Interest

A parent coordinator shall disclose any actual or potential conflict of interest as soon as this information is made known to the coordinator.

Standard VI: Confidentiality

A parent coordinator shall ensure confidentiality to the extent that it is defined in the court order or stipulation. He or she shall remind both parents that any form of mediation performed by a parent coordinator is not a confidential process since memos may be sent to attorneys and the court may request information regarding both parents. A parent coordinator shall maintain confidentiality with regard to storage and disposal of records. A parent coordinator shall speak to attorneys regarding only their own client and/or the coordination process.

Standard VII: Informed Consent

A parent coordinator shall provide each participant with a copy of an informed consent form in accordance with the Health Information Privacy Act. Since parent coordination is not considered psychotherapy, a written document shall also be provided that clarifies the limitations of the informed consent as it applies specifically to parent coordination.

A parent coordinator shall function as a mandated reporter. He or she shall provide parents with a copy of office policies prior to the first joint session addressing guidelines on mandated reporting.

Standard VIII: Encouraging Parental Independence

A parent coordinator shall encourage parents to make informed decisions regarding all child-rearing matters and avoid any impulsive or premature resolutions. A parent coordinator shall use caucus-style negotiations when attempting to reach agreements whenever an imbalance of power may exist between the parents. If the parents reach an impasse, a coordinator shall not prolong unproductive sessions that would result in emotional and monetary costs to either parent.

As soon as ongoing services are no longer necessary, a parent coordinator shall modify the frequency and intensity of his or her involvement with the family and change the status of the parents' participation to an as-needed basis. A parent coordinator shall not encourage parents to become dependent on the process of parent coordination. He or she shall not create a situation in which the parents will become dependent on the parent coordinator's guidance. A coordinator shall promote parental authority when appropriate, as well as parental decision making.

Standard IX: Appropriate Referrals

A parent coordinator shall make appropriate referrals on behalf of the parents for additional services as needed and be able to justify the reasoning behind any referral. He or she shall never make a referral to any professional through which he or she could profit in some manner.

A parent coordinator shall meet with the children only as necessary to enhance the process of parent coordination. If the children are in need of ongoing therapeutic services, a coordinator shall make an appropriate referral and ensure that the proper releases are signed in order to communicate with the child's therapist. Likewise, if the children are already involved in treatment, a coordinator shall obtain the proper releases and consult with the child's therapist to ensure continuity of care.

Standard X: Coordination of Services

A parent coordinator shall keep in close contact with other professionals working with the family in order to ensure continuity of care. He or she shall ensure that the proper releases have been obtained prior to consulting with professionals.

If a guardian has been assigned for the children, a parent coordinator shall establish and maintain contact with the guardian. He or she shall keep the guardian informed of the family's progress and shall contact the guardian immediately in situations deemed serious emergencies. Prior to making any "temporary" modifications to the existing court order or settlement agreements, a parent coordinator shall consult with the guardian.

Standard XI: Ex parte Communication

A parent coordinator shall not engage in ex parte communication with the judge by telephone, e-mail, fax, or in person.

A parent coordinator shall prepare and send written updates to both attorneys and the guardian regarding any noncompliance exhibited by either parent. Only when required by the court order shall a coordinator send a copy of the document to the judge.

Standard XII: Temporary Modifications

A parent coordinator shall document a rational justification for any temporary modification or recommendation. He or she shall recognize that the overall purpose of any change or directive shall be for the purpose of shielding the child from unnecessary conflict or stress. A parent coordinator shall reevaluate each modification at the end of a specified period of time. Temporary changes shall not be used as a negative consequence or sanction against one parent for inappropriate behaviors. If a temporary recommendation impacts the amount of time with one parent, arrangements shall be made to correct this as soon as possible so as not to reduce parent-child contact.

Standard XIII: Emergency Services

A parent coordinator shall be available to the family for child-focused emergencies, twenty-four hours a day. If the coordinator is out of town, he or she shall ensure that adequate twenty-four-hour services are available during the absence.

A parent coordinator shall immediately notify the other professionals involved with the family when an emergency situation is inevitable and the child may be in physical or severe emotional risk, to determine if an emergency hearing is warranted.

Standard XIV: Safety

A parent coordinator shall take reasonable safety precautions when domestic violence is suspected or documented.

Standard XV: Legal Advice

A parent coordinator shall not give legal advice. He or she may share basic knowledge of legal issues related to divorce such as legal terminology and the separation process. However, a coordinator must encourage parents to consult with their attorneys at any point in the process as needed.

Standard XVI: Dual Roles

A parent coordinator shall not perform more than one role with a family prior to or after offering the services of parent coordination. He or she shall not provide psychological testing or enter into a therapeutic relationship with either parent after providing the services of parent coordination. However, periodic sessions with the children or coaching sessions with the parents shall not be considered therapeutic but rather a part of the parent coordination process.

Standard XVII: Documentation

A parent coordinator shall keep detailed session and telephone notes for an indefinite period of time. If the case is transferred to a new coordinator a complete copy of the file shall remain with the previous coordinator.

Standard XVIII: Financial Matters

A parent coordinator may assist the parents in the resolution of all parenting matters. Major financial issues such as child support, assets, liabilities, and taxes shall be resolved in standard mediation, between attorneys, or by the court. However, a parent coordinator may address finances as they apply to parenting expenses such as, but not limited to, reimbursement of medical co-payments, fees associated with extracurricular activities, and the purchase of school supplies.

Standard XIX: Testimony

A parent coordinator required to testify shall do so on behalf of the child(ren) rather than for either parent or attorney.

A parent coordinator shall not offer recommendations for physical or legal custody. However, if asked to report back to court in the form of memo or testimony, a coordinator may reflect upon each parent's strengths and weakness, including observations regarding the effectiveness of the time-sharing plan.

Standard XX: Fees

The fees associated with the services of a parent coordinator shall be set as reasonably as possible with a sliding scale. The joint charge shall not be set higher than the therapist's standard hourly charge. A parent coordinator's hourly fee may be reduced as needed to assist low-income families. However, fees shall not be increased based upon the parents' ability to pay. Since parent coordination is not therapy, no third-party reimbursement shall be used.

Standard XXI. Professional Education

A parent coordinator shall have the education and training necessary to provide ethical and professional services to high-conflict families. Professional education shall include (1) adult psychopathology, (2) child development, (3) children's issues of divorce, (4) divorce recovery, (5) basic legal terminology and the legal process of divorce, (6) family systems theory, (7) domestic violence, and (8) mediation and conflict resolution training. In addition, the parent coordinator shall remain up-to-date on divorce issues and professional training requirements as determined by the jurisdiction in which he or she is providing services.

A parent coordinator shall participate in continuing education and be personally responsible for ongoing professional growth. A parent coordinator shall consult with other professionals when necessary, such as a family law attorney, child therapist, physician, and with at least one established parent coordinator. The parent coordinator shall not give information or advice in areas in which he or she is not qualified by training or experience.

ORDER APPOINTING A PARENT COORDINATOR

THIS CAUSE having come before this Court, and this Court having reviewed the file and being otherwise fully advised in the premises, based on a stipulation of the parties, this Court does:

ORDER AND ADJUDGE as follows:

1. *Parent Coordinator:* The parties shall agree on a parent coordinator within thirty (30) days of the date of this Order. If counsel and/or pro se litigant cannot agree on the designation of a parent coordinator, the Court, on Motion by either party, and without a hearing, shall appoint one through the Cooperative Parenting Institute. The parent coordinator shall have the following minimal qualifications:
   A. Licensed mental health provider trained in family therapy, child development, conflict resolution and;
   B. Certified family mediator and/or trained in the CPI model of parent coordination through the Cooperative Parenting Institute (404) 315-7474 Ext.1
   C. Is a current member of the National Association of Parent Coordinators
2. *Expense Shared Equality:* Initially, the parents shall equally share financial responsibility to pay the parent coordinator (the Court reserves the right to resolve any objection to the changes made and redistribute the cost on a pro rata basis if appropriate). Each parent shall promptly pay one-half of any reasonable bill submitted by the coordinator. If the parties fall behind thirty days or more on their balance they shall be responsible for a 15 percent finance charge each month. The Court shall enforce payment of any amounts owed to the parent coordinator (PC) by either party through contempt proceedings, if necessary.
3. *General Responsibilities of Parent Coordinator:* Under Georgia law, the children are entitled to access to both parties, without interference from either parent or anyone else, once the parties separate. The parent coordinator shall assist the parties and the children to promote the children's best interest in general. The PC is entitled to communicate with the parties, children, health care providers, psychological providers, teachers, and any other third parties deemed necessary by the

parent coordinator. The parties recognize that parent coordination is not psychotherapy and therefore is not confidential. The parties shall cooperate with the coordinator by executing any necessary releases.

4. *Role of Parent Coordinator:* The parent coordinator shall:

4.1. Make any recommendations relative to enforcing any shared parenting plan and parenting schedule and to minimize conflicts between the parties by addressing the particular patterns of behavior for the parties.

4.2. Assist the parents in implementing any plan or schedule so that the children have continuous and consistent contact with both parents.

4.3. Minimize conflict, loyalty binds, and unnecessary stress for the children.

4.4. The parent coordinator has the following broad responsibilities: To educate, mediate, monitor, and make recommendations as needed. In addition, the PC may:

4.4.1. Recommend approaches that will reduce conflict between parents and require parents to temporarily make adjustments to reduce conflict for the child/ren. However, the PC may not make changes to either parent's custodial time.

4.4.2. Recommend compliance with any parenting plan or parenting schedule in the Court's Order or Settlement Agreement. In addition the PC may monitor parental behaviors and program agreements and report any noncompliance to the parent's counsel if necessary.

4.4.3. Recommend outside resources as needed such as random drug screens, parenting classes, or psychotherapy.

4.4.4. Monitor parenting plan or parenting schedule and mediate the parents' disputes concerning parenting issues.

4.4.5. Write detailed guidelines or rules recommended for communication between parents and practicing those guidelines or rules with the parents. If parenting skills are lacking, the coordinator shall work with one or both parents to teach those skills.

4.4.6. Recommend modification of the parenting plan when agreement or consensus cannot be reached, as a means of reducing conflict and promoting the best interests of the children. Any recommended modification of a plan or schedule shall be in writing and submitted to the parents and their attorneys.

4.4.7. Prior to completion, write modifications of the parenting plan when mutual agreement has been made by both parents and their attorneys.

4.4.8. Prior to completion, recommend how a particular element of the parenting plan or schedule shall be implemented including, without limitation, the frequency and length of visitation, temporary changes in the schedule, holiday or vacation planning, logistics of pickup and drop-off, suitability of accommodations, issues dealing with stepparents and significant others.

4.4.9. Work with both parents and any significant others to update and fine-tune their parenting schedule over time. (All possible changes in the family's circumstances can not be foreseen when the parenting plan originated.) Parenting schedules, postdivorce, may need to be adjusted to children's changing developmental needs, schools, new blended families, or evolving outside interests. At the completion of the program, both parents shall be put on an as-needed basis to minimize problems and unnecessary litigation in the future;

4.4.10. Ensuring that both parents maintain ongoing relationships with the children; and

4.4.11. Recommend a final decision on any parenting issue over which the parents reach an impasse, by submission of a written recommendation to the parents and their counsel.

4.5. Educate the parents with a psychoeducational program such as *Cooperative Parenting and Divorce* in the areas of:

4.5.1. effective communication and negotiation skills

4.5.2. effective parenting skills

4.5.3. how to meet the developmental needs of their children

4.5.4. how to disengage from each other when it leads to conflict

4.5.5. how to keep their children out of the middle

The PC may determine if the educational component is completed in a group format with other divorcing parents or in joint sessions. If the parents participate in a group, the PC may determine if they participate in the same group or separately. The joint sessions may occur simultaneously or after the completion of an eight-week group.

4.6. The PC shall maintain communication among all parties by serving, if necessary, as a conduit for information. The PC is not the ally of either parent and the PC is not a neutral mediator. The parent coordinator's role is active and specifically focused on helping parents work together for the benefit of the children. The PC's fundamental role is to minimize the conflict to which the children are exposed by the parents.

4.7. The PC is not a custody evaluator, nor can he or she change the amount of custodial time either parent has been granted by the courts. Making decisions to place children in the residence and custody of one parent would seriously compromise the parent coordinator's neutrality. The PC shall not recommend primary residence of the children. The PC may make temporary changes to reduce conflict for the children or to better understand the needs of the children. Temporary changes are those changes that would not extend more than a few weeks such as minor changes in the transfer location, time of phone calls, and other parenting issues.

4.8. The PC shall recommend, if necessary, supervised visitation to protect the children but not as a sanction. The coordinator may also recommend a transition from supervised to unsupervised visitation in writing to counsel.

4.9. Assistance provided by the PC is not intended to be a crisis service except when a crisis directly impacts on the child. Unless an emergency directly impacts on the child neither parent shall contact the PC outside normal working hours.

4.10. Significant financial matters shall not be addressed by the parent coordinator

5. *Meeting with the Parent Coordinator*

5.1. The PC may meet with the parties, the children, and significant others jointly or separately. The parent coordinator shall determine if the appointments shall be joint or separate. The PC shall determine if the joint appointments are video- or audiotaped for educational purposes. The tapes may be reviewed by either parent during or after their appointments.

5.2. Both parent shall contact the parent coordinator to schedule appointments. Appointments may also be scheduled when the parent coordinator requests.

5.3. Each parent should direct any disagreements or concerns regarding the children to the PC during the active phase of the process. The PC shall work with both parents to resolve the conflict and, if necessary, shall recommend an appropriate resolution to the parents.

6. *Written and Oral Documents and Appearance in Court*

6.1. At the completion of the work, the PC may submit a final memo or written report to the parents' counsel describing any conflicts and the parent coordinator's recommended resolutions. The PC may also report to the parties and their counsel on parental compliance with and parental attitudes about any element of the parenting plan as amended by agreement or the parties or as determined by the PC. Copies of all memos or reports to the Court shall be sent to the parties and their attorneys, not to the Court directly.

6.2. If either parent subpoenas the PC to testify on any matter, a new parent coordinator may be assigned by the current parent coordinator to be available to the family after the hearing date.

7. *Terms of Appointment*

7.1. The parties shall honor the standard parent coordination guidelines outlined in the Agreement and Expectation materials.

7.2. The appointment of the PC is for an indefinite period of time. However, as soon as the parties have stabilized they shall be transferred to an as-needed basis. If the parties are unable to make progress and/or return to court, they may request that the appointment be terminated. The parent coordinator may be discharged by the Court or by written agreement of the parties. Both parties have the right to request a new parent coordinator one time. The former PC shall select the next PC through trained coordinators at the CPI. The previous PC shall remain appointed until both parents have started sessions with the new coordinator.

7.3. The parent coordinator reserves the right to withdraw from the role of coordinator should he or she feel that effective change is no longer occurring. The parents and their respective attorneys shall be given two-weeks notice of the decision to withdraw

along with the names of other coordinators. When the PC terminates services he or she shall continue to act as the PC for up to
two weeks to provide a smooth transition between coordinators.

7.4. At the completion of the work with the PC, a closing memo
shall be sent to the parties and their counsel indicating that they
have moved to an as-needed basis. At that time, the PC shall no
longer have any authority to make recommendations or temporary changes.

8. *Complaint Procedure*

8.1. If either parent believes that the PC is biased then he or she shall
write out the complaint on one page to send to the coordinator.
The next step is to schedule an individual appointment with the
PC in an attempt to resolve the matter prior to changing coordinators.

8.2. If either parent believes that a complaint should be lodged
against the court-appointed coordinator, the complaint shall be
presented only after:

8.2.1. The allegations are submitted to the Court; and

8.2.2. The appointed parent coordinator receives an opportunity to present a defense against the allegations in the
Court; and

8.2.3. The Court issues an order or judgment containing an express finding that the court-appointed parent coordinator did not perform services to the satisfaction of the
Court.

9. *Future Use of the Parent Coordinator*

9.1. At any point in the future, either parent may request a joint session to discuss a parenting impasse as long as they have documented a minimum of two attempts to communicate and resolve
the matter with the other parent prior to requesting a joint meeting.

9.2. Should any serious disputes arise between the parents pertaining to the child's welfare, before seeking modification through
the courts, the parents shall schedule the services of their parent
coordinator in an attempt to resolve the matter prior to taking
any adversarial action.

BY THE COURT, _____

This _____ day of _____ 200 ____

PARENT COORDINATION
AGREEMENT/EXPECTATIONS FORM

As of today, _____ / _____ / _____, I agree to the following program guidelines (26 points) for the appointment of a parent coordinator through the Cooperative Parenting Institute:

I. Parent Coordination versus Psychotherapy or Mediation

1. I understand that parent coordination is not psychotherapy. There is no therapist/client privilege and third-party reimbursement will not be accepted.
2. Since the appointment of a parent coordinator is either court ordered, recommended by a guardian ad litem, or a stipulation between the two parents, I understand that the process *is not confidential.* I understand that memos to the court and attorneys may be sent by my parent coordinator if we reach an impasse. I will provide a release for any and all parties/reports as requested by my parent coordinator.
3. Although parent coordination includes a form of high-conflict mediation, the process of parent coordination is not considered mediation.

II. Financial

4. I will be billed at $_____ per 50-minute hour and $_____ per 80-minute joint appointment. I will also be responsible for one-half of all other fees associated with this process such as, but not limited to, emergency phone calls, consultations, our child's session, memos, and the preparation of our Parenting Plan. I will be billed at a rate of $_____ per quarter hour during working hours and $_____ per quarter hour during after-business hours. My parent coordinator will determine if I am billed a portion of these fees or if I will be solely responsible for the fee.
5. I will either keep a retainer or pay as I go keeping a zero monthly balance. Monthly statements will be made available to me. Monthly balances may have a 15 percent finance charge added. If my account is referred to a collection agency or an attorney, I agree to pay all fees associated with the collection of my account.

---

6. I will be billed for a joint session along with my coparent's portion of the session if I am running late or unable to manage myself during that particular session. Likewise, I will be responsible for any cancellation made without twenty-four hour notice provided to both the institute and to my coparent. This applies no matter who has been ordered to pay for the joint sessions.

III. General Expectations/Agreements

7. I will schedule joint sessions at least every other week unless the parent coordinator recommends more frequent appointments. I understand that my child will be seen at least once for an intake appointment. I also understand that the coordinator will determine if and when other adults are included in our joint sessions.
8. I will allow the taping of our joint appointments for educational viewing exclusively by our parent coordinator, my coparent, and myself.
9. I will work on implementing new skills in joint sessions and ultimately outside sessions.
10. I will make child-focused decisions and sacrifices when necessary. I will stay solution focused rather than fight to win.
11. I will be responsible for my own behavior and not focus on the behavior of my coparent. I understand that I am expected to make progress and changes for the sake of my child.
12. I will take responsibility for the parenting issues I want to address and resolve at each joint session.
13. I will not call our parent coordinator unless I am having an emergency that is child focused, and I will not expect a return call unless I indicate the exact nature of the emergency on the voice mail or with the live emergency service.
14. If my attorney subpoenas the parent coordinator, I will be solely responsible for all charges associated with the time involved to prepare and testify one week prior to a court date. I understand that the coordinator will not testify for me or my coparent, nor will he or she have an opinion regarding custody. In addition, if the parent coordinator is required to testify, a new one will be assigned immediately after the court date.
15. If I feel my parent coordinator is biased, I will meet with him or her to discuss the issue prior to requesting a new coordinator. I understand that

I may request only one change in coordinators and after I have a zero balance. This change will include a consult between coordinators at my expense. The CPI will provide names of trained coordinators. The previous coordinator will continue to be responsible for our family and bill accordingly until the first joint session with the new coordinator.

16. If I believe a complaint should be lodged against the appointed parent coordinator, the complaint will be presented only after:
    a. The allegations are submitted to the Court; and
    b. The appointed parent coordinator receives an opportunity to present a defense against the allegations in the Court; and
    c. The Court issues an order or judgment containing an express finding that the court-appointed parent coordinator did not perform services to the satisfaction of the court.

IV. Parental Behaviors

17. I will act respectfully and acknowledge my coparent, no matter how I feel about them *every time* I see them and even when my child is *not* present. (This includes the waiting room.)
18. I will not block our child's contact with the other parent either by phone or visitation. I will ensure that our child returns calls to the other parent the same day whenever a voice message has been left for them. I will keep child calls and parent calls separate.
19. I will use impulse control and shield our child from parental conflict and negative comments.
20. I will minimize and eliminate my child's sense of loyalty binds.
21. I will "consult" with my coparent rather than "inform" my coparent regarding parenting decisions.
22. I will not schedule activities or appointments on the other parent's time without prior agreement.
23. I will honor the current order and any new agreements made in the joint sessions.
24. I will not call the police unless there is a clear threat of physical harm. I will not contact the department of child and family services unless I consult with the parent coordinator first. I will use the emergency number 24/7 to reach the coordinator rather than do anything adversarial or upsetting to our child.

25. I will not contact my attorney to take any adversarial action without first dealing with the issue in a joint session and indicating my plans during that joint session.

_____   _____

Parent Signature   Date

_____   _____

Parent Signature   Date

PARENT COORDINATION CHECKLIST

Prior to Intake Appointments

___1. Request a copy of the order or settlement agreement that makes reference to PC's appointment.
___2. Make sure the language of the order is specific and delineates PC role and authority. If not, contact both attorneys and request the language be changed. Fax them a copy of a sample order.
___3. Contact both parents by phone to schedule the intake appointment.
___4. Mail each parent a packet that includes assessment forms and directions.
___5. Review their packets prior to their individual intake appointments.
___6. Contact both attorneys and ask them to contact your office if they need to share their concerns.

During Parent Intake Appointments

___1. Allow each parent to share their history and their concerns without the other parent present.
___2. Secure a brief time line.
___3. Request a list of parental concerns regarding their child as well as their coparent.
___4. Create a list of their goals.
___5. Ask for clarification based on their assessment forms.
___6. Answer their questions regarding the program.
___7. Request retainers and provide them each with a copy of their workbook.
___8. Ask each parent to bring a large 8x11 photo of their child and a copy of any order(s).

First Joint Session

___1. Review Expectations and Agreement Form and Releases with both parents and have them initial.
___2. Create mutual goals with both parents and sign.
___3. Read the Divorce Rules together and initial.

___4. If time permits ask each parent what one issue they would like to resolve.

___5. Make a list of any agreements and initial.

___6. Copy their mutual goals, Expectation/Agreement form, and agreement for each parent.

___7. Schedule a minimum of four to five joint sessions at a time.

___8. After the first session send a brief memo to both attorneys indicating that the parents have begun the program. Attach copies of the expectation/agreement form and mutual goals.

Further Joint Sessions

___1. Prior to each session have parents sign the review sheet indicating that PC is not therapy and is therefore not confidential.

___2. If they are doing the education material in a group focus all the time on mediating a minimum of four or five parenting issues. Record, initial, and copy for both parents.

___3. If they are not participating in a group and they will benefit from the material, address at least fifteen to twenty minutes on their workbooks. Use the remaining time to mediate three to four parenting issues, record agreements, initial, and copy.

Make sure to get agreements about how they will communicate on a weekly basis and exactly how this will work.

Child's Intake Appointment

___1. Introduce yourself and explain why their parents are working with you.

___2. Show the child his or her photo in the parents' file.

___3. Let them know that everything you record in your notes will be confidential unless they want you to tell their parents. Tell the children that they can say anything they want and that you will read them back everything you wrote down. They will tell you "yes" or "no" depending if they want you to tell both their parents. Write a "yes" or "no" in the margins to remind yourself and to reassure the children.

Stepparent or Significant Other Intake Appointment

___1. Meet with new partners alone rather than with their current spouse.
___2. Ask what their concerns are for the child or children.
___3. Ask what their concerns are about the coparent.
___4. Ask them to be prepared to attend sessions when ready.
___5. Find out what name the child calls them.
___6. Ask if they speak with the child's other parent.
___7. Ask what role they play with the child, if they discipline, and how.

Stepparent/Significant Other with Same-Sex Parent

___1. Do not allow the current spouse into this meeting.
___2. Set up the child's photo in the stand.
___3. Use the term "stepparent" as such to help remind the stepparent and to reassure the biological parent.
___4. Ask the stepparent to share any positive information about the child with the biological parent. This should be a joining activity and reduce tension between them.

Four-Way Parenting Joint Sessions

Do not schedule these until the biological parents are clear they are the "primary parents." When ready, you may want to schedule with all parents about every other session.

___1. Encourage the stepparents to take a backseat to both biological parents.
___2. Do not allow the stepparent to speak for the household.

Prior to Moving to As-Needed Basis

If they have been fairly conflicted, wean them with sessions at one month, three months, six months, and one year.

___1. Review their previous order to make sure all loopholes have been resolved or clarified.

___2. Compile all their initialed agreements and type into a parenting plan.
___3. Review the parenting plan with the parents and edit in session or allow the parents to review it in the waiting room. Do not allow them to take a copy of the plan until it is signed.
___4. Revise parenting plan until ready to be signed by all parties. E-mail to both attorneys.
___5. Meet with both parents and the child to discuss relapse indicators.
___6. Send a memo to both attorneys (and court when appropriate) indicating that their status has gone to PRN.

PARENTING PLAN CHECKLIST

Many of the components contained in a parenting plan are enumerated in this checklist. Although most parenting plans share similar components, some may not be as detailed as others.

1. Custody Arrangement

_____ Have the parents determined who will have physical custody?
_____ Has a primary home been designated for the purposes of public school enrollment?

2. Joint Legal Custody: Access to Records and Parental Decision Making

_____ Have the parents determined if they will share joint legal custody?
_____ Will all major parenting decisions be discussed and agreed upon?
_____ How will parents resolve parenting disputes/impasses?

Optional:
_____ If required, determine if there will be a tiebreaker and if so on which parenting disputes?
_____ Indicate that both parents shall have access to school and all medical records.

3. Time-Sharing Arrangement/Living Arrangement

_____ Indicate the access schedule for each parent for the school year.
_____ Indicate if they want right of first refusal and, if so, over how many hours?
_____ Determine provisions for trade-offs equal in time and/or agreement to ensure make up of missed time.

4. Summer Schedule

The summer vacation schedule takes precedence over the regular schedule and the holiday schedule takes precedence over the regular and the summer schedule (e.g., Father's Day). Length and timing of vacation is usually

---

determined by the child's age, developmental stage, temperament, and school schedule.

_____ Do the parents desire any limitations regarding vacation sites such as in/out of state/country?

_____ Outline a deadline for each parent to select their vacation dates in writing.

_____ What will the schedule be during the parts of the summer that are not selected as vacations?

_____ If there is a midweek visit, what will happen when the parents are out of town?

_____ When parents travel out of town, will they share travel information and phone numbers prior to leaving with the child?

_____ If they equally share the weeks during the summer, how will parents do so? What happens if one child wants to go away to a summer camp? Whose week will it be?

5. Transfers

_____ Which parent will pick up the children? The parent beginning their custodial time or the parent ending their custodial period?

_____ Determine where the transfers shall take place.

_____ Stipulate how long each parent shall wait, and identify the procedure for getting the children if the parent leaves after having waited the designated period of time.

_____ If high-conflict parents, outline the details regarding the transfer, such as remaining in the car and saying good-bye to the children prior to the transfer.

Optional:

_____ Stipulate if the parent can wait in the living room at times of transition and if the child can take the parent briefly to his or her room.

6. Holiday Schedule

Holiday schedules generally take priority over the regularly scheduled living arrangement. It is recommended that specific days not be used in the definitions of holidays since each school system varies on when they get out of school on a particular holiday. For instance, Wednesday prior to Thanksgiving can become "the day the children are released from school for the Thanksgiving holiday until . . ." Discourage parents from breaking up holidays other than the winter holiday, which is usually about two weeks. Mother's Day and Father's Day does not alternate.

_____ Determine which holidays the parents want to include in their holiday rotation.
_____ Define each holiday with beginning and ending times.
_____ Alternate with even and odd years so that both parents have holidays each year.
_____ Determine if Mother's Day and Father's Day will include the whole weekend or just the Sunday.
_____ Explore options for holidays that may vary during the year such as the parents' and child's birthdays.

Optional:
_____ When the holiday schedule interrupts the normal rotation, do the parents want to prevent either parent from having more than two weekends in a row? How will this be accomplished?
_____ Stipulate when the child's birthday party will be held and which parent will host and pay for the child's birthday on the date of his or her birth.
_____ Determine if they have any special religious observances.

7. Extracurricular Activities

_____ Do they want any limitations on the number of activities per child or per year?
_____ Who will schedule and pay for the activities?
_____ Who will be responsible for transportation to the activity?
_____ Will there be any restrictions regarding adult attendance at extracurricular activities?

8. Parental Communication Expectations

See Chapter 9 for additional information on communication. Encourage parents to notify the coparent when traveling out of town without the children in the event of an emergency or in case the child would like to contact the absent parent.

_____ Determine frequency and method of communication, such as phone calls, e-mail, facsimile, meeting in public places, or written correspondence.

_____ Design a decision-making procedure regarding choice of physicians and assistance outside routine medical care, such as therapy and orthodontia, as well as payment arrangement.

_____ Do parents want any deadlines, such as "Written requests for change in schedule must be made 72 hours prior to the anticipated change in schedule. The receiving parent shall respond within 12 hours."

_____ Specify exact time and limits for weekly parental communication.

_____ Designate which parent should initiate contact with the other parent and clarify important communication ground rules, including topics that are off limits.

_____ Clarify when both parents should return to the parent coordinator to assist with issues.

_____ Develop a system with deadlines for sharing:
    _____ non–time-sensitive parenting information
    _____ time-sensitive information
    _____ emergencies
    _____ written schedules, report cards, etc.
    _____ child's school and activity schedule
    _____ notification of appointments

9. Inclusion Expectations

_____ Have the parents determined who will schedule the routine appointments?

_____ Will both parents be included in well check ups or consultations?

_____ Will both parents be invited to all school and extracurricular activities?

Optional:
_____ Would parents like to alternate school field trips?

_____ If the child is in therapy, will they take turns transporting the child?

10. Parent-to-Child Communication

_____ How often can the noncustodial parent call the children and during what periods of time?

_____ Determine when parents will get returned calls when they are unable to reach the child.

_____ Designate if and when the child can call the absent parent.

Optional:

_____ Determine if privacy for the child's calls will be expected.

11. Parental Behaviors

Consider outlining the Divorce Rules in this section. Any expectations the parents have of each other should be included in this section. Keep in mind that some of their expectations cannot be monitored without an involved parent coordinator. Be sure to inquire if these expectations will also apply to future stepparents or significant others.

_____ Determine if parents will commit to mature behavior in front of their child. If so, be specific.

_____ Decide if parents want a morality clause regarding overnight guests.

_____ Determine if parents want a travel expectation regarding significant others.

12. Safety Issues

Ask parents to consider safety issues. For example, drinking and driving with the children in the car, wearing helmets for certain activities, riding in the backseat, and guidelines regarding guns in the home.

13. Financial Responsibilities

In general, financial responsibilities of both parents will be determined through the legal system, particularly child support, child care fees, and medical costs. In many jurisdictions, written guidelines help determine financial matters. In situations of joint physical custody it is not unusual for the parents to share all expenses related to child rearing. Child support may or may not be designated. Encourage parents to keep these payments separate from any other payments. The checklist may or may not be necessary.

_____ Determine parental responsibility to purchase special attire, teacher gifts, yearbooks, car.

_____ Decide parental responsibility for fees for service beyond insurance premiums. Consider deductibles and noncovered expenses.

_____ Clarify how and when the parents will exchange receipts and make these payments.

_____ Determine type of education: preschool opportunities, public or private education, and tutoring, and how the costs will be paid.

_____ Explore exactly what will be considered separate from child support. For instance, daycare, private school, clothes, and overnight camps.

14. Optional Concerns

_____ Determine parental responsibility for maintenance and type of health insurance coverage.

_____ Explore whether parents are willing to include college expenses.

_____ Decide how clothes will be handled and returned to the primary home, or if clothes will be provided in both homes.

_____ Determine if the child will be permitted to move items between homes.

_____ Determine commitment to religious education.

_____ Discuss the rules and responsibilities the parents want to support in both homes.

_____ Decide if corporal punishment may be used by the parents.

_____ Determine if parents want to include a provision for maximum distance between homes.

_____ Discuss provisions for continued contact with former stepsiblings and/or stepparents.

Bibliography

Ahrons, C. R. (1979a). The binuclear family: Two households, one family. *Alternative Lifestyles, 2,* 499-515.

Ahrons, C. R. (1979b). The coparental divorce: Preliminary research findings and policy implications. In A. Milne (Ed.), *Joint custody: A handbook for judges, lawyers and counselors.* Portland, OR: Association of Family and Conciliation Courts.

Ahrons, C. R. (1990). Families of divorce: Choices, challenges, and changes. Plenary address at the annual meeting of the American Association for Marriage and Family Therapy, October 7, Washington, DC.

Ahrons, C. R. (1994). *The good divorce: Keeping your family together when your marriage comes apart.* New York: HarperCollins.

Ahrons, C. R. (2004). We're still a family: What grown children have to say about their parents' divorce. New York: HarperCollins.

Ainsworth, M. D. (1978). *Patterns of attachment: A psychological study of the strange solution.* Hillsdale, NJ: Erlbaum.

Allison, P. D. and Furstenberg, F. F. Jr. (1989). How marital dissolution affects children. *Developmental Psychology, 25,* 540-549.

Amato, P. and Keith, B. (1991). Consequences of parental divorce for the well-being of children: A meta-analysis. *Psychological Bulletin, 110,* 26-46.

American Psychiatric Association (2000). *Diagnostic and statistical manual of mental disorders* (Fourth edition, Text revision). Washington, DC: American Psychiatric Association.

Arbuthnot, J. and Gordon, D. A. (1993). *What about the children: A guide for divorced and divorcing parents.* Athens, OH: Center for Divorce Education.

Arizona State Legislature (2003). Arizona revised statutes. Available at <http://www.azleg.state.az.us/>.

Arizona Supreme Court (2003). The model parenting time plans for parent-child access. Available at <http://www.supreme.state.az.us/drt/>.

Association of Family and Conciliation Courts Task Force on Parenting Coordination (2002). Parenting coordination: Implementation issues. Available at <http://www.afccnet.org/catalog/>.

Baris, M. A., Coates, C. A., Duvall, B. B., Garrity, C. B., Johnson, E. T., and LaCrosse, E. R. (2001). *Working with high-conflict families of divorce.* Northvale, NJ: Jason Aronson.

Berger, S. (1983). *Divorce without victims.* Boston: Houghton Mifflin.

Biringen, Z., Greve-Spees, J., Howard, W., Leith, D., Tanner, L., Moore, S., Sakoguchi, S., and Williams, L. (2002). Commentary on Warshak's blanket restrictions: Overnight contact between parents and young children. *Family Court Review, 40*(2), 204-207.

Blau, M. (1993). *Families apart.* New York: G. P. Putnan's Sons.

Block, J., Block, J., and Gjerde, P. (1986). The personality of children prior to divorce: A prospective study. *Child Development, 57,* 827-840.

Borderline Central (2001). Assumptions held by BPD sufferers. Available at <http://www.bpdcentral.com/resources/>.

Bowlby, J. ([1969] 1982). *Attachment and loss.* New York: Basic Books.

Boyan, S. (2000). What is a parent coordinator? Specialized therapists and mandated high conflict families. *American Association of Marriage and Family Therapists Family Therapy Magazine,* June/July.

Boyan, S. (2002). Stepparents and high-conflict divorce: Asset or liablity? *The Peaceful Co-Parent.*

Boyan, S. and Termini, A. M. (1999). *Cooperative parenting and divorce: A parent guide to effective co-parenting.* Kennesaw, GA: Active Parenting.

Brotsky, M., Steinman, S., and Zemmelman, S. (1991). Joint custody through mediation: A longitudinal assessment of the children. In J. Folberg (Ed.), *Joint custody and shared parenting* (Second edition) (pp. 167-176). New York: The Guilford Press.

Bryan, P. E. (1994). Reclaiming professionalism: The lawyer's role in divorce mediation. *Family Law Quarterly, 177,* 193-207.

Burhans G. Jr., Blackman, M., Diaz, J., and Knight, J. (1998). Profiles of unified family courts. The Association of Family and Conciliation Courts and the Hofstra University School of Law.

Burns, D. D. (1999). *Feeling good: The new mood therapy.* New York: Avon.

Camara, K. and Resnick, G. (1988). Interparental conflict and cooperation: Factors mediating children's post divorce adjustment. In E. M. Hetherington and J. D. Arasteh (Eds.), *Impact of divorce, single parenting and stepparenting on children* (pp. 169-196). Hillside, NJ: Erlbaum.

Camara, K. and Resnick, G. (1989). Styles of conflict resolution and cooperation between divorced parents: Effects on child behavior and adjustment. *American Journal of Orthopsychiatry, 59,* 560-575.

Campbell, L. and Johnston, J. (1986). Multi-family mediation: The use of groups to resolve child custody disputes. In D. T. Saposnek (Ed.), *Applying family therapy perspectives to mediation.* San Francisco: Jossey-Bass.

Carter, L. and Minirth, F. (1993). *The anger workbook.* Nashville, TN: Thomas Nelson.

Clapp, G. (1992). *Divorce and new beginnings: An authoritive guide to recovery and growth, solo parenting, and stepfamilies.* New York: John Wiley and Sons.

Coates, C., Jones, W., Bushard, P., Deutsch, R., Hicks, B., Stahl, P., Sullivan, M., Sydlik, B., and Wistner, R. (2003). Parenting coordination: Implementation issues. *Family Court Review, 4,* 533-564.

Cowen, E. L., Pedro-Carroll, J. L., and Alpert-Gillis, L. J. (1990). Relationship between support and adjustment among children of divorce. *Journal of Child Psychology and Psychiatry, 31,* 727-735.

Cullen, M. (1992). *Cage your rage: An inmates guide to anger control.* Lanham, MD: American Correctional Association.

Darnell, D. (2001). Parental alienation: Three types of alienators. Available at <http://www.divorcesource.com/>.

Elgin, S. (1995). *You can't say that to me! Stopping the pain of verbal abuse.* Hoboken, NJ: John Wiley and Sons.

Elkin, M. (1991). Joint custody: In the best interest of the family. In J. Folberg (Ed.), *Joint custody and shared parenting* (Second edition) (pp. 11-15). New York: The Guilford Press.

Ellis, A. (1962). *Reason and emotion in psychotherapy.* Secaucus, NJ: Lyle Stuart.

Felner, R. D. and Terre, L. (1987). Child custody dispositions and children's adaptation following divorce. In L. A. Weithorn (Ed.), *Psychology and child custody determinations* (pp. 106-153). Lincoln: University of Nebraska Press.

Fisch, R., Weakland, J. H., and Segal, L. (1982). *The tactics of change: Doing therapy briefly.* San Francisco: Jossey-Bass.

Folberg, J. (Ed.) (1991). *Joint custody and shared parenting.* New York: The Guilford Press.

Forward, S. and Frazier, D. (1997). *Emotional blackmail: When the people in your life use fear, obligation, and guilt to manipulate you.* New York: Harper Collins.

Gardner, R. A. (1987). *The parental alienation syndrome and the differentiation between fabricated and genuine child sex abuse.* Cresskill, NJ: Creative Therapeutics.

Gardner, R. A. (1991). Joint custody is not for everyone. In J. Folberg (Ed.), *Joint custody and shared parenting* (Second edition) (pp. 88-96). New York: The Guilford Press.

Gardner, R. A. (1992). *The parental alienation syndrome.* Cresskill, NJ: Creative Therapeutics.

Gardner, R. A. (2002). Response to Kelly/Johnston article. *Speak Out for Children, 17*(2), 6-10.

Garrity, C. and Baris, M. (1994). *Caught in the middle: Protecting the children of high-conflict divorce.* San Francisco: Jossey-Bass.

Garrity, C. and Baris, M. (2002). Understanding and working with children in high-conflict families. Seminar presented at the meeting of the Association for Conflict Resolution Family Section Conference, Savannah, GA. February 28.

Gelman, D. (1991). The miracle of resiliency. *Newsweek, 117*(26), 44-47.

Gold, L. (1992). *Between love and hate: A guide to civilized divorce.* New York: Plenum Press.

Goldstein, J., Freud, A., and Solnet, A. (1979). *Before the best interests of the child.* New York: The Free Press.

Gottman, J. (1994a). *What predicts divorce? The relationship between marital processes and marital outcomes.* Hillside, NJ: Erlbaum.

Gottman, J. (1994b). *Why marriages succeed or fail.* New York: Simon and Schuster.

Gould, J. W. and Stahl, P. M. (2001). Never paint by numbers: A response to Kelly and Lamb (2000), Solomon and Biringen (2001), and Lamb and Kelly (2001). *Family Court Review, 39,* 372-376.

Grief, J. B. (1979). Fathers, children, and joint custody. *American Journal of Orthopsychiatry, 49,* 311-319.

Hallowell, E. M. and Ratey, J. J. (1995). *Driven to distraction: Recognizing and coping with attention deficit disorder from childhood to adulthood.* New York: Simon and Schuster.

Hess, R. D. and Camara, K. A. (1979). Post-divorce family relationships as mediating factors in the consequences of divorce for children. *Journal of Social Issues, 35,* 79-96.

Hetherington, E. M. and Arasteh, J. (Eds.) (1988). *Impact of divorce, single parenting, and stepparenting of children.* Hillside, NJ: Erlbaum.

Hetherington, E. M., Cox, M., and Cox, R. (1982). Effects of divorce on parents and children. In Lamb, M. E. (Ed.), *Nontraditional families: Parenting and child development* (pp. 233-262). Hillside, NJ: Erlbaum.

Hetherington, E. M., Cox, M., and Cox, R. (1985). Long-term effects of divorce and remarriage on the adjustment of children. *Journal of the American Academy of Child Psychiatry, 24,* 518-530.

Hetherington, E. M., Hagan, S., and Anderson, E. R. (1989). Marital transitions: A child's perspective. *The American Psychologist, 44*(2), 303-312.

Hewlett, S. J. (1991). *When the bough breaks.* New York: Basic Books.

Hirczy de Mino, W. P. (1997). Coparenting arrangements in a jurisdiction with statutory guidelines. *Family and Conciliation Courts Review, 35(4),* 443-446.

Hodges, W. F. (1991). *Interventions for children of divorce* (Second edition). New York: John Wiley.

Holman, E. and Irvine, J. (2002). Alienation, undermining, and obstruction: A field guide for professionals. Seminar presented at the Association of Family and Conciliation Courts 39th Annual Conference, Waikoloa, Hawaii, June.

Imber-Black, E. and Roberts, J. (1992). *Rituals for our times.* New York: Harper Collins.

Irving, H. and Benjamin, M. (1995). *Family mediation: Contemporary issues.* Newbury Park, CA: Sage.

Isaacs, M. B., Montalvo, B., and Abelsohn, D. (1986). *The difficult divorce.* New York: Basic.

Johnston, J. (1992). High-conflict and violent parents in family court: Findings on children's adjustment, and proposed guidelines for the resolution of custody and visitation disputes. Statewide Office of Family Court Services, Judicial Council of California, Administrative Office of the Courts. Available at <http://www.courtinfo.ca.gov/programs/cfcc>.

Johnston, J. (1997). Developing and testing a group intervention for families at impasse. Seminar presented at the Association of Family and Conciliation Courts Conference, CO, September.

Johnston, J. and Campbell, L. (1988). *Impasses of divorce: The dynamics and resolution of family conflict.* New York: Free Press/Macmillan.

Johnston, J., Campbell, L., and Tall, M. (1985). Impasses to the resolution of custody and visitation disputes. *American Journal of Orthopsychiatry, 55,* 112-129.

Johnston, J., Kline, M., and Tschann, J. M. (1991). Ongoing post-divorce conflict in families contesting custody: Do joint custody and frequent access help? In J.

Folberg (Ed.), *Joint custody and shared parenting* (Second edition) (pp. 177-184). New York: The Guilford Press.

Johnston, J. and Roseby, V. (1997). *In the name of the child: A developmental approach to understanding and helping children of conflicted and violent divorce.* New York: Simon and Schuster.

Kalter, N. (1990). *Growing up with divorce.* New York: Fawcett Columbine.

Katz, M. (1997). *On playing a poor hand well: Insights from the lives of those who have overcome childhood risks and adversities.* New York: W.W. Norton.

Kelly, J. B. (1988). Longer-term adjustment in children of divorce: Converging findings and implications for practice. *Journal of Family Psychology, 2*(2), 119-140.

Kelly, J. B. and Johnston, J. R. (2001). The alienated child: A reformation of parental alienation syndrome. *Family Court Review, 39*(3), 249-266.

Kelly, J. B. and Lamb, M. E., (2000) Using child development research to make appropriate custody and access decisions for young children. *Family and Conciliation Courts Review, 38,* 297-311.

Kempton, T., Armistead, L., Wierson, M., and Forehand, R. (1991). Presence of sibling as a potential buffer following parent divorce: An examination of young adolescents. *Journal of Clinical Child Psychology, 20,* 434-438.

Kline, M., Tschann, J. M., Johnston, J. R., and Wallerstein, J. S. (1989). Children's adjustment in joint and sole physical custody families. *Developmental Psychology 25,* 430-438.

Kopetski, L. (1991). Parental alienation syndrome: Recent research. Paper presented at the Fifteenth Annual Child Custody Conference, Keystone, CO.

Kriesman, J. J. and Straus, H. (1991). *I hate you—don't ever leave me: Understanding the borderline personality.* New York: Harper Collins.

Kübler-Ross, E. (1997). *On death and dying.* New York: Simon and Schuster

Lamb, M. E., Sternberg, K., and Thompson, R. A. (1997). The effects of divorce and custody arrangements on children's behavior, development, and adjustment. *Family and Conciliation Courts Review, 35,* 393-404.

Lester, G. W. (1999). Personality disorders in social work and healthcare. Cross Country University course material, Boca Raton, FL.

Lewin, T. (1990). Father's vanishing act called common drama. *The New York Times,* June 4, p. A18.

Lieberman, D. J. (2002). *Make peace with anyone: Breakthrough strategies to quickly end any conflict, feud, or estrangement.* New York: St. Martin's Press.

Linehan, M. (1993). *Cognitive-behavioral treatment of borderline personality disorder.* New York: Guilford Press.

Ludolph, P. and Viro, M. (1998). Attachment theory and research: Implications for professionals assisting families of high conflict divorce. Paper presented at the 35th Annual Conference for Association of Family and Conciliation Courts, Washington, DC, May 28.

Luepnitz, D. A. (1991). A comparison of maternal, paternal, and joint custody: Understanding the varieties of post-divorce family life. In J. Folberg (Ed.), *Joint custody and shared parenting* (pp. 105-113). New York: The Guilford Press.

Lund, M. (1995). A therapist's view of parental alienation syndrome. *Family and Conciliation Court Review, 33*(3), 308-316.

Maccoby, E., Depner, C., and Mnookin, R. (1991). Co-parenting in the second year after divorce. In J. Folberg (Ed.), *Joint custody and shared parenting* (Second edition) (pp. 132-152). New York: The Guilford Press.

Maccoby, E. E. and Mnookin, R. H. (1992). *Dividing the child: Dilemmas of custody.* Cambridge, MA: Harvard University Press.

Margulies, S. (1992). *Getting divorced without ruining your life: A reasoned practical guide to the legal, emotional, and financial ins and outs of negotiating a divorce settlement.* New York: Fireside/Simon and Schuster.

Marston, S. (1994). *The divorced parent.* New York: William Morrow and Company.

Mason, P. and Kreger, R. (1998). *Stop walking on eggshells: Taking your life back when someone you care about has borderline personality disorder.* Oakland, CA: New Harbinger.

McKinnon, R. and Wallerstein, J. S. (1986). Joint custody and the preschool child. *Behavioral Sciences and the Law, 4*(2), 169-183.

Meichenbaum, D. (2002). *Treatment of individuals with anger-control problems and aggressive behavior: A clinical handbook.* Clearwater, FL: Institute Press.

Mnookin, R. (1992). Dividing the child: How professionals can help make decisions. Paper presented at the 16th Annual Child Custody Conference, Keystone, CO.

Moore, C. (1996). *The mediation process* (Second edition). San Francisco: Jossey-Bass.

National Clearinghouse for the Defense of Battered Women (1992). *Georgia Network Against Domestic Violence.* Atlanta, GA: Author.

Neff, R. and Cooper, K. (2004). Parental conflict resolution: Six, twelve, and fifteen-month follow-ups of a high-conflict program. *AFCC Family Court Reiew, 42*(1), 99-114.

Oklahoma Parenting Coordinator Act (2001). 43 O.S. 120.1. Available at <http://www.oscn.net>.

Our Family Wizard (2003). Available at <http://www.ourfamilywizard.com>.

Page, R. (1993). Family courts: An effective approach to the resolution of family disputes. *Juvenile and Family Court Journal, 1,* 3-5.

Pasley, K. and Ihinger-Tallman, M. (1987). *Remarriage and stepparenting: Current research and theory.* New York: Guilford Press.

Potter-Efron, R. and Potter-Efron, P. (1995). *Letting go of anger: The ten most common anger styles and what to do about them.* Oakland, CA: New Harbinger.

Pruett, K. (2000). *Fatherneed: Why father care is as essential as mother care for your child.* New York: The Free Press.

Pruett, M. K., Ebling, R., and Glendessa, I. (2004). Critical aspects of parenting plans for young children interjecting data into the debate about overnights. *AFCC Family Court Review, 42*(1), 39-59.

Ricci, I. (1980). *Mom's house, Dad's house: Making shared custody work.* New York: Macmillian.

Ross, K. L. and Blush, G. J. (1990). Sex abuse validity discriminators in the divorced or divorcing family. *Issues in Child Abuse Accusations, 2*(1), 1-6.

Rutter, M. (1987). Psychosocial resilience and protective mechanisms. *American Journal of Orthopsychiatry, 57,* 316-331.

Sande, K. (1997). *The peacemaker* (Second edition). Grand Rapids, MI: Baker Books.

Sanders, C. H. (1993). When you suspect the worst: Bad faith relocation, fabricated child sexual abuse, and parental alienation. *Family Advocate, 15*(3), 54-56.

Sandler, I. N., Wolchik, S. A., and Braver, S. L. (1988). The stressors of children's postdivorce environments. In S. Wolchik and P. Karoly (Eds.), *Children of divorce: Empirical perspectives on adjustment* (pp. 111-143). New York: Gardner Books.

Sapolsky, R. M. (1998). *Why zebras don't get ulcers: An updated guide for stress, stress-related diseases and coping.* New York: W. H. Freeman.

Saposnek, D. T. (1983). *Mediating child custody disputes: A systematic guide for family therapists, court counselors, attorneys, and judges.* San Francisco: Jossey-Bass.

Saposnek, D. T. (1991). A guide to decisions about joint custody: The needs of children of divorce. In J. Folberg (Ed.), *Joint custody and shared parenting* (Second edition) (pp. 29-40). New York: The Guilford Press.

Saposnek, D. T., Hamburg, J., Delano, D. C., and Michaelson, H. (1984). How has mandatory mediation fared? Research findings of the first year's follow-up. *Conciliation Courts Review, 22,* 20.

Schaffer, H. R. and Emerson, P. E. (1964). *The development of social attachments in infancy.* Monographs of Social Research in Child Development 29(4). Lafayette, IN: Child Development Publications of the Society for Research in Child Development.

Seligman, M. E. (1996). *The optimistic child: A proven program to safeguard children against depression and build lifelong resilience.* New York: Harper Collins.

Shear, L. E., Drapkin, R., and Curtis, R. (2000). Legal custody and best interests: Assessing and allocating communication and decision-making authority. Paper presented at the ASCT/LACBA Child Custody Colloquium, 2000, and the meeting of the Association of Family and Conciliation Courts 39th Annual Conference, Waikoloa, Hawaii, June.

Siegel, J. C. and Langford, J. S. (1998). MMPI-2 validity scales and suspected parental alienation syndrome. *American Journal of Forensic Psychology, 16*(4), 5-14.

Silvestri, S. (1992). Marital instability in men from intact and divorced families: Interpersonal behavior, cognition and intimacy. *Journal of Divorce and Remarriage, 18,* 79-108.

Solomon, J. and George, C. (1999). The effects on attachment of overnight visitation in divorced and separated families: A longitudinal follow-up. In J. Solomon and C. George (Eds.), *Attachment disorganization* (pp. 243-264). New York: Guilford.

Stahl, P. (1999a). *Complex issues in child custody evaluations.* Newbury Park, CA: Sage.

Stahl, P. (1999b). Personality traits of parents and developmental needs of children in high-conflict families. Prepared for the Association of Family and Conciliation Courts meeting in Kiaweh, SC, November 13. This article is excerpted and adapted from P. Stahl (1999), *Complex Issues In Child Custody Evaluations.* Newbury Park, CA: Sage.

Steinman, S. B. (1983). Joint custody: What we know, what we have yet to learn, and the judicial and legislative implications. University of California-Davis Law Review, 16, 739-747.

Steinman, S. B., Zemmelman, S. E., and Knoblauch, T. M. (1985). A study of parents who sought joint custody following divorce: Who reaches agreement and sustains joint custody and who returns to court. *Journal of the American Academy of Child Psychiatry, 24,* 554-562.

Stolberg, A. L., Camplair, C., Currier, K., and Wells, M. J. (1987). Individual, familial, and environmental determinants of children's post divorce adjustment and maladjustment. *Journal of Divorce, 11,* 51-70.

Stolorow, R. D. and Lachman, F. M. (1980). *The psychoanalysis of developmental arrests: Theory and treatment.* New York: International Universities Press.

Stoltz, J. M. and Ney. T. (2002). Rethinking parental alienation and child alienation. *Family Court Review, 40*(2), 220-231.

Sullivan, M. (2004). Ethical, legal and professional practice issues involved in acting as a psychologist parent coordinator in child custody cares. *Family Court Review, 42*(3), 576-582.

Taylor, A. (1991). Shared parenting: What it takes to succeed. In J. Folberg (Eds.), *Joint custody and shared parenting* (Second edition) (pp. 41-54). New York: The Guilford Press.

Termini, A. M. (1991). Ecologically based interventions in residential and school facilities: Theory or practice? *Adolescence, 26*(102), 387-398.

Turkat, I. D. (1994). Child visitation interference in divorce. *Clinical Psychology Review, 14*(7), 737-749.

Turkat, I. D. (1995). Divorce-related malicious mother syndrome. *Family Violence, 10*(3), 253-264.

Wallerstein, J. (1983). Six psychological tasks of children of divorce. Unpublished raw data.

Wallerstein, J. (1989). Children of divorce. Workshop sponsored by Albert Einstein College of Medicine, Eastham, MA, August.

Wallerstein, J. (1991). The long-term effects of divorce on children: A review. *Journal of American Academy of Child Psychiatry, 30*(3), 349-360.

Wallerstein, J. and Blakeslee, S. (1989). *Second chances: Men, women, and children a decade after divorce.* New York: Ticknor and Fields.

Wallerstein, J. and Kelly, J. (1976). The effects of parental influence: Experiences of the child in later latency. *American Journal of Orthopsychiatry, 46,* 256-269.

Wallerstein, J. and Kelly, J. (1980). *Surviving the breakup: How children and parents cope with divorce.* New York: Basic Books.

Wallerstein, J. and Lewis, J. (1998). The long-term impact of divorce on children: A first report from a 25-year study. *Family and Conciliation Courts Review, 36*(3), 368-383.

Ward, P. (1997). Introduction to parenting coordination. Seminar presented at the Second World Congress on Family Law and the Rights of Children and Youth, Association of Family and Conciliation Courts, San Francisco, CA, June 2-7.

Ward, P. and Harvey, J. (1993). Family wars: The alienation of children. *The New Hampshire Bar Journal, 34,* 30-40. Also available at <http://www.divorcesource.com/NH/DS>.

Warshak, R. A. (2000). Blanket restrictions: Overnight contact between parents and young children. *Family Court Review, 38,* 422-445.

Webb, S. G. (1998). Collaborative law practice model. A program presented at the Family Dispute Resolution Continuum, Association of Family and Conciliation Courts, October 29-31.

Wexler, D. (n.d.). Therapeutic jurisprudence: An Overview. Available at <www.law.arizona.edu/depts/upr-intj/>.

Wexler, D. B. (1990). *Therapeutic jurisprudence: The law as a therapeutic agent.* Durham, NC: Carolina Academic Press.

Wexler, D. B. (2000). Therapeutic jurisprudence: An overview. *Thomas M. Coley Law Review, 17*(1), 125-134.

Wexler, D. B. and Winick, B. J. (1991). *Essays in therapeutic jurisprudence.* Durham, NC: Carolina Academic Press.

Whiteside, M. F. (1998). Custody for children age 5 and younger. *Family and Conciliation Courts Review, 36*(4), 479-502.

Williams, F. S. (1987). Child custody and parental cooperation. Paper presented at the American Bar Association Family Law Section Conference, August.

Williams, R. (1989). Curing type A: The trusting heart. *Psychology Today,* January-February, pp. 36-42.

Winick, B. J. (n.d.). Therapeutic jurisprudence defined. Available at <www.brucewinick.com>.

Worthington, E. (2001). *Five steps to forgiveness: The art and science of forgiving.* New York: Crown Publishers.

Index

Alienation *(continued)*
  parent behavior contributing to,
    296-298
  parental alienation syndrome, 290,
    292
  reunification sessions, 168
Alpert-Gillis, L. J., 22-23
Alternating weekend plan, 127-129
Alternative dispute resolution (ADR),
  defined, 76
American Association of Marriage and
  Family Therapy, 45
American Bar Association parent
  coordinator recommendations,
  31-32
Anderson, E. R., 21, 22
Anger
  after divorce, 3-4
  aggression versus, 195, 197
  causes, 196
  constructive versus destructive, 205
  cost of, 202
  domestic violence, 197-198. *See
    also* Domestic violence
  educational foundation, 63
  emotional abuse and, 200-201
  log or journal, 219-220
  management techniques. *See* Anger-
    management techniques
  metaphors, 206-207
  overview, 193-195
  rating, 205-206
  reframing, 205-206
  safety measures, 201-202
Anger-as-a-choice activity, 204-205
Anger-management techniques
  anger-as-a-choice activity, 204-205
  awareness, 202-207
  blame game, 220
  coaching, 217-220
  cognitive dissonance, 220-221
  cognitive restructuring, 211-217
  communication skills, 222
  cost-cost activity, 203-204
  dealing with noncompliance,
    225-226
  defusing anger, 228
  education, 222
  forgiveness, 223
  humor, 223-224

Anger-management techniques
  (continued)
  impulse-control, 207-211
  indirect criticism, 222
  overview, 202
  parental feedback, 224
  praise and encouragement, 221
  referral for treatment, 224
  reflective listening, 184-185, 220
  rejection of suggestions, 221
  reshaping self-esteem, 221
  use of consequences, 227-228
Anxiety reducing guidelines, 135-136
Arbitration
  defined, 77
  by parent coordinators, 48-49
Arbuthnot, J., 15
Arizona
  family court advisor, 38
  nonconfidential communication, 40
  parent coordinator authority, 37
  parent coordinator legislation, 33
  parent coordinator training, 39
  Supreme Court parenting time plans,
    129-131
Armistead, L., 22-23
Assessment
  CPI model, 66-68
  by parent coordinators, 47, 57
Assignments
  acceptance of coparent, 255
  courteous transitions, 255
  during sessions, 256
  incomplete, 228
  joint attendance at child's activities,
    255-256
  motivational, 253-256
  parent-child contact, 254
  waiting room, 254
Association of Family and Conciliation
  Courts (AFCC)
  Bowlby's attachment theory, 108-109
  common practices, 38
  "Parenting Coordination:
    Implementation Issues," 32
  quasi-judicial immunity, 39
  Task Force on Parent Coordination,
    29, 33-34
Attachment
  components, 108-109
  defined, 108

75162